Praise for *The Language of*

"In *The Language of Coaching*, Nick Winkelman has done something I previously thought to be impossible. He has combined a textbook-caliber education on motor learning with practical strategies that coaches of *all* levels from *all* disciplines can utilize *immediately*. It would take you an entire career of coaching to pick up, just by chance, some of the competencies he outlines—and even then, you'd come up short. Nick's work will fast-track coaches to effective communication—and, in turn, outstanding results—for their athletes and clients. I wish I'd had this book 20 years ago!"

—Eric Cressey, CSCS
President and Cofounder of Cressey Sports Performance
Director of Player Health and Performance for the New York Yankees

"Nick is one of the bright young minds in our field. *The Language of Coaching* continues Nick's excellent progression from coach, to speaker, and now to writer."

—Michael Boyle
Owner of Mike Boyle Strength and Conditioning

"Nick Winkelman is what I like to call a 'coaches' coach.' In the 10 years I have known Nick, he has proven himself to be one of the authorities in the industry for strength and conditioning as well as the art of coaching. Nick has the ability to convey information in such a relatable fashion, making his delivery warm and welcoming. He is one of the few people I like to lean on for advice in our industry, and I am excited to continue to use Nick as my go-to resource. I will be gifting *The Language of Coaching* to dozens of coaches and athletes."

—Don Saladino
Celebrity Trainer
Health and Performance Specialist
Founder and Owner of Drive Health Clubs

"Whether you are a sport coach, a strength and conditioning specialist, or a physical therapist, you need to effectively communicate with your athletes or clients. Nick Winkelman takes the science of effective coaching to another level with *The Language of Coaching* and delivers effective real-world strategies to improve not only communication but also the ultimate goal—clients results. *The Language of Coaching* is a masterpiece. In time it will become the ultimate guide to coaching. It's already mandatory reading for all my coaches."

—Alwyn Cosgrove
Fitness Coach
Owner of Results Fitness

"Nick Winkelman's passion, wisdom, and knowledge have helped to turn the science of motor learning into a digestible, applicable framework. His book, *The Language of Coaching*, will serve as an invaluable tool for driving results with athletes and clients."

—Alex Zimmerman
Senior Director of the Tier X Program at Equinox

"Nick Winkelman helped me gain an edge on the combine and take full advantage of my training. His book, *The Language of Coaching*, will help other athletes do the same."

—Dontari Poe
Defensive Tackle for the Carolina Panthers

"*The Language of Coaching* is a groundbreaking and meticulously researched book that delivers practical and user-friendly ways for a coach to connect for results. This book should be on every coach's shelf."

—Martin Rooney
Founder of Training for Warriors
Coach to Hundreds of NFL, UFC, NBA, WNBA, MLB, and Olympic Athletes
Author of *Coach to Coach*

"Nick Winkelman helped improve my mind-set and introduced me to a new way of performing at the highest level. With *The Language of Coaching*, he will do the same for you."

—Prince Amukamara
Cornerback for the Chicago Bears

"Using a logical, evidence guided approach, Nick essentially obliterates the communication barrier between coaches and athletes. If your job description includes conveying ideas with the intention of improving the physical capabilities of others, read *The Language of Coaching*."

—Andreo Spina, BKin, DC, FRCCSS(C)
Sports Specialist Chiropractor
Movement and Mobility Coach
CEO of Functional Anatomy Seminars

"Drawing on Winkelman's vast personal experience with high-level athletes, *The Language of Coaching* unpacks the flaws in our assumptions, examining how apparently small changes in what we say and how we say it can result in more durable learning for the athletes we teach. It will surely prove to be a significant and enduring contribution to the literature of coaching."

—Doug Lemov
Author of *Teach Like a Champion*, *Teach Like a Champion 2.0*, and *Practice Perfect*

"In *The Language of Coaching*, Nick has offered an important contribution to the coaching world. A combination of a comprehensive scientific text and practical operator's manual, this is a must-read for all coaches."

—Stuart McMillan
CEO of ALTIS
Sprint Coach

"I was privileged to spend an intense period learning from Nick in a formal workshop setting. These sessions were Olympic-coach-level workshops and presentations. I can honestly say that the guidance on cueing was evidence based, highly practical, and immediately applicable. Nick's knowledge, manner, and communication skills make available a level of athlete performance enhancement that is off the charts. His work and process are highly recommended across a broad spectrum of sports; his methods will make you a better coach—period!"

—Bobby McGee
Olympic Coach (With Medals in the Atlanta, London, and Rio Olympics)
Team Leader and High-Performance Support Staff

"As a coach of athletes who are blind, I am constantly looking for better ways to describe actions and motion without needing a visual reference. After working with Nick, I have the perfect set of verbal cueing skills to best teach my team!"

—**Jake Czechowski**
Head Coach of the USA Women's National Goalball Team

"Nick's guidance on cueing gave me the most effective coaching technique I have ever practiced. It has taught our coaching staff how to prevent manufacturing complexity and has given our athletes laser focus on what truly matters in performing at the highest level."

—**Mike Kohn**
USA Bobsled Head Coach

"Nick's work is a valuable component of our national team coach course, providing unique and practical insight on communicating with athletes to elicit better performance. His practical approach and methods help enhance coach–athlete understanding in a strategic, logical way. Coaches who have gone through his training as part of our course have seen significant results right away. Nick's work is a valuable tool that can be applied across a variety of levels and sports."

—**Christine Bolger**
Coaching Education Department of the United States Olympic and Paralympic Committee

"The very practical tactics I learned from Nick (at a USOC National Team Coach Seminar) helped immediately with my pair figure skating athletes. My improved understanding of cueing and the use of purposeful and targeted analogies guided faster skill acquisition, specifically with triple twists."

—**Bobby Martin**
U.S. Figure Skating Coach

"Nick has unlocked the superpower shared by highly effective coaches around the world. Great coaching is directly correlated to precise and purposeful communication. Cleaning up communication is as critical as correcting compensatory movement patterns. Nick has relentlessly worked through the research and has the practical knowledge that comes only from thousands of coaching sessions. *The Language of Coaching* will make you and our field better."

—**Mark Verstegen**
Founder and President of EXOS

"Knowing your stuff is only part of the coach's task: The more important part is transmitting that knowledge. That takes not only advanced speaking skills—mastering both what to say and how to say it—but also conscious listening, because listening is the doorway to understanding, and understanding is the access to effective relationships, not to mention motivation. Nick's excellent book is long overdue, focusing as it does on communication, the most critical and long-overlooked aspect of performance coaching."

—**Julian Treasure**
Five-Time TED Speaker
Author of the Award-Winning Book *How to Be Heard*

"The longer I'm in the 'movement game,' from rehabilitation to performance, the more I appreciate it when equal value is placed on information, experience, and reflection. In The Language of Coaching, Nick guides us to not overvalue one aspect and undervalue the others."

—**Gray Cook, MSPT, OCS, CSCS**
Cofounder of Functional Movement Systems
Author of *Movement*

"Now we can all have access to the most powerful tool in our toolbox—language. In The Language of Coaching, Nick captures the importance of intentional and effective communication in creating a movement experience for our athletes that will maximize their performance!"

—**Anna Hartman, ATC**
Founder of MovementREV

"In *The Language of Coaching*, Nick Winkelman has taken a complex topic and its large amounts of research and evidence, paired it with his expertise on the subject, and compressed it down to an extremely practical and easily digestible book. This is a must-read for anyone who works with people and seeks to make them better."

—**Brandon Marcello, PhD**
High-Performance Strategist

"Bottom line: What we say matters. Our words are what bridges the gap from the science of coaching to the art of coaching. In this book, Nick does a beautiful job of helping coaches bring their programming to life via the most important tool we all have: communication. Not only will this book help you improve as a coach, it will help you connect better to your client, ultimately improving their results."

—**Sue Falsone, MS, PT, SCS, ATC, CSCS, COMT**
President of Structure & Function Education
Author of *Bridging the Gap From Rehab to Performance*

THE LANGUAGE
OF COACHING

The Art & Science of Teaching Movement

NICK WINKELMAN

HUMAN KINETICS

Library of Congress Cataloging in Publication Data

Names: Winkelman, Nick, 1984- author. | Human Kinetics (Organization)
Title: The language of coaching : the art & science of teaching movement /
  Nick Winkelman, PhD, CSCS, NSCA-CPT, Head of Athletic Performance &
  Science, Irish Rugby Football Union.
Description: Champaign, Illinois : Human Kinetics Inc., 2020. | Includes
  bibliographical references and index.
Identifiers: LCCN 2019052286 (print) | LCCN 2019052287 (ebook) | ISBN
  9781492567363 (Paperback) | ISBN 9781492591450 (ePub) | ISBN
  9781492567370 (PDF)
Subjects: LCSH: Coaching (Athletics) | Performance.
Classification: LCC GV711 .W56 2020 (print) | LCC GV711 (ebook) | DDC
  796.07/7--dc23
LC record available at https://lccn.loc.gov/2019052286
LC ebook record available at https://lccn.loc.gov/2019052287

ISBN: 978-1-4925-6736-3 (print)

Permission notices for material reprinted in this book from other sources can be found on pages xx-xx
The web addresses cited in this text were current as of October 2019, unless otherwise noted.

Senior Acquisitions Editor: Roger W. Earle; **Developmental Editor:** Laura Pulliam; **Managing Editor**
Shawn Donnelly; **Copyeditor:** Erin Cler; **Indexer:** Rebecca L. McCorkle; **Permissions Manager:** Marth
Gullo; **Computer Graphic Art Director:** Sean Roosevelt; **Cover Designer:** Keri Evans; **Cover Design**
Specialist: Susan Rothermel Allen; **Photograph (cover):** msan10 / Getty Images; **Photographs (inte**
rior): © Human Kinetics, unless otherwise noted; **Photo Asset Manager:** Laura Fitch; **Photo Productio:**
Specialist: Amy M. Rose; **Photo Production Manager:** Jason Allen; **Senior Art Manager:** Kelly
Hendren; **Illustrations:** © Human Kinetics; **Printer:** Walsworth

Human Kinetics books are available at special discounts for bulk purchase. Special editions or book
excerpts can also be created to specification. For details, contact the Special Sales Manager at Humar
Kinetics.

Printed in the United States of America   10 9 8 7 6 5 4 3 2

The paper in this book was manufactured using responsible forestry methods.

Human Kinetics
1607 N. Market Street
Champaign, IL 61820
USA

United States and International
Website: **US.HumanKinetics.com**
Email: info@hkusa.com
Phone: 1-800-747-4457

Canada
Website: **Canada.HumanKinetics.com**
Email: info@hkcanada.com

E7315

Tell us what you think!
Human Kinetics would love to hear what we
can do to improve the customer experience.

To my love: You are my truth, my best friend, and my inspiration.

To Gracie and Madden: Find what you love and give it your all.

To Maddy, Roxy, and Keg: You will forever be our chaos.

CONTENTS

PART I LEARN

PART II COACH

PART III CUE

FOREWORD

Every great moment in sports happens twice.

First, it happens in the moment of achievement, in that breathless, electric instant when an athlete scores a game-winning goal, makes a spectacular fingertip catch, or wins an important race. That's the moment captured in the highlights—the one most of us remember.

But there's another moment that happens a few seconds later, away from the bright lights. It's the moment of private celebration when the athlete and coach connect. The moment when they bump fists, or hug, or just smile at each other with big goofball smiles. No words are needed, because there's nothing to say. Just a warm, shared truth: Hey, we did it.

The first moment of achievement is thrilling—it's why we love sports. But I love this second moment more, because it's bigger. It contains the whole crazy, exasperating, painful, inspiring journey that happens between athlete and coach. And every time we witness this happy moment, it raises a question: How do we make it happen more often? In other words, what is great coaching really made of?

That's exactly what this book is about.

Historically and traditionally, great coaching has been seen as a kind of magic. In this way of thinking, the magic is located mostly inside the coach—in their keen eye, their intuition, and their way with people. Thus we've assumed great coaches (Wooden, Lombardi, Stengel, Popovich) to be wizards. This way of thinking makes sense, but it also leads to some problems.

For one, it's unscientific. We live in a world where the skill sets of doctors, engineers, architects, and every other professional are built on foundations of evidence-based research and continuously improving methods. Coaching culture, for whatever mysterious reason, has proved mostly immune to science, leaving coaches to guide themselves by the hazy, unreliable stars of tradition, intuition, and anecdote. Sometimes it works well. But down deep, it's unclear. Even the most fundamental questions echo with uncertainty: What's the best way to design practice? What's the best way to give feedback?

For another, it creates a world of copycats. If you see successful coaches yelling at athletes, you naturally assume that that must be the best way to coach. If you see other successful coaches whispering to athletes, you assume that they are right. If you see still other coaches buddying up to their athletes, you assume that they're right. But which is it, really?

Fortunately there's a better way, led by a new generation of researchers and coaches who are building a bridge from the world of science to the craft of coaching. And no one is doing that more effectively than Nick Winkelman.

I met Winkelman in September 2017 in a meeting room of a Hampton Inn in Goodyear, Arizona. Winkelman had come to speak with the Cleveland Indians, a team I consult for. Unlike our big-market competitors, the Indians can't afford to buy talent; we have to build it, and thus we are obsessed with understanding and improving at the craft of coaching. On that day, the

room was packed with 50 people, including coaches, baseball operations people, player development staff, the general manager, and the team president—a big crowd. Most didn't know much about Winkelman; they knew only that he had worked in rugby, had a background in high performance, had earned his PhD in motor learning, and had done some fascinating research on attentional focus and cueing. The room was expectant and maybe a little skeptical. Then he started.

"To create players who can adjust, we must be coaches who can do the same," he said. Then he showed us how. For two days, Winkelman took the group inside the landscape between the athlete and the coach, mapping it. He taught from the bottom up, starting with Gabriele Wulf's research on internal and external cues and then working outward toward the craft of practice design. He delivered a tool kit of clear, actionable ideas. It was riveting, useful, and mind-expanding. Afterward, I told Winkelman that he should write a book. He smiled and said, "I already started."

And so here it is. I will leave it to him to explain his work, but let me give you two quick pieces of advice: (1) Read with a pencil or a highlighter, because you'll want to take notes, and (2) make a list of the important coaches in your life, because you'll want to get them a copy too.

In a larger sense, this book arrives at the right time, because the sports world is changing fast. In the past few years, the data revolution has radically redefined the relationship between athlete and coach. We live in a world where weekend golfers and joggers have access to a level of performance data that pro athletes could not have dreamed of just 10 years ago, and this new world has spawned urgent questions: How do coaches provide value in a world where the athlete has access to accurate feedback? Can you be coached by artificial intelligence? What does coaching really mean?

While some fear that this data revolution means the end of coaching, I would argue the opposite: Coaches are becoming ever more valuable. We see proof in the way that the coaching model continues to expand from sports into business and other walks of life. It is not inconceivable that in the not-so-distant future, everyone will have a coach to help guide them in work, relationships, fitness, nutrition, leadership—whatever they need. That means that the questions Winkelman explores in this book are precisely those that will guide us in the future: How do you talk to people in a way that unlocks their abilities? How do you identify and overcome obstacles? Those are not just questions for sports; they are questions for life. And as we explore them, we'll continue to learn the larger lesson that Winkelman teaches us in these pages: The magic is not in who the coach is but in what the coach does.

—**Daniel Coyle**
Author of *The Talent Code*

PREFACE

Let's cut to the chase. You want to know what this book is about and why you should care.

Before I answer these questions, however, I need to share two assumptions I'm going to make.

1. You're interested in teaching movement. By *teaching movement*, I mean that you want to know how you can help others learn to move better. Moving better could be as basic as helping a child learn how to ride a bike or as complex as helping a professional golfer refine their swing. Ultimately, movement is movement, and I'm assuming that you want to get better at teaching it.

2. You're interested in coaching language. By *coaching language*, I mean the stuff you say to influence the way a person moves. This includes the instructions a personal trainer uses when teaching a client how to lunge, the short cues a basketball coach uses to help a player refine their jump shot, or the feedback a physical therapist provides when helping a stroke survivor retrain their gait. No matter the context, I'm assuming that you want to know how your words affect movement.

If my assumptions are off the mark, then this might not be the book for you. However, if you found yourself nodding in agreement, then I suggest you read on.

I believe this book's potential is best revealed through the lens of your own circumstances. Therefore, I'd like you to imagine the context in which you're hoping to apply the ideas contained within this book. For example, if you're an American football coach, you'd visualize yourself during practice; if you're a physical education teacher, you'd visualize yourself during class; and if you're a physical therapist, you'd visualize yourself during a rehabilitation session.

Now that you've visualized your context, I want you to populate it with an actual teaching scenario you've faced in the past. For our American football coach, this could be a time you were teaching tackle technique; for our physical education teacher, this could be a time you were teaching elementary students how to pass a soccer ball; and for our physical therapist, this could be a time you were helping a patient relearn a squat pattern.

Like a mental movie, I'd like you to let your teaching scenario play out in your mind. As you watch, I'd like you to notice the way you're communicating with those in front of you. Specifically, I'd like you to focus on the relationship between *what you're saying and how they're moving*.

Here are some questions to consider as you watch yourself in action:

- How did you know what to say?
- How did you know when to say it?
- How did you know how much to say?
- How did you know whether it made a difference?

The scenario that just played out in your mind represents a singular teaching moment. Although any one of these moments, in isolation, may seem insignificant, it is their summation that ultimately determines what a person learns. Here, learning is what the person walks away with. It is their capacity to own the improvements in their movement. It is their ability to express these changes independent of you—the trainer, coach, or therapist that facilitated them.

Thus, inside of each teaching moment hides the potential for learning. However, as anyone who teaches movement can attest, there are no guarantees. Whether we're working with a client who seems to forget everything once they've left the gym or an athlete who struggles to perform as well as they practice, all movement professionals know how elusive learning can be.

It is here, at the intersection of teaching and learning, that our story begins.

Before I continue, however, it is important that I clarify a few terms. If we're going to talk about teaching and learning, then we must agree on what we're going to call the person doing the teaching and the person doing the learning. This pairing can go by many names: teacher–student, trainer–client, therapist–patient, parent–child, coach–athlete, and so on. Only because my background is in strength and conditioning have I decided to use the *coach–athlete* pairing in this book.

I stress the reason for this selection because it is important that you see yourself in the word *coach* and those you work with in the word *athlete*. Thus, even though my wording implies a coach–athlete pairing, please know that this book is universally applicable to *all movement professionals*.

Throughout my career, I've committed myself to understanding how people learn to move. To be precise, I've committed myself to understanding the portion of the learning process that coaches have the greatest influence on. After years of studying, applying, and reflecting, I believe a coach's influence on learning is best understood when broken into two categories: *programming* and *coaching*.

Programming represents all the *physical stuff* the athlete is being asked to do (e.g., drills, games, exercises, movements, or skills) in the context of a progressive training program; I call this the *what*. Coaching represents everything a *coach says* to influence how that physical stuff is performed; I call this the *how*.

Now, I want you to ask yourself two questions:

1. Which of these two learning influencers—programming or coaching—would you be more comfortable delivering a presentation on to a hundred peers?
2. Which of these two learning influencers—programming or coaching—do you spend more time engaged in on a daily basis?

If I had been asked these questions earlier in my career, I would have quickly said that I would much rather deliver a presentation on *programming* and that, obviously, I spend more time *coaching* on a daily basis. If I had to guess, I'd say my answers reflect those of the vast majority of people reading these words. In fact, my experience suggests that this is how most movement professionals would answer these questions.

Do you see the irony in this?

We spend far more time coaching than we do programming, yet most of us would find the latter far easier to talk about than the former. Why is this? I believe the reason has two parts. First, if you examine the education of movement professionals, you'll find that degrees and certifications emphasize the *what* far more than the *how*. Second, the *what* is emphasized more because it is visible, it is tangible, and it is the foundation on which the movement profession is built. Thus, it makes sense that people are more comfortable talking about *what* they do than about *how* they do it. However, in the process of developing movement professionals, we've committed a crime of omission. Unknowingly, we've neglected to develop the invisible skill of coaching. We've forgotten that a *what* without a *how* is like a car without a driver. We've left movement professionals to fend for themselves and learn through an unguided process of trial and error that is more chance than choice.

This stops with *The Language of Coaching.*

This book seeks to make the invisible...visible, examining the interplay between a coach's words and an athlete's movement. At its core, this is a book about communication and relationships. It is about understanding how a coach's ideas, through their words, turn into an athlete's movement. It is about revealing that the art of coaching has a scientific sibling and that the great coaches, knowingly or not, get this art and science to mesh in a manner that best serves the athlete.

If you agree that *how* you coach is as important as *what* you coach, then I welcome you to join me on my mission to help coaches help the world move better, one word at a time. To achieve this, I have written a book that is designed to help movement professionals of all levels and backgrounds learn the skills necessary to wield words with the same precision as a surgeon with a scalpel.

This book is broken into three parts. Parts I and II each contain three chapters, and part III has four. Each part begins with an opener that chronicles my own coaching journey and the profound impact committing yourself to the *how* can have on you and those under your care.

In part I, Learn, we focus on the way people learn to move, emphasizing the factors that coaches have the greatest influence on. Chapter 1, Learn This, is broken into three sections to help you identify (1) what needs to be coached (using the 3P Performance Profile), (2) what learning looks like, and (3) the difference between short-term changes in performance and the long-term learning we desire. With an understanding of what learning is, we transition into an exploration of the factors that influence it.

Chapter 2, Pay Attention, covers the first step in learning anything—paying attention. Broken into three sections, this chapter tours the brain and examines the mind when it is (1) wandering and out of focus, (2) captured and coming into focus, and (3) kept in focus. Along the way, I'll discuss the simple strategies you can use to capture and keep your athletes' attention.

Chapter 3, Remember When, covers the final step in learning anything: remembering it. Broken into three sections, this chapter first introduces you to short-term and long-term memory. After seeing where memories live, we'll check out how memories are made. Along the way, I'll share the keys to becoming a memorable coach who triggers learning that sticks.

In part II, Coach, we examine how a coach's words influence an athlete's focus and the impact this focus has on learning or refining a movement. Chapter 4, Finding Focus, opens with a breakdown of the *coaching communication loop*, which outlines when and how coaching language is used to teach or refine a movement pattern. With an understanding of the different categories of coaching language, we'll focus on the category known as *cueing*. Cues are the brief phrases that coaches use right before an athlete moves. As you'll see, the cue receives the majority of our attention because it has the greatest influence on what an athlete will focus on and, therefore, what they'll learn. This three-section chapter goes on to discuss a continuum of cues and the compelling research narrative that outlines the type of cues coaches should use to optimize learning and performance.

Chapter 5, Cue It Up, focuses on helping you build the skills of creating and adapting your cues to fit the movement and the athlete performing it. To achieve this, you'll learn about the 3D cueing model, which provides you with a systematic way to create and manipulate your cues to serve the individual you're working with. Along the way, I'll share a wide range of pointers (what I like to call Cue Tips!) that will help you refine your cues for the toughest of coaching scenarios.

Chapter 6, Going Analog, focuses on a specific type of cue known as the analogy, which is nothing more than a comparison between something an athlete is familiar with and a feature of the movement they're learning. Using an analogy model, you'll learn how to apply one of the most powerful coaching tools I've ever come across. By learning how to compress your athletes' experiences and language into the analogies you use to coach them, you'll fast-track understanding while building stronger relationships.

In part III, Cue, we focus on cultivating the cueing behaviors you established in part II. Chapter 7, The Road Map, was written for you, the reader, because I know how difficult it can be to change the way you communicate. In this chapter, I lay out a plan to help you create a habit of cueing. Only by examining a habit can we disrupt it, challenge it, and build it into something new. Understanding the content in this chapter is critically important if you want to take everything from the first six chapters and bring it into the real world.

Chapter 8, Strong Cueing; chapter 9, Powerful Cueing; and chapter 10, Fast Cueing, contain a total of 27 movement sequences. These examples bring the cueing models and tips to life through beautiful imagery that captures what is possible when motion meets language that moves us. These are meant to illustrate the concepts in this book, inspire your own creativity, and provide you with a foundation on which to build your habit of cueing.

I wrote this book for you. Why? Because you know that your impact on people is more than reps and sets; you know that what you say matters; and you know that what ultimately determines your impact is the space between you and your athlete.

The question is this: What will you fill it with?

ACKNOWLEDGMENTS

Of all the emotions I felt while writing this book, gratitude stands above them all.

To my parents: Thank you for giving me this gift called life and the tools to live it to the fullest. Mom, you filled my childhood with wonder, whimsy, and imagination. If not for you, I would've never told this story the way that I did. Dad, you taught me to finish what I start and be committed to excellence. It was your voice that echoed in my mind when I thought about taking the easy path or questioned my ability to finish this book.

To my grandfather: Thank you for your endless support. You know where this journey started, and I know how proud you would be if you were still with us.

To my high school strength and conditioning coach, Rudy: Thank you for showing me what it means to be a great coach and, more importantly, a great person. You taught me that coaching the person is as important as coaching the player.

To my mentor, J.C.: Thank you for teaching me the value of coaching language. It was your precise use of coaching cues that opened my eyes to the fact that *how* we coach is as important as *what* we coach.

To my mentor, Guido Van Ryssegem: Thank you for your steadfast belief, support, and challenge. It was in your office that I shared my very first ideas about coaching language and said that one day I'd write a book on the topic. Many would've laughed at my youthful dreams, but you didn't. Instead, you told me to get to work.

To my mentor, Mark Verstegen: You taught me what it means to be a humble servant—to wake up every day and commit yourself to your craft, to give someone your all and expect nothing in return, and to serve so that others can succeed. I wrote this book as a humble servant. My hope is that it can do for others what you did for me.

To the team (past and present) at Athletes' Performance (now EXOS), including Craig Friedman, Luke Richesson, Darryl Eto, Ken Croner, Joe Gomes, John Stemmerman, Jeff Sassone, Masa Sakihana, Katz Abe, Kevin Elsey, Eric Dannenberg, Ben Dubin, Denis Logan, Percy Knox, Tristan Rice, J.P. Major, John Barlow, Joel Sanders, Nicole Rodriguez, Brett Bartholomew, Brent Callaway, Victor Hall, Russ Orr, Anthony Hobgood, Scott Hopson, Amanda Carlson-Phillips, Danielle Lafata, Michelle Riccardi, Bob Calvin, Debbie Martell, Sue Falsone, Anna Hartman, Darcy Norman, Omi Iwasaki, Graeme Lauriston, Trent Wilfinger, and Dan Zieky: You are more than colleagues; you are friends. I hope each of you finds yourself in this book in some way, because our time together is indelibly etched into every word I write.

To all of my past and present athletes: Thank you for trusting me with your goals and aspirations. I can't say I always got it right, but I can say that I always did my best. Without you, this book would not have been possible, and because of you many athletes and coaches will benefit.

To Chris Poirier, the team at Perform Better, and Anthony Renna: You gave my ideas on coaching language and cueing a platform. Anthony, it was on *The Strength Coach Podcast* that I first shared my views on cueing and communication. Chris, it was on the *Perform Better* stage that I first presented the cueing models in this book. Without you guys, the groundswell of awareness needed to justify *The Language of Coaching* would have never been possible.

To Gabriele Wulf and Jared Porter: Words cannot capture my gratitude for you and your contribution to the field of motor learning and coaching. There is not a section in this book that isn't somehow influenced by your work. I will be forever grateful for the time we spent together discussing the intersection between thinking and moving.

To the many researchers and professionals who have contributed to the fields of attentional focus, language, and coaching, including Sian Beilock, Anne Benjaminse, Nikolai Bernstein, Suzete Chiviacowsky, Dave Collins, Edward Coughlan, Mihaly Csikszentmihalyi, Anders Ericsson, Damian Farrow, Paul Fitts, Timothy Gallwey, Dedre Gentner, Alli Gokeler, Rob Gray, Nicola Hodges, William James, Marc Jeannerod, Daniel Kahneman, Rebecca Lewthwaite, Keith Lohse, Richard Magill, Cliff Mallett, David Marchant, Richard Masters, Nancy McNevin, Wolfgang Prinz, Friedemann Pulvermüller, Thomas Schack, Richard Schmidt, Charles Shea, Robert Singer, Mark Williams, Daniel Wolpert, Will Wu, Rolf Zwaan: Thank you for committing your lives to making the invisible visible.

To Michael Posner: Thank you for taking time to review my chapter on attention. Your insights and feedback were invaluable.

To Daniel Schacter: Thank you for taking time to review my chapter on memory. Your insights and feedback were invaluable.

To Lisa Feldman Barrett, Benjamin Bergen, Nick Chater, and Julian Treasure: Thank you for taking time to discuss your respective books and how they relate to the language of coaching. Your nuanced perspectives influenced many sections of this book.

To my friend, Matt Wilkie, and my wife, Brittany Winkelman: Thank you for providing the earliest review of each chapter of this book. I do not believe the outcome we achieved would have been possible if not for your consistent feedback and support.

To Mike Boyle, Alwyn Cosgrove, Eric Cressey, Doug Lemov, Brandon Marcello, Stuart McMillan, Bryan Miller, Martin Rooney, Don Saladino, Andreo Spina, and Alex Zimmerman: Thank you for reviewing the earliest versions of the complete manuscript. I am so grateful for your support and belief in the book's message.

To Daniel Coyle: Thank you for your ongoing support and advice throughout the writing process. Your insights and feedback on the manuscript have been invaluable and most certainly improved the final product.

To Jason Muzinic, vice president and division director at Human Kinetics: Thank you for taking a chance on my book and believing in me. When other publishers said *the world isn't ready for this*, you said *this is exactly why we need to publish it*.

To Roger Earle, my acquisitions editor at Human Kinetics: From the bottom of my heart, thank you. You have spent hours on the other side of that phone listening, advising, and supporting. I consider you a true friend, and I will never forget what you have done for me.

To Laura Pulliam, my developmental editor at Human Kinetics: Thank you for committing to the spirit of this book and ensuring that it kept its voice throughout the editorial process. You have been a joy to work with, and I can't thank you enough for your support and editorial guidance.

To Sean Roosevelt, Joanne Brummett, Keri Evans, and Lisa Lyness, the artistic geniuses behind the cover and visuals in this book: Thank you for taking my ideas and bringing them to life. You have shown the reader what is possible when imagination meets movement.

To the rest of my Human Kinetics team, Julie Marx Goodreau, Shawn Donnelly, Doug Fink, Alexis Koontz, Jenny Lokshin, Karla Walsh, Martha Gullo, Susan Allen, Susan Sumner, Amy Rose, Jason Allen, Matt Harshbarger, Laura Fitch, Kelly Hendren, and Dona Abel: Thank you for making this book possible. Even though I've had varied amounts of interaction with each of you, it does not diminish my gratitude for your support and contributions.

And to you, the reader: Thank you for spending your time and money to get better so that you can help others. It is because of you and those you serve that I wrote this book.

PHOTO CREDITS

PART I
LEARN

Like a fast-approaching siren, the rising pitch of my alarm shattered my sleep, alerting me to the start of a new day. Orienting to the darkness, I was struck by a sudden pounding in my chest, an unrelenting thud that refused to be ignored. The magnitude of this feeling was such that, had this been any other day, I might have called 911. However, this was no ordinary day, no, this was the kind of day that defines a career. A day that marks the transition from apprentice to master, student to teacher. For me, this was the day I took over the National Football League (NFL) Combine preparation program at EXOS.

First run in 1982, the NFL Scouting Combine has become the premier event for NFL hopefuls to showcase their readiness to enter the league. Staged at Lucas Oil Stadium in Indianapolis, Indiana, the NFL Combine is a yearly event that occurs during the last week of February, two months before the NFL Draft. Over the course of three grueling days, an average of 330 of the country's top prospects are invited to complete an extensive battery of physical and mental tests, earning it the title of *The Biggest Interview of Your Life*, an apt name, when you consider that more people get into Harvard each year than are drafted into the NFL.

While the first two days require players to deal with 5:00 a.m. wake-up calls, extensive medical assessments, and late-night interviews, it is the final day that has earned the NFL Combine its international appeal (Australian rules football has followed suit with its own AFL Draft Combine). Nationally televised, during the final day, players are asked to show off their physical skills in a spectacle that has been called the *Underwear Olympics*. Every player is required to complete a vertical jump, broad jump, 40-yard (37 m) dash, pro-agility drill, three-cone drill, and a selection of position-specific drills. With only a few reps to show what you've got and your future employer scrutinizing your every move, it is no surprise that players and agents put a premium on preparing for this pressurized event.

I had been working at EXOS for three years, having started with the company when it was still called Athletes' Performance (AP). During that first year, I got my first taste of the Combine preparation program. I soon learned that AP was the most sought-after "finishing school" for premier college football players looking to physically and mentally prepare for the Combine, hoping that an elite performance in February would help their draft status in April. To say I was hooked would be an understatement — I told myself, "I will run this program one day."

AP had become a sanctuary for professional or soon-to-be professional athletes. Through the leadership and vision of Mark Verstegen, founder and president of AP, the organization had become a recognized leader in human performance. This status was a consequence of Verstegen integrating some of the best minds and methods, across mindset, nutrition, movement, and recovery, to produce a training environment and system that, to this day, influence the way the world thinks about performance.

In that first year at AP, I had the privilege of meeting Combine coaching elites Luke Richesson, Darryl Eto, and Joe Gomes. For the next three years, I worked alongside and learned from these coaches as we supported the NFL stars of the future. I saw the immense responsibility placed on each of them, the tireless and, at times, thankless effort required to improve the program year after year, ensuring that the legacy lives on and another generation of athletes are given a chance to maximize their performance during the biggest interview of their life.

As darkness gave way to light, the realization that this responsibility was now mine flooded my awareness, triggering the inescapable pounding in my chest. However, any sense of fear or uncertainty was quickly replaced with focus and determination as I turned into the driveway of our performance center in Phoenix, Arizona.

Luke had since gone to the Jacksonville Jaguars, fulfilling his goal of working in the NFL. Darryl had also transitioned, taking a position with the Houston Rockets. This meant that Joe Gomes and I would be co-coaching the speed portion of the Combine preparation program, with the expectation that I would inevitably run solo. As with most things in life, plans changed, and I received the news that I'd be taking over the program sooner than anticipated.

Now in the driver's seat, I focused on executing the program to the dotted *i* and crossed *t*. At the time, I defined a successful session as one in which movements were explained with clinical detail, time was managed with military accuracy, and every rep and set was accounted for. The fact that this program had been born out of years of work by some of the most successful athletic performance coaches of our time was not lost on me. I was not going to be the coach who tainted a legacy and the coaches who'd built it. This is why I continued to sweat the smallest detail and, in the process, ensured that my athletes did as well.

It is through the lens of this last point, and the impact this type of coaching can have on learning movement, that I discovered the path to this book. It all started on a Monday morning in early January. We were on the track going through a series of drills in preparation for the sprint session that followed. I recall providing detailed instructions before, during, and after each group's turn, wielding words and correcting movement with surgical precision. In my mind, everything I was saying was well articulated and correctly timed. If my words sounded good and had substance, I was happy, end of story. However, it wasn't the end of the story; in fact, it was just the beginning because I soon realized that, just because my words made sense, didn't mean they made a difference.

I am not sure why this session stood out in my mind, but I am grateful that it did, as the ensuing reflection led me to interrogate how I coach, revealing a number of sobering truths. First, I was providing the athletes with so much information, it would be unfair to expect them to remember and apply everything I was saying. While experience and education told me that attention and memory are finite resources, I consistently ignored this fact when it came to my coaching. Despite being well intentioned, I, like so many coaches, was a chronic over-communicator. Second, a consequence of this overcommunication meant that I was unaware of what my athletes were focusing on. I was giving so many cues that there was no way to know which cues got in, let alone which ones helped and which ones hindered. Considering these observations, I asked myself a series of hard questions: What effect does cue quality and quantity have on my athletes' ability to learn and develop? How much further could I push my athletes' gains by first simplifying and then optimizing their focus during training? Is there a coaching science that can inform what is so often referred to as an art?

This story, a true reflection of my early years as a coach, provides the basis for part one of this book. Above all else, that first year taught me that it's not enough to coach the program, you also need to coach the person. We need to consider all the factors that influence how a person learns, notably the impact of attention and memory. By understanding the way attention shapes memory and, as a consequence, the way memory serves learning, we'll be far better at deploying coaching language that sparks lasting change.

LEARN THIS

1

Learning: A Primer

Stepping off the plane in late February, the brisk Indianapolis air seemed to sharpen the senses, preparing the coaches and athletes for the unforgiving environment that is the NFL Combine. As this was my first time attending, I didn't know what to expect beyond the stories I'd heard. However, I knew one thing for sure—the pounding in my chest was back, and this time the reason was clear. In just three days, my athletes would be competing against the best in their position for all the world to see.

While the effectiveness of our eight-week program would be tested on the final day of the Combine, athletes had to first endure two days of intensive interviews and medical assessments. From drug testing at daybreak to meetings at midnight, athletes had their character tested, knowledge assessed, and health screened. Thus, to avoid unnecessary stress and anxiety, we prepared for the particulars and controlled the controllable. From packed lunches at baggage claim to a temporary performance center in a hotel ballroom, our EXOS team was running a home away from home.

The suspense was suffocating at times as we waited for our athletes to run on that final day. While we knew that draft status was determined by more than the Combine, we also knew that a surprisingly fast 40-yard (37 m) time could encourage a team to take a second look. Thus, we sat quietly, crowded around a TV in our hotel ballroom, each coach waiting for their athlete to run. When your athlete finally appears, time seems to slow as your heart starts to race. In an instant, they explode off the line, and five or so seconds later, the time appears on the screen, sealing your athlete's 40-yard (37 m) fate.

As I watched my athletes perform that first year, I assessed their times, checking them against our pretest scores, and I reviewed the tape, evaluating the evolution of their sprint technique from start to finish. The goal was to understand where changes, if any, had emerged. Did my athletes run faster because they had gotten stronger and could produce more force, a quality known to affect sprint speed (20), or did they run faster due to changes in coordination that optimized the direction of that force, a hallmark trait of elite sprinters (8, 16)? In truth, any combination of these factors could improve sprint performance, but, in my case, one factor seemed to stand above the rest.

Although the athletes were running faster over 40 yards (37 m), my coaching eye suggested that this had more to do with an upgrade to the car (i.e., strength and magnitude of force) than the skill of the driver (i.e., coordination and direction of force). In replaying each 40-yard (37 m) dash, I consistently saw movement errors that I thought we'd changed during the preparation process. For example, athletes who were able to maintain a flat back as they came out of their stance were now hunched over, appearing to almost fall as they took off toward the finish line. Other athletes, who'd been taught the importance of a powerful forward knee drive, were now reverting to the short and choppy steps one would expect to see from a two-year-old having a temper tantrum. The unavoidable truth was that something had happened between my athletes' leaving our training facility in Phoenix and their running the 40-yard (37 m) dash in Indianapolis.

While my athletes' performance had changed, the technique they'd used to achieve it had not. From this observation came a simple question: Why were my athletes able to perform with improved sprint technique and times during training but unable to perform at this same level during the Combine? How can we explain the difference, better or worse, between performance during practice and that observed during a future practice or competition? In answering this question, we'd surely find a fundamental truth about the way humans learn to move and, as a consequence, the way we should coach them to do so.

PART 1: THE PROFILE

When discussing the changes, positive or negative, that emerge from practice to practice or practice to competition, we must first align on the changes we're referring to. It is beyond the scope of this book to discuss every type of adaptation that the body will undergo over time; rather, we are chiefly concerned with the adaptive process connected to improving one's ability to move, coordinate, and express a skill, a process known as **motor-skill learning**. Therefore, to better understand what motor-skill learning is, there is value in briefly discussing what it is not. To this end, it is useful to frame our discussion through the lens of a familiar analogy.

Consider the following analogy and fill in the blank:

> **Car is to human body as driver is to human**_____.

Do you have your answer? The word that likely jumped to mind was *brain*. A car, like a body, provides the potential for motion; however, without a driver, specifically, the driver's brain, there would be little in the way of movement. Even self-driving cars require a *driver* to be modeled into the car's operating system. Thus, the analogy serves to provide us with a useful framework to discuss peripheral adaptation—represented by the car—and its relationship to central adaptation—represented by the driver—in terms of motor-skill learning.

3P Performance Profile

To begin, it is helpful to visit the birthplace of this analogy and, in doing so, discuss its utility as a mental model (or short-cut) coaches can use to prioritize the movement problems they're trying to solve. Throughout my years preparing athletes for the NFL Combine and, really, sport in general, one observation became clear: each athlete must take a very different pathway to achieve their potential. To illustrate this, let's imagine that we have three defensive backs (DBs) preparing for the NFL Combine. Upon arrival, our DBs go through a series of assessments and screens that're used to construct an individualized athletic profile. This athletic profile is then used to prioritize the athletic qualities that, if improved, will help the DBs turn their aspirations into abilities. The athletic profile we will use, referred to as the **3P Performance Profile**[1] (see figure 1.1), was born out of the need to quickly identify the limiting factors that influence the performance of a given movement (e.g., jumping, sprinting, and agility). Notably, this approach to prioritization is not unique to athletes and, therefore, can be used to profile any movement within any population, providing coaches, trainers, and therapists alike, with an individualized path to progress motor-skill learning. Now, before we return to our DB story, let's briefly consider each element of the 3P Performance Profile and the effect this approach can have on developing motor skills.

---

[1] The inspiration for the 3P Performance Profile (short for *position*, *power*, and *pattern*) comes from my former colleague Victor Hall. In 2010, Coach Hall produced an instructional video for the power clean and posted it on his blog, "Coach 'Em Up," under the title "Clean It Up." In the video, Coach Hall outlines a three-step prioritization list for correcting the power clean: Step 1: Can they get in the correct body *position*? Step 2: Can they execute the correct movement *pattern*? and Step 3: Can they move at the correct *speed*? I evolved this model into the 3P Performance Profile while I was at EXOS. This profile was eventually integrated into the EXOS training system and its educational offerings.

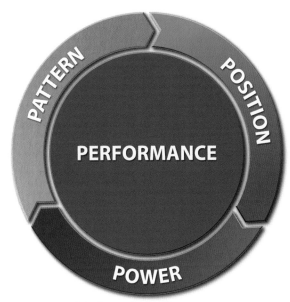

FIGURE 1.1   3P Performance Profile.

POSITION

Position, the first *P*, asks the question, does the athlete have the required mobility and stability needed to effectively perform the movement? Put differently, can the athlete get in and stay in the body positions associated with the motor skill? For example, when teaching an athlete how to accelerate over 10 yards (9 m), as depicted in figure 1.2*a*, we would like to see that they can simultaneously flex and extend their hips while maintaining a neutral spine. This ensures that they are able to work within the range of motion required to execute a biomechanically desired pattern while still allowing for individual variation. Further, we would want to see that the athlete has adequate stability in the joints associated with acceleration (e.g., trunk stability, hip stability, and ankle and feet stability). This stability, or control, provides the foundation on which more-complex patterns of movement or coordination can be built.

POWER

Power, the second *P*, asks the question, does the athlete have the required strength and power qualities needed to effectively perform the movement?[2] While power is important for all movements, it is particularly important when one needs to quickly overcome their own body mass. Therefore, any ballistic movements that require an athlete to project their body in a specific direction would qualify as a power-dependent pattern. For example, as depicted in figure 1.2*b*, when an athlete begins to run (jump or change direction), they must counteract their body weight by producing a large force, in the right direction, at the right time. If the athlete lacks an adequate level of power, they will have a difficult time maximizing their performance because the effectiveness of these movement patterns is, in part, determined by the force-generating characteristics of the associated muscles. In contrast, movements with limited ballistic demands (e.g., squats, kettlebell swings, and biceps curls) are less dependent on maximizing power, as the coach can manipulate the weight if a change in the movement pattern is desired, notably, during instances when the weight is too heavy. Thus, the type of movement and associated context dictate the relative importance of power and, as a result, the influence it has on the movement pattern.

---

[2] In this context, I use the word *power* to represent the collective strength and power qualities associated with the performance of a given movement. As such, when I use the word *power*, I am using it as an inclusive term, recognizing that it is a product of Force × Velocity, which accounts for the kinetic characteristics of any movement.

PATTERN

Pattern, the third *P*, asks the question, does the athlete have the required coordination needed to effectively perform the movement? In this context, **coordination** refers to the spatial and temporal organization of joint motion associated with the execution of a movement pattern, as depicted in figure 1.2*c*. Thus, by definition, we can see that the coordination, or pattern, is inextricably linked to the characteristics associated with the position and power categories. Observed through the lens of our opening analogy, the physical qualities represented by position and power are like a car, which contains the capacity for performance, while the pattern is like the driver, which is required for that performance to be realized. And just as a high-performance sports car is ineffective without an experienced driver, an experienced driver is equally ineffective without a high-performance sports car. Thus, the principal responsibility of the coach is to use the 3P Performance Profile to identify whether they have a car issue, a driver issue, or some combination of both.

PERFORMANCE

Once combined, the three *P*s give rise to a final *P*, **performance**, which can be defined as the measured output of a motor skill (e.g., weight lifted, time achieved, or points scored). Applied to our DBs, we're interested in the position, power, and pattern that influence performance on a 40-yard (37 m) dash. To unpack this, let's look at how our DBs stack up across the 3P Performance Profile. In table 1.1, we see an example of a breakdown of the relevant assessments and screens that could be used to profile the three *P*s. Further, figure 1.3 provides the profiles for each DB. Each profile is built based on the DB's performance across the three *P*s, scaled from –5 to +5, with 0 representing an average outcome. For the purpose of this example, it is not important to discuss the performance on any one measure; however, it is important to understand how the relative performance in one area compares to the relative performance in another.

FIGURE 1.2 *(a)* The mobility and stability needed to achieve the correct body *position*, *(b)* the musculature involved in producing the *power* needed to perform the movement, and *(c)* the coordination associated with the *pattern* on which the movement is based.

(a)　　　　　　　　　　*(b)*　　　　　　　　　　*(c)*

TABLE 1.1   3P Performance Profile: Examples of Assessments and Screenings for the 40-Yard (37 m) Dash

Category	Quality	Examples of assessments and screens	Measure/metric
Position	Mobility and stability	Range of motion	Degrees of motion
		Functional Movement Screen	Score out of 21
Power	Relative strength	Lower-body push (front squat)	Lb lifted per lb of body weight
	Relative power	Lower-body push (vertical jump)	Watts produced per lb of body weight
Pattern	Coordination	0-10 yd (acceleration)	Video analysis: technique
		10-20 yd (transition)	Video analysis: technique
		20-40 yd (absolute speed)	Video analysis: technique
Performance	Outcome	0-10 yd split	Split time
		10-20 yd split	Split time
		20-40 yd split	Split time
		0-40 yd split	Split time

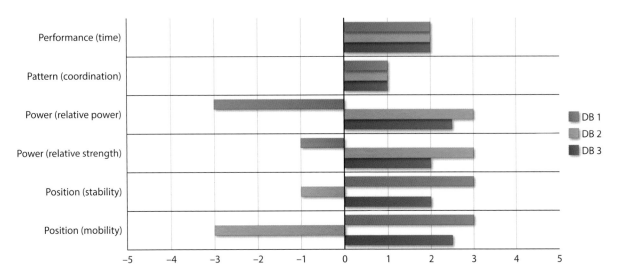

FIGURE 1.3   DBs' performance profiles on the assessments and screens that are outlined in table 1.1. Results are represented on a scale from −5 to +5, where 0 represents positional average. A positive score is above average, while a negative score is below average. Training priorities are established based on individual DBs' strengths compared to weaknesses.

Applying the 3P Performance Profile

If we examine each profile (see figure 1.3), starting at the top, we see that all three DBs performed similarly in their outcome performance and pattern, which is to say that they used a common sprinting technique to cover 40 yards (37 m) in a similar time. This is an important point, as it is normal to find athletes with similar movement patterns and performance outcomes; however, the pathway to improving these baseline measures is invariably unique to each athlete.

Unlike the DBs' patterns and performances, we see that all three of them vary across the measures of power and position. That is to say, each athlete is dealing with a unique car, which, if taken to a mechanic, would require service on different parts of the vehicle. Thus, a key responsibility of the coach is to understand how the car and driver are interacting to achieve the measured outcome performance, providing insights on where service is needed.

To illustrate this last point, it is important to anchor position and power to the observed pattern. As we noted, the DBs use a similar sprint pattern, which, in this case, we will describe as an excessively quick leg action. This means that they are taking more steps than are required to cover a given distance and, in the process, produce less overall force and speed than would otherwise be possible. A consequence of this sprinting technique, or the possible cause, is reduced hip flexion and extension, which visually conveys that temper tantrum–type leg action that is unique to this sprint pattern. To understand why this technique is emerging, however, we need to consider the position and power characteristics of each DB.

Take a moment to look at the profiles in figure 1.3 with the intention of prioritizing each DB's biggest area for improvement. What did you notice? Likely, you saw that DB 1 has adequate mobility and stability (i.e., position), with deficits relating to the expression of relative strength and power (i.e., power); DB 2 has adequate relative strength and power, with deficits relating to mobility and stability; and DB 3 has no distinct deficits that are apparent. When taken collectively and applied to the sprint pattern previously described, we now have three possible explanations for the same sprint pattern. Specifically, it is not unreasonable to think that DB 1 adopts a choppy sprint pattern due to an inability to generate large forces quickly, as represented by deficit in power, while one could speculate that the reason DB 2 adopts this sprinting style may have to do with an inability to achieve and maintain the required flexion and extension at the hip. Furthermore, due to the fact that DB 3 doesn't have any distinct deficits within their athletic profile, it would be fair to reason that their sprint style is a pure consequence of their natural coordination, as opposed to some underpinning physical deficit.

While this approach is somewhat reductionist, it does convey a practical way of understanding the nature of the movement problem we're dealing with. For example, let's assume we are four weeks into working with our three DBs. We begin to find that, while all three athletes are progressing, DB 1 and DB 2 are not progressing as fast as DB 3. Logic suggests that this isn't a result of the coaching because all three athletes are receiving similar instruction and going through the same program. Thus, our dealings with the driver, so to speak, seem to be working for DB 3, while the mechanical issues associated with the cars of DB 1 and DB 2 appear to be impeding progress. Therefore, DB 3 is benefitting from *driver's school*, while DB 1 and DB 2 need to spend a bit more time *in the shop*. To this end, all three athletes can continue to follow a similar sprint program; however, DB 1 and DB 2 would require specific strategies to overcome their deficits. Once resolved, their patterns and resulting performances should respond quickly.

Although hypothetical, this example reflects a situation that I've found myself in time and time again and, based on numerous conversations, reflects a common phenomenon within coaching and rehabilitation. Thus, born out of necessity and utility, the 3P Performance Profile and the associated car and driver analogy have served to provide a practical framework for developing motor patterns and their physical dependencies (i.e., position and power). Therefore, when we discuss motor learning, which we'll define in greater detail in the next section, we must recognize that there are physical factors that have a material impact on coordination.

Consequently, what can sometimes appear to be a driver problem can, in reality, be a misdiagnosed issue with the car. For this reason, to clarify the message of this book, we will focus solely on the motor learning strategies, notably cueing, that're best suited for developing movement *patterns*. Accordingly, it is the coach's responsibility to understand that, when an effective coaching strategy fails, the failure may in fact be a physical deficit in disguise.

PART 2: THE PROCESS

The previous section provided us with a framework for understanding the factors that underpin the development of a movement pattern. We will now turn our attention back to the question that concluded the first section of this chapter: How can we explain the differences observed between performance during practice and performance during a future practice or competition? Specifically, while the structural (peripheral) adaptations associated with improvements in position and power have lasting effects that change the physical body, the neural (central) adaptations associated with changes to the pattern tend be far less stable and are highly responsive to the conditions that gave rise to them. Put another way, if we stretch enough, we will become mobile; if we lift enough, we will become strong. However, the act of performing a movement pattern does not guarantee its optimization.

To demonstrate this, go no further than to reflect on a time when you observed a tangible improvement in an athlete's movement pattern early in a week, followed by a complete regression back to the original (undesirable) pattern later that same week. This scenario is all too common for coaches and athletes and suggests that there is something fundamentally different between the appearance of motor learning in the short term and its sustained expression in the long term. To understand why acute changes (to a motor skill) are not always lasting, we need to establish several definitions. To frame these definitions, consider the following stories:

▶ **Story A**

An athletic performance coach is working with an athlete on Olympic lifting. The athlete is a freshman in a college football program and has never been coached on how to lift properly. After working with the athlete for a number of weeks, the coach identifies a consistent trend. Specifically, when the coach engages the athlete, providing individualized cues, they respond favorably with a distinct improvement in their technique. However, any changes are brief, as the coach notices that the athlete's technique quickly regresses back to baseline in subsequent training sessions.

▶ **Story B**

A personal trainer is working with a client on squats. The client tells the personal trainer that their knees ache when they play with their kids. After assessing the client's squat technique, the personal trainer notices that the client's knees shift inward as they descend into the squat. Identifying that this may be a contributing factor, the personal trainer attempts to cue the client out of this pattern. Despite telling the client to "keep your knees over your toes" and "push your knees out," the client continues to revert back to old habits, session after session. After consulting with a colleague, the personal trainer shifts tactics by placing a mini band just above the client's knees and encouraging the client to "keep tension through the band" as they squat. The new strategy results in a noticeable change to the client's squat pattern, which, after a few training sessions, is easily maintained with or without the prompting of the band or the personal trainer.

For many coaches, the scenarios presented in stories A and B are all too familiar. We can see the echo of story A in every athlete who practices well and plays poorly, while story B captures the outcome that every coach is chasing. Thus, to help coaches move their athletes' narrative from story A to story B, it is essential that we understand the fundamental differences between the two scenarios.

Motor Performance Versus Motor Learning

The defining difference between story A and story B is the ending. That is, in story A, the coach was perplexed, as the athlete was only able to perform at the desired standard when reminded to do so. In contrast, the personal trainer in story B redirected their coaching strategy and was able to instigate a lasting change to their client's squat technique. In both stories, the coach and personal trainer were able to improve **motor performance**, which refers to short-term shifts in motor behavior that can be observed and measured during or immediately after a practice session, while only the personal trainer was able to facilitate **motor learning**, which reflects relatively permanent changes in motor behavior that underpin long-term retention of motor skills (15). Thus, as highlighted by the distinction between the stories, a change in motor performance is not necessarily indicative of a change in motor learning. What's more, many methods have been shown to improve motor performance in a practice context, while only a select few consistently promote long-term motor learning. For this reason, we'll turn our attention to defining the contexts used to develop and assess motor skills, providing coaches with a natural framework for evaluating the effectiveness of their coaching methods.

Acquisition Phase Versus Retention Phase

In both stories, there is a period of time where the athlete and client practice a motor skill while receiving input from their athletic performance coach and personal trainer. This initial practice period, whether a single practice session or a series of practice sessions, describes the **acquisition phase**. This phase of motor skill development is commonly characterized by coaches providing their athletes with instructions before and feedback after a movement is performed. Further, coaches may also manipulate features of the motor skill (e.g., putting a mini band above the knees in story B) to help encourage a desirable change. Practically speaking, any attempt to influence a motor skill, whether through explicit or implicit means, can be considered an identifying feature of the acquisition phase. Thus, even in the case of a well-learned movement, further attempts to improve motor performance would be categorized as a reentry into acquisition mode.

While coaches will often use changes during an acquisition phase as a barometer for progress, the ultimate assessment of motor learning requires a **retention phase**, which takes place at some point in the future, is within a relevant context, and is void of any coaching influence. In story A, for example, each practice session can serve as a retention phase, as the coach is able to watch the athlete execute the Olympic lift before providing input. However, if the coach were quick to remind the athlete of essential cues, then the coach would lose the opportunity to directly assess retention and, therefore, learning. Thus, as we'll see in the next section, we must be cautious not to assume that coach-induced changes in the present are indicative of sustained, athlete-owned changes in the future.

PART 3: THE DISTINCTION

For many of us, one of our most memorable childhood experiences was learning how to ride a bike. Knowing this, when the day finally came for my daughter to learn how to ride her first two-wheeler, I summoned the memories from my own experience that seemed useful. While I didn't want her to end up in the bushes as I had on my first solo attempt, I did recognize the value in the approach my dad used to teach me, which included simple reminders like "focus forward," "push through the pedals," and "balance the bike." Armed with these cues and my dad's voice echoing the importance of "just giving it a go," we made our way to the park to start practicing.

As expected, the first few sessions were marked by my daughter yelling "don't let go" and me reaffirming that "I won't," all the while slowly letting her ride without the support of my hand. Inevitably, her comfort and balance grew, and she was happy for me to run alongside her. In the weeks leading up to this moment, there was a consistent phenomenon. My daughter would end one practice session, having made small gains in her riding ability, and she would start the next session with a noticeable improvement beyond where we'd finished. That is, the improvement she experienced in one practice session seemed to amplify in the lead-up, typically a few days, to our next. While my daughter was content in the fact that she was finally learning how to ride her bike, I was excited to see one of the most important motor-learning principles at work.

This observation, which is common for anyone learning a new skill, is a perfect example of the **performance-learning distinction**, which contrasts short-term changes to a motor skill (i.e., motor performance), commonly prompted by the influence of a coach, with long-term changes that can be expressed independent of a coaching presence (i.e., motor learning) (7, 13). Thus, the improvements I observed in my daughter's motor performance during one practice session did not indicate the full extent to which motor learning had taken place. This is an important consideration for coaches, as we often assess our effectiveness in terms of the improvements we see within a single practice session. However, as discussed in the previous section, this is ill-advised, as there is well-established evidence that acute motor performance is not always indicative of chronic changes to motor learning (3, 15).

Before providing evidence for this last point, let's consider three outcomes that can be explained by the performance-learning distinction (see figure 1.4). The first outcome is that the motor performance achieved during the acquisition phase is better than the motor performance achieved during the retention phase. This was the case in story A, where the athlete's lifting technique was effective when the coach was available to cue them (i.e., acquisition phase) but quickly regressed once the coaching influence was removed (i.e., retention phase). As coaches, we need to be quick to spot this scenario because a regression in motor performance is a sign that the athlete is either dependent on our coaching tactics or isn't adapting to the learning environment we've designed. The second possible outcome is that the motor performance achieved during the acquisition phase is maintained during the retention phase. This was the case in story B, where the improvements in the client's squat technique were sustained from acquisition to retention. This maintenance or stabilization in motor performance is often a strong indication that, while retention and thus learning have occurred, a change in coaching tactic or programming is required if further improvements are needed. The third possible outcome, which was the case with my daughter learning to ride her bike (story C), is that motor performance during the retention phase is better than the motor performance during the acquisition phase. This third outcome, which is common in individuals learning a new skill, is a good sign that the coach has used effective coaching tactics, as the practice conditions encouraged changes to the motor system that are only fully realized after a period of memory storage and motor adaptation has occurred.

The three scenarios described in figure 1.4 provide a learning GPS of sorts that tells the coach if the athlete is moving in the right direction. This information will help the coach redirect coaching tactics based on where the athlete falls on this continuum. Further, coaches are encouraged to consistently use the movement pattern and performance outcome when assessing motor learning during these retention phases. Assuming there is a metric associated with the motor skill (e.g., weight lifted, time to run a distance, or pass accuracy), the coach is looking to see whether there are positive shifts in the pattern, the performance, or both.

In applying this strategy, coaches can use what I like to call **silent sets**. For example, let's say our coach from story A tried out new cues for the Olympic lift and wanted to see if they resulted in improved motor skill retention. To test this, rather than immediately reminding the athlete of these cues during a subsequent training session, the coach would employ one or more silent sets, where they say nothing and simply observe the athlete perform the movement. If the athlete maintains or betters the changes seen in past training sessions, then the coach can be confident that learning has occurred. Conversely, if the athlete still regresses, then the coach knows that more time is needed for the athlete to fully adapt or they may need to evolve their coaching strategy. Ultimately, athletes should come to value silent sets, as they're an opportunity to show their coaches (and themselves) that they've mastered or are on their way to mastering a movement.

Now that we've established the key terms associated with the performance-learning distinction, let's examine two research areas that provide us with a glimpse of this distinction at work.

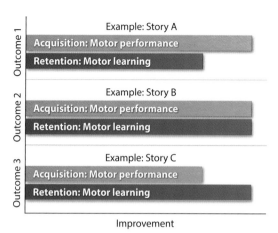

FIGURE 1.4   Three possible outcomes that can emerge between a learning stimulus (acquisition phase) and the assessment of that learning stimulus (retention phase). Each outcome represents one of the stories discussed, where outcome 1 represents story A, outcome 2 represents story B, and outcome 3 represents story C.

Practice and Learning

Have you ever watched a basketball or soccer team practice? If you have, then you've undoubtedly seen athletes lining up to go through drills—shooting, kicking, and passing—performing repetition after repetition. At first glance, this physical form of rote memorization doesn't seem dissimilar to the approach one would have used to study vocabulary as a kid: step 1, put a word on one side of an index card and the definition on the other; step 2, stare at the word and definition until you think you can remember it; step 3, spell and define the word aloud; and step 4, check if you were correct and repeat. While this method works well when deployed moments before a pop quiz, it is unlikely to do the trick if the teacher sprung a retention test three days later, requiring you to use each word in a sentence. Sport, as we'll see, is no different, with the way one practices determining, to a large degree, how well they play.

The idea that there is an optimal way to design practice to support learning has been an area of interest for researchers, coaches, and teachers for the better part of 40 years (14). In principle, researchers agree that practice needs to impose a level of *desirable difficulty* on the athlete if learning is to be optimized (1). While this might seem counterintuitive at first, a child's perspective helps reveal the logic.

When my son was three, he became interested in puzzles after seeing his big sister complete a number of junior jigsaws. While he wasn't ready for the 100-piece princess palace his sister was working on, he was more than capable of tackling her old 8-piece wooden puzzles. After he had conquered a number of these puzzles, he quickly became disinterested and looked for something more challenging. His failed attempts to help his sister suggested that he wasn't quite ready for a 100-piece puzzle; however, he was more than capable of completing a 20-piece puzzle depicting some of his favorite Disney characters. Although simple,

this example depicts two underpinning truths about learning. First, you have to be interested in what you are learning about, and, second, there needs to be something for you to learn. That is, once the 8-piece puzzle ceased to present a challenge, my son lost interest because there wasn't anything new to learn. Equally, when faced with the 100-piece puzzle, he hadn't yet developed the skills necessary to deal with such complexity and, consequently, lost interest after repeated failures. However, when presented with the 20-piece puzzle, his interest was piqued, as there was a new challenge that he was both motivated by and capable of overcoming.

GOLDILOCKS PRINCIPLE

This story captures what is commonly referred to as the **Goldilocks principle**, which proposes that a given exposure (e.g., difficulty) needs to be within a certain bandwidth (i.e., "just right") to encourage a desired change (e.g., learning). In motor learning, this idea has been translated into what Guadagnoli and Lee (5) call the **challenge point hypothesis**, which proposes that learning is a consequence of the information available to the learner (see figure 1.5). In other words, learning is limited if there is too little or too much information and optimized when the available information aligns with the learner's readiness to absorb it. Practically speaking, the relative difficulty of a task determines how much information is available to the learner. Hence, if I'm a novice at something, a small challenge will initially result in a large learning effect, as I'm able to consume all available information about a task (e.g., hitting a baseball off a tee). However, if I'm faced with a challenge that stretches beyond my capabilities, then I won't be able to take in the overflow of information on offer (e.g., hitting a thrown baseball). Conversely, if I'm an expert on the other end of the continuum, the challenge needs to be high for me to extract new information about a given motor skill (e.g., hitting off a live pitcher). Ultimately, information, whether it be implicit or explicit, is the reward that comes from working through the puzzle, or, in our case, solving the movement problem. As coaches, our job is to create the learning conditions that stretch the athlete just beyond their comfort zone, ensuring that a fresh dose of information is always available.

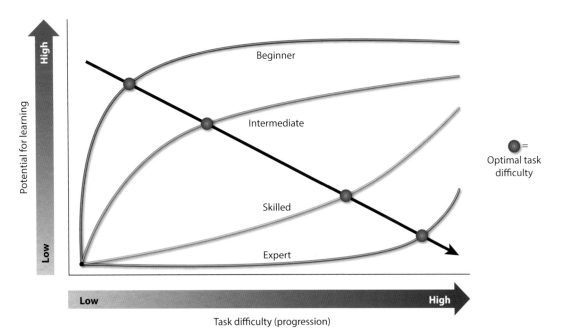

FIGURE 1.5   Challenge point hypothesis.

Adapted by permission from M.A. Guadagnoli and T.D. Lee, "Challenge Point: A Framework for Conceptualizing the Effects of Various Practice Conditions in Motor Learning," *Journal of Motor Behavior* 36, no. 2 (2004): 212-224.

PRACTICE VARIABILITY

To further demonstrate the importance of the practice environment, let's consider a series of studies by Porter and colleagues. Based on the concept of *desirable difficulty*, Porter and Magill (10) examined the influence of practice variability,[3] commonly referred to as *contextual interference*, on basketball passing accuracy in a group of novices. The participants were broken into three groups: a low-variability group, which performed a block of repetitions of one pass type (e.g., two-hand overhead pass) before moving on to a second and third pass type (i.e., blocked practice group); a high-variability group, which performed all three pass types in a randomized order (i.e., random practice group); and a progression group, which transitioned from a low-variability (i.e., blocked practice) to a high-variability (i.e., random practice) practice structure. The results, which were later confirmed by Porter and Saemi (11) and extended by Porter and Beckerman (9), showed that, while there were no between-group differences during the acquisition phase, the progression group outperformed the blocked and random practice groups during the retention phase (see figure 1.6). This means that a systematic increase in practice variability results in greater motor learning than simply practicing under low- or high-variability conditions (i.e., the Goldilocks principle).

This study and others like it provide our first clear example of the performance-learning distinction at work (2). Even though low-, high-, and progressive-practice variability result in similar performance during an acquisition phase, this similarity dissolves in favor of progressive-practice variability when learning is assessed during a retention phase.[4] Thus, from a coaching perspective, we see that the structure of practice

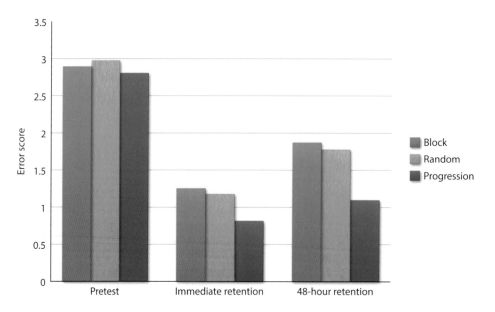

FIGURE 1.6   Average absolute error (AE) scores for pretest, immediate retention test, and 48-hour retention test.

Reprinted by permission from J.M. Porter and E. Saemi, "Moderately Skilled Learners Benefit by Practicing With Systematic Increases in Contextual Interference," *International Journal of Coaching Science* 4, no. 2 (2010): 61-71.

---

[3] Both practice variability and contextual interference are terms used to describe how often the context changes during a practice session. Thus, for example, if a coach were to have a practice where the athletes did the exact same passing drill for the entire session, then we would say there is minimal practice variability. In contrast, if a coach were to change the drill every minute, then we would say that the session had high-practice variability. Now, the right amount of practice variability is dependent on the skill level of the athlete; however, in principle, we know that as someone improves in ability, they benefit from increased practice variability. If you consider that most sports, especially team sports, by their very nature are variable, then this finding should make sense.

[4] Contextual interference research has traditionally examined the difference between blocked and random practice, showing that, while blocked practice supports better short-term performance, random practice tends to support superior long-term learning (i.e., the performance-learning distinction). However, we cannot reduce all practice design down to blocked, random, or progressive; rather, as stated, we must match the right level of variability to the athlete and skill they are learning. That said, if we make a training session too easy or too easy too often, we run the risk of being coaxed into a false sense of security by the fact that the athlete appears to be improving in practice and simply "hasn't figured it out yet in competition."

has a direct impact on long-term motor learning. This comes as a consequence of manipulating practice variability in proportion to an athlete's current level of performance, whereby the right level of variability or challenge keeps the athlete engaged and their attention tuned to task-relevant information (4). As we will begin to see in the next section, it is this tuning of attention that not only underpins effective practice design but also effective coaching.

Coaching and Learning

If you're a student of coaching, you'll inevitably come across a video called "Funny Golf Tip from J.C. Anderson" (21). While this satirical take on coaching cues is over the top, it is also strikingly familiar, as it conveys threads of truth that most coaches come to realize later in their careers. As coaches, we easily fall into the trap of saying too much, too often (this was definitely true for me early in my career). For example, have you ever served up a sermon on squatting only to have your athlete look back at you and ask "So what do you want me to do?" or give your athletes a soapbox speech on sprinting only to have them do the exact opposite of what you intended? These examples, a small sampling of the possible coaching blunders, capture the ease with which coaches can inadvertently misuse language—often, none the wiser. In contrast, a coach who is familiar with the intersection between coaching language and motor-skill learning will understand what to say; when to say it; and how much to say to encourage improvements that are stable over time. To illustrate this, let's look at the "what to say" portion of the coaching conversation and highlight another example of the performance-learning distinction in action.

COACHING CUES

To examine the influence coaching language (i.e., "what to say") has on performance and learning, we'll consider two studies from Dr. Gabriele Wulf, a researcher you'll come to know quite well by the end of this book. Interested in the effect different types of coaching cues have on learning a volleyball serve, Wulf and colleagues invited a group of *novices* with no volleyball experience and a group of *advanced* participants with some volleyball experience, to take part in their study (19). The task required participants to set up on the right side of a volleyball court and serve a ball over a standard net, trying to hit the middle of a 3- × 3-meter target (surrounded by a 4- × 4-meter and a 5- × 5-meter target), which was centered on the opposite side of the court (3, 2, and 1 points awarded for each zone, respectively, with 0 points awarded if outside target). The coaching intervention involved half of the participants (i.e., half of the novices and half of the advanced) receiving coaching cues related to the movement of the body, what is known as an *internal focus*, while the other half received coaching cues related to the outcome they were trying to achieve, what is known as an *external focus* (see table 1.2*a*). The coaching cues were delivered across two practice sessions (acquisition), set one week apart (see table 1.2*b*). Participants performed five blocks of five serves; following each block, an experimenter would give the participants a single, individualized coaching cue (external or internal) based on their most obvious technical error. A week after the second practice session, the participants came back to complete a 15-serve retention test where no cues, prompts, or reminders were given (see table 1.2*b*). As expected, the *advanced* participants outperformed the *novices*, independent of whether they were in the internal or external focus group. However, what was interesting was the fact that, within both the *advanced* and *novice* groups, those who'd received external focus cues achieved higher accuracy scores than those who'd received internal focus cues. What's more, this performance gap widened during the retention test, showing a distinct learning advantage for those who adopted an external focus, as opposed to an internal focus (see figure 1.7).

TABLE 1.2a   Internal and External Cues Used Across the Novice and Advanced Participants

Internal focus	External focus
Toss the ball high enough in front of the hitting *arm*.	*Toss the ball* straight up.
Snap your *wrist* while hitting the ball to produce a forward rotation of the ball.	Imagine holding a bowl in your hand and *cupping the ball* with it to produce a forward rotation of the ball.
Shortly before hitting the ball, shift your weight from the *back leg to the front leg*.	Shortly before hitting the ball, shift your *weight toward the target*.
Arch your *back* and accelerate the *shoulder* first, then the *upper arm*, the *lower arm*, and finally your *hand*.	*Hit the ball* as if using a whip, like an equestrian driving horses.

TABLE 1.2b   Volleyball Coaching Study Design

Acquisition		Retention
Day 1 (week 1)	**Day 2 (week 2)**	**Day 3 (week 3)**
5 blocks × 5 serves Individualized cue following each block of serves (5 total) (25 serves)	5 blocks × 5 serves Individualized cue following each block of serves (5 total) (25 serves)	3 blocks × 5 serves No cues, prompts, or reminders (15 serves)

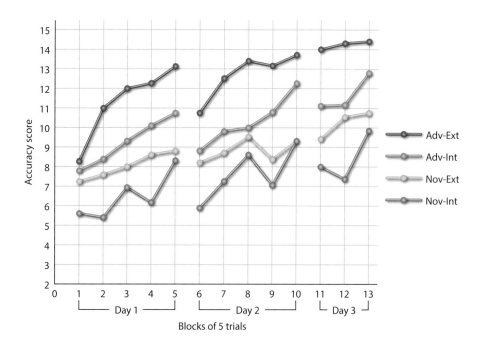

FIGURE 1.7   Accuracy results for the advanced and novice participants across the internal and external focus groups.

Reprinted by permission from G. Wulf, N. McConnel, M. Gartner, and A. Schwarz, "Enhancing the Learning of Sport Skills Through External-Focus Feedback," *Journal of Motor Behavior* 34, no. 2 (2002): 171-182.

In a follow-up study published alongside the volleyball experiment, Wulf and colleagues extended their findings to the soccer field. This time they recruited university students who had *some experience* playing soccer but were not considered advanced. The task required participants to kick a soccer ball at a target that was suspended 15 meters (16 yd) away (square target 1.4 × 1.4 m, suspended 1 m [1.1 yd] off the ground; central target 80 × 80 cm with two outer zones, each 15 cm [6 in.] wide; 3, 2, and 1 points awarded for each zone, respectively, with 0 points awarded if outside target). Participants were randomly assigned to one of four groups: an external focus group that received a coaching cue after every trial (EXT100%), an external focus group that received a coaching cue after every third trial (EXT33%), an internal focus group that received a coaching cue after every trial (INT100%), or an internal focus group that received a coaching cue after every third trial (EXT33%) (see tables 1.3a and 1.3b). The coaching cues were delivered across a single practice session (acquisition), with a retention test occurring one week later. The practice session was divided into six blocks of five kicks, and the retention test was divided into two blocks of five kicks. Similar to the volleyball study, the experimenter provided participants with a single, individualized coaching cue (EXT or INT) based on the participants' assigned cueing frequency (100% or 33%). Once again, the results showed that both external focus groups achieved greater overall kicking accuracy than both internal focus groups during the practice session; the EXT100% group performed similarly to the EXT33% group, and the INT33% outperformed the INT100%. During the retention test, accuracy continued to improve, and the relative performance of each group remained constant (see figure 1.8).

TABLE 1.3a   Internal and External Cues Provided Across the 100 and 33 Percent Feedback Frequency Groups

Internal focus	External focus
Position your *foot* below the ball's midline to lift the ball.	*Strike the ball* below its midline to lift it; that is, kick underneath it.
Position your body weight and the nonkicking *foot* behind the ball.	*Be behind the ball*, not over it, and lean back.
Lock your *ankle* down and use the instep to strike the ball.	Stroke the *ball toward the target* as if passing to another athlete.
Keep your *knee bent* as you swing your *leg back*, and *straighten your knee* before contact.	Use a long-lever action like the swing of a golf club before *contact with the ball*.
To strike the ball, the *swing of the leg* should be as long as possible.	To *strike the ball*, create a pendulum-like motion with as long a duration as possible.

TABLE 1.3b   Soccer Coaching Study Design

Acquisition	Retention
Day 1 (week 1)	**Day 2 (week 2)**
6 blocks × 5 kicks	2 blocks × 5 kicks
100% received individualized cue after every kick (30 total)	No cues, prompts, or reminders
33% received individualized cue after every 3rd kick (10 total)	(10 kicks)
(30 kicks)	

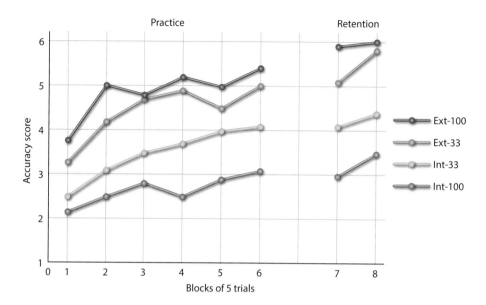

FIGURE 1.8   Accuracy results for participants receiving feedback 33 and 100 percent of the time across the internal and external focus groups.

Reprinted by permission from G. Wulf, N. McConnel, M. Gartner, and A. Schwarz, "Enhancing the Learning of Sport Skills Through External-Focus Feedback," *Journal of Motor Behavior* 34, no. 2 (2002): 171-182.

Collectively, these studies spotlight one of the most robust findings in all of motor learning (17): Focusing externally on the movement environment (e.g., "strike under the ball") or outcome (e.g., "hit the ball toward the target"), whether facilitated by literal language or analogy, consistently results in superior performance and learning compared to focusing internally on the movement process itself (e.g., "lock your ankle"). As we saw in the soccer study, this finding is so robust that we actually see participants benefit from a reduction in internal cue exposure (i.e., INT33% outperformed INT100% during practice and retention).

Unlike practice variability, there does not appear to be a middle ground whereby a progressive shift from an internal focus to an external focus is warranted, although this has yet to be explicitly studied. To the contrary, more than 20 years of research, championed by the immense contributions of Gabriele Wulf, have consistently shown that coaches should encourage athletes to adopt an external focus of attention while they move (17). By doing this, coaches will not only promote improved performance during practice, but, more importantly, they'll be promoting learning that sticks. Thus, we have our second example of the performance-learning distinction, an example that brightens the fact that it is not simply the contents of practice that determine learning but also the contents of one's mind.

And it is to this last point that we turn next. Despite the more than 20 years of research backing the learning benefits of adopting an external focus, evidence and my own experience suggest that the uptake from the broader coaching (e.g., 12) and rehabilitation (e.g., 6) communities has been slow. For this reason, we will dedicate the remaining pages of this book to understanding how coaching language influences attention and, in turn, the impact one's attention has on motor-skill learning. I will attempt to make the invisible visible, showing coaches, trainers, and therapists alike how to interrogate the coaching tool they use more than any other—their voice.

SUMMARY

Considered by many to be one of the greatest coaches of all time, John Wooden famously said "you haven't taught until they've learned." Befitting the narrative of this chapter, Coach Wooden's words suggest that, no matter your title—coach, trainer, or therapist—you're responsible for creating the conditions for learning to thrive and, thus, you're a teacher first. Bearing the gravity of this responsibility, I have written this book for everyone who teaches movement and those who'd like to get better at it. Whether you're a physical education teacher nurturing an early love for movement, a physical therapist helping an individual regain their movement independence, or a coach seeking to help an athlete push their movement to the edge of possible, this book will provide you with the necessary tools to create learning that sticks.

We started our journey by reviewing a mental model that we called the 3P Performance Profile. As you'll recall, the three *P*s are *position*, *power*, and *pattern*, which, when taken as a collective, give rise to *performance*. Knowing that this is a book exclusively focused on language and motor-skill learning, we used a car and driver analogy to frame what motor learning is and what it is not. If the car represents the peripheral characteristics of the body (mobility, stability, strength, power, etc.), we will be focusing on the driver, who serves as the analog for the central adaptation contained within the nervous system, notably, the brain. Thus, the successful application of the strategies contained herein require us to presuppose that we are dealing with a driver, as opposed to a car, problem. This is not to say that we don't develop the car and driver in parallel, we do. However, to get the most out of this book, you must be able to identify when a problem is *coachable* and, therefore, subject to being influenced by coaching language, and when a problem is *trainable* and, therefore, in need of a sustained training stimulus to overcome a physical limitation.

We continued by considering the key terms and context in which motor learning will be discussed. Specifically, we demonstrated that the learning intervention, or acquisition phase, allows a coach to measure and assess acute motor performance, whereas the assessment of long-term motor learning must occur during a delayed retention phase. We defined this performance-learning distinction as the differences that emerge between motor performance and motor learning and cited evidence in the domains of practice design (i.e., practice variability) and coaching cues (i.e., cueing). What's more, attention, or attentional focus, surfaced as a probable mediator of learning due to its connection to theories explaining the benefits of practice variability (7) and effective cueing (18). Thus, in chapter 2, we'll shift our focus to attention and start to unpack the cognitive phenomenon that underpins intentional movement.

PAY ATTENTION

Attention: A Primer

Have you ever woken up to find that you can suddenly speak and understand a new language? Alternatively, have you ever sat down at a piano and instead of playing your nostalgia-inducing go-to, Chopsticks, Beethoven's Fifth Symphony magically jumped from your fingertips—dun dun dun dunnn? You likely answered no, for waking to these newfound abilities would quickly suggest that you are not awake at all, as these are the things of dreams. And while there may come a day when downloading a new ability is as easy as downloading a new app, for now, we must resign ourselves to learning motor skills the old-fashioned way: through practice.

However, as we discussed at the end of chapter 1, if we desire to continuously improve motor skill learning, it is not enough to simply practice. Rather, the quality of practice needs to be considered equal to, if not more important than, the quantity of practice (16). But what counts as high-quality practice, and how is it influenced by the way we pay attention throughout it? To answer this question, it is useful to briefly consider the growing body of evidence that explores the underpinnings of expertise.

Developing Expertise

Dr. Anders Ericsson is a Swedish-born psychologist working at Florida State University. While Dr. Ericsson has made notable contributions in a number of scientific areas, he is most well known for his research on the influence of practice on expertise. In their seminal paper, *The role of deliberate practice in the acquisition of expert performance*, Dr. Ericsson and colleagues (16) recruited three cohorts of violinists from the Music Academy of West Berlin. Matched for age and gender, 10 violinists were identified as the "best violinists"; 10 were identified as the "good violinists"; and 10 were identified as the "music teachers," based on their enrollment in the music education department. Over the course of three interview sessions, students provided the researchers with information about when they started playing the violin and the average amount of solo practice they'd accumulated each year since starting to play. This data allowed Ericsson and his team to identify if it was the accumulation of practice or practice habits that explained the differences in musical ability.

The now famous result showed a clear trend. The "best violinists" had accumulated significantly more solo practice hours (7,410 hours on average) by the time they were 18 than had the "good violinists" (5,301 hours on average), with both groups accumulating far more practice hours than the "music teachers" (3,420 hours on average). Further support for this finding was provided by a secondary analysis of 10 "expert violinists," who were members of two internationally recognized orchestras in Berlin. Similar to the "best violinists," the experts had accumulated an average of 7,336 hours of solo practice by the time they were 18. Thus, the data clearly showed that the accumulation of solo practice hours explained a portion of the expertise pathway.

Ericsson's paper has now been cited over 8,000 times and has inspired further inquiry into the intersection between practice and expertise, with a distinct emphasis on expertise in sport. For example, Baker, Côté, and Abernethy (4) found that expert (national level) team sport athletes accumulate significantly more sport-specific practice hours (~5,709 hours) after 15 years of involvement in their sport compared to nonexpert (provincial or state level) team sport athletes (~2,900 hours). Further, the expert athletes were practicing their sport 20 hours per week by the time they had qualified for a national team, while the nonexpert athletes had achieved only nine hours of practice per week for the same years of sport involvement.

While logic would suggest that hours of practice is the primary factor determining the development of expertise, researchers agree that the quality of practice is the key. For example, in a follow-up publication using the same data set, Baker, Côté, and Abernethy (5) showed that, compared to nonexperts, the expert athletes spent significantly more time competing, practicing, and receiving individualized instruction, while non-experts spent significantly more time playing sports with friends, weight training, and conditioning aerobically. Confirming the importance of where and how practice hours are spent, Ward, Hodges, Starkes, and Williams (51) found that, compared to age- and experience-matched recreational soccer players, elite players not only engaged in more practice hours; they specifically engaged in practice that contained a higher level of decision-making activities.

While we can't discount the effect of genetic factors that give each athlete their unique physical and psychological tool kit (e.g., height, weight, morphology, and personality) (25, 48), there is no question that accumulating hours and hours of high-quality practice is an essential part of the expertise equation (31). Because of this, it is important to examine the underpinning features of effective practice and identify the mediating role of attention.

Deliberate Practice

While Ericsson and others have clearly shown that both quantity and quality of practice matter, popular media have latched on to the seductive idea of a "10,000-hour rule." This interpretation, which many believe stems from Malcolm Gladwell's summation of Ericsson's work in his book *Outliers* (53), unintentionally suggests that expertise is a short 10,000-hour jaunt away. Put in your time, and you too can become an expert. As attractive as this idea is, there is one small problem—it's false.

In his own book *Peak*, Ericsson sets the story straight by saying that "The rule is irresistibly appealing. … Unfortunately, this rule—which is the only thing that many people today know about the effects of practice—is wrong" (14). The fact is that many studies, especially in team sports, have shown that there is large variability in the practice hours required to reach an expert level of performance, with many examples citing national-level qualifications being achieved in less than 10,000 hours (24). Thus, as Ericsson pointed out in the 1993 paper, "the differences between expert performers and normal adults reflect a life-long period of deliberate effort to improve performance in a specific domain" (16). This quote, reflecting the original definition of deliberate practice, suggests that underpinning effective practice is a deliberate, focused effort. Highlighting this feature, Ericsson expanded the definition of **deliberate practice**, proposing that it "involves the provision of immediate feedback, time for problem-solving and evaluation, and opportunities for repeated performance to refine behavior" (15). Building on this definition, Ericsson recommends that deliberate practice include clear goals, a distinct focus, relevant feedback, and an appropriate level of challenge (see figure 2.1).

GOALS

It is not surprising that Ericsson identified goal setting as one of the four pillars of deliberate practice, as the positive impact of goal setting on performance is one of the most stable findings in psychology (29). Well-defined goals bring purpose to the learning environment and, by default, guide what we pay attention to.

In their 1993 paper, Dr. Ericsson and colleagues (16) described the properties of goals that affect performance. First, goals help athletes direct their attention to goal-relevant features of a motor skill. For example,

FIGURE 2.1   Primary and secondary features of Anders Ericsson's deliberate practice model.

if I am just learning how to return a serve in tennis using a forehand shot, then watching the ball through contact makes much more sense than focusing on footwork or arm position because the latter is guided by the former. Second, challenging goals lead to greater persistence and effort than easy or vague goals. Think back to chapter 1 and our discussion of my son's desire to identify an appropriately challenging puzzle. If the goal is too easy, then there is less satisfaction when it is achieved. And, once the perceived satisfaction of achieving the goal is gone, effort and persistence quickly erode.

While there are many types of goals, for the purpose of developing motor skills, two general categories are relevant. In one instance, a coach or an athlete can identify **process-oriented goals**, which relate to a specific technical feature of the motor skill being practiced. For example, imagine a rugby coach who would like to improve the speed of a player's pass to the left. The coach identifies that the reason the player takes so long is due to a forward-looping motion, as opposed to moving the ball straight across the body. To correct this, the rugby coach devises a scenario whereby the player moves forward as a defender comes straight at them, creating a game-relevant situation. The coach then provides a simple cue by telling the player to make the pass to the left at the last possible moment. This cue serves to limit the defender's ability to make a play on the ball and forces a quick, straight pass from the player to their teammate. The coach proceeds to run the drill and provides the player with the goal of completing 10 successful passes to a teammate who is running 6.5 yards (6 m) to the player's left. Considering that the coach can change how quickly the defender approaches the attacking player, easily modifying the difficulty of the task, and the fact that external feedback is built into every repetition, confirms that the attributes of this scenario are sufficient for encouraging a change in motor skill performance (30).

In addition to process-oriented goals, a coach or an athlete can establish **outcome-oriented goals**, which focus on the outcome, or result, of the motor skill being practiced. Building on our rugby example, let's assume that the player has been successful in modifying their technique and, consequently, improving the speed of release and flight path of the ball. A natural progression is to shift the goal to a feature of the desired outcome. In this case, the goal could be **spatial** (i.e., accuracy) and require the player to pass the ball so that their teammate receives it in front of their chest, as opposed to having to turn back to catch the ball. Alternatively, the goal could be **temporal** (i.e., speed), and the rugby coach could use a radar gun to establish the actual speed of the pass. Thus, the coach could set parameters around how fast he wants the player to pass the ball, establishing a speed × accuracy relationship that is appropriately challenging.

While we typically see goals through the lens of short-, medium-, and long-term time scales, principles of deliberate practice would suggest that we should identify micro-goals that can be applied at the repetition level of motor skill practice. In essence, this approach puts the *why* (goal) in the *what* (action) and provides the necessary conditions for directing focus.

FOCUS

When my daughter turned five, she became interested in Legos. As someone who loved playing Legos as a kid, I was excited to see my daughter find that same joy and whimsy in the little bricks. During one of our building sessions we were constructing a futuristic ninja castle and I casually asked my daughter how school was. Without looking up, immersed in piecing together the ninja villain, my daughter said, "Dad, I am trying to focus. Can you please wait a minute?" Both amused and surprised, my daughter's response reminded me of the second feature of deliberate practice, the importance of focus.

Intuitively, we know that to focus on something means that we can't focus on everything. This is why you stop talking to the passenger in your car or turn down the music as you approach unexpected traffic on a freeway. Similarly, this is why libraries are quiet, music studios are loud, and team sports only use one ball, as our capacity for focus is innately limited. Not surprisingly, science has long understood that there is a trade-off between the number of choices available to someone and the speed with which they can make a selection. This principle is known as **Hick's law** (30), and it describes the time a person takes to make a decision as a function of the number of options available to them. For example, if there were 10 lights arranged in a circle on a wall and you were asked to quickly react and tap the lights as they turn on (one at a time), you would find that your average reaction time during the 10-light condition would be far slower than if you were to complete the same task with only five lights. As we'll discuss later on, this phenomenon is a function of limitations in attentional capacity, which explains why distributing attention across 10 things is far more difficult than distributing it across five.

The "so what" from a coaching perspective is quite simple: If our athletes don't focus on something, ideally, the right thing, they can become distracted by anything, especially as the number of choices increase. Therefore, an important part of facilitating deliberate practice is to direct focus **explicitly** through the use of verbal cues (i.e., "On your next rep, I want you to focus on X") or **implicitly** by designing activities that connect a successful outcome to a specific focus. In many ways, an effective verbal cue (which will be the focus of part II of this book) is a micro-goal in disguise. That is, the outcome goal for a sprinter may be to run 10 m (11 yards) in 1.85 seconds; however, to achieve this, the coach may ask the sprinter to focus on "driving low out of the blocks as fast as you can." This cue illustrates how the micro-goal of each rep, set, or session can be nested within the focus adopted by the athlete, leaving them inextricably linked.

However, as the adage goes, you can lead a horse to water, but you can't make it drink. Translated into coach-speak, we know that we can't always provide the answer and there comes a time when athletes need to figure things out for themselves. For example, a movement scenario may be so complex that no single verbal cue captures the entirety of the task (e.g., a quarterback needing to scan the field to select the best receiver to throw to), or we may want the athlete to figure out how to solve the movement problem on their own (e.g., evading an oncoming defender in a one-on-one drill). Considering these contextual motives, to help our athletes achieve the desired ends, coaches need to understand how to build movement scenarios that can be solved only if focus is directed correctly.

To illustrate this last point, consider a coach who wants to improve an ice hockey player's ability to make better decisions during one-on-one defensive scenarios. It is evident to the coach that, at times, the player loses, or misplaces, focus during defensive scenarios and is vulnerable when isolated on the wing. Evidence suggests that this type of rapid decision-making can be partly explained by an athlete's ability to focus, or fixate, on relevant features of the task while disregarding the irrelevant (22). Hence, our coach wants to generate a movement scenario that provides the hockey player with the opportunity to direct their focus in a way that improves their

defensive decisions in one-on-one scenarios. From a defensive tracking perspective, we know that the motion of an attacker's center of mass (COM) is directly related to the ultimate motion of their body and the direction it will move (7). As such, experts in team sports will commonly focus on the COM, or torso, longer than nonexperts, who, as it turns out, are more susceptible to being misdirected by head and limb motion (8). Knowing this, the coach creates a 13-yard (12 m) channel between the boards and center ice (movement zone) and places the attacking winger 16 yards (15 m) away from the defending winger (decision zone). To manipulate decision time, the coach has the defensive winger start with their back to the attacker, turning around only when alerted to do so. Practically, the coach blows the first whistle to trigger the forward motion of the attacker and the second whistle to trigger our defender to turn and play. Ultimately, our player's success or failure hangs on their ability to quickly read the motion of the attacker (i.e., anticipate) and use this information to make a defensive maneuver that results in delaying forward progress or a turnover. Assuming our player is physically fast and strong enough, failure in this scenario is a direct reflection of misplaced or mistimed focus. Thus, given enough repetitions, feedback from the outcome would condition the player to focus correctly so that their rate of success increases.

Whether through explicit or implicit means, the way we focus in practice, or the way practice encourages us to focus, has a direct effect on the quality of the learning that ensues. Thus, our goals and focus serve to define the attentional spotlight for a given repetition. The coach has a responsibility to ensure that the goal is appropriate for the skill and the focus is relevant to the goal. Since motor skills are ever evolving, however, coaches and athletes require timely feedback to know when to reboot goals and refresh focus.

FEEDBACK

Known for his relentless work ethic and attitude in practice, Michael Jordan famously said, "I've missed more than 9,000 shots in my career. I've lost almost 300 games. Twenty-six times, I've been trusted to take the game-winning shot and missed. I've failed over and over and over again in my life. And that is why I succeed." Like so many kids in the 1990s, I had these words plastered on my wall, but I didn't come to appreciate their meaning until I realized that "there is no failure, only feedback" (Robert Allen).

Of all the ingredients inherent to deliberate practice, feedback is the most essential. Without feedback, athletes have no sense of progress and are unable to make adjustments when improvements stagnate. Fortunately, there are many forms of feedback, some of which are hardwired right into the motor skill itself. Specifically, sports involving a ball or equivalent piece of equipment ultimately have an accuracy element and are therefore naturally rich with feedback. From basketball to badminton, cricket to curling, these sports provide the athlete with immediate feedback around the success of a scoring attempt (e.g., a basket, a goal, a hit, shot placement, or proximity to a target). Equally, these same sports provide valuable feedback on the consequences of actions in the dynamic play that leads to scoring opportunities (e.g., accuracy of a pass; success of a catch; or outcome of an offensive or defensive decision, such as a line break in rugby). However, sports do not necessarily require a ball to provide feedback. To the contrary, any sport that has built-in sensory information (i.e., visual, auditory, tactile, and proprioceptive) about the outcome of a given motor skill is said to have **task-intrinsic feedback**.

While all motor skills have, at least, a level of task-intrinsic feedback, this form of feedback can, at times, be insufficient to encourage changes in motor performance that will elicit an improved outcome (e.g., accuracy of a goal kick). As such, the necessity of a coach is seated in the fact that athletes require some form of supplemental feedback from an external source, which is commonly referred to as **augmented feedback**. For example, consider sports that are based on subjective scoring criteria (i.e., judges), as opposed to objective scoring criteria (e.g., points, time, distance, or weight). These sports, which include gymnastics, diving, and figure skating, always require some form of external feedback to convey whether the technical marks and artistry associated with a motor skill are at the desired standard. Moreover, as implied at the beginning of this paragraph, even if a motor skill has built-in feedback (e.g., accuracy of a header in soccer), there can be technical errors that are hidden within the outcome error. As such, if the feedback around an accuracy error is not sufficient to drive implicit or explicit changes to the motor skill, then a coach is required to introduce augmented feedback that can assist the athlete in making the necessary change.

Within the domain of augmented feedback, there are two primary forms that emerge. The first, which aligns with our description of outcome-oriented goals, is referred to as **knowledge of results (KR)** and is defined as externally presented information pertaining to the outcome of the motor skill. This can be as simple as telling an athlete whether or not a trial was successful (e.g., if a target time or velocity was achieved during a sprint). Alternatively, and more commonly, a coach can provide a specific description of the outcome (e.g., distance jumped, height achieved, time run, points scored, shot distance, etc.). This information alerts the athlete to the proximity of the achieved outcome to the expected outcome. If the expected and achieved outcomes are close (e.g., goal: make 75 percent of my free throws; outcome: made 77 percent of my free throws), then the athlete associates their current motor strategy with success, and the motor skill behaviors are reinforced. Conversely, if the expected and achieved outcomes are far apart (e.g., goal: place 60 percent of chip shots from the bunker within five feet [1.5 m] of the hole; outcome: placed 30 percent of chip shots from the bunker within five feet [1.5 m] of the hole), then the athlete is immediately alerted to a possible error in the movement strategy, and additional information is required to elicit a change.

This additional information comes in the form of **knowledge of performance (KP)**, which is defined as externally presented information pertaining to the movement characteristics or process that led to the performance outcome. Again, this is well aligned with our earlier description of process-oriented goals. Thinking back to chapter 1 and our discussion of the 3P Performance Profile, we can see that KP maps directly onto our discussion of the motor pattern, or coordination, of the motor skill. Thus, once a coach feels that they're observing a stable movement pattern, which is to say that the error or effectiveness of the pattern is consistent, then the coach has met the requirement for using KP feedback.[1] Once this requirement is met, the coach has two types of feedback they can leverage. The first type of KP feedback is referred to as **descriptive KP**, which outlines the pattern in descriptive terms (e.g., "during the second pull of the power clean, you did not fully extend your hips" or "during your vertical jump, you were effective at fully extending your hips"). The second type of KP feedback is referred to as **prescriptive KP**, which not only describes the nature of the movement pattern but also prescribes a focus cue to either correct or confirm the current movement strategy (e.g., "as you struck the rugby ball from the tee, you looked up; focus on the logo as you strike the ball during your next repetition" or "as you hit the golf ball off the tee, you kept your head down; continue to focus on the ball through contact").

A logical question emerges at this point: Which type of feedback is better? Like most things, there is no single answer to this question, as it depends on a number of contextual factors, the least of which being the experience level of the athlete. That said, there are a number of learning theories that can help us narrow in on a possible answer. One of the most widely accepted and relevant to our discussion of feedback is the three-stage model of learning first presented by Fitts (19) and later popularized by Fitts and Posner (20). Specifically, Fitts and Posner proposed that learning, while nonlinear in nature, follows a general path that is paved by a cognitive stage, associative stage, and an autonomous stage. Simply put, humans go from having to explicitly focus on the performance of a motor skill (i.e., low experience, such as first learning to walk or ride a bike) to being able to perform the motor skill with no explicit focus (i.e., high experience, such as being able to hold a conversation while walking or riding a bike). As such, we can assume that a low-experience athlete doesn't fully understand the inner workings of a given motor skill and, therefore, is ill-equipped to self-correct any movement features that are not somehow linked to task-intrinsic feedback. Thus, in reference to augmented feedback, those with low experience will generally benefit from KP of a prescriptive nature, while those with high experience are better equipped to make use of KR or KP of a descriptive nature. In practice, coaches will use all three types of feedback and should ultimately be guided by their athletes' responsiveness to a given coaching prompt (motor performance) and their stable expression of any improvements over time (motor learning).

---

[1]You don't want to start providing feedback on technique (i.e., KP) until you are certain of the movement error you're trying to correct or the feature of the technique you'd like to reinforce. As such, before you provide KP feedback, it is important that you've watched enough repetitions (i.e., think back to silent sets) to ascertain the athletes' authentic movement patterns. Too often coaches will coach before they watch, thereby introducing new information that could mask the athletes' normal movement pattern. This is why it is so important to watch athletes move before you try to change the way they move.

While there is more that can be said about feedback, the preceding paragraphs provide a road map for coaches to effectively apply the core principles underpinning its various forms. Interested coaches are encouraged to read about augmented feedback in Magill and Anderson's book *Motor Learning and Control: Concepts and Applications* (32) for an in-depth discussion of feedback and the contextual factors that influence its application.

To summarize, feedback, independent of the source, is the metaphorical heartbeat of deliberate practice. Pulsing through every movement, it brings forth the learning from one repetition and infuses it into the life of the next. As coaches, if we're uncompromising in our adherence to facilitating a feedback-rich environment, then we need only observe our athletes' progress to know when they're ready for a new challenge.

CHALLENGE

The final quadrant of deliberate practice is represented by the challenge imposed on the athlete. As we discussed in chapter 1, the appropriate level of challenge is necessary for the athlete to stay engaged in practice without getting discouraged. Discussing this topic, Daniel Coyle, in *The Little Book of Talent*, outlines 52 tips for improving talent. Relevant to challenge is Tip 13, in which Coyle refers to the idea of "find[ing] the sweet spot" (10). Having spent years studying why certain areas of the world produced an inordinate amount of talent in a given sport, known as talent hotbeds, Coyle concluded that talent is earned by "stretch[ing] yourself slightly beyond your current ability, spending time in the zone of difficulty called the 'sweet spot.' It means embracing the power of repetition, so the action becomes fast and automatic. It means creating a practice space that enables you to reach and repeat, stay engaged, and improve your skills over time" (10).

This sweet spot, similar to our description of the Goldilocks principle in chapter 1, sits at the center of a continuum flanked by a "comfort zone" and a "survival zone." As the names imply, the comfort zone is characterized by an athlete having success 80 percent of the time—whether qualitatively or quantitatively assessed—and experiencing a general sense of effortlessness and ease. Conversely, the survival zone is characterized by an athlete having success less than 50 percent of the time and experiencing confusion and desperation. However, between these poles is the sweet spot, which is characterized by an athlete having success approximately 50 to 80 percent of the time and dealing with a manageable level of frustration and difficulty, or what we can call an achievable challenge.

The sweet spot is analogous to Guadagnoli and Lee's (23) challenge point hypothesis and Bjork and Bjork's (6) concept of creating desirable difficulties. Thus, independent of the model you subscribe to, the message is clear—coaches need to manipulate features of their coaching language (i.e., what they say, how much they say, and when they say it) and practice design (i.e., type, number, and order of the drills or activities) to generate a net challenge that is appropriate for the level of the athletes they're working with.

DJ-ing Deliberate Practice

The preceding sections laid out the functional components of a deliberate practice framework. While we understand that each component can be individually manipulated, we also know that the combined influence of the four variables serves a singular purpose—to focus attention on the most relevant feature of the motor skill being learned. In this way, we can think of goals, focus, feedback, and challenge like the gain dials on a DJ mixer, collectively tuning the attention that plays out in every rep (see figure 2.2). Through this lens, the coach is the DJ, turning the gain up or down on each variable, ensuring that the attentional mix is just right for the mood, the moment, and the movement.

Although we started with the end in mind, handing you the mixer, so to speak, we will now step back and examine the underlying properties and behaviors of the attentional system we seek to influence. For just as DJs need to understand the structure of music, coaches need to understand the structure of attention.

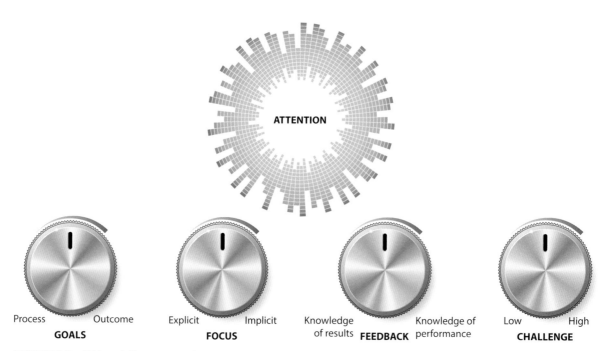

FIGURE 2.2   DJ-ing deliberate practice.

ATTENTION AT WORK

When you first move to Phoenix, Arizona, you're acutely aware of two things: the heat and the rattlesnakes. This perception is confirmed by the blast of hot air that hits you as you enter the airport terminal and the spattering of tiled snakes that seem to follow you on your way to baggage claim. In my case, the tiled snakes turned into real snakes that populated my mind and, it seemed, every bush that I walked by. Thus, while walking past a row of bushes on my way into work, I could be lost in thought, my mind wandering, and suddenly hear a rustling in the brush. Without fail, I would sidestep the sound, swivel my head, and focus my attention, waiting for the reptile to strike.

While sensationalized, this story is true and captures the essence of how our attentional system operates. As we'll discuss in depth, our attentional focus is constantly being updated with the most important information for a given context. Thus, the speed program I was thinking about on my way into work is quickly deprioritized when the rustling in the bushes alerts me to a possible danger. And, although this distractibility can, at times, be at odds with our ability to focus, ultimately, it's a distinct survival advantage to have an attentional system that's constantly on autopilot, scanning the world for danger. Once the threat of danger is gone, however, we want the capacity to quickly redirect our focus toward that which is most important to us.

In a way, our attentional system is like the movie theater of the mind, with the feature film seamlessly flowing between our own thoughts and the world around us, providing an uninterrupted sense of what we call consciousness. In line with this view of attention, William James (52), in his seminal book *The Principles of Psychology*, rightly stated the following:

> Millions of items of the outward order are present to my senses which never properly enter into my experience. Why? Because they have no interest for me. My experience is what I agree to attend to. Only those items which I notice shape my mind—without selective interest, experience is utter chaos. (p. 402)

More recently, the researcher who illuminated the flow state, Mihaly Csikszentmihalyi (12), described attention in this way:

> *Because attention determines what will or will not appear in consciousness, and because it is also required to make any other mental events—such as remembering, thinking, feeling, and making decisions—happen there, it is useful to think of it as [cognitive] energy. Attention is like energy in that without it no work can be done, and in doing work it is dissipated. We create ourselves by how we invest this energy. Memories, thoughts, and feelings are all shaped by how we use it. And it is an energy under our control, to do with as we please; hence, attention is our most important tool in the task of improving the quality of experience. (p. 79)*

Both Williams and Csikszentmihalyi capture the beauty and complexity that is our capacity to attend. Functionally, only that which we attend to can we become aware of. As such, attention can be seen as the currency of learning—to be paid or invested—and the feature of an athlete's mind that coaches must be most astute at influencing. However, to be masterful in your ability to influence another's attention, it is important to first appreciate how our attentional system is organized. Specifically, attention operates like an automatic switchboard, rapidly changing our focus as the situation demands, leaving us none the wiser. Surprisingly, however, our attention, while providing a unified sense of our world, is in fact functionally distributed throughout the brain in what has been termed an attention network (17). This global network is made up of three sub-networks, filters if you will, that are named according to their function—alerting, orienting, and the central executive (37). This global attention network is so critical to human functioning that some researchers believe that it operates like an organ system, providing the contents of consciousness in a manner analogous to an organ releasing life-sustaining hormones (39). However, before we discuss what gives rise to focused attention, it is instructive to first discuss the basis for unfocused attention, also known as mind wandering.

PART 1: OUT OF FOCUS

Let's consider a coaching scenario that is all too familiar to those working in team sports—the pre-session team talk. For context, our basketball coach and players are in a classroom setting and the coach is previewing film on the team's defensive strategy for the game that weekend.

Coach: *"OK, settle down and take a seat. It goes without saying that this weekend marks our biggest challenge of the year. Bradenton Central have one of the best offenses in the state and it will take our best defensive performance of the year to win. As always, we want to play up-tempo basketball. Ashley, what does that mean within our defensive system?"*

Player (Ashley): *"Constant communication and clarity in our zone defense, first on the ground for the scraps, first in the air for the boards, and maintain inside position and spacing in our zone press."*

Coach: *"Excellent, Ashley. Katie, what kind of zone press are we looking to run? (Silence)*

Coach: *"Katie?"*

Player (Katie): *"Oh, sorry, Coach. What did you say?"*

As coaches, all of us have experienced this type of response, or lack thereof. Whether speaking with a team or directly to an athlete, all of us have been on the receiving end of a wandering mind. However, before we are quick to judge others for their loss of focus, let's quickly consider how ubiquitous this is in our own lives. Consider, for example, how many times you forgot you were reading a book or were snapped back into reality when the person you were speaking with said "So what do you think?" Better, yet, how many times have you been sitting at a red light only to be reminded that green means go by a symphony of car horns?

The truth is, we're all susceptible to mind wandering, and we should not take personal offense if an athlete lapses into la-la land. Rather, we should seek to understand why mind wandering occurs and what we, as coaches, can do about it.

The Wandering Mind

Mind wandering can be defined as a mental shift away from primary task goals to the processing of personal or unrelated goals (46). In principle, mind wandering is the opposite of focused attention and, therefore, presents one of the greatest threats to learning. But why does it happen?

Relevant to the narrative of this book, there are two primary reasons for mind wandering to emerge. First, mind wandering has been shown to vary in proportion to an individual's working memory capacity (45). That is, on average, if you have a harder time storing information in your short-term memory, a phone number, for example, then you will be more inclined to have your mind wander off (33). In this case, athletes with lower working memory capacity would have greater difficulty recalling a large number of plays or a series of coaching cues compared to those with higher working memory. Consequently, they are more likely to mentally drift off when confronted with too much information, reducing their comprehension of what was said or read. Thus, from a coaching perspective, we should seek to be clear and concise with every message we deliver, remembering that less is in fact more when it comes to retaining spoken information.

Second, mind wandering, unsurprisingly, is influenced by motivation and interest in the topic being learned (50). Thus, just as reading an uninteresting book triggers mind wandering, so too will a lengthy speech on the nuances of an upcoming training session. Therefore, as we'll talk about in the sections that follow, coaches should attempt to craft messages that are personally important to their athletes, captivating, and easily understood.

While mind wandering can negatively affect the comprehension and retention of information (35), there is a silver lining that coaches should be aware of. First, considering how much time we spend mind wandering throughout the day (50 percent by some estimates), it should come as no surprise that there are certain benefits. Specifically, mind wandering has been associated with autobiographical planning, which is to say that we plan for the future during our moments of rumination. While spending too much time in the past or future can result in an unhappy mind (27), the right amount of contemplation can be positive. Practically speaking, prior to training, consider giving athletes 5 to 10 minutes to reflect and relax, prompting them to consider what they would like to get out of the session while performing basic preparatory exercises. This scenario serves as an ideal forum to allow for prospective mind wandering ahead of the detail that will follow.

The second, and arguably more important, benefit of mind wandering comes in the form of creative insight. Specifically, while many of us intuitively know that a break from intense focus is all that is required for a breakthrough, limited research has been conducted on the benefits of mind wandering for creative endeavors. However, Baird and colleagues (3) have now shown that taking mental breaks and allowing the mind to wander actually benefits creative problem solving, which is yet another reason to strategically program breaks into training, especially when teaching complex skills or asking athletes to engage in intense periods of decision-making. As Friedrich Nietzsche said, "all truly great thoughts are conceived by walking." In our case, a short walk and a shot of water might be all a player needs to get that next rep right.

Default Mode Network

As it turns out, mind wandering has a home within our brain, and it has been termed the **default mode network**. Specifically, the default mode network is a cluster of brain regions that consistently show higher brain activity during resting states and are involved in spontaneous cognition, or mind wandering (42). Raichle and colleagues (43) were the first to identify that there are three primary brain regions that increase in activity during rest—eyes open or closed—and decrease in activity in response to goal-directed thoughts and behavior. Thus, returning to our DJ mixer analogy, we can think of the default mode network as channel A, which is active when the crossfader is in the left-hand position, and the attention network as channel B, which is active when the crossfader is in the right-hand position. Just as sliding the fader back and forth changes the song being played over the speakers, so too will shifting brain networks change the contents of the mind.

The three primary brain regions that make up the default mode network are the ventral medial prefrontal cortex (VMPC), the dorsal medial prefrontal cortex (DMPC), and the posterior cingulate cortex (PCC). While it is of no great consequence if you don't remember these brain regions, it is quite interesting to note their function in terms of mind wandering. Specifically, the VMPC is associated with social behavior, mood control, and motivational drive; the DMPC is associated with self-directed judgments and thoughts; and the PCC has a direct link to autobiographical memory formation in the hippocampus (42). If we consider that mind wandering is usually subject to ideas about our past, our future, or a creative struggle, it should come as no surprise that these functional brain regions make up the default mode network. What's more, you may find it interesting to know that the default mode network accounts for 60 to 80 percent of the brain's energy budget, which is significant when you consider that the brain represents 2 percent of the body and consumes 20 percent of its total energy requirements (44). Thus, to overcome this natural tendency to stay in our head, we must help our athletes change the channel and move their minds from wandering to wondering.

PART 2: COMING INTO FOCUS

Let's pick up where we left off. Katie was just brought back to reality when her coach asked her a question at the team meeting.

Player (Katie): *"Oh, sorry, Coach. What did you say?"*

Coach: *"I asked you to remind the team what kind of zone press we run."*

Player (Katie): *"Oh yeah. We run a 2-2-1 zone press, Coach."*

Coach: *"Exactly. What are we looking to achieve with the 2-2-1?"*

Player (Katie): *"We want to keep pressure on the inbound pass, pressing 75 percent of the court. We also want to keep inside position, not letting them shift the ball to the center."*

Coach: *"Why is it important to keep inside position?"*

Player (Katie): *"This allows us to shade the offense to the sideline, creating a possible opportunity to trap the player with the ball."*

As we discussed earlier, the brain defaults into a mind-wandering, or daydreaming, mode when (a) there is no perceived threat and thus no reason to monitor the external world, (b) no novel or interesting information is present in one's surroundings, or (c) there is no perceived requirement to focus attention on an internal thought or external stimulus. Thus, just as a computer inevitably goes into sleep mode if it is not used, so too do we go into sleep mode when there is no thought or stimulus worth considering. For coaches, then, it is important to understand what triggers the switch from the default mode network to the attention network.

Dr. Daniel Levitin is a professor in the department of psychology at McGill University in Canada. I first became aware of Dr. Levitin after reading his best-selling book, *The Organized Mind: Thinking Straight in the Age of Information Overload*. This tour de force, which I recommend to anyone interested in understanding the human mind, revealed valuable insights about our brain's "attentional switch" (28). In this instance, the word *switch*, like a light switch or a railroad switch, literally represents a mind shift from the default mode network to the attention network. Thus, at the moment when our coach had to repeat Katie's name, we saw the switch occur. Retreating from the depth of her own thoughts, Katie reemerged, ready to see what she had missed.

Consider, for yourself, how many times in your day, let alone your career, you've seen this kind of switch take place: eyes going from glazed to glistening, heads going from down to up, posture shifting from slumped to strong; and mood shifting from discouraged to determined. We've all seen the consequence of effective communication and effective session design, as the evidence is built into the behavior of our athletes. Thus, as we did in our discussion of mind wandering, let's consider how this shift takes place, where it occurs in the brain, and what we can do to encourage it.

The Novelty-Seeking Mind

In discussing the mind as a novelty-seeking machine, Winifred Gallagher, in her book *New: Understanding Our Need for Novelty and Change*, states that "vital information about potential threats and resources is likelier to come from things that are new or unfamiliar than from the same old same old" (21). She goes on to quote Alexander Pope, who said, "be not the first by whom the new are tried, nor yet the last to lay the old aside." The wisdom and wit of these quotes should not be understated because it is clear that, before one has the opportunity to fight, flee, freeze, or befriend, they must first be alerted to do so. As such, we should think of our brain, to borrow another line from Dr. Levitin, as a "change detector."

We experience this change detection all the time and are easily fooled into believing that we are the causal agent flipping the switch. The reality couldn't be further from the truth, as our brains process sensory information from our external and internal worlds (i.e., visual, auditory, tactile, proprioceptive, and interoceptive), referred to as **bottom-up processing**, long before we are able to make conscious decisions associated with that information, referred to as **top-down processing** (34). Thus, when I look up from my oatmeal to see a fox in my backyard, grip the wheel harder when I suddenly feel bumps on the road, turn my head and duck when I hear a loud noise, or put my hands in the air when we score the game-winning drop goal, I can be quite certain that my reactions were automatically triggered by a meaningful change in my environment. We should not be coaxed into feeling that we have no control, however, as once I am aware that there is a fox in my backyard, I can make the conscious decision not to let my excited dog out just as I can look back to see that the loud noise was a balloon popping and that it is safe for me to continue walking. Thus, our change detector is simply alerting us to the fact that something unexpected has happened, what we do with that information is up to us.

From an evolutionary perspective, it is quite apparent that this novelty-seeking behavior would have supported survival. And, while some might find my jumping at the sound of a rustling bush hilarious, others would be quick to remind them that this served us well on the African savannah. The reality, however, is that, in today's world, we are more likely to die from a heart attack than an animal attack and, consequently, we've found new ways of satisfying our underlying need for novelty. This need has led to the creation of what some call an attention economy whereby every business and body is vying for a piece of our attention, continuously seeking new and better ways to get us to engage, click, or buy. Practically speaking, go into any locker-room or pre-session area, assuming they allow phones, and you'll see heads down, thumbs up. In a way, our phones have become homing devices for novelty-seeking behavior. While the battle for our attention wages on, my goal isn't to focus on the doom and gloom of the matter; rather, let's examine how coaches can use this to their advantage.

To understand what makes something novel or interesting to pay attention to, it is important to define the concept of **saliency**, which can be described as a stimulus, whether inside or outside the body, that stands out or is different from others (49). Specifically, a salient stimulus is said to have one or more of the following characteristics (13):

- **Context-dependent salience**
An athlete may consider a stimulus salient if it has utility to them, which is to say that it is relevant. Just as an image of Waldo becomes salient when looking through a Where's Waldo book, so too is a hole in a defensive line if you're a running back or a foothold in a mountain if you're a rock climber. Think of context-dependent salience like priming, in a way—the greater the perceived utility, the greater the likelihood that you'll notice it.

- **Intensity-dependent salience**
An athlete may consider a stimulus salient if the intensity or suddenness is at a sufficient level. Thus, the yell of a normally quiet coach or the sudden shriek of a whistle will likely suffice in drawing an athlete's attention.

- **Frequency-dependent salience**
An athlete may consider a stimulus salient if it is presented frequently enough. Thus, a mundane stimulus that is presented over and over again may, by the nature of its frequency, catch the athletes' attention. In marketing, they call this the "rule of seven," which states that people need to see an ad seven times before they click or buy. As coaches, we can use the Aristotelian triptych (Greek for *threefold*) to ensure that (a) we tell them what we're going to say, (b) we say it, and (c) we tell them what we said. This way, everyone can be quite clear that the most important message was heard.

- **Novelty-dependent salience**
While we're discussing salience in terms of novelty, sometimes, the most salient stimuli are, in fact, those that are simply new or different. Thus, as coaches, one of our greatest tools for capturing attention is to simply change it up. This can be as easy as facilitating a warm-up in a large circle, as opposed to a straight line; asking questions, as opposed to always dictating; or giving options (e.g., between two different conditioning sessions) rather than always prescribing.

Further, the saliency of a stimulus is said to be influenced by the following factors (49):

- **Previous experience and memory**
A stimulus that is associated with distinctly positive or negative emotions will likely be perceived as salient. This is why my three-year-old tears up when he hears he is going to the doctor, immediately assuming he will get a shot (i.e., the most salient memory at the doctor's office). Because of this, coaches have it within their control to create memories laced with polarizing emotions that, if stimulated again through a similar scenario, will likely grab their athletes' attention. Go no further than to mention a particular conditioning session or allude to practice finishing early, and watch your athletes stand at attention, patiently waiting for the rules of engagement.

- **Current physical state**
The relative benefit of a stimulus to one's current physical state will influence the stimulus's salience. That is, if someone is in the midst of a repeat-sprint conditioning session and is absolutely exhausted, it's probably not the best time to yell coaching cues from the sideline. Conversely, if a weightlifter is struggling to complete a lift, then they'll likely be open to any coaching cues that might help.

- **Goals and motives**
If a stimulus doesn't align with one's goals and motives, then it will likely be de-prioritized for a salient stimulus that does. Athletic performance coaches deal with this all the time in that we are teaching athletes skills (e.g., sprinting or squatting) that are associated with their sport but are not the sport itself. Thus, we hear things like "I just want to play" or "how is this going to help improve my shot" in response to asking certain athletes to get in the weight room. Because of this, coaches need to be able to draw

on metaphor and analogy to connect the mundane to the meaningful—"this isn't a squat; this is the body position during the scrum" or "this isn't a jump; this is you going up to make the game-winning block at the net" (see chapter 6).

- **The name game**
  From a coaching perspective, one of the easiest ways to flip this attentional switch is to use your athletes' names, a phenomenon coined the "cocktail party" effect. Evidence has shown that, even in a loud environment, like that of a party, a certain percentage of the population will detect their name, even if it is spoken in an unrelated conversation to the one they're having (9). Thus, we are conditioned to respond to our name from early on (it is the only tool parents have when their young child bolts for the street or reaches for a hot stove), and it is a simple strategy all coaches can use (i.e., insert name here, give instruction, cue, or feedback).

Collectively, we can see that context, our internal state, and the external world around us combine to achieve a net saliency score for any given stimulus and, if the score is high enough, a change is detected and attended to. Consequently, to flip this "saliency switch," coaches need to create experiences, through words, actions, and environments, that compel the athletes to pay attention. Practically speaking, I encourage you to weave these strategies into your current coaching curriculum and simply see what happens. If a strategy gets a laugh, a positive nonverbal response, or a shift in behavior, then stick with it. As I like to say, if they're laughing, they're listening. Alternatively, if the strategy isn't working, try something different, and keep iterating until you get the response you want. In the end, this book is full of strategies but has no rules. Just like an athlete, we need to use the feedback from our surroundings to guide our behaviors. Next, we will briefly examine the electronics hardwiring our saliency switch.

The Salience Network

Just as the default mode network has its own neuroanatomical real estate, so too does the salience network. But, before we go on a tour, let's experience it in action. Take a look at the following three photos, and see what jumps out in each of the pictures.

OK, what did you see? I'm going to guess that you saw nothing peculiar in photo A if you are from a country that drives on the right, such as Canada; however, if you're from a country that drives on the left, such as South Africa, then the lane orientation would've caught your eye. Photo B should be universal, which means you probably spotted the little red person in the middle without any trouble. Finally, for those of us not used to taking the subway on Halloween or *Star Wars* Day, Darth Vader would've jumped out as odd in photo C. Thus, just as linemen in pass protection keep their heads up to scan for any wayward defenders looking to hit the quarterback, so too was your attention scanning the images to find "which one of these things is not like the others." In either case, the salience network is hard at work, pinpointing where attention should be deployed next.

Whether you're woken from a dream by your cat stepping on your face or someone suddenly calls your name from across the room at a party, there are two distinct brain regions that will activate and trigger your response. The first brain region, and arguably the more famous of the two, is the insula, or, more specifically, the anterior insular (AI). The AI, popularized by Dr. Antonio Damasio in his book *Descartes' Error: Emotion, Reason, and the Human Brain* (54), plays a central role in routing the sensory information from inside the body (e.g., pain, temperature, muscular and visceral sensations, hunger, and thirst), commonly referred to as interoception, to the attentional network so it can receive an emotional tag (e.g., joy, sadness, anger, fear, or disgust) or be acted upon (e.g., eat if hungry, lean in if interested, run away if scared, or ask for a phone number if intrigued) (11). Considering that the AI, among other brain regions, notably, the parietal cortex, responds to salient sensory information from outside of the body, we should not be surprised that the AI is central to the salience network (13).

The second brain region implicated in the salience network is the anterior cingulate cortex (ACC). While it shares some responsibilities with the AI, it plays a more prominent role in controlling the cognitive and motor responses that come as a result of salient stimuli (34, 36). A consequence of routing life-sustaining information to the brain is that the AI and ACC are centrally located and connect the default mode network and the attention network through a grouping of unique fibers called the von Economo neurons (VENs) (47). Commenting on this connection and the function of the salience network, Menon and Uddin (34) state that, "[t]aken together, the AI and ACC help to integrate bottom-up attention switching with top-down control. With these differential anatomical pathways and von Economo neurons that facilitate rapid signaling between the AI and the ACC, the salience network is well positioned to influence not only attention but also motor responses to salient sensory stimuli" (p. 9).

In a sea of ordinary, the salience network ensures that we find the extraordinary or, at least, the information that is relevant to us. Thus, as coaches, we need to use the strategies and insights described above to ensure that the switch is flipped and the athlete's attention is being directed at the most relevant focus cues or stimuli within the environment. Let me be clear; if you don't get this right, then nothing else in this book will be of use. The benefit of delivering an effective focus cue is predicated on the athlete hearing, understanding, and actively focusing on the cue while they move. As such, the salience of our training sessions and the quality of our communication will ultimately determine how good we are at *capturing* our athlete's attention; however, to understand how to *keep* our athletes' attention, we need to understand one final network.

PART 3: IN FOCUS

Over the years, I've found that one of the best ways to capture and keep an athlete's attention is to let them experience it at work. To do this, I employ sleight of hand and misdirection, but rather than stealing their watch, I steal their strength. To illustrate how you too can improve your athletes' attitude about attention, I've described the scenario and technique here:

Coach: *"Bring it in. . . . As we consider the session in front of us, we have to ask ourselves a critical question: What am I going to do to ensure that I get better today? While each of you will answer that question differently, one fact holds true, we only improve the skills and abilities that we focus on. That is, if you're unfocused and distracted during training, the best you can hope for is underdeveloped skills and inconsistent results. To show you this, let me have one of you step to the center.*

"Robert, I want you to face the team, place your feet shoulder width apart, and extend your stronger arm straight out, away from your body. Now, I want you to imagine that your arm and body are made of steel. So, when I press down on your wrist, don't let me push your arm down."

Action: *Slowly press on the athlete's wrist, encouraging them to keep their arm straight and as strong as possible. Get the other athletes to cheer them on. Press slowly, ramping up force until the arm moves down a bit, and hold for five seconds. Overall, the athlete will be strong, and it should be difficult to move their arm through a significant range of motion.*

Coach: *"Robert, how did that feel? Were you strong or weak?"*

Athlete (Robert): *"I felt strong, Coach."*

Coach: *"Exactly. You put your full focus and attention on the task, and you were successful. Let's do the same thing but with a small tweak. Keep your stance wide and your arm straight. I now want you to count backwards from 100 . . . out loud . . . by twos. Oh, and I also want you to track my finger with your eyes. While you're doing all this, don't let me push your arm down. Ready?"*

Athlete (Robert): *"Yeah!" (cheers from the team)*

Action: *The athlete will count aloud backward by twos from 100. You will face them with one hand on their wrist, as before, and the index finger of your opposite hand in front of their eyes. As they start to count, move your finger around, encouraging them to keep their eyes fixed on your finger. While this is happening, slowly apply pressure to their wrist (same time and pressure as before). Their arm will be significantly easier to move, and they will want to stop talking and following your finger in an effort to focus on their arm. Encourage them not to.*

Coach: *"Robert, how did that feel? Were you strong or weak?"*

Athlete (Robert): *"A lot weaker that time."*

Coach: *"Team, just like that, I can take your strength away by distracting you from the task at hand. There is no difference between this demonstration and your not being focused on the task in front of you. Your mind mediates your performance; never forget that."*

This activity, which I highly encourage you to try with your athletes, illuminates the most important feature of our attention network—it requires concentrated effort. As we've seen, however, this concentrated effort is being diluted by the gravity of our own thoughts and motives and our inherent need to seek novelty. Therefore, building on the last section, once we flip the salience switch and turn the lights on, we need to deploy coaching tactics that pay the bills and keep the lights on. To unpack how we do this, we will briefly discuss the organization of the attention network and then move on to a final discussion of the primary factors that mediate our ability to sustain focused attention.

The Attention Network: Alerting, Orienting, and Executive Control

Dr. Michael Posner is a cognitive neuroscientist at the University of Oregon and a professor emeritus in the psychology department. Known for immense contributions in the psychological sciences, Dr. Posner's seminal work came through his illumination of the attention network. Using a number of brain imaging techniques, Dr. Posner and his colleagues identified three distinct brain networks that collectively make up the attention network (17). In describing the three brain networks in his book *Attention in a Social World*, Dr. Posner says that "we can view attention as involving specialized networks to carry out functions such as achieving and maintaining the alert state, orienting to sensory events, and controlling thoughts and feelings [through our executive system]" (38). In defining the three networks, Posner and Rothbart (40) describe the **alerting network** "as achieving and maintaining a state of high sensitivity to incoming stimuli"; the **orienting network** as "[selecting] information from sensory input"; and the **executive control** network as "monitoring and resolving conflict among thoughts, feelings, and responses" (p. 7).

As you may have noticed, the alerting and orienting networks seem to be very similar to the salience network described in the last section, and that is because they are. Specifically, they share common neuroanatomical real estate and collectively determine what enters our executive attention network—our conscious awareness—through what has been termed a priority map. As the name implies, a **priority map** integrates bottom-up sensory information via the salience network—sensory information from our internal and external world—with top-down information from the attention network—relevance, rewards, and goals—to ultimately decide where attention is directed (18, 41). Once attention is locked in on its target, we can be confident that it is comfortably seated within the neuroanatomy of our executive control network, importantly, the prefrontal cortex. However, as coaches, our job isn't done—capturing attention is the easy part; it's keeping our athletes' attention that's the key.

Mastering Attention

Throughout this chapter, we've used music production and DJ-ing as an analogy to help us understand the role of attention within a deliberate practice framework. Fittingly, then, we will turn to music one final time as we discuss how to master attention. Mastering, in a musical sense, is the final process in producing a song—our net attentional focus if you will. It is characterized by *compression*, which glues the track together, unifying the sound; ensuring that each song element is at the right volume; and equalizing, or *EQing*, which ensures that the most important elements of the song stand out. Mastering attention, from a coaching perspective, is no different, as we need to compress, or shorten, our message to avoid information overload while EQing our language to ensure that the most important and interesting bits stand out.

COMPRESSING ATTENTION: LESS IS MORE

Speaking about attentional capacity, Dr. Daniel Kahneman, Nobel Prize winner and author of *Thinking Fast and Slow*, said that we "dispose of a limited budget of attention that you can allocate to activities, and if you try to go beyond your budget, you will fail" (26). In sport, we have a name for this—"paralysis by analysis." And, while we often project this back on the athletes, saying things like "they choked,""they're not mentally strong enough," or "they just don't listen," we just as easily could say that "our message wasn't clear and concise,""we didn't arm them with the right focus," or "we said too much." Now, I am not proposing that the athletes don't deserve some of the credit for performance missteps; however, my point, brash as it is, is meant to turn the mirror back on us, coaches, so we can accept our portion of the blame.

To illustrate this, consider figure 2.3. Here, we have our metaphorical attentional spotlight, fixed in size and able to handle only so much information at a time. As we discussed at the beginning of this section, we have a general requirement to deploy attention to physical tasks. While the amount of attention is proportional to our experience with and the complexity of the task, we can be confident that every physical task requires a portion of our attentional real estate. Thus, as represented by the upper crescent moon, a portion of our athletes' attention is taken by the task itself. Additionally, it is likely that you'll provide some type of verbal instruction, and, even if you don't, the odds are that the athletes will focus on something. Hence, the athletes' thoughts—represented by the lower crescent moon—will also take up a portion of their attentional real estate. As such, the shorter the message and the more familiar it is to the athletes, the less attention that is required,

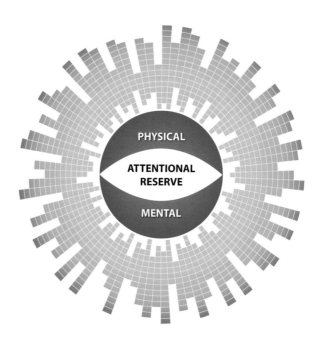

FIGURE 2.3   Attentional capacity.

Adapted from R.A. Magill and D.L. Anderson, *Motor Learning and Control: Concepts and Applications,* 11th ed. (New York: McGraw-Hill Education, 2017), 203.

with the opposite also being true. What we're left with can be called our attentional reserve. As coaches, we should endeavor to always leave as much attentional reserve as possible, especially if we are coaching sport skills or scenarios that require decision-making on top of everything we've already discussed. Thus, we can conclude this section with one of the most important recommendations in the entire book: say the most with the least and use the attention saving principle of 'one cue per rep.'

To be clear, we can provide extensive feedback and engage in a discussion about the movement skill or scenario (see chapter 4); however, when it comes time for the athletes to move, we need to make every effort to summarize our ideas into one cue, one focus point, at a time. The alternative is to give the athletes more information than they can mentally tolerate, after which, one of three things will likely happen: (a) Because of information overload, they will disregard everything you said and focus on something else; (b) they will attempt to focus on everything simultaneously, unsuccessfully; or (c) they will pick the most interesting or the last point to focus on. The key takeaway here is that you really have no idea what they're focusing on, which, consequently, means you cannot use their movement performance to judge the effect of your language. Thus, if you want to move the impact of your coaching from chance to choice, then you should provide only one cue at a time and allow the feedback from one rep to influence the focus you encourage on the next.

EQ-ING ATTENTION: RELEVANCE, REWARDS, AND GOALS

In a previous section, we discussed novelty- and salience-driven attentional triggering. We sampled various strategies coaches can use to leverage the brain's natural affinity for salient stimuli. However, it is not reasonable to expect that every cue, session, or experience will be distinct from the last. Thus, once attention has been captured, we still have a responsibility to help the athlete identify how best to invest it so it sticks.

Considering this last point, taking the perspective of your athlete, what kind of information would you want to focus on for extended periods of time? What did you come up with? My guess is that you said something like "ideas that I value," "information that will help me achieve a goal," or "thoughts that are somehow rewarding to me." If my views are somewhere in the vicinity of your own, then we're moving in the right direction, as there is plenty of science to back up our intuitions on what gives a thought staying power.

Dr. Brian Anderson, assistant professor in the psychology department at Texas A&M University, argues that, in addition to salience- and novelty-driven triggers, we also have goal- and value-driven triggers (1, 2). Consequently, assuming there is no immediate threat to our life that requires our attention, we are free to attend to goal-oriented thoughts. Thus, as we discussed earlier, clearly outlining how a given focus will help your athlete achieve a goal will increase the likelihood that it stays top of mind. Further, if our attention is somehow rewarded, then that thought, or environmental stimulus, will receive higher prioritization the next time it is available.

From a coaching standpoint, we can quickly see how attentional value can be generated through the effect of our cues. For example, let's say we provide an athlete with a single cue and assess its influence on performance. Assuming the cue had a favorable effect, the repetition is rewarded with positive feedback and, as a result, so is the focus that led to the change. At this point, the cue becomes prioritized in terms of its attentional value, as the athlete associates the sound of the cue and the focus it encourages with a positive experience.

Along the same line, we can prepopulate our coaching language with words, phrases, and examples that we know our athletes are familiar with and interested in. Thus, if I'm working with a group of young athletes, for example, and I'd like to encourage them to jump higher during a plyometric drill, I could tell them to "explode to the sky like Iron Man." Assuming these athletes are into Marvel movies, I am more likely to have success with this cue than telling them to "explode through their hips as fast as they can." Ultimately, the language we use to convey a cue will literally determine its staying power, so choose wisely.

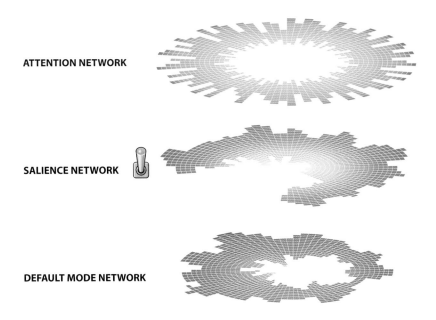

ATTENTION NETWORK

SALIENCE NETWORK

DEFAULT MODE NETWORK

FIGURE 2.4   Three integrated networks that make up the various modes through which our attention can shift.

SUMMARY

We started the chapter with a primer on attention, discussing the attention-influencing features of deliberate practice: goals, focus, feedback, and challenge. In starting with the end in mind, we were able to sketch a picture of effective practice, providing you with a blueprint of sorts. However, as we know, a sketch isn't a sculpture just as a blueprint isn't a building. Thus, to bring these concepts into the three-dimensional world, we needed to discuss the lifeblood of learning, attention.

In discussing attention, we went on a journey through three distinct states of mind (see figure 2.4, previous page). First, we discussed the out-of-focus mind, what we called mind wandering, and the associated cost-benefit analysis of this headspace. We then toured the default mode network, the neuroanatomical home of mind wandering, and revealed how form is tied to function. Second, we discussed the mind that is coming into focus through the process of flipping a salience switch. That is, our brains are constantly prioritizing the most important information for us to attend to, and the salience network is at the center of this prioritization process. Finally, we discussed the linchpin of learning, the attention network, focusing on its capacity to alert, orient, and control the contents of our attentional spotlight. Importantly, we discussed how compressing information—saying the most with the least—and EQing information—ensuring we connect language back to what is most important to the athletes—provide the basic ingredients needed to bake stickiness into every cue.

To conclude, the goal of this chapter was to provide you with a backroom tour of the brain and our attentional networks at work. Understanding this information provides the foundation on which the rest of this book is built. Whether or not you know it now, if the preceding information made sense, then you are well on your way to applying the recommendations that will follow. However, before we get to the treasure trove of practical insights, we need to go on one last tour, the final resting place of learning, our memory system.

REMEMBER WHEN

Memory: A Primer

Before we begin our journey down memory lane, let's take your memory out for a quick test-drive. To start, we'll play a series of games designed to test your memory in the short- and long-term. In each game, you'll be given a simple set of instructions, a series of words or a passage to read, and then a quick retention test to see how much you can remember. Read carefully, focus, and we'll catch up on the other side to see how you did.

Working-Memory Games

To begin, let's play two games designed to test your working (short-term) memory. In the first game, you'll be asked to read and recall a list of words. In the second game, you'll be asked to recall the same number of words, only this time the words will be embedded in a passage. In both games, your goal is to remember as many words as possible.

Memory Game 1

Following are 15 random words (don't peek). Before you begin reading through the list, set a timer for 30 seconds. Start your timer, and intently study the words until the time runs out. Have a pen and paper ready because, as soon as you're done, you will close the book and see how many words you can remember.

Set your timer for 30 seconds . . . and start.

Horse	Pencil	Folder	Bunny	Brake
Table	Strawberry	Tire	Giraffe	Chalk
Wheel	Milk	Window	Floor	Peanuts

Quickly, close the book and write down as many of the words as you can. Now, check your memory, out of the 15 words, how many did you get correct? Once you're done, we can go on to the next game.

Memory Game 2

John's daughter is turning seven, and John needs to go to the store to pick up 15 items for her birthday party. The following passage describes John's outing and the items he picked up at the store. Before you begin reading the passage, set a timer for 60 seconds. Start your timer; then, read through the passage with the intention of remembering the 15 items. Have a pen and paper ready because, as soon as you're done, you will close the book and see how many items you can remember.

Set your timer for 60 seconds . . . and start.

When John arrived at the store, he looked at his shopping list and saw that it was broken into three sections—food, barbecue, and party. Because John had entered on the food side of the store, he picked up those items first. In the produce section, John got the first two items on his list—*lettuce* and *tomato*. John then moved to the bread and snacks aisle to get his next two items—*buns* and *chips*. Finally, John went to the meat counter to pick up his final food item—*turkey burgers*. John quickly moved to the outdoor section of the store to get his barbecue items. Because this was the first barbecue of the season, John picked up a *new grill*, a *metal flipper*, a *grill brush*, *lighter fluid*, and a *bag of briquettes*. Finally, John went to the party section of the store and picked up princess-themed *plates, goody bags, balloons, wrapping paper,* and a *piñata*. Leaving the store, having successfully finished his shopping, John made his way home to set up for his daughter's birthday party.

Quickly, close the book and write down as many of the items John picked up at the store as you can. Now, check your list against the 15 italicized items in the passage. How many did you get correct?

So, if you were in a casino, which game would you prefer to place a bet on? I would wager a fair sum that you would select game 2 over game 1. But why? Seeing as both games contained 15 words or phrases, why did they stay in your mind after game 2 while they seemed to stray from your mind in game 1?

For starters, in game 1, you were given a list of words with no context, and, in game 2, the words came with extensive context and were embedded in the narrative of a story. Further, game 1 did not make any associations between the words and your existing knowledge, while game 2 clustered, or chunked together, related words and associated them with knowledge categories (i.e., the kind of stuff you buy for a birthday party and a barbecue). As such, game 2 encouraged you to visualize John's experience and the items he was purchasing, which allowed you to associate, or anchor, this new information with knowledge you already have. Conversely, in game 1, unless you generated a story around the words (more on this later), you likely attempted to hold each word in your mind through rapid rehearsal, hoping to get all the words down on paper before you ran out of memory. Similar to holding a phone number in your head long enough to write it down, game 1 exposed the limitations of your working memory. However, as game 2 shows, these apparent limitations can be overcome or bypassed if new information is presented through the lens of something we already know. Hence, the memory games illustrate how the framing of information can affect its mental stickiness regardless of the quantity of information presented.

Long-Term Memory Games

Now that we've looked at your mind in the short term, let's rewind and see how your memory operates in the long term. The following memory game is quite simple. Read the passage, and try to remember, in as much detail as possible, the experience being described. As best you can, hold the memory in your mind, and replay it as you would a video on a high-definition television.

Take a moment to scan your memory for the following experiences:

▶ **Memory A**

Think back over the past few years and identify a very positive memory. Maybe you went on an amazing vacation or just got married. Perhaps you had your first child or just graduated from college. Whatever the memory, hold it in your mind and allow your senses to be transported back in time. Try and notice where you were, what you were doing, what you were wearing, and how you were feeling.

▶ **Memory B**

Think back to one week ago from today (e.g., if it is Wednesday, then think back to the previous Wednesday). Again, try and notice where you were, what you were doing, what you were wearing, and how you were feeling.

How did you do? Odds are that you quickly flipped through your memory channels and found memory A in high definition, an obvious choice. To the contrary, identifying memory B probably felt more like adjusting the antenna on an old television set as you tried to make out the memory through the mental static. The question is why. That is, why is it effortless to retrieve some memories and effortful or seemingly impossible to retrieve others? Reflecting back to chapter 2, a large portion of this answer lives in the way we deploy attention. As we discussed, the brain is more sensitive to novelty than it is constancy. As such, if there is nothing unexpected or interesting within our immediate surroundings, then our attention won't be alerted. Because of this, we typically don't remember experiences of the common variety, instead, we sum up these experiences to create an averaged memory that can be called on as needed. You can tell people what you typically wear to work or typically eat for dinner; however, if you are put on the spot to recall a specific outfit or meal, you'll surely have trouble. Conversely, the briefest of experiences, scoring the winning goal or crashing a car, for example, can become instantly imprinted on our memory in remarkable detail, no practice required. In reality, you'd find it easier to remember the make and model of your first car than you would the title of the first chapter in this book. The reason for this is simple: The more uncommon and personally important an experience is, the more likely we are to have total recall.

WHAT'S IN A MEMORY?

One of my favorite movies growing up was the 1990 version of *Total Recall*. Set in the "not too distant future," the plot is built around Rekall, a company that specializes in implanting memories: "Do you dream of a vacation at the bottom of the ocean, but you can't float the bill? Have you always wanted to climb the mountains of Mars, but now you're over the hill? Then, come to Rekall Incorporated, where you can buy the memory of your ideal vacation—cheaper, safer, and better than the real thing." Persuaded by this pitch, Douglas Quaid, played by Arnold Schwarzenegger, goes in to get an implant of a two-week trip to Mars as a secret agent; however, something goes wrong, and Douglas is left to navigate an unfamiliar world with memories he doesn't trust.

While this movie seems well divorced from reality, a moment of reflection reveals a parallel between coaches and Rekall. For example, Rekall charges people to put fake memories in their head, coaches charge people to put in real ones; Rekall wants its clients to walk away with unforgettable experiences, coaches want their athletes to experience unforgettable performances; Rekall uses advanced technology to directly implant memories, coaches use—what? That's the question, right? What do we, the coaches, use to implant unforgettable memories into our athletes' heads—and not just memories of the verbal variety but also the motor memories required to perform the right movement, at the right time, in the right place, no thought required? To answer this question, we need to start by answering a simpler one. Before we can understand how memories get in, we must first appreciate what a memory is.

Our understanding of memory received a boost when famed Canadian psychologist D.O. Hebb published *The Organization of Behavior* in 1949 (75). In this iconic text, Hebb proposed that memory, and thus learning, is represented by networks of interconnected neurons, which he called "cell assemblies." Hebb suggested that these neural networks fire in response to sensory input (e.g., coaching cues, a sunset, or a foul-smelling tuna fish sandwich), with the resultant brain activity representing the perception of that stimulus. If these same neural networks were to fire in the absence of the sensory input, the resulting activity was said to represent the concept of the stimulus, or a memory. This would explain our unique ability to recall an interesting bit of information, relive an experience in vivid detail, or visualize a future that is constructed from our past. Ultimately, if these neural networks are activated often enough, associations are drawn, and the brain undergoes changes that fuse neuronal connections, etching our perception of the world into the anatomy of our brain. While the nuance and details underpinning memory have progressed since Hebb's original publication, what hasn't changed is the view that the brain is an adaptable—some would say, plastic—network of neurons with an infinite capacity for association. Through this lens, we can start to appreciate how 86 billion neurons and 100 trillion connections power our consciousness, turning brains into beings.

While D.O. Hebb provided a sound explanation for the structure of a memory, William James in his 1890 book, *The Principles of Psychology* (40), provided one of the first explanations for the organization of memory. In describing memory, James eloquently stated the following:

> *The stream of thought flows on; but most of its segments fall into the bottomless abyss of oblivion. Of some, no memory survives the instant of their passage. Of others, it is confined to a few moments, hours, or days. Others, again, leave vestiges which are indestructible, and by means of which they may be recalled as long as life endures. (p. 1286)*

In unpacking this statement, James goes on to describe this momentary memory as our primary memory, what we now call working memory, and this indestructible memory as secondary memory, or memory proper, what we now call long-term memory. However, James also asks an important question, "Can we explain these differences?" That is, how does our external world become our internal world, and why do certain memories get a lifetime membership, while others only get a day pass? This brings us back to Rekall and our question, how do we implant unforgettable memories into the heads of our athletes?

To answer this question, leveraging decades of research and practical insights powered by Hebb, James and so many others, we will tour our memory systems as any new memory might, starting with a jaunt around our working memory, followed by a journey into our long-term memory. Upon entering our long-term memory, we'll notice a fork in the road, with one path leading us to our explicit memories, the variety of memory associated with knowing, and another path leading us to our implicit memories, the variety of memory associated with doing. At this juncture, we will consider the mental processes that give rise to these distinct forms of memory. Finally, in the spirit of one of my favorite childhood shows, *The Magic School Bus*, we will join Ms. Frizzle's class as we dive into the brain and take a detailed look at how memories are formed through a process of encoding, consolidation, and retrieval.

PART 1: WORKING MEMORY

We've all experienced the difference between a well-written book that flows and one that doesn't. Reading the former is effortless, whereas reading the latter strains the mind. And, while some would attribute this to story quality, those same people might be surprised to know that working memory had a role to play. To illustrate this, consider the following sentences:

1. The athlete kicks the ball over the goal.
2. The ball goes over the goal after the athlete kicks it.

Which sentence did you find easier to read? If you're like most, you preferred the first sentence. The reason for this is quite simple. Sentence one uses the active voice, where actions occur in the sequence they would in life (i.e., athlete kicks ball, ball goes over goal), while the second sentence is written in passive voice, where you don't find out who performed the action until the end of the sentence (i.e., ball goes over goal, athlete kicks ball). This is like a comedian giving you a punch line before you've heard the joke. Poor grammar aside, you are still able to understand the meaning of both sentences, a faculty you can thank your working memory for. Specifically, the second sentence tapped your working memory to a greater degree than sentence one, as you had to hold the outcome in your mind until you got to the end of the sentence and found out whodunnit. Thus, your brain had to work harder to comprehend the second sentence than it did the first sentence.

This simple exercise showcases the first memory system on our tour—short-term or working memory. While the terms are often used interchangeably, researchers agree that **short-term memory** refers to the temporary storage of information, whereas **working memory** refers to a system that is for the temporary storage and manipulation of information necessary for comprehension, learning, and reasoning (4, 6). From a motor-learning standpoint, we can extend this definition to include working memory's role in integrating new information with that from long-term memory to support decision-making and movement execution (47). For clarity, considering that the storage feature of short-term memory is accounted for in the definition of working memory, we will use working memory throughout the remainder of this book.

As humans, we're well acquainted with this memory system, as it is the subject of our frustration every time we forget the phone number we just looked up or draw a blank on the name of the person we just met. While on the surface, these "sins of memory" appear to be a flaw within the system, an "evolutionary mishap" if you will; a closer look reveals that this flaw is actually a feature designed to filter information into actionable "chunks," where only the meaningful survive (62).

As famed Harvard researcher Daniel Schacter points out in his compelling book *The Seven Sins of Memory: How the Mind Forgets and Remembers* (76), if **absentmindedness**, the inattentiveness that leads to weak memories or forgetting to do something, weren't built into the brain, then we would be subject to remembering everything, the mundane and the magnificent, with little control over what was stored. And, while some would view this capacity for total recall as a superpower, a vastly different interpretation is suggested when we consult with the small minority of the population for whom this is true.

Known as *highly superior autobiographical memory*, or HSAM, for short, people with this condition can recall, in remarkable detail, every experience they've ever had from childhood forward (43). When asked about the condition (52), Jill Price, the first person ever diagnosed with HSAM, provided a surprising response:

> *Whenever I see a date flash on the television (or anywhere else for that matter), I automatically go back to that day and remember where I was, what I was doing, what day it fell on, and on and on. It is non-stop, uncontrollable and totally exhausting. . . . Most have called it a gift, but I call it a burden. I run my entire life through my head every day and it drives me crazy!*

As we discussed in chapter 2, attention serves as working memory's gatekeeper—the mind's bouncer—allowing only the most relevant, interesting, or important information in. Just as you wouldn't go to the store and buy one of everything, you wouldn't want every memory to stand equal in the mind, leaving you unable to tell the dull from the distinct. Thus, the next time you forget a number or a new acquaintance's name, consider the alternative, and be thankful that your memory is working.

Even if we accept that working memory's apparent limitations are features, rather than flaws, it doesn't change the fact that there is limited seating in the theater of our mind. As such, coaches will always be challenged to ensure that the right ideas are getting a front-row seat. For this reason, we will build on the concepts from chapter 2 and examine the structure and function of working memory, laying the foundation to understand how the soundwaves of words transform into the mechanics of movement.

Working-Memory Structure

Born in Great Britain in 1934, Alan Baddeley is best known for his seminal research on a theoretical, multicomponent model for working memory (7). While working-memory models existed at the time (3, 14) and have since been proposed (19), the model established by Baddeley and Graham Hitch in 1974 is widely accepted as our most accurate representation of the form and function of working memory. For this reason, we'll use Baddeley's most recent interpretation of working memory, which was presented in his paper "Working Memory: Theories, Models, and Controversies."

Baddeley and Hitch's original model (7) proposed that working memory, rather than being one unitary system (3), is comprised of three distinct subsystems, just like attention. This was born out of decades of research evaluating the human capacity for remembering newly presented verbal and visual information and, in select studies, considering that information in terms of long-term memories.

If we consider the categories of information we typically contemplate, it is not surprising that Baddeley and Hitch proposed that the three subsystems of working memory include a phonological loop (i.e., a verbal and an acoustic system), a visuospatial sketch pad (i.e., a visual, spatial, and kinesthetic system), and a central executive (i.e., an attentional system; see chapter 2) (7). The **phonological loop** is defined as a subsystem for momentarily storing and subvocally rehearsing verbal information of the written or spoken variety. Thus, your athletes' ability to comprehend, consider, and apply your instructions, cues, and feedback requires a well-oiled phonological loop. Further, the **visuospatial sketch pad** is defined as a subsystem for momentarily storing and manipulating information of the visual, spatial, and kinesthetic kind. Thus, if you provide a cue that encouraged your sprinter to 'imagine a cheetah was creeping up behind them' before the starting pistol goes off; had your player breakdown film and explain how they could have put their teammate into space with a better pass; or asked your diver to explain how they felt in the air prior to water entry, then you'd be tapping into their visuospatial sketch pad. Finally, the **central executive**, which we defined in chapter 2 for its role in the *attention network*, operates as a conductor—the maestro of the mind—combining and considering information from the phonological loop and the visuospatial sketchpad, creating the mental music that we call conscious experience.

Collectively, these three subsystems made up Baddeley and Hitch's multicomponent working-memory model for twenty-five years until it became apparent that the model couldn't explain how all this information was integrated and bound to existing information within long-term memory. Therefore, in 2000, Baddeley proposed the fourth pillar of the model, the **episodic buffer**, which is said to bind information across the phonological loop, the visuospatial sketch pad, and long-term memory to create a coherent stream of consciousness that can be accessed and interrogated by our central executive. In his most recent theoretical discussion of the model, Baddeley stated that he views "working memory as a complex interactive system that is able to provide an interface between cognition and action, an interface that is capable of handling information in a range of modalities and stages of processing" (6).

Working-Memory Capacity

If we view working memory as a hangout where cognition and action meet up, we should also consider its size and discuss how working-memory capacity influences learning.

By way of analogy, we can think of working memory as a dark room, fixed in size, and attention as the spotlight we use to search it. This room, however, can't hold much information and, lesser still, is the amount we can pay attention to.

Because of this, athletes are required to constantly reprioritize and update working memory with the most relevant information for the moment. With this in mind, we can see why coaches need to be, as Daniel Coyle once put it to me, *communication athletes*, ensuring that they provide enough information for the athlete to progress, but not so much as to push beyond the perimeter of their working memory.

Working-memory capacity can be broken down into verbal recall and visual recall, which includes our ability to turn demonstrated actions into our own movements. In his 1956 paper, "The Magical Number Seven, Plus or Minus Two" (77), George Miller proposed that the human capacity for verbal recall is, as the title suggests, seven, plus or minus, two pieces of information. However, in that same article, Miller argued that we can obviously remember more information if we "chunk" bits of it together. For example, consider the following 12 letters:

N   B   A   M   L   B   N   H   L   N   F   L

By Miller's estimates, you'd only remember a fraction of these letters; however, if your brain picked up the pattern, then you could chunk this information into three-letter sequences representing the NBA, MLB, NHL, and NFL. Research now suggests that our working memory can entertain four, plus or minus, two chunks of information at a time, although there is no consensus on what defines the limits of a chunk (20, 21).

A WORKING-MEMORY PALACE

To illustrate this last point, consider the World Memory Championships. Held annually, this event brings together the best memory athletes in the world to flex their mental muscle and crown the ruler of recall. Just to give you a taste, in 2017, Munkhshur Narmandakh, from Mongolia, set a new world record after recalling 1,924 playing cards in under two hours. What makes this feat amazing is that Munkhshur had only an hour to memorize the cards, which means she had to consume the cards at a rate of 1 per 1.87 seconds.

While we may think that there must be something special about Munkhshur, we'd be surprised to know that her brain is no different from ours (49). Sure, she may have a better-than-average working memory but not 1,924 playing cards better. So how do we explain these results? Fortunately, Joshua Foer, a freelance journalist and the author of *Moonwalking With Einstein: The Art and Science of Remembering Everything* (78), answered this question while chronicling his journey from average joe to memory pro. In his 2012 TED talk (84), Josh shares the story of going to cover the U.S. Memory Championship in 2005 and meeting Ed Cooke, an eccentric memory grand master from England. Ed explained that everyone at the championship had an average memory and that even Josh could become a high-achieving memory athlete if he applied himself. Compelled by this idea, Josh spent all of 2005 applying the techniques he had learned from Ed and others with prodigious memories, including Kim Peek, the savant who inspired Dustin Hoffman's character in the Hollywood classic *Rain Man*. In 2006, after training his memory every day for a year, Josh showed up at the U.S. Memory Championship he had covered a year earlier, not as a journalist, but as a competitor, and, to Josh's surprise, he took first place.

How did Josh do this; what does it tell us about working memory; and, most importantly, how can we leverage these insights to help our athletes master their memory? To answer these questions, we need to go back 2,500 years to the moment that Simonides of Ceos, a Greek poet, finished his poem in celebration of Scopas, a Thessalian nobleman. About to sit down, Simonides was suddenly called outside to meet two men with an urgent message. As he was making his way out of the banquet hall, the stillness of the night was suddenly fractured by the sound of the building collapsing. With laughter replaced by screams, it quickly became apparent that the devastation of the accident had left the deceased in an unrecognizable state, leaving their mourning families to agonize over which remains to bury. In shock, Simonides willed his mind to transport him back to the moment when he had stood at the head of the table, giving him a clear view of all those attending and where they'd been seated. With relief and remorse, Simonides carefully guided each family to where their loved ones had been sitting, providing them with the consolation and closure they so desperately desired.

This classic story, while shrouded in sadness, has a silver lining. It shows us that memories are far stronger when they're placed in a vivid context, especially when that context is emotionally salient and experientially unique. As Josh came to learn, this story gave rise to a mnemonic technique known as the **memory palace**, or the method of loci (Latin for "places"). To apply the memory palace, you first need to have something you'd like to recall, let's say all the names of the athletes on a team you just joined. As you sit down, instead of trying to bring the names and faces into your memory through brute force, you visualize the entry to your home—yes, I said your home. Now, as you look at the first athlete's headshot, let's say his name is Jordan Hanson, you will place Jordan at the threshold to your house. You notice that Jordan is wearing an Air Jordan T-shirt and you are pleasantly surprised that Jordan is opening the door for you and welcoming you home. As you walk into your house, you notice that Vinny Larson, your second athlete, is sitting on the bottom of the staircase playing the violin; you compliment him on his playing ability as you make your way into the kitchen. Upon entering, you see Charlie Franklin, your third athlete, dressed as Charlie Chaplin with his well-worn suit, bowling hat, and cane. You compliment Charlie on his dancing and continue moving through the house until you've placed each athlete in your memory palace. The moral of the story is that it is far easier to recall new information when it is wrapped in the context of something we already know.

HACKING WORKING MEMORY

While the memory palace might seem silly or over-the-top, it is for this very reason that it is so effective. Specifically, the memory palace technique uses a well-established learning strategy called **elaborative encoding**, which can be defined as the improved retention that comes as a consequence of associating to-be-learned information with information that already exists within memory. First presented in terms of levels of processing, Craik and Lockhart (22) argued that the "depth" of processing during the early stages of learning could explain how well something would be recalled in the future. For example, in a classic study, Craik and Tulving (23) had subjects encode words using four strategies that went from "shallow" to "deep." In strategy 1, subjects were asked to comment on whether a word was written in uppercase or lowercase. In strategy 2, subjects were asked whether the target word rhymed with the presented word (e.g., presented word: Does the word rhyme with possum; target word: awesome; answer: yes). In strategy 3, subjects were asked to make an association between a target word and a presented word (e.g., presented word: Is the word a type of car; target word: apple; answer: no). In strategy 4, subjects were asked to identify whether the target word would contextually fit within a presented sentence (e.g., presented sentence: The boy played _____ with his friends; target word: swimming; answer: no). Following the encoding strategies, subjects were given a surprise retention test to see how many target words they could recall. As one would expect, those who encoded target words using deeper levels of processing (i.e., strategies 3 and 4) performed better than those who encoded using shallow processing (i.e., strategies 1 and 2). To be clear, deep, or elaborative, encoding requires people to consider the meaning, not just a superficial feature, of the to-be-remembered information and integrate this information with existing semantic, visual, spatial, kinesthetic, or acoustic knowledge structures through a process of rehearsal.

Thus, the memory palace is elaborative encoding at its best. Leveraging working memory's episodic buffer, we are able to use our central executive to associate information that enters the mind via the phonological loop or the visuospatial sketch pad with information that exists within long-term memory. Without the need to create a memory from scratch, the established neural networks fire up and welcome the new information in, no different than editing an existing Word document on your desktop.

You don't have to be a memory champion to use these memory-editing techniques. They are available to you right now as a coach. All it takes is a bit of consideration when preparing to give an athlete instruction, cues, or feedback. That is, if you can connect the information you want them to bring on board to ideas and concepts that already have a home in their head, then you'll find that comprehension and recall will improve. As we'll talk about in chapter 6, one of the best ways to deploy this technique is by using analogies and metaphors, which is to say, you describe something unfamiliar in terms of something your athlete is familiar with. To capture this idea, consider the following example:

> *Jane is a strength and conditioning coach working with Ben on his squatting technique. Ben struggles to squat effectively, consistently allowing his knees to travel well in front of his toes as he descends into the squat. Concerned that this may cause Ben to have knee pain in the future, Jane is trying to identify cues that will help him make the necessary technical changes. After considering the problem, Jane comes up with two cues she thinks might work:*
>
> ► *Cue A: "Reach your hips back behind your heels as you lower into the squat."*
>
> ► *Cue B: "Reach your hips back as you would to sit down on an unstable park bench."*

Which cue would you prefer to focus on? For most, the second cue provides a relatable image that has an emotional essence. That is, you can visualize and simulate what it would feel like to sit down on an unstable park bench. In contrast, telling someone to "keep your hips behind your heels" is like asking them to remember a word by commenting on whether it is uppercase or lowercase. It draws attention to the *what* but neglects the *how*. This is similar to trying to learn a word by studying its letters instead of its meaning. Hence, the analogy of a park bench gives meaning that can be transformed into the way one performs the squat. Thus, using associative language that encourages elaborative encoding can support your athletes' learning by helping them hang new concepts on existing memory hooks, making a mini-memory palace, one cue at a time.

WORKING MEMORY AND COACHING BEHAVIORS

While most coaches would agree that overcoaching, or over-cueing, can tax working memory and increase the odds of paralysis by analysis, their behaviors often reflect a different set of beliefs. For example, in their study "Understanding Power and the Coach's Role in Professional English Soccer," Potrac, Jones, and Cushion (57) found that elite coaches spent 8.9 percent of their time providing instruction before skill execution, 22.9 percent of their time providing instruction during skill execution, and 22.6 percent of their time providing feedback after skill execution. This sits in contrast to the 2.3 percent of the time used to ask questions and the 14.54 percent of the time spent being silent. Notably, this result is not unique, as an overdependence on instruction is one of the most common findings within the coaching-behavior literature (24, 31).

While we know that not all instructions are created equal, meaning some are easier to process and remember than others (e.g., analogies), it doesn't take away from the fact that there are capacity limits within our working memory. Hence, the amount of information we provide an athlete needs to be proportional to the amount of information they can comprehend and focus on while still performing a movement. Highlighting this point, Buszard and colleagues (15) evaluated the interaction between working memory and instruction on children's ability to learn a basketball shooting task. With all children asked to read the same five instructions before each block of practice (12 blocks of 20 shots spread over three days), the researchers found that children who tested high on assessments of working memory (i.e., verbal, visuospatial, and attention) saw distinct improvements in shooting performance from pre- to posttest with a pronounced increase in performance during a retention test that occurred one week later. Conversely, children who tested low on the dimensions of working memory showed the opposite pattern, with their performance progressively worsening from pretest through retention. This result is not surprising because research has shown that visuospatial working memory and attention are predictors of motor learning (66).

Three key takeaways can be derived from the evidence presented in this section. First, coaches use instruction to a far greater degree than any other coaching tool (e.g., questioning or guided discovery). As such, coaches run the risk of providing too much information or framing information in a way that does not support comprehension and learning. For this reason, coaches are encouraged to use the one-cue-per-rep strategy to avoid working-memory overload and ensure that observed changes in technique are associated with the updated focus. Second, while everyone's working memory has a limited capacity, this varies across individuals. This explains why certain athletes can handle a lot of instruction with no negative effect on performance and learning, whereas other athletes cannot. Consequently, there is no replacement for getting to know your athletes and adapting your language to their limits – this is the art in the science. Finally, as we've shown through our discussion of the memory palace, the way information is framed or interpreted directly affects how much information can be actively attended to. This is why we say a picture is worth a thousand words and why coaches should endeavor to provide instructions, cues, and feedback that excite the theater of the mind.

PART 2: LONG-TERM MEMORY

As we discussed in the previous section, the brain employs working memory to let relevant information in and keep irrelevant information out. As such, the brain tends to invest in thoughts that pique curiosity, align with motives, or provide life-sustaining insights. However, working memory is like a waiting room, only allowing information to occupy a limited space for a short period of time. Once the mind decides that a thought or an experience is worth keeping, it needs a place to put it. This memory bank as it were, which we call **long-term memory**, allows us to relive the past so that we might benefit from those experiences in the present (69). Our capacity for this type of mental time travel is truly unique within the animal kingdom and marks the next stop on our tour.

The Man Who Couldn't Make Memories

If you read a book on memory, you're likely to come across the story of H.M. (Henry Molaison). As a boy, H.M. was knocked down by a bicycle and subsequently hit his head, leaving him unconscious for five minutes. The ensuing brain damage led to debilitating seizures that were deemed untreatable. After suffering from this condition for over 10 years and being unable to work, H.M. underwent a groundbreaking surgery in 1953 to have his hippocampus, amygdala, and portions of his medial temporal cortex removed.

Following the surgery, H.M.'s seizures were reduced, with no apparent changes to his intelligence and personality. Despite this success, however, it quickly became apparent that H.M. had a new problem: He could no longer generate new memories (65). To be clear, H.M. retained most of his early long-term memories that preceded the surgery. He also had an intact working memory, which meant he could remember the name of a person he'd just met. However, if that person were to come back the next day, H.M. would have no recollection of ever meeting them. As such, no matter how many times H.M. relived an experience, he lacked the mental machinery to commit it to memory.

A young psychologist at the time, Brenda Milner, a student of D.O. Hebb, set out to understand H.M.'s unique mind and what it might reveal about the nature of memory. After visiting H.M. every month for many years, Milner made a historic finding. She observed that, while H.M. could not recall people, places, or facts, he retained the ability to develop new motor skills (54). Notably, when asked to trace a five-pointed star by looking at his hand and the star in a mirror, H.M. displayed excellent retention across three days of practice, despite having no recollection of ever performing the task (67).

This observation, and the many that followed, provided evidence for the existence of multiple long-term memory systems: one system for storing facts and events and another for storing skills and habits. While distinguishable in an amnesia patient like H.M., a person without brain damage will have no sense of separate memory systems. In everyday life, this has its advantages. However, developing an appreciation for the particulars of each system can help coaches learn to boost, rather than block, their athletes' capacity for making memories.

Multiple Memories: A Short History

While Milner and her colleagues provided some of the earliest evidence for multiple long-term memory systems, there have been many scientists and philosophers who have made similar observations about the nature of long-term memory. For example, in 1804, Maine de Biran, a French philosopher, published "The Influence of Habit on the Faculty of Thinking," in which he provided one of the earliest descriptions of a conscious and an unconscious memory system (11). In describing de Biran's view of an unconscious memory system, Daniel Schacter states that, "after sufficient repetition, a habit can eventually be executed automatically and unconsciously without awareness of the act itself or of the previous episodes in which the habit was learned" (61).

Support for this viewpoint was born out of early research on patients with amnesia. In a now famous, albeit, devious study from 1911, Edouard Claparède (79) pricked the hand of an unsuspecting patient. Upon subsequent meetings, the patient refused to shake Claparède's hand even though she had no recollection of the painful experience. This provided further evidence that there was a form of memory that could be acted out without conscious recall of the inciting experience that gave rise to it.

In the same year that Claparède was pricking the fingers of unwitting patients, Henri Bergson in *Matter and Memory*, suggested that "the past survives under two distinct forms: first, in motor mechanisms; secondly, in independent recollections" (10). This idea—that some experiences lead to "doing" memories, whereby the mechanisms governing a physical change in behavior (motor learning) are locked away within our unconscious, whereas other experiences lead to "knowing" memories, whereby information about people, places, and facts can be consciously recalled—provided theoretical fuel for what would become the golden age of memory research. And, if the 20th century was the golden age for memory research, then Daniel Schacter was one of its "golden boys."

Multiple Memories: Knowing Versus Doing

In the mid-1980s, Daniel Schacter and his colleagues (80, 81) produced a series of papers that provided theoretical justification for the set of terms we now use to describe these distinct forms of memory. Specifically, **explicit memory** is a form of memory that supports the conscious recall of information derived from past experiences (e.g., people, places, facts, and ideas), whereas **implicit memory** is a form of memory that supports skilled performance without conscious control (e.g., reading, riding a bike, and driving a car). In describing the two forms of memory, Schacter (61) notes that "implicit memory is revealed when previous experiences facilitate performance on a task that does not require conscious or intentional recollection of those experiences, [whereas] explicit memory is revealed when performance on a task requires conscious recollection of previous experiences" (61). By way of analogy, we can think of explicit memories as what we know and implicit memories as what we do. Equally, drawing on sport, we can think of explicit memories as the rules of the game, while implicit memories are the actions required to play by those rules.

Within each form of memory, various subcategories have been identified. Specifically, explicit memories are commonly categorized as **episodic**, which is defined as memories of personal experiences that occurred at a specific time and within a unique context, or **semantic**, which is defined as experience independent knowledge (i.e., facts, ideas, and concepts) (68). Simply put, episodic memories provide the basis for mental "time travel," allowing you to revisit past experiences and fast-forward to experiences yet to be, whereas semantic memories can be summed up as your "world knowledge" (28). In a coaching context, we tap our athletes' episodic memories when information provokes an image or experience to be visualized and their semantic memory when information prompts facts, rules, or ideas to be conceptualized or abstracted. In many instances, both forms of memory will map onto each other because we use our semantic memory to derive meaning from experience: Why did I shoot when I should have passed? What should I do the next time I am in that defensive situation? How can I improve my technique so I don't miss that lift next time?

Similarly, our implicit memory can be divided into multiple subcategories of which two are relevant here. First, implicit memories can emerge in the form of **priming**, where one can access perceptual or conceptual knowledge quicker due to a prior exposure to that information. For example, in sport we often review film with the hope of identifying an opponent's tells: The basketball player prefers to drive to their left; the pitcher drops their glove before the windup when it's a fastball; or the rugby player tucks the ball under the side they intend to run. With these visuals on board, the athlete is perceptually *primed* to pick up these cues in games and make quicker decisions than if they hadn't reviewed the film.

The second type of implicit memory comes in the form of **procedural** memories, which are the complex motor skills that are coordinated by and organized within subcortical regions of the brain and spinal cord. This category of memory represents the neural networks that coaches are trying to interact with and modify every time they have an athlete practice a skill. From walking to running, cutting to jumping, every motor skill is controlled and deployed at an unconscious level of the nervous system. You might be thinking, but what about intention and attention, conscious control, goal-directed behavior; don't we consciously control and manipulate all of our movement? The answer is complex but, in short, no. We do not consciously control every degree of freedom, muscular contraction, and cellular process underpinning our movements.

To illustrate this point, let's imagine a simple motor task such as picking up a glass of water. Once you notice you're thirsty, your brain sets in motion a series of actions that require the seamless integration of implicit and explicit memories. First, you associate thirst with the action that will quench it. This requires a level of semantic knowledge that tells you that water, as opposed to Windex, is the better fluid to consume when thirsty. Second, you require the episodic knowledge to recall that you recently put a glass of water on the table next to you. Third, you deploy an implicit motor plan that allows you to reach for the glass, bring it to your mouth, and put it back down on the table. If all goes well, the only thing you are consciously aware of is that you had a goal—quench your thirst—and that the goal was achieved—thirst was quenched. At no time did you have to set the subgoals of picking up your arm 10 degrees, extending your elbow 90 degrees, opening your hand, grasping the glass, and so on. The reality is, unless you missed the glass or knocked it over, you were not alerted to the details of your movement. To the contrary, your movement operated in covert silence, guided by a continuum of explicit thoughts that started with a goal and ended with its achievement.

From getting out of bed in the morning to making the game-winning shot, our explicit (conscious) memory establishes the goal, and our implicit (unconscious) memory establishes the motor patterns required to achieve it. The question we now have to tackle is, how does our coaching language, which interacts with an athlete's explicit memory, influence and adapt the motor patterns locked within their implicit memory? To answer this question, we will examine how memories are formed through a process of encoding, consolidation, and retrieval.

PART 3: MAKING MEMORIES

Now that we've explored our primary forms of memory, we are ready to discuss the process by which memories are created and etched into our minds. To do this, we'll continue our tour and examine how we make memories through stages of encoding, consolidating, and retrieving. At each stage of the memory-forming process, we will give consideration to the interaction between memory type (i.e., implicit vs. explicit) and the associated brain regions that the memory will soon call home.

In an effort to keep this discussion as clear as possible, it is valuable to briefly align on the variety of memories coaches would like to see enter into the brains and, as a consequence, the bodies of their athletes. Specifically, with a firm focus on motor-skill learning, we can divide these memories into three distinct categories. The first category of memory that coaches seek to generate, is what we'll call **sport knowledge**, which refers to the context in which a motor skill is to be executed. In this case, context may include the rules of the game and an understanding of tactics and the opponent. This is useful knowledge that constrains how one deploys motor skills to achieve an outcome, although it is not representative of the motor skill itself.

We will call the second category of memory **motor-skill knowledge**, which refers to knowledge directly related to executing a motor skill. As we'll discuss at length in the coming chapters, this includes information pertaining to the movement process, what most coaches refer to as technique or technical knowledge, and the movement outcome, which relates to the outcome that should be achieved as a consequence of executing the motor skill. In simple terms, this is all of the information contained within our instructions, cues, and feedback.

The final category of memory is **motor-skill execution**, which refers to accurately executing a motor skill in the context in which it needs to be performed. This means that the athlete is not only able to perform the movement in isolation (e.g., change of direction) but also under the perceptual constraints of their sport (e.g., changing direction in response to an oncoming defender). As such, we can categorically think of motor-skill execution as being synonymous with the motor memories (i.e., motor patterns) that emerge in response to motor learning.

Considered as a collective, we can see that sport knowledge is a type of explicit memory that has both semantic and episodic features. Similarly, motor-skill knowledge is also a type of explicit memory that allows coaches to describe a physical movement using language. Finally, motor-skill execution is a type of implicit memory that is primed by motor-skill knowledge, through practice, and printed on unconscious regions of the brain. Considering the focus of this book, we will discuss the memory-forming process in terms of motor-skill execution and the associated motor-skill knowledge.

Encoding Memories

The first stage of the memory-forming process is referred to as **encoding**, which is the process of associating information that is currently being attended to with existing information in a person's memory (63). Quite literally, we have neural networks, biologically equivalent to cellular networks, that represent perceptions, actions, concepts, and categories. When we attend to something with the intention of remembering it, our brains will fire neurons associated with the constellation of neurons that represent the information being considered (think back to D.O. Hebb's "cell assemblies") (28). As one might expect, the more often these neural networks fire, the greater the likelihood that a memory will be formed, expanded, and strengthened. Hence, *neurons that fire together wire together.*

While the brain still holds many mysteries, our understanding of the neuroanatomy associated with the encoding process is quite good. To demonstrate this, we'll follow Marcus, a high school soccer player who, on the advice of his coach, is engaging in a summer sprint program to improve his speed for next season. While Marcus will continue playing soccer throughout the summer, he will also engage in speed-development sessions specifically designed to improve his coordination and performance. Because Marcus is not a sprinter and has never been formally coached on how to sprint, we will assume that his learning will traverse the cognitive, associative, and autonomous learning stages proposed by Fitts and Posner (see chapter 2).

ENCODING CUES

Let's begin our story at Marcus' first speed-development session. He has just finished his warm-up and a series of submaximal 20-yard (18 m) sprints. Now that his coach feels he has a good understanding of Marcus' preferred sprinting style, he provides him with a single focus cue, for example, "As you sprint, focus on driving your knees forward as if to shatter a pane of glass," and asks him to focus intently on this throughout the next sprint.

With the cue well situated in Marcus' mind, his working memory kicks into high gear to hold this information for immediate access and application. If we zoom into Marcus' brain at the very moment the cue penetrates his consciousness, we would see distinct regions of his cerebral cortex activate in proportion to their role in processing the type of information contained within the cue. As a refresher, the cerebral cortex is the outermost layer of the brain that supports consciousness, perception, action, and goal-directed behavior. We know that Marcus would require his phonological loop to store and rehearse the words contained within the cue. In doing so, Marcus would recruit Broca's area, a lateral portion of the frontal lobe associated with language rehearsal, so that he could repeat the cue back to himself, while also recruiting his temporoparietal region in an effort to store the content of the cue itself (5).

While Marcus would use his phonological loop to process the language within the cue, he would enlist his visuospatial sketch pad to extract the visual meaning from the cue. To do this, we would find that Marcus' occipital cortex, the back of the brain, activates to store visually generated information while regions of his parietal cortex, prefrontal cortex, and premotor cortex activate to allow him to interrogate, integrate, and interpret any visual information that is triggered as a consequence of the cue (5). Moreover, Marcus' phonological loop and visuospatial sketch pad require his central executive to deploy attention to ensure that the content of the cue pervades the intention he brings to the next sprint. Accordingly, this would require Marcus to activate his prefrontal cortex, the brain region that commands the attentional component of working memory (42).

While the cue is now in the driver's seat of Marcus' mind, he still needs to interpret its meaning if he wants the language to get to his legs. To do this, his working memory requires access to his long-term memory via the episodic buffer, which means that he will need to tap into the neural networks representing sprinting and glass breaking so that his association networks can weave these ideas together (i.e., "Focus on driving your knees forward as if to shatter a pane of glass"). If these representations turn out to be weak or nonexistent in Marcus' mind, then this cue will fail to make a significant difference when he sprints. However, if Marcus has a strong representation of these concepts, he'll be able to color his next sprint with the information contained within the cue. That is, to break a pane of glass, an object is first projected at high speeds before an ensuing collision launches shards of glass in all directions. Thus, assuming Marcus understands the contents of the cue, he can easily run a simulation by transforming his knee into a ballistic projectile that explodes through a pane of glass with every stride.

This simulation, or any simulation, is dependent on our ability to take a new piece of information, a cue in this case, and integrate it with information in long-term memory. Like a Hollywood movie producer, the mind takes different memory clips and edits them together until a new thought emerges. If successful, the theater of our mind is updated and starts playing the new release, allowing us to consider an idea or an image for the first time.

To achieve this movie magic, three distinct brain regions are called into action (28). First, as we've discussed, the cerebral cortex receives and processes incoming sensory information (i.e., sight, sound, smell, taste, and touch). Second, this information is sent to a subcortical area of the brain called the parahippocampal region, which is responsible for integrating and refining

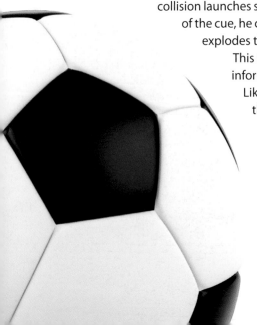

sensory information via a "what" and a "where" pathway. Functionally, the "what" pathway processes the contents of thought and experience (i.e., people, places, objects, etc.), whereas the "where" pathway processes context (i.e., when and where). These pathways converge on the hippocampus, where content is placed in context. This new information is then compared to and integrated with information contained within our long-term memory. This refined information is then redirected back to the original cortical regions from which the initial sensory information came, and a new thought is born.[1]

Describing this process in *The Cognitive Neuroscience of Memory*, Howard Eichenbaum notes that "the role of the medial temporal lobe [hippocampal circuit] is to enhance the storage of, change the organization of, or otherwise modify the nature of cortical representations" (28). Thus, every time information passes through the hippocampus, it doesn't just modify our immediate thoughts; it modifies our memory. This is why we practice: The more often we recall a piece of information, the stronger the network that represents that information becomes. To the contrary, if people lack a hippocampus, which was the case with H.M., they lose all capacity to generate new or modify existing explicit memories. As such, we can think of the hippocampus as a composer, authoring memories in the same way one would compose a musical score, one note and one synapse at a time, whereas the prefrontal cortex is a conductor, orchestrating our memories as one would musicians, shaping the features of the mind to fit the mood of the moment (53).

As we zoom out of Marcus' brain, you will be surprised to know that the entire process we just navigated took a fraction of a second (64). Marcus was able to convert his coach's cue into conscious intentions faster than Usain Bolt can cover the first 10 m of a sprint. Thus, Marcus has completed the first step in the memory-forming process: He has encoded his coach's cue, which allows him to simulate or visualize his motor intentions before his next sprint, in essence, test-driving his focus before bringing it online. Assuming the cue passes the driving test, Marcus is now ready to sprint. Let's zoom back into Marcus' brain to see what happens when motor intentions turn into motor actions.

ENCODING ACTIONS

Similar to encoding cues, encoding actions requires a number of connected brain regions operating in parallel to convert a motor plan into a motor action. This is an important point because every voluntary movement requires explicit memory formation to support motor intention, the conscious part, and implicit memory formation to support motor action, the unconscious part. The essential role of the coach is to ensure that each memory system is delegated the task it is best suited to achieve. Our explicit memory is very good at establishing the goal, or outcome, of the movement task (e.g., "Push the bar to the ceiling" or "Throw the ball to the wide receiver"), whereas our implicit memory is very good at deploying and adapting the motor actions required to achieve that goal (i.e., coordination—the spatial, temporal, and force characteristics of motion). In this way, the explicit memories associated with movement intentions provide the brain with the "what," similar to putting a location into a GPS, whereas the implicit memories associated with the movement action provide the brain with the "how," the directions, or process, required to achieve the "what." With this information, let's rejoin Marcus and peer into his brain as this neural narrative unfolds.

As Marcus lowers into his stance, his muscles tense in preparation for the ensuing sprint. At the same time, his mind makes final preparations before deploying the motor actions that will propel him down the field. With the last bit of mental rehearsal complete, Marcus' brain revs into action, sending a cascade of neural fireworks through distinct motor loops that have evolved to support motor intentions (planning) and motor actions (execution). Like a Formula 1 race car around a track, neural signals circulate between cortical and subcortical brain regions, creating a continuous flow of information that turns intentions into actions. While these motor loops share responsibilities and neural real estate, it does appear that one loop guides motor planning while the other guides motor execution. For this reason, we will explore each loop separately, knowing that these loops are united in controlling movement.

---

[1] While this process of converting cues into consciousness appears to be very linear, like an assembly line, the reality is that many of these processes are occurring in parallel, with a number of feedback loops connecting one brain region to another, a kind of checks and balances if you will. I've highlighted the main brain regions and mental processes that are implicated in encoding explicit information for future use; however, there is still much that is unknown within this area of cognitive neuroscience.

Planning Loop   Operating like a neurological trigger for voluntary movement, the **planning loop** is anchored to anatomical pit stops that include areas within the motor cortex and the basal ganglia, a seedlike structure nestled deep within the subcortical centerfold of the brain. We know this based on a diversity of studies examining those with and without damage to structures within their planning loop. For example, in a group of surgical experiments straight out of the *Black Mirror* series on Netflix, researchers showed that direct stimulation to the supplementary motor cortex (33), a key region associated with motor planning, resulted in patients' reporting a voluntary "urge to move," whereas stimulation applied to the primary motor cortex (32), a key brain region associated with motor execution, resulted in motor actions that patients reported as involuntary, or not their own. Notably, this last point is further supported by the fact that motor-planning regions of the cortex illuminate when movements are self-initiated, whereas the same brain regions go dark when movements are triggered by an external stimulus, such as a light or sound (41). Thus, evidence supports the notion that motor planning and motor execution, while inextricably linked, are associated with distinct brain regions, with the nature of the task dictating how much involvement is required from each brain area.

While the motor cortex clearly supports motor planning, evidence has now shown that the basal ganglia serves as an anatomical primer (2), with activity appearing in this brain region seconds before movement begins (46). Notably, outputs from the basal ganglia to the motor cortex are modulated by dopamine, the neurotransmitter associated with reward (72). These dopamine inputs are proposed to affect motor planning by rewarding intentional states that have led to positive movement outcomes in the past (56). Consequently, if dopamine levels diminish in the basal ganglia, a feature of Parkinson's disease, then output to the motor cortex is reduced, resulting in tremors and reduced motor control (25). These changes to motor control are so debilitating that even the simplest of voluntary actions become taxing. However, toss a ball to an individual with Parkinson's or ask them to move in response to an external stimulus, and you'll be amazed to see how many can catch the ball and react normally (a phenomenon known as paradoxical Parkinson's) because the planning loop doesn't appear to be implicated in the automatic motor actions that are the responsibility of the action loop (8, 35).

A notable example of this comes from an interview with Michael J. Fox, who was diagnosed with Parkinson's in 1991 at the age of 29. In the interview (85), you can visibly see Michael's resting tremors as he discusses the effect Parkinson's has had on his life; however, a glimmer of hope is revealed when the *Back to the Future* star showed a video of himself ice skating with no trouble at all. What appears to be a miracle is further evidence that motor-planning and motor-action loops are anatomically distinct, allowing those who suffer from motor-control diseases like Parkinson's to bypass their compromised planning loop by using external as opposed to internal stimuli to guide their motor control. Quite literally, the use of rhythmical sounds (44) or visual prompts (8) can be used to cadence movement, allowing the action loop to be triggered by an external sensory source, which does not require excessive contribution from the planning loop (39). This provides powerful evidence that the contents of attention and intention have significant effects on motor control, especially when one's motor system has been compromised by disease. We will revisit this idea in subsequent chapters, as therein lies a clue to understanding how the focus encouraged by a coaching cue can have dramatic effects on the way we learn to move.

Action Loop   While Marcus' planning loop supports his intention to move, he ultimately needs to convert these intentions into actions. To do this, he will require the assistance of an **action loop**, a neural circuit that connects his motor cortex, notably his primary motor cortex, and his cerebellum, a butterfly-shaped subcortical region that is positioned at the base of the brain. This action loop serves two essential purposes: (a) It converts motor intentions into motor actions and (b) adapts movement in real time based on sensory feedback (45). Specifically, the primary motor cortex has detailed maps of the body etched into its cells. These maps appear to contain motor code for controlling the kinetic and kinematic features of all possible movement (60). Thus, for intention to drive action, the action loop requires the planning loop so that it knows which patterns to activate and which patterns to inhibit (55). To do this, the planning loop provides information in the form of sensory predictions (59), which means that intentions are converted into the sensory goals the motor actions are attempting to achieve.

To illustrate this, imagine that you're moving to a new house and you're putting boxes onto a moving truck. You have one box left labeled kitchen pots and pans. Prepared to lift a heavy box, you squat down, but, to your surprise, you shoot up because the box is lighter than you expected. This experience violated your expectations because your motor system had predicted a much heavier box and, consequently, deployed far more neuromuscular resources than the situation required. This story demonstrates how motor actions are coded in terms of their predicted sensory consequences. Simply put, our motor actions are guided by the sense we should have once they are completed. When this sense is violated, the motor system receives an error signal, and motor learning ensues, often through a process of self-correction, while a confirmatory signal serves to strengthen the motor patterns already on the hard drive.

The "Little Brain"   While the primary motor cortex is often referred to as the "final common path" in motor control due to its direct link to the spinal cord, the cerebellum (Latin for "little brain") is the unsung hero within the action loop. Notably, while the cerebellum makes up only 10 percent of your brain's volume, it's home to just over 80 percent of the 86 billion neurons in your head (37). To echo the title of Daniel Wolpert's insightful TED talk (86), the "real reason for brains" resides in our ability to use movement as a means of linking intentions to outcomes, and, for this, we need to give thanks to our little brain, the cerebellum.

The cerebellum connects to the motor cortex via a closed loop, allowing the cerebellum to influence and modify the motor signals being sent from the primary motor cortex to the spinal cord. At the same time, the cerebellum also has a direct line to the spinal cord, allowing it to tune and adapt movement patterns that are already in progress. This tuning is a reflection of the cerebellum's role in synchronizing the timing of movement, which possibly explains why rhythm cues help Parkinson's patients improve their gait control—their cerebellum is well suited to control movement when attention is focused on a musical cue. Further support for this tuning feature comes from research on stroke patients with cerebellar lesions who can learn spatial parameters of a movement (i.e., where to move) but struggle to learn the temporal parameters of movement (i.e., when to move) (13). Thus, just as kinetic (force) maps seem to predominate the primary motor cortex, it appears the kinematic (motion) maps seem to predominate the cerebellum (50), supporting their partnership in controlling movement.

In addition to tuning the motor system, the cerebellum can compare the motor signal deployed by the primary motor cortex to what actually occurred, acting as a "comparator," as it is often called (73). Specifically, the cerebellum is said to receive a copy of the motor signal deployed by the primary motor cortex—a sensory blueprint, or efference copy, as it is known (50). The cerebellum can then compare this sensory blueprint with real-time sensory feedback coming in from the spinal cord. A consequence of this comparison is that the cerebellum can adapt movements in real time by redirecting a motor pattern that has gone off course. Hence, the reason we're pretty good at not spilling our steaming latte when trying to navigate a busy coffee shop during the morning rush.

Beyond real-time motor adjustments, the cerebellum's comparative abilities also benefit motor learning. Specifically, when a movement is performed quickly, the cerebellum doesn't always have enough time to make real-time changes. For those of us who have ever bitten our tongue, tripped and fallen while running, or made any variety of motor mistakes, we know this truth all too well. However, do not fear, as the cerebellum is still here; that is, when our motor actions misalign with our motor intentions, the cerebellum is still able to compare what happened with what we wanted to happen. When these puzzle pieces don't fit, our brain generates an error signal, the "that just didn't feel right" signal, alerting us to the mismatch. This built-in alerting system sits at the heart of motor learning because errors serve to support our ability to self-correct; this is true of learning how to walk, ride a bike, or just about anything else you can think of. Errors emerge as sensory sirens that tell us when something is off. In most cases, athletes are aware of these errors and can use this information to self-correct. However, there are many cases in which the athlete feels the error but doesn't know how to make the change. If this is the case and you have confirmed there are no physical limitations, then this is where you step in with your cues or constraints and help guide the athlete toward a new movement pattern.

As we link up again with Marcus, we can see that his coach's cue has materialized into a surge of activation flowing from his basal ganglia to his motor cortex. As this intentional signal hits his primary motor cortex, the motor plan is converted into a motor action, which is coded in terms of predicted sensory consequences—the feel. With the conversion complete, the motor action is communicated to the motor system via direct connections to the spinal cord. In the same moment, the cerebellum receives a copy of the motor plan and readies itself for a sensory storm, prepared to align Marcus' intentions and actions by tuning his motor system through a process of constant comparison. Like the kickback of a shotgun, Marcus explodes off the line, a fury of activation pulsing through his muscles. With every stride, Marcus blasts his knee through a "pane of glass," leaving a trail of shards in his mental wake. Moments later, Marcus drives through the finish line, the sprint is over. As he starts to slow down, the sensory scanning begins: "How did the sprint feel?" "Did the cue help?" "What did I do well?" "What should I focus on next?" Marcus' internal dialogue is quickly met with insights and ideas from his coach. Minutes later, having waded through the information provided by the previous rep, Marcus and his coach identify a new focus, a new cue, and, with that, Marcus is back on the starting line ready to go again.

Consolidating Memories

Once memories have been invited into the brain via the encoding process, the consolidation of those memories can begin. Spanning minutes to years, **consolidation** is the process of converting unstable memories that are being temporarily stored into stable memories that receive permanent residence within the brain (63). Occurring in two distinct stages (29), memories will initially exist in a fluid state, represented by a cascade of molecular changes within the neural networks associated with the contents of our memories, what we will call **chemical consolidation**. As practice continues, memory networks are repeatedly activated, leading to the structural changes in the brain that come to reflect our long-term memories and learning, what we will call **structural consolidation**.

As we've discussed at length, the contents of information heavily influence how memorable something is. You'll recall that information high in emotional value is well suited to capture and keep our attention, a precursor to memory formation, whereas information low in emotional value has trouble staying within our mind's theater. This being true, it will come as no surprise that the first stage of memory consolidation is associated with neurochemical changes that are partly mediated by the amygdala, the brain's emotion center (51).

When an experience is tagged as high in emotional value, it triggers the release of hormones from the adrenal glands, the triangular patch of tissue that sits atop your kidneys. These hormones, epinephrine and glucocorticoids, target the amygdala, which in turn modulates the release of the neurotransmitter norepinephrine, which has a direct effect on the synapses firing within the neural networks representing the to-be-learned information. To illustrate the importance of this process to memory consolidation, Cahill and colleagues (17) presented a group of participants with a three-part story that had an emotionally neutral beginning, an emotionally charged middle (a boy getting hit by a car and going to the hospital), and an emotionally neutral end. During a retention test, the researchers found that people could remember more from the emotionally charged section of the story than from the emotionally neutral sections, which is what one might expect. However, when a portion of participants received a drug to block the uptake of epinephrine and norepinephrine, their ability to remember the emotionally charged content fell to that of the emotionally neutral content. This study clearly shows the importance of chemically induced consolidation, but it also shows that emotionally charged information gets preferential treatment in the brain, a consideration that should not be forgotten when thinking about your coaching narrative.

Echoing this last point, the level of amygdala activation during encoding, which coaches can ultimately influence, directly correlates to how much information is remembered (16). Moreover, if someone has a damaged amygdala or have had their amygdala removed, as in the case of H.M., their ability to form new explicit memories, especially those of the emotional variety, becomes severely limited (1). From this, we can clearly see that the amygdala and the cocktail of chemicals it controls are central to early memory consolidation, especially for explicit memories. Give due consideration to this when you approach the design of your session and the delivery of your coaching cues because memory kicks into motion when triggered by emotion.

The second stage of memory consolidation can be compared to the way I do laundry at my house. First, I bring the clean clothes upstairs in the hamper and dump them out on the bed; this is analogous to a fresh memory that is still in an unstable (unfolded) state. I then fold the clothes and organize them by clothing type; this is analogous to memory-triggering associative networks that represent similar content. Finally, I stack all the clothes and put them in the drawer, shelf, or closet to which they belong; this last step is the hallmark of structural consolidation, where memories are physically reorganized, or moved, into the brain networks designed to house that specific type of long-term memory. To demonstrate this, let's check back in with Marcus and see what his brain has been up to now that he has been going to sprint school for a few weeks.

CONSOLIDATING CUES

After working with his coach for a number of weeks, Marcus has accumulated significant motor-skill knowledge connected with sprinting. By way of instructions, cues, and feedback, Marcus now has a clear understanding of the motor skill he has been learning and, more importantly, the focus points that help him perform. As we discussed, the processing of this explicit information required a seamless interaction between Marcus' cerebral cortex and hippocampal circuit. Thus, it should not be surprising that both of these brain regions are involved in the structural consolidation of memories.

As discussed by Howard Eichenbaum in "To Cortex: Thanks for the Memories" (82), both the hippocampus and the cortex play a role in early memory consolidation, which spans weeks to years. However, once a memory has been activated enough times, it no longer requires anatomical support from the hippocampus and will eventually call the cortex home. To illustrate this, recall the story of H.M. Although he no longer had a hippocampus and an amygdala and, thus, couldn't form new memories, he was still able to recall most of his memories from before his surgery, which suggests that his long-term memories had moved out of his hippocampus and into the cortex. Interestingly, however, H.M. didn't retain all of his long-term memories. In fact, H.M. was unable to recall most of the memories he'd accumulated in the few years leading up to the surgery. This observation supports the notion that the hippocampus is initially involved in long-term memory storage, holding the memory for an unspecified period of time, after which, the memory moves permanently to its associated cortical region. Thus, when the surgical team "evicted" H.M.'s hippocampus, they also evicted the memories that still called it home.

CONSOLIDATING ACTIONS

Just as explicit memories undergo structural and organizational changes, so too will implicit memories be required to move around the brain until they find a permanent home. As a reminder, two cortical areas, the motor and parietal cortices, and two subcortical areas, the basal ganglia and the cerebellum, are involved in encoding implicit motor memories. The nature of the skill, however, dictates where the implicit memory is stored long term.

Voluntary Movements As outlined by Doyon and colleagues (27), when learning a discrete or continuous skill that will be deployed voluntarily, which is to say under conditions of explicit awareness, the areas in the brain that will initially be involved are the prefrontal cortex, the motor cortex, the basal ganglia, and the cerebellum. However, with practice, activation will subside in the prefrontal cortex, indicating reduced attentional requirements; reorganize within the motor cortex; lessen within the cerebellum; and be maintained within the striatal region of the basal ganglia. To support your comprehension of this, let's anchor these findings to a discrete skill, such as the golf swing.

When you first learn to swing a club, you have to deploy many attentional resources (prefrontal cortex) to support motor planning (motor cortex and basal ganglia), and there will be quite a bit of movement error (cerebellum) in your swing. However, as time passes, your motor planning becomes efficient and focused, no longer requiring an attentional boost from your central executive. Moreover, your pattern will begin to stabilize, and fewer errors will arise. Further, because there is no expectation of a sudden perturbation on the course, the cerebellum is not overly active during the execution of a well-learned swing. Taken collectively, the planning loop and the noncerebellar branch of the action loop take ownership of this long-term implicit memory, with the cerebellum and prefrontal cortex ready to step in when errors or novelty emerges.

Reactive Movements While many of the movements we coach fall into a discrete or continuous skill bucket, the reality is that many of these same skills need to be deployed in a chaotic sporting environment that requires real-time adaptability. Marcus is a perfect example of this. As a soccer player, he will rarely sprint unopposed. Knowing this, his sprint coach would inevitably introduce sprinting with the ball or in response to a defender, galvanizing his ability to sprint in a contextually relevant environment. This adaptability, which requires the motor system to constantly correct errors and provide feedback, would undoubtedly require the assistance of his cerebellum to a far greater degree than performing a well-learned sprint unopposed. As such, the more a movement requires an individual to deal with variability and adaptability, the greater the contribution of the cerebellum to long-term memory consolidation.

The "Plastic Brain" With the advent of brain-imaging technology, notably, functional magnetic resonance imaging, or fMRI, we can easily peer into the mind of elite individuals and see these structural changes for ourselves. For example, Maguire and colleagues (48), in their study of London taxi drivers, showed that the hippocampal regions associated with spatial mapping were larger in taxi drivers than in regular subjects, with the size of the brain region related to years on the job. Similar findings have been observed in musicians, with researchers showing that cortical regions associated with the musical skill (e.g., fingers in string-instrument players) enlarge in proportion to the amount of practice completed (30, 34). Interestingly, despite all of these structural changes within the brain, the net outcome of a highly proceduralized skill is an overall reduction in brain activity (36, 74). This observation makes sense when you map it against your own experience of learning a new skill. At first, it is mentally and physically exhausting; however, as time progresses, you don't feel like you have to deploy the same level of mental and physical resources to get the same amount of work done. As such, the structural reorganization of memories seems to be accompanied by a process designed to improve the efficiency of storage and retrieval.

While Marcus will undoubtedly continue his sprint training, he can at least leave his summer speed camp knowing, implicitly and explicitly, that new memories have materialized within his mind. What started out as an idea in his coach's head—a cue—has now matured into a memory within his own. While this screams of science fiction, this is the reality for every coach and athlete and every teacher and student.

Retrieving Memories

When we hear the opening of the Bon Jovi song about being shot through the heart and being to blame, it's virtually impossible not to shout out the next line. Don't you find it interesting that a song lyric that would normally elude us is easily remembered if we are given the opening lines? Similarly, have you ever found that, while listening to an old playlist, your mind will start playing the intro of the next song just as the current song is ending? It's as if your mind knew the exact order of the songs, even though you hadn't listened to the playlist in years.

These examples showcase our final feature of memory formation, what is known as **retrieval**, or the ability to recall stored information. In principle, we've been talking about recall from the outset of this chapter because any thought that enters your mind is a rendering of a stored memory. From the stories that flood your mind after seeing an old friend to an athlete's ability to call the right play, these examples illustrate the brain's capacity to bring our past into the present. However, our retrieval process doesn't always behave as we'd like it to, at times, leaving memories balancing on the tip of our tongue. And this isn't just the case for explicit memories; this can also be true for motor memories. Whether it is the clients who seem to rely on your cues to get a move right or the athletes who struggle to play like they practice, there are countless examples of motor memories appearing to have gone missing. Hence, it is important for coaches to understand the inner workings of memory retrieval and the strategies that make it tick.

As the previous examples demonstrate, memories materialize in our mind when cued to do so. To use a relatable example, consider the following conversation between two friends:

Mark: *"Hey, Mary, how have you been? I feel like I haven't seen you in forever."*

Mary: *"I know, it's been too long. I think the last time I saw you was at the Bon Jovi concert."*

Mark: *"Oh, yeah, what a great night. His instrumental version of 'Livin' on a Prayer' was amazing."*

Mary: *"That whole night was amazing. How's your mom doing? I heard she had a bad fall."*

Mark: *"Thanks for asking. It was pretty scary, but she's back on her feet and fully recovered."*

Mary: *"I am so happy to hear that. My dad had a similar injury last year, and it took him a few months to bounce back."*

If we unpack this conversation, we can see memory cueing in action. When Mary sees Mark, the sight of him immediately triggers the memory of their last encounter. This prompts Mark to comment on the standout moment of the night. Mark's mention of the song, "Livin' on a Prayer," reminds Mary that she had been thinking about Mark's mom. Following Mark's update, Mary is compelled to share a relatable story from her own life. If you think back to a recent conversation you've had with a friend, you'll find that a similar reciprocal cueing powered every thought that entered your mind. As such, cueing, in all its forms, is a prerequisite for any memory to be retrieved.

ENCODING SPECIFICITY

While cues are important, they don't influence memory retrieval in isolation. Specifically, the way a memory was encoded directly influences the conditions required for that memory to be retrieved. This concept, known as **encoding specificity**, asserts that specific encoding of what is perceived (to-be-learned content + learning context + mood) determines what memory is stored and what is stored determines what retrieval cues will elicit access (70). To illustrate this feature of memory retrieval, Craig Barclay and colleagues (9) asked participants to consider a variety of target sentences, such as "The man lifted the piano." During a retention test, which was designed to identify the best cue for prompting memory retrieval, "something heavy" was a better retrieval cue for recalling the target word *piano* than "something with a nice sound." However, the opposite result was found for the target sentence "The man tuned the piano." Even though *piano* was the target word in both examples, the content within the sentence had a direct effect on cued recall. This feature of encoding specificity is supported by fMRI research that has shown that the areas of the brain active during encoding are also active during retrieval, which provides further support that memories are stored in the same brain regions in which they're processed (71).

At this point you might be thinking "I don't use cues to trigger my athletes' memory of sentences; I use them to trigger their memory of movement." Therefore, it is worth considering the effect verbal cues have on the recall of movement. To shed light on this topic, Olaf Hauk, Friedemann Pulvermüller, and colleagues have produced a number of studies showing the interaction between language processing and motor regions of the brain.

Specifically, in a 2004 study, they scanned participants in an fMRI machine and showed that reading action verbs, such as *lick*, *pick*, and *kick*, activated the same brain regions associated with movement of the tongue, hand, and foot. To further illustrate the role of the motor cortex in language processing, the same research group used transcranial magnetic stimulation to heighten activation in motor regions associated with either the legs or the arms and hands. The results showed that, when leg regions of the motor cortex are activated, the participants can identify action verbs (e.g., *kick*, *hike*, and *step*) associated with the leg faster than without the stimulus, with the same being true for identifying arm- and hand-related action verbs (e.g., *fold*, *beat*, and *grasp*) after those motor regions have been stimulated (58). Collectively, this research supports the idea that the meaning of a word is processed in the same brain regions that allow that meaning to be acted out in the world (i.e., to move). Thus, coaches should see language as a gateway into their athletes' motor cortex, selectively identifying cues that best represent the movement outcomes they'd like to see their athletes achieve.

CONTEXT SPECIFICITY

While symmetry between the retrieval cue and the memory target is important, the context in which learning occurs also influences future recall. This is called the **law of specificity**, and it states that learning is a by-product of what is practiced and where it is practiced, which is to say that memories are encoded based on the interaction between perception (sensory information) and action (motor information). Thus, if you work to improve an athlete's agility within a closed environment in which, for example, there are no decision-making requirements (e.g., opponents) or competition elements (e.g., loud noise or pressure), then you would find incomplete transfer to the context of sport. However, progress the athlete toward deploying these motor skills within a contextually accurate environment (e.g., working against an opponent), and you will have generated a formula for transfer. It is worth noting that, while this book is primarily focused on the language of coaching, the learning context (e.g., physical environment, drill or exercise selection, variability, and difficulty), independent of a coach's verbal prompts, has tremendous influence on memory retrieval and the expression of learned material. To further your knowledge in this area, I recommend that you read "Learning Versus Performance: An Integrative Review" by Soderstrom and Bjork (83), as they thoroughly cover the contextual factors that influence both verbal and motor learning.

MOOD SPECIFICITY

Just as there are extrinsic contextual factors that influence retrieval, there are also intrinsic contextual factors that are worth considering. Research has shown that we find it easier to recall positive memories when we are in a positive mood, with the same being true for negative memories (38). This is known as **mood-congruent memory**. Similarly, we tend to encode information that aligns with our current mood (12). This is known as **mood-dependent memory**. That is, we are more likely to encode information with negative emotion associations when we are in a bad mood and information with positive emotion associations when we are in a good mood. Moreover, this interaction between current mood state and memory encoding extends to our current physical state. Specifically, researchers found that when the body posture adopted during memory retrieval was the same as that during encoding, participants could recall more information at a faster rate (26). This idea, that our physical state is somehow encoded in memories, is so engrained in us that researchers have shown that we can recall more positive memories when rolling marbles up a hill (a metaphorical association with progress and positivity) and more negative memories when rolling marbles down a hill (a metaphorical association with regression and negativity) (18). Like a Twitter post, our memories seem to receive physical and emotional hashtags at encoding that can be used for later recall.

MISLABELING MEMORIES

A final disclaimer. Memories are malleable and subject to change and manipulation over time. Specifically, every time we retrieve a memory, firing up the associated neural networks, we are reopening the Word document, so to speak. Thus, features of encoding and, therefore, the hashtags associated with the memory, can change over time. This is a key consideration for coaches, as a lack of transfer from practice to play could reflect incongruent learning (i.e., practicing the wrong thing and therefore encoding the wrong memories), or it could reflect incongruent retrieval, which is to say that, although you're practicing the right motor skills, the features of encoding are misaligned with the features of retrieval, notably, the learning context. Thus, the more we practice a skill, the greater the possibility for learning. And the more that practice (encoding) reflects the demands of competition (retrieval), the greater the possibility of transfer.

Taken collectively, we can see that memories are a reflection of our experience during encoding. As such, memory retrieval is optimized when the features of the present map to features of the past. As we will discuss at length in the following chapters, coaches should think of verbal cues as movement triggers that alert athletes to the key outcomes associated with the movement they're performing. As such, the best cues will be those that most completely capture how a movement should be performed in terms of the outcome the movement is meant to achieve (e.g., "Explode up, catching the ball at its highest point" vs. "Explode through your hips"). Similarly, coaches need to remember that we only get better at what we practice and where we practice. For this reason, the learning context needs to map onto the competitive context that the athlete wishes to excel in. Finally, consider how mood and physical states influence memory encoding and retrieval. From an encoding standpoint, you should probably have athletes adopt a posture that embodies the information you're giving them, meaning that, if you're talking about physical power and speed of execution, it would be far better to have the athlete standing than sitting. Similarly, we should look to encode feedback using positive, rather than negative, speech. For example, even if athletes have errors, let's say they aren't getting enough hip extension during a sprint, there isn't any reason you can't frame the feedback or cue positively. In this instance, rather than saying "*You're not* getting enough hip extension," you could simply say "*Focus on* pushing the ground away." Assuming we want our athletes to operate in a positive headspace, it would behoove us to encode cues using positivity, the cueing equivalent to rolling a marble up a hill.

SUMMARY

Endel Tulving eloquently described **memory** as "the capacity that permits organisms to benefit from their past experiences" (69). This, in its purest form, is the responsibility of every coach and teacher. While we do not have the fancy machinery of Rekall, we do have the capacity to use cues to alert attention, trigger memory, and encourage a process that converts language into learning. However, to do this effectively, coaches need to consider the quantity and quality of the information they put in their athletes' heads. If we present too much information, we run the risk of short-circuiting working memory, limiting our ability to know which cues worked or, worse, triggering a state of paralysis by analysis. Moreover, we know that the quality and accuracy of our language are fundamental to motor learning. That is, presenting language that is emotionally charged and visually intriguing is far more memorable than serving up sentences that are visually mute and motivationally mundane. What's more, the best of cues will not work unless they align with the most important features of the to-be-learned motor skill. Therefore, the accuracy of a cue is dependent on its ability to represent the desired movement outcome (e.g., "Sprint here," "Jump there," "Tackle him," and "Sidestep her") while accounting for the movement features that underpin that outcome (e.g., "Push the ground away," "Explode toward the sky," "Squeeze your opponent like a handcuff around a criminal's wrist," and "Step to the space like you're dodging a truck").

Just as you can't move into a house until it is built, you can't appreciate the nuance of effective coaching until you understand the science of learning. Thus, with part I in our rearview mirror, we are well suited to drive on to part II. Over the next three chapters, we will explore the inner workings of language, unpacking the interaction between motor-skill learning and the contents of cues. Using evidence, my own experiences, and a bit of storytelling, we will work through a series of practical models that will help you learn to quickly generate and update your language to fit the needs of your athletes and the motor skills they hope to develop.

As my Phoenix-bound flight departed Indianapolis, I felt relieved that our EXOS athletes had performed as expected at the NFL Combine. Seeing as I was a rookie coach and my athletes were pursuing rookie status, there were plenty of opportunities for this house of cards to come tumbling down. Luckily, we kept it together, and the athletes did what they do best—perform when it counts. Considering this good fortune, you'd think I would have been ecstatic; however, I was barely content. I had finally received the chance of a lifetime, the responsibility of leading the most respected Combine preparation program in the country, but I saw fractures everywhere I looked. Despite seven years of coaching experience under my belt, I felt as though I had to start again.

As my headspace cleared following that first year, I experienced a number of clarifying thoughts that, to this day, shape the way I think about coaching. The first idea came in the form of a thought experiment. Imagine that we recruited 10 coaches for a 10-week speed-development study. We can assume that the coaches have similar experience and education levels. Each coach will facilitate their training sessions using the exact same field, training equipment, program, and athletes. Because it would be unreasonable for the same 10 athletes to work with each coach, we will imagine that we cloned our 10 athletes so that each coach received a biologically matched group of participants. Thus, the program, the people, and the place are all the same; the only defining difference is the coach. Here is the question to consider: After 10 weeks, would all 10 groups achieve the exact same results?

Over my career, I have presented this scenario and question to thousands of coaches and the answer is always the same, a resounding no. I believe this thought experiment exposes a core intuition that exists within every coach—we know that *how* we coach has as much to do with the outcome as *what* we coach. Recognizing this is in no way meant to undermine the importance of programming and planning (the *what*); to the contrary, it is paramount that coaches know that running laps won't improve a bench press in the same way that sprinting won't improve one's ability to catch a ball. However, we'd be naïve to think that results are purely a consequence of programming. A far more charitable view gives coaching and communication (the *how*) a seat at the table, elevating the coach from designer of programs to developer of people.

In the midst of my meditations on coaching, my good friend Chris Poirier recommended that I read *Aspire: Discovering Your Purpose Through the Power of Words.*[1] In this short and accessible book, Kevin Hall invites you to reconsider the meaning and heritage of our words. As I opened the book and scanned the table of contents, Chapter 9, "Coach," caught my attention. As it turns out, the word *coach* comes from the Hungarian city, Kocs, which is best known for manufacturing the first spring suspension carriages. Designed for the nobility of the time, these "coaches" made for a more comfortable journey, absorbing the bumps and bends of the unkempt roads. Over time, the word *coach*, like so many other words, evolved, giving rise to an expanded definition that represents "something, or someone, who carries a valued person from where they are to where they want to be" (p. 222).

But how do we, the coaches, do this? What vehicle do we use to steward our athletes' journey? What energy source powers this process? With a bit of reflection, the answer soon reveals itself. In the same way that stagecoaches were powered by horses and modern coaches (buses) are powered by fuel, we, the coaches, use information to power our athletes' learning journey. That is, we spend years learning about physical development so that we can teach our athletes how to apply that learning to their own bodies. Through this lens, we could just as easily call ourselves tutors, mentors, or teachers.

The realization echoed in this last point struck a chord with me and served to illuminate a second important idea about coaching: Coaches are teachers, athletes are students, and our subject matter is movement. As this idea floated across the surface of my mind, the coaching solution I'd been searching for became clear and, as it turns out, had been collecting dust in a box in my garage.

As I dusted off the cover of *Motor Learning and Control: Concepts and Applications* by Richard Magill and David Anderson, I was transported back to college, where I recalled the only class I'd taken on teaching movement, a 300-level course on motor learning. Unfortunately, at the time, I failed to appreciate the gravity of motor learning, especially when I compared it to the value I, and my chosen industry, placed on technical sciences: anatomy, physiology, and biomechanics. Consequently, the technical language my education and industry used to teach me about movement ultimately transformed into the language I used to coach it—mechanical, detailed, and rigid.

As I started reading, highlighter in hand, white pages quickly turned yellow, as I struggled to find an idea that didn't matter. With each passing page my intuitions were validated—a coaching science does exist, and it has existed for a long time. Rooted in the demands World War II placed on developing a skilled labor force, the field of motor learning emerged to help answer a fundamental question: How do people learn motor skills? While there is no single answer to this question, I found what, or should I say who, I'd been looking for in Magill and Anderson's discussion of coaching language – her name was Dr. Gabriele Wulf.

A professor at the University of Nevada, Las Vegas, Dr. Wulf has a diverse portfolio of motor learning research; however, her work on the effect of cueing (attentional focus) on motor skill learning was what initially piqued my interest. With over 60 publications and a book on the topic, Dr. Wulf is the uncontested thought leader on the relationship between coaching language and motor-skill learning.

Hall, K. *Aspire: Discovering Your Purpose Through the Power of Words*. New York: HarperCollins, 2010.

After reading Dr. Wulf's masterful book, *Attention and Motor Skill Learning*, I was compelled to reach out and learn more from her. We finally had our chance during a National Strength and Conditioning Association conference that was being hosted in Las Vegas. Soft spoken and deliberate, Dr. Wulf welcomed me into her well-organized office. I couldn't help but feel a bit star struck, as I was standing in front of motor-learning royalty. Poised and patient, Dr. Wulf answered my questions with great precision, clearly dissociating fact from fiction, known from unknown. She was a professional in every sense of the word.

As our conversation drew to a close, I felt a sudden wave of responsibility overtake my thinking. While I had the good fortune to come to know Dr. Wulf and her work, how many coaches would remain content, unaware that a path to better coaching was within their grasp? How many coaches would remain oblivious to their own shortcomings, violating basic principles of motor learning on a daily basis yet none the wiser? Something had to be done.

Over the ensuing years, I remained relentless, developing and disseminating ideas related to the language of coaching. Loaded with passion and ready to persuade, I put everything I had into becoming a better coach and echoing my learnings to anyone who'd listen. The goal was simple: elevate how we coach to the same level as what we coach, one word at a time. The pages that follow chronicle this journey and showcase all that I've learned on optimizing what we say so that athletes can optimize how they move.

FINDING FOCUS

4

Cueing: A Primer

In part I, we explored the impact of attention and memory on learning. We built this foundation on the argument that attention is the currency of learning, where mental investments determine motor returns. In demonstrating this link between thought and action, we repeatedly asserted that a coach's chief responsibility is to capture, keep, and direct their athlete's attention (see figure 4.1). Considering our emphasis on the first two steps of this process in part I, we will now focus on the art and science of directing attention in part II. To begin, let's interrogate our own intuition about the interaction between cues, thoughts, and actions.

FIGURE 4.1 Three-step approach to engaging your athlete's attention.

Cue It Up

In chapter 3, we met Marcus and his summer sprint coach. In an attempt to help him net more hip flexion at a faster rate, Marcus's coach cued him to "drive his knee forward as if to break a pane of glass." An equally plausible scenario could've had Marcus lacking adequate hip, knee, and ankle extension, the biomechanical bits associated with pushing. This is your athlete who appears to have watched too many episodes of *Road*

Runner as a kid and has since adopted a choppy leg action, taking 10 steps when 5 would do. Athletes with this type of technical error usually benefit from a cue that encourages them to push longer, optimizing force production and, consequently, the rate at which they accelerate.

With this new movement error uploaded in your mind, let's rejoin Marcus and his coach. We will imagine that Marcus' coach is now trying to formulate a cue to improve Marcus' leg extension over the first 10 yards (9 m) of his next sprint. Following is the short list of cues Marcus' coach is considering. Marcus' coach would like your help in identifying the cue that would most likely encourage the desired technical change while preserving a focus on speed of execution. To help Marcus' coach, follow the four steps outlined here.

STEP 1: Read through the list of cues.

Cue A: Focus on *extending your hips* as explosively as possible.

Cue B: Focus on *driving off the ground* as explosively as possible.

Cue C: Focus on *extending your legs* as explosively as possible.

Cue D: Focus on *driving toward the finish* as explosively as possible.

STEP 2: Based on your intuition or experience, rank the cues from most effective (#1) to least effective (#4):

1. _____

2. _____

3. _____

4. _____

STEP 3: Considering the imagery triggered by the cues, rank the cues from most vivid (#1) to least vivid (#4):

1. _____

2. _____

3. _____

4. _____

STEP 4: Considering the content of the cues, rank the cues from most technical (#1) to least technical (#4):

1. _____

2. _____

3. _____

4. _____

Before I reveal my predictions, take a moment to reflect on the exercise. What did you notice about your answers? Were there any trends? When you reflect on the language you use to coach movement, how similar or different is it to the essence of the cues you ranked as most effective? Had you not read part I of this book, would you have ranked the cues differently?

Now, for my predictions. In terms of cue *effectiveness* and *vividness*, I am going to guess that cues B and D filled your top spots, while cues A and C were at the bottom. To the contrary, I suspect you reversed this order when asked to rank the cues for *technical* specificity. Whether or not you ranked your cues as I've predicted is of no consequence, as the purpose of this chapter is to convince you that this is in fact how the cues should be ordered.

Let me start by briefly outlining the premise of my argument. Assuming the correct movement error has been identified, the effectiveness of a cue is partly anchored to the accuracy and vividness of the imagery it provokes. Accuracy, in this case, requires the cue to capture the most relevant feature of the movement in the context of the desired outcome. To illustrate, let's compare cue A, "extending your hips," to cue B, "driving off the ground."

Considering our desire to see Marcus' improve his leg extension, we could argue that both cues target a relevant feature of the movement but do so by directing attention at different levels of the task. Specifically, cue A asks Marcus to focus on "extending your hips," which is one joint within the series of joints involved in leg extension. By contrast, cue B encourages Marcus to focus on "driving off the ground," which is an outcome that depends on leg extension. Through this lens, we can see that cue A is nested within cue B, as Marcus would need to orchestrate hip, knee, and ankle extension to effectively "drive off the ground." This being so, we can argue that cue B is a more accurate representation of the desired action because it embeds lower-level technical features within a higher-level outcome, all the while preserving the ultimate goal of running fast. If we apply this logic to all four cues, we can categorically state that cues B and D encourage a more accurate focus than do cues A and C.

Let's see if the same logic holds for vividness. By definition, a vivid image is one that is both clear and powerful in the feelings it incites. Thus, we can say that a cue is vivid if it encourages an image that accurately represents the target features of a movement (the *what*) while also capturing the essence or feeling one should have while performing the movement (the *how*). To test this out, let's compare cue C, "extending your legs," to cue D, "driving toward the finish." In terms of imagery, cue C draws attention to a technical feature of the task, a muted concept to anyone who is not a coach or biomechanist, while cue D triggers the mind's theater by mapping a race car–like visual onto a sprinting context. As for essence, cue C doesn't improve its standing, as "extending your hips" is contextually indistinct and uninteresting, while cue D is rich with meaning and interpretative latitude. *Drive*, in this case, can map onto *driving* a race car, *driving* a golf ball, or *driving* a nail, while *finish* clearly outlines the goal or end-point the athlete is *driving* toward. The list goes on, but the point is clear. "Driving toward the finish" is a triple threat with the imagery it excites, the force it encourages, and its relevance to sprinting. Everything considered, we can comfortably state that cues B and D encourage a far more vivid focus than do cues A and C.

It is interesting that, on one hand, we are trying to make a highly technical change, but, on the other, the most effective cues, at least using the logic I've proposed, are the least technical. We can refer to this contradiction as the **zoom fallacy**, where the more our cues zoom into the technical error, the harder it is to change. Why? Well, that is what the rest of the chapter is for, but, in short, what is gained by focusing on the micro is lost in the execution of the macro. As the saying goes, the closer you get to an elephant, the harder it is to know you're looking at an elephant.

So where are you placing your bets? I think Marcus and his coach are growing impatient.

Coaching Loop

Before we launch into the cueing cosmos, it's important that you know what you're getting into, and for that you'll need a map. What kind of map, you ask? Well, this isn't your conventional map of *wheres*; rather, this is a map of *whens*.

As you know, this is a book about language; it's about the last idea we put in our athlete's head before they move, what we coaches call **cues**. However, as we're all aware, we depend on language for far more than creating interesting sound bites worth our athlete's attention. Realistically, we are communicating with them before, during, and after sessions. This being true, if we're going to discuss the role of language in directing attention and the effect it has on motor-skill learning, we need to be very clear on *when* the strategies in this chapter should be used. Hence, the map.

Let's start by stating the obvious: We are talking about the words we use to compel movement patterns to change. Thus, the following recommendations should be considered for their relevance to the moments when your message is about movement. To the contrary, while the principles contained herein may excite ideas that transcend movement-based discussions, this is not the primary focus of the strategies or the science that underpins them. Hence, we will not discuss how to give a rousing pregame speech or console a player after just being cut from your team. Instead, we will parachute into your whistle-to-whistle training sessions and unpack the language you use to freshen up footwork, renovate running, and, generally, troubleshoot technique.

With our boots on the ground and the session about to start, we're in a position to map out our messaging. We know that we will need to open and close a session with some form of communication. While distinct from cueing, this bookend messaging is still important for previewing and reviewing the focus and outcomes of training. Specifically, to open a session, it is always valuable to start with some **WWH**. And no, this is not some new wrestling syndicate, it stands for three simple questions: *What* are we doing? *Why* is it important? and *How* will we achieve it? In this case, the *what* is nothing more than a description of the movements, drills, or scenarios that will be covered (e.g., "Today, we're focusing on change of direction"); the *why* is a short explanation as to how this connects to a central goal (e.g., "This is going to improve your ability to evade defenders in open-field play"); and the *how* summarizes the key focus points for the session (e.g., "Throughout the session, let the three *L*s of lateral movement guide you—stay low, stay light, and stay loose"). Similarly, to close a session, you can review and add a two-plus-two at the end, meaning that you review your original *what*, *why*, and *how* and give your athletes the opportunity to comment on two aspects of the session that went well and thus should be maintained, plus two areas for improvement that can be targeted in future sessions. While there are many other ways to approach the fringes of a session, this approach ensures that focus is always calibrated and learning becomes the red thread connecting one session to the next.

While the beginning and end of each training session allows for preplanned messaging, the middle requires an adaptable yet repeatable pattern of communication that can be molded to the learning needs of the athlete. To achieve this balance of structure and flexibility, it is important that coaches have a communication model that can circle the movement, providing guidance on what to say before, possibly during, and after an athlete moves. Recognizing the necessity and utility of such a model, I conceptualized the **coaching communication loop**, which simply calls attention to the five most important coaching moments surrounding each rep or set of a movement. These five moments, represented by the acronym **DDCDD**, recognize that, when it comes to teaching a motor skill, coaches will DESCRIBE it, DEMONSTRATE it, and CUE it; athletes will DO it; and both will DEBRIEF it.

Like a song on a loop, you'll find that the DDCDD repeats throughout the training session. If it's a new rep or set and you want to reset focus, DDCDD. If it's a new movement or drill that requires an explanation, DDCDD. If it's a new game scenario that needs context, DDCDD. You get the point; the DDCDD represents the communication loop that surrounds the core elements, or content, of your session, with each step requiring a slightly different coaching tool. To see the coaching loop in action, consider the following story about Jack and Diane.

► **Story Context**

Diane is the head strength and conditioning coach at New Haven High School, and Jack is a freshman shortstop on the varsity baseball team. Diane is working with Jack on his change of direction, as the head coach feels Jack's base stealing would benefit from a faster transition from crossover to acceleration. Considering the fact that Jack will likely start as a freshman, the coach has asked Diane to spend some extra time working with him on his speed. We now join Jack and Diane as they kick off their second training session on base-stealing speed.

► **Step 1: DESCRIBE it**

Diane: *"Jack, building on our last session, the first skill we're going to work on is stealing second from your lead position. Do you remember the key focus points we're looking for?"*

Jack: *"Yeah, I should try to keep tension, balance, and width in my base position (lower body)."*

Diane: *"That's right. Now, what're the keys once we pull the trigger to go [sprint]?"*

Jack: *"Um, stay low and drive hard off my inside leg. Then, run like hell."*

Diane: *(Laughing) "That's right, Jack. Good memory!"*

The DESCRIBE it section is used to introduce new movements or remind athletes about the structure or setup of a skill. You will explain or discuss the details of the movement, avoiding nonessential technical language. You will not, nor should you, describe a movement each time your athlete performs it because this places an unnecessary tax on working memory. The goal should be to provide the least amount of information required to give context and support safety. As we can see in the story, Diane has already taught the crossover to Jack during their first session and, therefore, asks Jack to recall the key features of the movement. This illustrates that, while coaches will often be the ones describing a movement, there is no reason the athletes can't be involved, as their inclusion will improve engagement, support autonomy, and allow the coach to check for learning.

► **Step 2: DEMONSTRATE it**

After having Jack describe the key tenets of the crossover to acceleration, Diane proceeds to demonstrate the movement sequence, highlighting the importance of a low body height, a strong inside leg push, and an aggressive acceleration toward second base.

Like the DESCRIBE it section, you'll DEMONSTRATE it any time you're teaching a new movement or want to provide a refresher. It's valuable to let your athletes know that you're always willing to demonstrate again if they'd like a second or third look. Further, unless you're using one-word action statements to accent the demonstration (e.g., *long*, *snap*, *pop*, *quick*, or *tight*), it is best to keep talking to a minimum so that you avoid placing an unnecessary strain on your athletes' attention. Once your athletes are familiar with the drill or movement you're teaching, it's not necessary to re-demonstrate, unless you have a new athlete join the group or you're using the demonstration to revisit or emphasize a coaching point.

In practice, the demonstration can be completed by a coach, an athlete, or a video. For the initial demonstration, it is valuable to show the athlete what effective movement looks like. However, as time progresses, there is value in athletes' observing the difference between effective and ineffective movement strategies (3, 4, 56).[1] This will occur naturally if athletes are working in a group and provided with an opportunity to watch others move (e.g., have athletes partner up and alternate within a drill, or use a waterfall or domino start, where each athlete performs the skill one at a time, triggering the next athlete to go once they've completed their rep). Coaches can also trigger an implicit comparison between effective and ineffective movement by using an A and B demonstration, where A, for example, is how the movement should be performed, and B is how it should not. After demonstrating the A and B versions of the movement, the coach simply asks the athletes to comment on which movement is preferred and why. I've yet to see a group of athletes guess wrong.

---

[1] Evidence has shown that watching both novice and expert performers leads to better learning than watching novices or experts alone. This is based on the premise that the observer (athlete) is able to compare the novice and expert performers, increasing the salience of errors. This salience acts as an implicit information source that the athlete can apply to their own movement execution.

▶ **Step 3: CUE it**

Diane: *"Jack, I want you to go ahead and give this a go. Let's see you take your lead off first and settle into your base position. Once our pitcher commits to the windup, hit it. For this first rep, focus on **pushing hard toward second.**"*

The CUE it section is where you help **one** final idea get into your athlete's head before they move. This will be the one prioritized thought that you believe will help improve execution. This cue can come from you or the athlete; the only rule is the **rule of one**: one rep, one cue, one focus. To build athlete autonomy and ownership, you'll find many instances where there is no need to cue, especially as an athlete's experience and skill level increases. That said, there is always a need to focus, as an unoccupied mind is easily distracted. Thus, the CUE it section should be considered the brief moment each athlete takes to get their mind set before each rep. In the case of Jack and Diane, everything said (DESCRIBE it) and observed (DEMONSTRATE it) has been filtered into a four-word *cue*, "pushing hard toward second."

▶ **Step 4: DO it**

Jack proceeds to execute the movement as advised. Diane stands in the outfield so she can get a clear view of Jack's read on the pitcher and the timing and execution of his crossover to sprint (base stealing).

The most important aspect of the DO it section is to ensure that you're positioned in such a way that you can see the target features of the movement unfold. Place yourself in a position to extract the information from the movement on which you may want to provide feedback (e.g., Diane stands side-on to Jack so she can clearly see him transition from a crossover to acceleration). The second most important aspect of the DO it section is to stay silent; avoid unnecessary prompts that may distract the athlete from the task at hand. The only time it is advisable to talk during the execution of a movement is when you're cueing the tempo of a continuous pattern (e.g., you might say "push, push, push," synchronized with the first three steps of a sprint, or "pop—*clap* . . . *clap*—pop," to denote timing during a skipping pattern with a desired tempo). Similarly, during a discrete, one-repetition pattern, like a jump, a coach might use a single word, such as *explode*, to accent the takeoff, adding energy to the stimulus. Alternatively, a coach might say "lon*ggggg*," holding the sound of the last letter as an athlete lowers into a single-leg Romanian deadlift, for example, reinforcing the timing of the motion and the fact that they want the athlete to stay long from head to heel throughout the motion. Unless a coach is trying to support timing using simple, familiar language, they should avoid all commentary, until they arrive at the DEBRIEF it portion of the coaching loop.

▶ **Step 5: DEBRIEF it**

Diane: *"Jack, first rep in the books, how did your transition feel?"*
Jack: *"Not bad. I felt like I got a pretty good push off my inside leg."*
Diane: *"Did you feel balanced and square (to second base) as you accelerated?"*
Jack: *"Not sure. I just know I got out of my stance quickly."*
(Loop restarts at CUE it section.)
Diane: *"OK, very good. Let's go again, same focus—'push hard towards second.' However, this time, continue to focus on 'pushing hard' until you get through second base."*

The DEBRIEF it section is synonymous with feedback. As we discussed in chapter 2, this feedback can come from the coach or the athlete and can relate to either movement performance or movement outcome. Put differently, a coach should see the DEBRIEF it section as an opportunity to ask questions and engage; to comment and nudge; and to, generally, collaborate with their athlete on their next best focus (72).[2] Ulti-

---

[2] The concept of self-controlled feedback has consistently been shown to improve motor learning. Specifically, self-controlled feedback is when the athlete is involved in the feedback process, given partial or complete control of when they receive feedback and, to varying degrees, the type of feedback they're receiving. As described in Wulf and Lewthwaite's OPTIMAL theory of motor learning, self-control supports autonomy, a critical dimension of motivation, as outlined in the self-determination theory, while increasing the attention invested in the task, which emerges as a consequence of having influence over when feedback is provided and what type (e.g., knowledge of results, knowledge of performance, or demonstration). Notably, this is one of the many ways a coach can organize the DEBRIEF it section of the coaching loop.

mately, the way a coach uses the DEBRIEF it section comes down to the needs of the athlete, their level of experience, the type of movement or drill, and the goal of the next rep or set. In Jack's case, Diane wanted to pull task-intrinsic feedback from him, which focused on movement performance (the feel), rather than the outcome. As is evident in the previous narrative, Diane was interested in when Jack had applied the focus cue (i.e., during the transition, during the acceleration, or both). As Jack's feedback illustrates, he seemed to focus on the transition out of the crossover more than the acceleration itself. As such, Diane sought to maintain and extend this focus to the remaining foot strikes throughout the sprint to second base.

As we can see, the coaching loop provides a map to guide communication throughout a session. As previously noted, each step in the process will leverage a slightly different communication tool. However, like a chemist trying to synthesize an antidote, we're trying to synthesize the next best thought to share with our athlete's mind. Thus, DESCRIBE it, DEMONSTRATE it, and DEBRIEF it should be used only to the extent that they assist the coach's ability to CUE it and the athlete's ability to DO it. As an athlete progresses, we should see the DDCDD, what we can call the **long loop**, start to trim down, leaving us with the cyclical application of CDD—CUE it, DO it, and DEBRIEF it, or, simply put, the **short loop** (see figure 4.2).[3]

Map in hand and premises outlined, we are well prepared to begin unpacking how best to direct attention through the cues we use. Before we continue, however, let me make something very clear.

> **Unless otherwise stated, everything that will be discussed from here on specifically relates to the language we use during the CUE it portion of the coaching loop.**

To be clear, this is the last idea we put in our athlete's head moments before they move, the thoughts, as we'll see, that serve performance and learning and the mindsets we'll come to welcome when the game is on the line.

LONG LOOP (DDCDD)		SHORT LOOP (CDD)		
DESCRIBE IT	**DEMONSTRATE IT**	**CUE IT**	**DO IT**	**DEBRIEF IT**
Extended description of the movement	Physical demonstration of the movement	Brief phrase used to focus attention on the movement	Athlete maintains focus while performing the movement	Athlete + Coach feedback is considered
The WHAT	**The HOW**			**The WHAT**
Internal or external language	Silence, single words to highlight, or A/B demonstration	Last phrase is an external cue or analogy	Silence or single words/sounds to highlight tempo	Questions, comments, and collaboration

FIGURE 4.2   Coaching communication loop.

---

[3] It is important to recognize that there are entire texts dedicated to the nuances of scheduling of descriptions, demonstrations, and debriefs (feedback). As such, there may be instances where you withhold feedback, for example, allowing the athletes to work through a skill for a number of repetitions before commenting, what is known as summary, or average, feedback. These feedback schedules, as they're often referred to, manipulate the timing and type of information you provide your athlete with, all in an attempt to support their ownership with and engagement in the learning process. While many books are available on this topic, I recommend *Skill Acquisition in Sport: Research, Theory, and Practice* by Nicola Hodges and Mark Williams (32).

PART 1: A CUE IS BORN

The year 1974 saw its fair share of big moments. Richard Nixon became the first U.S. president to resign from office; Muhammed Ali regained his heavyweight title after knocking out George Forman in the Rumble in the Jungle; and Stephen King published his debut novel, *Carrie*. However, they weren't the only big moments, as 1974 also witnessed the publication of one of the most important coaching books ever written. With over a million copies sold and an unlikely author, a Harvard English student turned tennis pro, *The Inner Game of Tennis* (78) has maintained its status atop coaches' recommended reading lists.

A former captain of the Harvard tennis team, Timothy Gallwey penned *The Inner Game* to address many of the common complaints he dealt with as a tennis pro. These included the usual suspects:

> *I know what to do; I just can't seem to do it.*
> *I'm fine when I practice, but everything falls apart when I play.*

A recovering coach-aholic, Gallwey began saying less and seeing more. He noticed that "errors [he] didn't mention were correcting themselves" (p. 35) and that some "verbal instruction [actually] decreased the probability of the desired correction occurring" (p. 36). What was happening here? Gallwey's observations stood in contrast to the conventional wisdom of the day, which emphasized quantity, rather than quality, of instruction. Thus, Gallwey set out to write about the inner game, hoping to provide an antidote to the "habits of mind which inhibit performance" (p. 24).

Influenced by the meditative teachings of the East, Gallwey's approach centered on the importance of "learning how to get the clearest possible picture of your desired outcome" (p. 65). He professed that "images are better than words, showing better than telling, [and] too much instruction worse than none" (p. 42). Despite having minimal scientific support for these ideas at the time, we can see that Gallwey's intuition hadn't deceived him.

In fact, Gallwey's instincts align perfectly well with our premise, that the most effective cues, verbal or not, accurately represent goals within a vivid mental image. Whether this image is a snapshot from a demonstration or assembled from visually rich language is of no consequence; the key is that an image focuses the mind, trading distraction for direction. In his own words, Gallwey notes that "the concentrated mind has no room for thinking how well the body is doing" (p. 48). He continues by stating that "it is almost impossible to feel or see anything well if you are thinking about how you should be moving" (p. 372).

Echoing this perspective in *The Mind Is Flat* (79), Dr. Nick Chater states that "tasks and problems needing conscious attention engage swathes of our neural machinery; and each part of that machinery can only do one thing at a time" (p. 392). In support of this surprising claim is clear evidence showing that we process only one word at a time while reading, one color at a time while seeing, and one thought at a time while thinking. As such, the sense that we are simultaneously experiencing all that our inner and outer worlds have to offer is nothing more than an illusion, a spell of the mind. Rather, the brain operates like a spotlight, only becoming aware of or interacting with that which it shines its light on. Thus, as discussed in chapter 2, coaches must master the art of directing attention, as the brain can only do, and, therefore, focus on, one thing at a time.[4]

This being true, Chater would undoubtedly agree with Gallwey when he states that "to still the mind one must learn to put it somewhere. It cannot just be let go; it must be focused. If peak performance is a function of a still mind, then we are led to the question of where and how to focus it" (p. 372). While Gallwey provides many insightful and practical answers to this question, the evidence required to turn his suggestions into science wouldn't mature for another 24 years.

---

[4] It is important that we recognize that our sense of being able to focus on multiple things simultaneously is just that, a sense. In fact, it is our ability to easily and rapidly switch from one focus to the next that paints the illusion of a limitless attentional window. However, in the world of movement, where thoughts are meant to sit alongside the patterns they're influencing, we cannot afford to ask the mind to consider more than one idea, one cue, for any given moment of movement.

A Wulf in the Water

A flash of brilliance, a stroke of genius, a lightbulb moment—every scientist hopes for one, but very few ever experience it. Fortunately, for us, Dr. Gabriele Wulf just so happens to be one of those lucky scientists.

If you pick up a copy of Wulf's book, *Attention and Motor Skill Learning* (80), you'll see a windsurfer on the cover. While it is perfectly common for a book about movement to have an action shot on the cover, a windsurfer does seem like an odd choice. That's until you get to chapter 2 and you meet the windsurfer once again.

Wulf opens the chapter with a story about a windsurfer who is trying to learn a new skill called the "power jibe." Before getting out on the water and giving this complex maneuver a go, the windsurfer decides to purchase a magazine that provides detailed instruction and imagery of the skill being performed. To give you a flavor of the kind of instructions a magazine like this would have, I pulled an actual list of instructions from a windsurfing website (81):

- *Step 1:* Hands into position, palms down, reach back hand back on the boom, slow down, and hook out.

- *Step 2:* Take your back foot out of the strap and put it on the leeward rail of the board.

- *Step 3:* Start engaging your rail, as soon as your rail starts to bite, put your body weight into it, bend your knees, lean your body in, and try to keep your sail upright.

There are seven more steps like this, but I think you get the point.

With our windsurfer's working memory well stocked with step-by-step instructions, they set out for a day on the water. After several hours of practice, the windsurfer is still struggling to make the expected progress. With each pass at the power jibe, our windsurfer's frustration grows, as they find it nearly impossible to simultaneously control their body, balance on a surfboard, flip a sail, and try to have a bit of fun in the process. The windsurfer inevitably realizes that (a) trying to focus on every step offered by the magazine is futile and (b) focusing on the motion of the board seems to be far more effective than focusing on their body.

With a renewed focus, our windsurfer is back on the water, only this time, they are purely focusing on the motion of the board opposed to the movement of the body. With the excess attentional baggage gone and a clear goal in mind, *shift and turn the board*, our windsurfer has their eureka moment, and failure soon gives way to fluency. The takeaway is clear: If you focus on too many things or the wrong things while learning a new skill, you'll spend far more time in the *water* than you will in the *wind*.

As Wulf ends the story, if you're like me, you are left wondering why she had decided to dramatize such an obscure movement. I mean, the story is relatable, but come on, the power jibe? If you're trying to open a chapter with a story meant to foreshadow a point, at least use a movement people can relate to, right? Wrong!

As quickly as it came, this fleeting thought was extinguished, for this wasn't some random story being used for effect; it was a depiction of actual events. In a plot twist, you find out that the would-be windsurfer was none other than Dr. Gabriele Wulf herself. As she notes, this experience, which occurred in 1996 in Italy on Lake Garda, triggered her curiosity. Wulf wondered whether the shift in performance that had accompanied her shift in focus was a one-off or whether she had found a fundamental relationship between attentional focus and motor learning.

If Archimedes found buoyancy in a bathtub and Newton witnessed gravity in a falling apple, why couldn't Wulf figure out focus while windsurfing?

The Year Was 1998

A researcher at the renowned Max Planck Institute in Munich, Germany, at the time, Wulf returned home from windsurfing, excited to put her theory to test. Intrigued by the performance change that had followed her shift in focus from body to board, Wulf wanted to see whether focusing on the effect of a movement would result in superior performance and learning compared to focusing on the body itself.

Steps 1-3 reprinted by permission from P. Bijl, "10 Step Plan to the Perfect Power Gybe." Accessed Sept 6, 2019, http://pieterbijlwindsurfing.com/tutorialpowergybe/.

To test her hunch, Wulf and colleagues, Markus Höß and Wolfgang Prinz, designed a study whereby subjects would practice a slalom-type movement on a ski simulator over the course of three days. The goal of the task was simple: Push a platform, which sits atop a set of wheels that are tethered by elastic bands, as far to the left and right of a bowed track as possible (see figure 4.3). The maximum distance the platform could travel in either direction was 1.8 feet (55 cm) from the center. Thus, the participants would attempt to progressively increase the distance they could move the platform over the course of the three days.

The study consisted of twenty-two 90-second trials, with eight trials being completed on days 1 and 2, and six trials being completed on day 3. The researchers compared the average distance covered by the platform for the first and last trial of each day, allowing them to examine changes within and across testing sessions. Finally, the researchers provided the

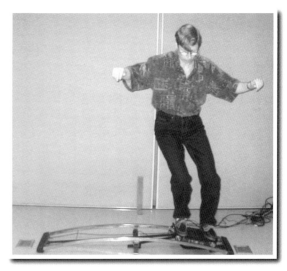

FIGURE 4.3   Ski simulator being used by Gabriele Wulf.
Reprinted by permission from G. Wulf, *Attention and Motor Skill Learning* (Champaign, IL: Human Kinetics, 2007), 9.

participants with specific focus cues on days 1 and 2, what we could call the acquisition period, and no cues or reminders on day 3, what we could call the retention period.

Thirty-three participants with no ski-simulator experience were recruited and randomly assigned to the three groups, each representing a different type of focus. Group 1, the external-focus group, was instructed to "exert force on the outer wheels" of the platform, while group 2, the internal-focus group, was instructed to "exert force on the outer foot." Group 3, the normal-focus, or control, group did not receive any instructions and were allowed to focus as they normally would.

After two days of practice using their respective focus cues, clear group differences emerged (see figure 4.4). Having all started with an average movement distance of 0.7 feet (20 cm), the participants in the external-focus group took the lead with an average distance of 1.5 feet (47 cm), while the participants in the internal-focus and normal-focus groups were averaging 1.2 feet (35 cm) and 1.4 feet (41 cm), respectively. After the third day of testing, which didn't include any cues, prompts, or reminders, a clear winner emerged. The external-focus group had maintained its position atop the leaderboard, exiting the study with an average movement distance that was significantly greater than that of the other two groups, which, as it turns out, did not differ from one another.

As you can imagine, Wulf and her colleagues were ecstatic; their hunch-turned-hypothesis now had scientific support. Just as a shift in focus from body to board had helped Wulf improve her windsurfing, her participants saw their slalom performance maximize when they focused on the platform opposed to their feet. Despite this encouraging finding, Wulf's excitement was short lived, as her first attempt to publish the study was met with reviewer skepticism and a journal rejection notice. Admittedly, even Wulf found it hard to believe that such a small difference in focus—realistically, the foot was no more than a few centimeters from the wheel—could make such a measurable difference in performance. However, all was not lost because one of the reviewers asked Wulf and her colleagues to replicate their findings using a different task. If their findings generalized, they would have the first published record of an external-focus cue leading to superior learning compared to an internal-focus cue; if not, they would be back at square one.[5]

With the challenge accepted, Wulf and her colleagues set out to find a new motor skill to assess. Knowing that they wanted to continue with their theme of balance and postural control, the research team settled on using a stabilometer, which is a technical word for a single-axis balance board. Other than the task being different, Wulf used a very similar protocol. Notably, 16 participants, who were unfamiliar with the task, took

---

[5] It is worth noting that prior to Wulf's 1998 paper, other authors had researched the effect of focus on performance; however, this was the first paper, as far as I can tell, that explicitly examined internal- versus external-focus cues, with the intention of understanding how focusing on the body versus an outcome would affect performance and learning.

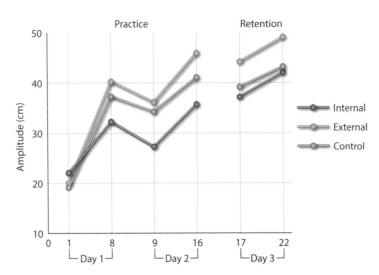

FIGURE 4.4   Average amplitudes of the internal-focus, external-focus, and control groups. during practice (days 1 and 2) and retention (day 3) on the ski simulator in experiment 1.

Reprinted by permission from G. Wulf, M. Hoss, and W. Prinz, "Instructions for Motor Learning: Differential Effects of Internal Versus External Focus of Attention," *Journal of Motor Behavior* 30, no. 2 (1998): 169-179.

part in a three-day study that included twenty-one 90-second trials, seven on each day. The goal of the task was to keep the balance board as still as possible, where small, frequent adjustments would lead to better performance than large, infrequent adjustments.

Just as before, participants were randomly assigned to different focus groups. This time, the external-focus group was asked to "focus on the red markers (tape placed in front of the feet) and try to keep the markers at the same height," whereas the internal-focus group was asked to "focus on their feet and try to keep them at the same height." Note that both groups looked straight ahead because Wulf did not want a visual focus on feet versus tape to be confused with the intended mental focus. In contrast to the ski-simulator experiment, these groups made similar improvements to their balance over the first two days of the study, when cues were present; however, on day 3, when the cues were removed, the external-focus group pushed ahead once again, achieving a net improvement in balance that was greater than that of the internal-focus group.

With undeniable proof in hand, Wulf and colleagues went back to the *Journal of Motor Behavior*, who later published "Instructions for Motor Learning: Differential Effects of Internal Versus External Focus of Attention" (82) in the summer of 1998, two years after Wulf had gone windsurfing. At the time, these findings likely seemed nuanced and limited in application. Just as the reviewers had questioned Wulf's initial findings, you couldn't blame a coach for asking what focusing on wheels or little pieces of red tape had to do with improving their athletes' performance. However, as coaches would soon realize, wheels and tape were just the beginning, for hidden inside these simple cues was the language of coaching.

The Start of a Movement

Two decades after Wulf's landmark study, the evidence for the benefits of an external focus is still rolling in—a crescendo with no end in sight. When queried for research explicitly evaluating *internal focus* versus *external focus*, the U.S. National Library of Medicine reports that over 160 original studies have been completed since 1998. Thus, Wulf helped build one of the most complete research narratives the field of motor learning has ever seen. In the same way that an archaeologist reveals buried remains, one brushstroke at a time, Wulf and the many researchers who have followed continue to reveal the interplay between cues, thoughts, and actions, one precise study at a time.

FROM THE LAB

Not long after Wulf published her 1998 paper, she began working on a number of follow-up studies. Interestingly, Wulf's next study was with none other than Charles Shea, the reviewer who had suggested she complete a second experiment back in 1998. Obviously excited by the prospect of Wulf's results, Shea and Wulf (60) set out to replicate and extend her original findings. Using the same stabilometer task as described earlier, Shea and Wulf broke participants into four groups, each practicing for two days before completing a retention test on day 3. Two of the groups were assigned the same cues Wulf had used in 1998 (experiment 2), whereas two additional groups received continuous visual feedback about the balance board via a computer screen and were told that either the "line on the screen should be thought of as representing their feet" (internal-feedback group) or the "line represented the lines in front of their feet" (external-feedback group).

Confirming the 1998 findings, the external-focus group that kept the "lines in front of their feet at the same height" was able to stabilize the balance board with greater control than the internal-focus group that attempted to keep their "feet at the same height." Interestingly, the same effect was found in the groups receiving visual feedback, with the external-feedback group outperforming the internal-feedback group. Collectively, these findings added further support to the growing suspicion that encouraging an external focus during practice leads to superior motor learning compared to an internal focus. But what about individual preference? Surely, the benefit of any focus is predicated on an individual's affinity for it.

To answer this question, Wulf, Shea, and Park (76) came up with a clever study to examine the effect of focus preference on learning. Using the same stabilometer task and cues as were used in Wulf's 1998 study, the researchers devised two experiments to test their intuitions about the effectiveness of an external focus. In experiment one, 17 participants, who were unfamiliar with the balance task, alternated between using an internal focus (i.e., "feet at the same height") and an external focus (i.e., "lines at the same height) on day 1 and practiced using their preferred focus on day 2. On day 3, the participants completed a retention test. Upon completion of the retention test, the researchers interviewed the participants to see what focus they'd self-selected. The results showed that 12 participants had selected an external focus and 5 had selected an internal focus. After controlling for the selected focus, the results showed that those who adopted an external focus showed greater balance control than those who focused internally. The researchers went on to replicate those findings in a second experiment, providing evidence that, when given the option, most people will eventually self-select an external focus, supporting the intuition that Wulf herself had had while windsurfing.

Wulf and others went on to reveal a number of interesting findings that only served to strengthen the hypotheses developing around the benefits of an external focus. By 2017, two systematic reviews had been completed, and the verdict was in—balance is maximized when you adopt an external focus (36, 49). If you have any doubt about these results, consider a time in your life when you were trying to learn a demanding balance task. Recall where your mind was when everything clicked. Whether you were surfing, skateboarding, or snowboarding, I guarantee you weren't humming "head, shoulders, knees, and toes, knees and toes," at least not for long, as you would've inevitably realized that a far better ditty would have been "board, balance, find an edge, find an edge."

FROM THE FIELD

While showing that an external focus improves balance was a good first step, Wulf and her colleagues knew that a theory supporting the universal benefits of an external focus would need to generalize to all categories of movement. With this is mind, Wulf and others set out to examine the differential effect of internal- and external-focus cues on learning sport skills.

In the same year that Shea and Wulf replicated Wulf's 1998 findings, Wulf, Lauterbach, and Toole (70) devised a study to examine the effect of focus on learning a chip shot in novice golfers. Twenty-one participants were randomly assigned to either an internal-focus group, which focused on "the swinging motion of their arms," or an external-focus group, which focused on "the pendulum-like motion of the club." The objective was to hit balls into a circular target, 1.5 feet (45 cm) in diameter, which was positioned 16.4 yards (15 m) away from where the participants were standing. Using a nine iron, participants completed 80 shots on day 1, the practice phase, and 30 shots on day 2, the retention phase. In agreement with the studies discussed so far, the results showed that those who focused externally were far more accurate during practice and retention than those who focused internally.

With the benefits of an external focus appearing to generalize, Wulf and colleagues wanted to see whether the type of external focus adopted would affect the results. To test this, they designed two experiments that evaluated the influence of two different external-focus cues on learning a forehand in tennis and a chip shot in golf (75). In the first study, 36 novice tennis players were randomly assigned to an incoming- or outgoing-focus group; the incoming group members were told to focus on "the trajectory of the ball coming from the ball machine until it contacted the racket," and the outgoing group members were told to focus on "the (anticipated) trajectory of the ball and to imagine the ball landing on the target" after they'd hit it. While the results did not differ during practice, which is not surprising considering that both cues required an external focus on the ball, the outgoing-focus group edged out the win with a slightly better performance during the retention test. In principle this makes sense, as the outgoing focus embedded the ultimate task goal (hit the ball here) within the cue, whereas the incoming focus cue did not.

In their second experiment, Wulf and colleagues resurrected the chip-shot task used by Wulf, Lauterbach, and Toole in 1999. Twenty-six novice golfers were randomly assigned to either a close external-focus group, which focused on "the pendulum-like motion of the club," or a far external-focus group, which "anticipated the ball's arc and imagined the ball landing on the target." The results showed a clear advantage for the close external-focus group during practice and the retention test. Taken collectively, we can see that, while external-focus cues encourage better performance compared to internal-focus cues, there is still a need to find the optimal external cue for the task and experience levels of the athletes. We will revisit this idea in chapter 5 and discuss the factors coaches should consider when trying to identify the best cue to guide their athletes' focus.

As research in the applied setting continued, support for the beneficial effects of an external focus only grew stronger. From basketball (1, 77) to baseball (15, 28), soccer (22, 73) to swimming (23, 62), the research consistently showed that adopting an external focus of attention leads to superior performance and learning compared to focusing internally. In her 2013 review, "Attentional Focus and Motor Learning: A Review of 15 Years" (91), Gabriele Wulf summarizes this nicely:

> *The breadth of this effect is reflected in its generalizability to different skills, levels of expertise, and populations, as well as its impact on both the effectiveness and efficiency of performance. Evidently, subtle differences in the wording of instructions or feedback can have significantly different effects on performance and learning (p. 99).*

It's a Cue

No doubt, you have a lot of questions at this point. I know I did once I started reading the literature on attentional focus and cueing. However, I am confident that all questions will be answered in the coming pages. To begin, let's lay out some key definitions that will summarize what we've discussed so far and guide our discussion of cueing moving forward.

You've probably noticed the term *attentional focus* being thrown around. Notably, *attentional focus* is the formal term used within the motor-learning literature to describe the focus adopted by a participant while performing a motor skill. This focus can be encouraged by a coaching cue or self-selected by the athlete themselves. We can define **attentional focus** as the conscious effort of an individual to focus their attention on explicit thoughts or feelings in an effort to execute a task with superior performance. Thus, from a coaching standpoint, we can use language to guide the attentional focus or intention of our athletes, with the hope that words turn into thoughts; thoughts turn into actions; and those actions, in time, reflect improved performance and learning.

INTERNAL- AND EXTERNAL-FOCUS CUES

Throughout our discussion of the evidence, we've referenced two attentional focus categories—internal and external. As we've seen, an **internal-focus cue** encourages individuals to focus on a feature of their body (e.g., muscles, joints, and limbs) or the associated movement process (e.g., "activate" muscle X or "extend" joint Y), whereas an **external-focus cue** encourages the individual to focus on a feature of the environment (e.g., "drive off the *ground*" or "strike through the *ball*") or the associated movement outcome (e.g., "sprint through the *finish line*" or "kick the ball through the *center of the posts*"). To ensure we understand the difference between internal and external cues, let's do a quick check for understanding. Imagine that a coach is working with an athlete on a countermovement vertical jump. Similar to the observation made by Marcus' sprint coach, this coach has noticed that their athlete isn't maximizing hip extension at takeoff, which the coach believes is affecting jump height. Based on this finding, the coach has identified five cues that they think will improve hip extension, which I've listed below. Take a moment to circle internal (INT) or external (EXT) to denote which type of focus the cue is encouraging.

Cue A	**"Focus on pushing the ground away."**	**(INT | EXT)**
Cue B	**"Focus on driving through your legs."**	**(INT | EXT)**
Cue C	**"Focus on blasting through your hips."**	**(INT | EXT)**
Cue D	**"Focus on jumping as high as you can."**	**(INT | EXT)**
Cue E	**"Focus on exploding toward the ceiling."**	**(INT | EXT)**

How'd you do? Were you able to spot the internal cues from the external? The key is to identify whether the subject of the sentence is referencing the body or the environment. In cue A, for example, the athlete is encouraged to "push the ground," which is an external cue because of the interaction with the environment. To the contrary, cues B and C are internal because "driving legs" and "blasting hips" emphasize actions within the body. Cues D and E, on the other hand, with their focus on "jumping high" and "exploding toward the ceiling," prompt an external focus by drawing attention to the movement outcome and, once again, an interaction with the environment. Despite the fact that all five cues target the same movement error, incomplete hip extension, they do so using categorically different words, which have a material effect on performance and learning.

Before we continue, let me address the suspicion that has likely taken-up residence in your mind. Reflecting on your own experience as a coach, I suspect you will, if you haven't already, start considering all the situations where you believe an internal cue may be beneficial, if not preferred. For example, an athlete returning from injury, wouldn't the isolated nature of some of the tasks (e.g., glute bridges) benefit from an internal cue? Or, an athlete looking to increase muscle hypertrophy, isn't there a mind–muscle connection that feeds off of an internal focus? And what about the athlete looking to make a nuanced technical change? Don't they require an internal focus to zoom into the error they are trying to correct? While these questions and others may be floating around in your head, let me ask you to park them for just a bit longer, as we'll discuss the role of internally directed language in the coming pages. In the meantime, let's reflect on what we know so far. There is overwhelming evidence that, when looking to optimize motor skill performance and learning, externally oriented cues provide a measurable advantage over internal cues. This doesn't mean that you don't improve using internal cues, you do, just not to the same degree as learning via external cues. Thus, considering the nature of the tasks we've discussed so far, we can comfortably state that, when teaching a complex, multijoint movement, we should promote an external focus during the CUE it portion of our coaching loop.

Shifting back to our discussion of cue spotting, let's reverse tactics and give you a chance to work through some cue creation of your own. Take a look at the text box below. Use "movement name" to write down a movement of your choosing, use "movement error" to describe the error or aspect of the technique you would like your cues to target, use "internal cue 1 and 2" to denote examples of internal cues, and use "external cue 1 and 2" to denote examples of external cues. Note that I am having you write down both internal and external cues not because they are equally beneficial—because we know this isn't the case—but, rather, because I want you to easily discern between the different cueing categories, allowing you to spot this language within your own coaching.

Movement name _____

Movement error _____

Internal cue 1 _____

Internal cue 2 _____

External cue 1 _____

External cue 2 _____

CONTINUUM OF CUES

With a clear understanding of the difference between internal and external cues, we can now discuss what I refer to as the continuum of coaching cues. That is, while the research would suggest that selecting a cue is a binary, black-and-white process, the lived truth suggests that there are multiple shades of internal and external cues worth considering. Figure 4.5 shows a description of five categories that span the internal to external cueing continuum.

FIGURE 4.5   The continuum of coaching cues.

1 NARROW **INTERNAL**   "Extend your hips as explosively as you can"

2 BROAD **INTERNAL**   "Drive your leg back as explosively as you can"

3 HYBRID   "Drive your leg back into the ground as explosively as you can"

4 CLOSE **EXTERNAL**   "Drive the ground back as explosively as you can"

5 FAR **EXTERNAL**   "Drive towards the finish as explosively as you can"

▶ Narrow Internal Cue

Fully zoomed in, a narrow internal cue asks the athlete to focus on the action of a single muscle (e.g., single leg squat: "squeeze your glute") or a single joint (e.g., sprint: "flex your hip"). This cue prioritizes the part at the possible expense of the whole.

▶ Broad Internal Cue

A broad internal cue zooms out a level and asks the athlete to focus on the action of an entire limb (e.g., sprint: "extend or drive your leg back") or a global region of the body (e.g., squat: "keep your back flat or spine straight"). This cue doesn't comment on the action of any one muscle or joint; rather, it provides general guidance on where a limb or body region should move or be positioned in space.[6]

▶ Hybrid Cue

A hybrid cue asks the athlete to focus on the interaction between a body region and the environment (e.g., sprint: "drive your knees toward the finish line"; bench press: "punch your fists through the ceiling") or the orientation of a body region to the environment (e.g., plank: "keep your body parallel to the ground"). Notably, combative (e.g., mixed martial arts) and contact (e.g., rugby and American football) sports will use hybrid cues when teaching many of the sports techniques. For example, when teaching a front-on tackle, coaches will provide cues like "shoulder through the hip pocket" or "cheek to cheek" to denote safe head and shoulder positions. In these instances, the opponent's body becomes a feature of the environment being targeted. Notably, in the instances when a hybrid cue ends with an external focus, drawing the athletes' attention to a feature of the environment, we can treat it as a close cousin to the external cue.[7]

▶ Close External Cue

Zooming out of the body, a close external cue asks the athlete to focus on a feature of the environment that is close to them (e.g., bent over row: "pull the dumbbell to your pocket"; lateral bound: "push the ground away and stick the landing"). Ultimately, if there is an implement involved, whether it be sport related (e.g., balls, bats, and rackets) or performance related (e.g., dumbbell, barbell, or medicine ball), it will commonly serve as the primary focal point for the athlete. Alternatively, if there is no implement involved, then the ground or an environmental feature in the athlete's immediate surroundings becomes the focus (e.g., wall).

▶ Far External Cue

Completely zoomed out, a far external cue asks the athlete to focus on a feature of the environment that is far from them. In this case, far is relative to the goal of the task, which is influenced by whether or not there is an implement involved.

- *Implement:* Sports and certain exercises with one implement (e.g., ball, javelin, shot put, barbell, and medicine ball) or two implements (e.g., ball + bat, club, racket, or hurley) commonly require discrete, often ballistic, actions to do such things as move or project the implement in a specific direction, throw it as far as possible, pass to a teammate, hit a target, or take a shot on goal. With a premium placed on speed, accuracy, or distance, it is important for athletes to get their focus right. While a close external cue encourages the athlete to focus on the implement itself, a far external cue encourages the athlete to focus on a trajectory (path in the air or on the ground) or a target (teammate or goal), which is, sometimes, referred to as the end point.

---

[6] Collectively, narrow and broad internal cues categorically make up the types of cues one would find in the current literature. However, outside of the paper by Kevin Becker and Peter Smith, "Attentional Focus Effects in Standing Long Jump Performance: Influence of a Broad and Narrow Internal Focus," authors have yet to consistently adopt this distinction (7). My hope is that this book will inspire a greater number of researchers to examine this distinction, as my experience suggests that narrow internal cues are far more detrimental to performance and learning than are broad internal cues.

[7] While studies have looked at mixed-focus cues (i.e., internal + external or internal + analogy), to my knowledge, no one has explicitly looked at cues that contain both internal and external language (17, 37). For this reason, I am speculating that hybrid cues that end with an external focus would operate more like external cues, while those ending with an internal focus would operate more like internal cues. While I use hybrid cues in my own practice, they're a minority among the pure external cues and analogies. Note that this cue type is *not* the same as using internal language in the DESCRIBE it section + external language in the CUE it section of our coaching loop because a hybrid cue requires that all cue content to be framed in a single phrase.

- *No implement:* Sports (e.g., sprints and gymnastics) and certain exercises (e.g., jump, hop, and bound) with no implements or implements that aren't meant to leave the body (e.g., snowboarding, surfing, and skiing) commonly require discrete and, sometimes, ballistic actions to move or project the body as far as possible or with enough airtime to complete a series of tricks or maneuvers before landing. Because the body is the projectile in these instances, close external cues encourage the athlete to focus on the generation of force off the ground, whereas far external cues encourage the athlete to focus on trajectory (path or motion in the air) or target (finish line, goal distance, or landing spot).

Through the lens of the cueing continuum, you can see that the language we use to guide motor learning operates like the zoom on a camera, drawing attention in toward the smallest units of movement and progressively moving out toward the ultimate objective of the task. While research is fundamentally correct in suggesting that the perimeter of the body creates a border between an internal and external focus, there are still gradations of focus that can have practical consequences. Hence, in chapter 5, we'll discuss considerations for identifying the gradation of external cues that will best serve the task and experience level of the athlete, while considering the role of internal language within a holistic coaching narrative.

To sustain our focus on application and to check for understanding, below you'll find an example of the cueing continuum applied to cutting or side-stepping an opponent, with a specific emphasis on the pushing or extension phase of the motion:

Movement name: Cut or sidestep

Movement error: Incomplete extension or speed during cut or sidestep that is characterized by a long ground contact; excessive flexion in the hip, knee, and ankle; or a lateral bending of the body toward the cut leg.

Narrow internal cue: "Focus on rapidly extending your <u>knee</u>."

Broad internal cue: "Focus on rapidly extending your <u>leg</u>."

Hybrid cue: "Focus on keeping your <u>leg</u> stiff as you explode off the <u>ground</u>."

Close external cue: "Focus on exploding <u>off the ground</u> as you step (past) the defender."

Far external cue: "Focus on exploding <u>toward the space</u> as you step (past) the defender."

Now, it's your turn. Modeling the example above, pick a new movement, a movement error you commonly correct, and develop the full continuum of cues for the five categories provided.

Movement name _____

Movement error _____

Narrow internal cue _____

Broad internal cue _____

Hybrid cue _____

Close external cue _____

Far external cue _____

CUEING CONSIDERATIONS

Before we dive into the compelling evidence underpinning the mechanisms behind the external-focus advantage, it is important to briefly consider the practical utility of internally directed language within the context of our coaching loop, which, as you'll recall, is represented by five key coaching moments: DESCRIBE it, DEMONSTRATE it, CUE it, DO it, and DEBRIEF it. As we noted earlier, when introducing a new movement to an athlete, it is necessary to go through the entire coaching loop, what we called the long loop; however, once an athlete has a working mental model of the skill being learned, the coach can shed the excess communication weight and cycle through the CUE it, DO it, and DEBRIEF it segments that make up the short loop.

While the benefits of an external focus are undeniable, it doesn't change the fact that an external-focus cue, by itself, is often insufficient when initially teaching a motor skill. For example, consider a coach teaching an athlete how to back squat for the first time. It is paramount, notably for reasons of safety, that the athlete knows how to get set up before performing the movement. This requires the coach to describe and demonstrate how to get under the bar, step back into the rack, set the feet, set the posture, and then begin the actual squat. Similarly, a coach teaching an athlete how to tackle would be compelled, often by a governing body, to help the athlete understand the exact body positions that will lead to safe and effective technique. In both examples, we can see that the DESCRIBE it portion of the coaching loop is critical for explaining *what* to do, providing the athlete with an overall understanding of the task, while the DEMONSTRATE it and CUE it portions of the coaching loop provide insights into *how* to do it, a singular focus point.

While I'm not suggesting you infuse the DESCRIBE it portion of the coaching loop with unnecessary internal language, I am saying that we cannot dismiss the role of body-oriented words in explaining key features of movement, especially when a deviation from a given body position presents a clear risk of injury. Thus, considering the continuum of cues, we are on solid ground in recommending that any internal language reside within the DESCRIBE it section of the coaching loop, leaving external language to occupy the CUE it section. Notably, this recommendation extends to any video analysis a coach might do or any technical conversation they might have with an interested athlete, as both instances likely require an explanation of biomechanics (the *what*) and, therefore, the use of targeted internal language. The only rule, if you will, is that we always have an external cue acting as a buffer between the athlete's mind and their movement (the *how*). To illustrate this, let's examine how a coach might teach the back squat using the first three steps (DDC) of the coaching loop.

▶ Step 1: DESCRIBE it

"Today, we're going to introduce the barbell back squat."
"As I am demonstrating the lift, I'd like you to notice the following five steps."
"One, get under the bar so that it's centered atop your traps, gripping the bar as if to create a W."
"Two, firmly gripping the bar, stand up slowly and step back so you're centered in the rack."
"Three, widen your stance so your feet are just outside your shoulders and slightly flared out."
"Four, moving at a controlled pace, squat as deep as you can while keeping a tall, tight trunk."
"Five, maintaining this same posture, stand up in a controlled manner."

▶ Step 2: DEMONSTRATE it

These points can be made before and highlighted again during the demonstration. Alternatively, some coaches may prefer to make these points only during the demonstration. This works only during movements that are slow; otherwise, descriptions should be separate from the demonstration to avoid distraction.

▶ Step 3: CUE it

"For the first couple of sets, I am going to put a low box just behind you."
"Focus on squatting down so that you just tap the center of the box without actually sitting on it."

To summarize, describe a movement only if the absence of a description will make it unnecessarily difficult to learn or it will put the athlete at an increased risk of injury. When describing a movement, keep the word count low, prioritize visually rich language, and keep internally directed language to a minimum. No matter what, a demonstration should be used so the athlete can create an image of the movement. Coaches are encouraged to consistently use demonstrations to update and refresh the visual image in the athlete's head. Finally, by way of cueing or guided questioning (e.g., "What do you think you should focus on to achieve X?"), coaches should encourage an external focus during movement execution. In this way, coaches frame the movement by DESCRIBING it and DEMONSTRATING it and filter out a singular external focus when CUEING it.

PART 2: THE DARK SIDE OF THE CUE

While Gabriele Wulf's 1998 study was instrumental in establishing the benefits of an external focus of attention, psychologists have long suspected that effective movement is a by-product of a goal-oriented focus. Notably, in his second volume of *The Principles of Psychology*, published in 1890 (83), William James, the father of American psychology, said the following about the role of focus and movement:

> We walk a beam better the less we think of the position of our feet upon it. . . . Keep your eye on the place aimed at, and your hand will fetch it; think of your hand, and you will very likely miss your aim. (p. 1435)

This is one of the earliest recorded statements outlining the benefits of an external focus over an internal focus. However, James is not alone, as many others have since championed the benefits of getting out of one's head by focusing on the movement effects, opposed to the movement itself. Unsurprisingly, Timothy Gallwey was one such individual who advocated this approach. Referencing tennis, Gallwey said the following about focus:

> Someone playing "out of his mind" is more aware of the ball, the court and, when necessary, his opponent. But he is not aware of giving himself a lot of instructions, thinking about how to hit the ball, how to correct past mistakes or how to repeat what he just did (p. 44).

Describing his own views on instruction and cueing, Gallwey continues:

> I believe the best use of technical knowledge is to communicate a hint toward a desired destination. The hint can be delivered verbally or demonstrated in action, but it is best seen as an approximation of a desirable goal to be discovered by paying attention to each stroke (p. 232).

While we've examined considerable evidence supporting the intuitions of James, Gallwey, and Wulf, we've yet to explore the mechanisms underpinning this external-focus advantage. Fortunately, there is a diverse body of research that has created the scaffolding for a simple and elegant theory to emerge.

The Idea of Movement

When driving a car, do you focus on your foot atop the gas pedal or the road ahead? When typing on a computer, do you focus on the motion of your fingers or the letters you intend to press? When kicking a ball, do you focus on the mechanics of your leg or the person on the end of the pass? These questions and the infinite equivalents that could take their place highlight a fundamental feature of movement; that is, we organize our movement in terms of the goals we hope to achieve.

Ask yourself, what is movement, if not a vehicle for goal achievement? What purpose would any movement serve, if not as a means of acting out our inner wants and needs? I challenge you to identify an intentional, voluntary action that isn't the echo of an intended outcome. Even dance, in its abstract and boundless forms, is guided by the music it serves. Movement, then, can be conceived as a means to an end, where the end, in this case, justifies the means.

As outlined by Armin and Claudia Scott in "A Short History of Ideo-Motor Action" (84), this idea was first documented by Thomas Laycock (1812-1876), a British physician, who, while working with patients suffering from hydrophobia, discovered that touching, seeing, or imagining water would consistently result in involuntary movement, including spasms, gasping, and convulsions. Laycock went on to hypothesize that ideas were somehow connected to and embedded in motor actions, even if those ideas were imagined.

While Laycock provided early evidence for the connection between intention and action, it was his colleague, William Carpenter (1813-1885), who first gave this observation a name. Standing among his peers at the Royal Institution of Great Britain in 1852, Carpenter described the phenomena, akin to those described by Laycock, as **ideo-motor actions**—actions (motor) triggered by ideas (ideo).

As Laycock and Carpenter were examining the ideo-motor reflexes in patients with compromised nervous systems, Johann Herbart (1776-1841), the German philosopher who founded pedagogy, had independently considered a global theory of ideo-motor action. Motivated to show the connection between mind and body, Herbart argued that movements are controlled in terms of their intended sensory consequences, which is to say, the sensory experience associated with achieving a goal. Thus, once a sensory experience of a movement is registered (e.g., first time walking), it becomes the blueprint the motor system uses the next time the movement is performed (i.e., walk to achieve the same sensory experience as before).

In practical terms, our focus establishes the goal; our brain predicts the actions required to achieve that goal; these actions are documented in a sensory blueprint (i.e., this is what should happen); and the motor system then deploys the action, checking it against the blueprint. Our actions are then updated each time the movement is performed until the motor system ceases to register a difference between what we intend to do and what actually happened. In this way, our actions are organized in terms of our ideas (our goals), with the former undergoing constant updates until the latter is achieved (see chapter 3).

The Constrained Action Hypothesis

If you scroll to the bottom of Wulf's 1998 paper, you'll find a possible explanation as to why participants improved their ability to shred on the ski simulator and balance on the stabilometer. She concludes by referencing her coauthor Wolfgang Prinz's *action effect hypothesis* (52): "[A]ctions should be more effective if they are planned in terms of their intended outcome . . . rather than in terms of the specific movement pattern" (p. 148). Sound familiar? As it were, Prinz is part of a select group of researchers, including, notably, Bernhard Hommel (33), Marc Jeannerod (35), and Daniel Wolpert (67), who've provided recent theoretical and empirical support for the ideas originally postulated by Laycock and Herbart more than 150 years earlier.

With the ideo-motor theory of action operating as the explanatory backbone for Wulf's findings, she set out to answer the following questions: Why is it that an external focus leads to superior performance and learning compared to an internal focus? What changes in the motor system when it is under the influence of an internal focus?

To begin answering these questions, Wulf teamed up with Nancy McNevin and Charles Shea in 2001 (85). Using the same stabilometer study design from 1998, cues and all, the researchers added one small twist to the study. While the members of the internal group focused on keeping their "feet parallel" and the external group focused on keeping "markers parallel," the researchers would randomly trigger an auditory signal that each group had to react to as fast as possible by pressing a handheld trigger. These "probe reaction times" gave the researchers an indication of the attentional demands placed on the participants by focusing internally versus externally. That is, one could reasonably assume that the less attention a given focus requires, the faster the reaction time would be and vice versa. As it turns out, this is exactly what Wulf and colleagues found, with the results showing that the external-focus group was quicker on the trigger, posting faster reaction times than the internal-focus group. Fast-forward and we find that this result has been extended to sprint starts, where reaction time can mean the difference between winning and losing (34, 46).

Considered collectively, these results provide clear evidence that an external focus takes up less attentional real estate than does an internal focus, freeing up mental resources to do other things, such as hitting a baseball, returning a serve, or being first out of the blocks. But how can this be? It's not as if external cues are shorter than internal cues; in fact, most studies match the content and length of cues, with a one- to two-word difference delineating focus type.

Having contemplated this question many times, the answer finally revealed itself to me. The reason an internal focus slows down reaction time is because it always requires athletes to switch between two focus points, whereas an external focus only requires the athlete to focus on one. Consider, for example, the following cues for teaching a broad jump.

Cue A: "Explode through your hips."
Cue B: "Explode off the ground."

When evaluating cue A, the internal focus, I want you to ask yourself this question: Are the hips the only joint involved in performing a broad jump? Of course, the answer is no, as one would not be able to get off the ground without the help of knees, ankles, a trunk, and the rest of the body. Therefore, assuming we're talking about a multijoint movement, an internal cue always puts a micro-goal at odds with a macro-goal. That is, the athlete has to quickly switch between a hip-centric focus and an outcome-centric focus (i.e., jump far), creating competing demands on the attentional system. To the contrary, cue B, the external focus, embeds the task goal within the cued focus. To jump far, one needs to generate a large propulsive force; thus, a focus on "exploding off the ground" serves the goal by defining the means required to achieve it. In principle, an effective external cue will help the athlete identify how best to interact with the environment (i.e., the ground, a piece of equipment, or an opponent) to achieve a desired outcome. Moreover, once that athlete has developed a mental model of the skill and is highly experienced, they can spend more time simply focusing on

"Explode through your hips"

"Explode off the ground"

the outcome itself (i.e., run fast, jump high, throw far, strike here, hit there, etc.). Thus, once our focus passes the perimeter of the body and targets a relevant feature of the environment or the outcome itself, we free up attentional resources to focus on the most relevant component of goal achievement, allowing the body to do what it does best, automate the movement solution.

Arriving at a similar conclusion in 2001, Wulf and colleagues (74, 92) had one thing left to do, give their new discovery a name. And so, the **constrained action hypothesis** was born, a simple and elegant theory proposing that an internal focus "constrains the motor system by interfering with automatic motor control processes that would 'normally' regulate the movement," while focusing externally "allows the motor system to more naturally self-organize, unconstrained by the interference caused by conscious control attempts—resulting in more effective performance and learning" (74). The *constrained action hypothesis*, as you may have noticed, maps nicely onto our *zoom fallacy*, where the more we zoom into micro the harder it becomes to execute the macro. The brain, as we've discussed at length, can only handle one focus at any given moment. Hence, the more effective we are at defining the outcome to be achieved, the better the body is at achieving it.

The ensuing years brought forth a wave of evidence that would level any doubts directed at the external-focus advantage. From darts to driving, muscles to movements, the paper trail is clear, an external focus is here to stay.

MUSCLES

If we mine the depths of motor control, we should find evidence for the external-focus advantage everywhere we look. To begin, let's interrogate the micro-unit of movement, the action and operation of muscles. Like two people dancing to a common song, our muscles must work together to achieve a common goal. This neuromuscular dance requires a muscle to fire at the right time, with the right amount of force, and in harmony with its fellow motion makers. As such, a muscle that misfires or becomes overactive will immediately affect the rhythm and coordination of movement, producing a cascade of undesirable results.

To examine the effect of focus on neuromuscular function, Vance and colleagues (63) set out to ask a simple question: How do internal versus external cues affect muscle activation? To test this, they used a very basic task, a bilateral biceps curl. Similar to how coaches use cues in practice, each participant performed sets of 10 repetitions using an internal focus "on their biceps muscles" and an external focus "on the curl bar." The results confirmed suspicions around how a muscle responds to focus type, showing that, compared to an internal focus, an external focus leads to increased bar speed and lower muscle activation, measured by integrated electromyography (iEMG). Notably, an internal focus resulted in higher muscle activation in both the biceps and the triceps during the concentric, or upward, phase of the curl. This increase in cocontraction around the elbow joint provides a possible explanation for the reduced bar speed under an internal focus, as the harder the triceps fire during the curl, the harder the biceps have to work to move the bar.

Following the evidence to the present day, and we find that this result has been replicated (43) and extended time and time again. For example, Lohse and colleagues (40), using a task similar to a seated calf raise, had participants press the ball of their foot against an angled force platform by focusing externally on "pushing against the platform" or internally on "contracting the muscle in your calf." The researchers observed that, while the activation of the calf muscle (i.e., agonist: soleus) was the same in both conditions, the anterior muscles (i.e., antagonist: tibialis anterior) were far more active when participants focused internally. In a second study, Lohse and his team replicated these findings and showed that an external focus also leads to improved force-production accuracy at 30, 60, and 100 percent of a maximal voluntary contraction. Interestingly, Lohse observed that force-production error was correlated with the level of muscle cocontraction. This means that the more muscles on both sides of a joint fire simultaneously, the harder it is for the primary muscle, the calf, in this instance, to accurately produce force.

To help summarize these findings, imagine two basketball players going up for a slam dunk. As the players approach the hoop, they load into their legs to generate as much stored energy as possible. As they go vertical, we'd expect the activation in their hip flexors to quiet down so their hip extensors can get loud. The alternative is that both sets of muscle fire loudly, which is something like trying to drive on the freeway with your parking brake on, as one set of muscles resists the action of the other. With this in mind, imagine that we have player A, who was taught to jump by "focusing on exploding through their hips," and player B, who was taught to jump by "focusing on exploding toward the hoop." Based on our evidence, we can say that player A would be the one jumping with the parking brake on, while player B would be free to shift into fifth gear.

This idea of the parking brake has a name in motor learning; we call it the **freezing of degrees of freedom**, which literally means the reduction of motion due to the coactivation of muscles around a joint. Originally proposed by Nikolai Bernstein in his 1967 book, *The Co-ordination and Regulation of Movements* (93), the theory is based on the idea that, when initially learning a skill, the body pursues stability over fluidity. Over time, however, learning ensues, and the joints that were once *frozen* begin to *thaw*, allowing for a more efficient pattern of coordination to emerge (64).

This concept should tap into your own intuition. Think of the first time you got on a skateboard, rollerblades, or any other piece of equipment requiring balance. Literally, you felt frozen, hoping the wind wouldn't blow you over. It's kind of like the Tin Man in the *Wizard of Oz*, who is stuck until Dorothy oils up his joints. In our case, practice is the oil our joints need to become free and, one might say, *let it go*.

Map this insight onto the findings we've shared—not to mention those that have been extended to free throw shooting (77), dart throwing (31, 41, 42), and jumping (69)—and we can see that internal cues encourage an overt control mechanism that is similar to the one used when initially trying to learn a movement. Conversely, freed from unnecessary micro-management of muscles, an external focus encourages a more automatic form of motor control that leverages the fact that the motor system is very good at organizing movement as long as it has a clear outcome it is trying to achieve.

MOVEMENTS

Now that we've examined how a muscle operates under an external focus of attention, we can zoom out and survey the interaction between our focus and the movement as a whole. Building on their earlier work in examining the effect of focus at the level of the muscle, Lohse and colleagues (40-42) set out to extend their findings to coordinated movement. Using a dart-throwing task, novices practiced by alternating between an internal focus on the "movement of your arm" and an external focus on the "flight of the dart." As you've now come to expect, the external focus resulted in better accuracy and, echoing the evidence in the previous section, lower muscle activity in the biceps muscle.

What was surprising was the manner in which the motor system achieved this outcome. Specifically, Lohse and colleagues observed that, while the external-focus condition resulted in low-movement variability at the point of release (explaining the improved accuracy), the same participants had higher rep-to-rep variability in their shoulder angle during the throw itself. Thus, compared to an internal focus, an external focus preserved the desired outcome by allowing the body to automatically identify the optimal pairing of dart speed and shoulder motion to achieve the goal of hitting the bull's-eye. This finding, known as **functional variability** (47), states that the motor system will reduce variability in the desired outcome (i.e., kick a goal, make a shot, hit a ball, finish a lift, etc.) by increasing the number of movement options one has to achieve it.

Intrigued by this finding, Lohse and colleagues engaged in a follow-up study to see whether the results could be replicated and extended. In this study, there were four focus conditions that novice participants adopted: an internal focus on "the motion of your arm," a hybrid focus on "the dart leaving your hand," a close external focus on "the flight of the dart," or a far external focus on "the bull's-eye." As expected, both external-focus conditions resulted in better accuracy compared to the internal and hybrid conditions. Notably, when the sum variability of the involved joints was calculated, the researchers found that an external focus resulted in significantly higher functional variability compared to the internal-focus condition. This result provides further support that an external focus leads to an optimal control strategy, reducing variability in the outcome by increasing the flexibility of the pattern itself.

While this result shows that focus interacts with motor control, this finding isn't new. To the contrary, coaches have long suspected and researchers have often observed that experienced athletes *find a way*. Thus, it shouldn't be surprising that evidence from hammering (14) to handball (57) and jumping (38, 59) to shooting (53) has shown that experts reduce variability in outcomes by increasing variability in the process. How else could Cristiano Ronaldo dribble a soccer ball at the same time he is navigating unpredictable defenders while Rafael Nadal returns *impossible shots* from unconventional positions, still placing the ball just beyond the reach of his opponents?

Granted, while Lohse and colleagues' findings provide concrete evidence that an external focus underpins an optimal control strategy in dart throwing, I'm sure you're wondering whether an external focus has been shown to influence the technique of any other movements. As you've likely guessed, the answer is yes, as facilitating an external focus has been shown to encourage positive technical shifts in golf (2, 16), hitting (28), rowing (50), jumping (24, 65, 68), hopping (20), Olympic lifting (58), and change of direction (12, 13). What's more, we now have strong evidence, championed by Alli Gokeler and Anne Benjaminse, showing that an external focus when applied to hopping (24) and sidestepping (13) positively influences biomechanical risk factors associated with anterior cruciate ligament rupture (ACLR). This evidence has important implications for those at risk of an ACLR and those recovering from one (25).

All told, if we consider the evidence from the previous two sections, a clear story emerges—the body does what we say. When you give an individual an internal cue about a joint or a muscle, the body takes this cue as an invitation to oppress joint motion through increased muscle coactivation. Conversely, giving an individual an external focus serves to reduce variability, or noise, in the outcome by opening up the available movement pathways equipped to achieve it. In this way, an external focus is much like a dual-suspension mountain bike, allowing you to focus on the goal—the trail—while your body, with its full suspension, is free to adapt as the environment demands.

MIND, BRAIN, AND BODY

If you go on YouTube and type in "dancing dystonia," you'll find a video titled "Choosing Music over Meds, One Man's Quest to Retrain His Brain to Overcome Dystonia" posted by the *Globe and Mail* (89). The story profiles an Italian journalist named Federico Bitti, who suffers from focal dystonia, a movement disorder that affects the voluntary control of movement. In Bitti's case, he has involuntary muscle contractions that rotate and pull his trunk and neck to one side.

Unphased by medication and unwilling to go under the knife, Bitti put his 10-year battle with dystonia in the hands of Toronto-based therapist Joaquin Farias. In describing Farias' method, Bitti says that "sometimes you just have to use the body as a tool to get to your brain." Under the guidance of Farias' movement-based approach, Bitti started seeing the improvements that had evaded him for so many years. As exciting as this was, it was a chance meeting with Madonna's single "Vogue" that accelerated Bitti's progress. As described by Bitti himself, he was walking down the street listening to the 1990 hit and noticed that "as I followed the beat of the music, I realized that my walking was better." So excited by this change, Bitti wondered what other movements might be unblocked by the beat.

Upon showing up to therapy the next day, Bitti couldn't wait to show Farias the video he had shot of himself shortly after returning home from his walk. Farias' response says it all: "Oh my God, this is your treatment . . . this is your treatment, I mean you are another person when you dance." In a scene whose beauty is matched only by the hope it conveys, you see a nearly symptomless Bitti proceed to "Vogue," capturing the iconic dance moves of Madonna in a flawless number that can only be described as breathtaking. As the video plays on, Farias shares his views as to why dance works so well for Bitti, providing hope for so many others who suffer from this debilitating condition.

Since producing this video, both Bitti and Farias have been on TEDx. Amazingly, in his presentation titled "Dystonia: Rewiring the Brain through Movement and Dance," Bitti delivers an unblemished talk that is void of the tremors and involuntary movement that had haunted him for years. While his story is inspiring, Bitti's experience is not unique. To the contrary, many people who suffer from similar movement disorders, notably, Parkinson's disease, have also found relief by turning their focus inside out (see chapter 3).

For those of us with uncompromised nervous systems, we enjoy a body that, for the most part, does what we ask. We take for granted that, when we request one movement, opening a door let's say, our body doesn't do something completely different, for example, shake and convulse. However, for a portion of the population, the specificity of movement enjoyed by neurotypicals has been replaced with tremors, spasms, and involuntary movement. While there is no silver bullet or cure for these movement disorders, there is great promise emerging from research that examines the effect of focus on motor (re)learning.

Imagine, for a moment, a concert pianist. Picture their fingers dancing across the keys, each digit moving as if it has a mind of its own. As we enjoy the music that pours from the piano, we never consider that our experience wouldn't be possible if not for the nervous system's ability to be as gifted at turning muscles off as it is at turning them on. This phenomenon, known as **surround inhibition**, allows involved motor neurons to inhibit the uninvolved motor neurons in surrounding muscles. Hence, when our pianist presses middle C, they don't also press D, its neighbor, by mistake.

While neurotypical individuals don't have to give this a second thought, those with movement disorders appear to suffer from an inability to inhibit surrounding muscles that aren't involved in the task at hand, causing tremors or other unwanted actions. This isn't due to a bug in the muscle or the peripheral nervous system; rather, researchers believe that this has to do with a dysfunction within the basal ganglia and the motor planning loop (recall our discussion of this in chapter 3) (54). Luckily, however, we can bypass or suppress the contribution of this faulty wiring by simply switching our focus from controlling the motion (internal) to pursuing an outcome (external).

For example, Kuhn and colleagues (42) found that focusing externally on the movement outcome (e.g., pressing a key) increased surround inhibition to a greater degree than focusing internally on the movement process (e.g., contracting your finger muscles). Supporting the findings in the previous two sections, an external focus serves to tune the neuromuscular signal in terms of the task goal. For this reason, individuals with a diversity of movement disorders experience various levels of relief when they off-load their movement planning onto the environment, using sounds to guide step frequency (55) and visual lines to guide step length (61), or by simply placing stickers on their joints and focusing on the motion of the stickers, instead of focusing on the body itself (6).

While voluntary motor actions appear to be compromised in many movement disorders, an external focus provides a clear workaround, whereby individuals can learn to organize their movement in terms of the environment. In the same way, we can react to a fast-approaching car or catch a mistimed throw without much thought. We can teach the brain to leverage this environmentally guided form of movement on a regular basis. All that is required is that we learn to default to an external focus of attention, recognizing that we are ill equipped to voluntarily manage our movement one step or one joint at a time, a truth only fully appreciated by those with certain movement disorders.

PART 3: YOU GOTTA BE CHOKING ME

Consider the following thought experiment. I want you to imagine you're in a perfectly white room, void of color, sound, and smell. As the nothingness descends on you, notice the calmness that follows. With each breath, slower and deeper than the last, allow tension to evaporate and thought to dissolve until you feel absolutely present. . . . Take a moment, and, for 10 deep breaths, close your eyes and allow yourself to get lost in this image.

Feeling calm? Let's continue.

Still surrounded by white, you sense the faintest vibration of a faraway sound, fast approaching. Looking down, the floor comes to life as you're lifted by lush green grass that starts beneath you and cascades outward in all directions. As your vision rises, white lines begin to flow through the blades of grass, as if by the hand of some invisible painter, making it clear where you are . . . a soccer pitch. At the same instant, in a single, violent motion, the white walls are shattered as a stadium drives skyward, consuming the space surrounding the pitch. In the moments that follow, silence is suffocated by 60,000 crazed fans screaming with anticipation. You are at the center of the mayhem, 12 yards from the goal and a goalkeeper at the ready with a ball standing by. With everyone staring at you and your heart rate on the rise, you realize the penalty shot is yours to take . . . you glide forward and strike the ball.

How did you respond as your mind shifted from peaceful to pressurized, calm to chaotic? Did you see the ball as a challenge to be conquered or a threat to be avoided? Did you make the shot, or did you miss it? Suffice it to say that, no matter what your response, you can cite plenty of examples, personal or public, when you've observed big moments make or break an athlete. During the 1993 Wimbledon finals, for example, one might say that Steffi Graf mounted a comeback, going from 4-1 down in the final set to 6-4 up, while others may feel that Jana Novotná cracked under pressure. By the same logic, one could argue that Nick Faldo won the 1996 Masters by dropping five strokes on Sunday or that Greg Norman lost it by unraveling his six-stroke lead. Equally, during the 2017 Super Bowl, some would say New England rose, while many more would say Atlanta froze. No matter the example, one thing is clear—history is well stocked with these reversals of fortune. But why? How is it that an athlete or a team can go from an insurmountable lead to an unbelievable loss in mere moments? What changes?

Streak Versus Slump

As it turns out, Rob Gray, a professor at Arizona State University, asked the exact same question. However, before we get to Professor Gray's research, a little background is necessary. As you'll recall from chapter 1, there is little debate that athletes, or anyone, really, move from a cognitive stage of learning, thinking about the movement, to an autonomous stage, not thinking about the movement, as they transition from inexperienced to experienced. This Fitts and Posner (21) model of learning has received significant empirical support, including the finding that we discussed in chapter 3, showing that we initially rely on executive (thinking) areas of the brain when learning a movement (e.g., cognitive: prefrontal cortex) and that activation shifts to brain regions associated with the automatic control of motion (e.g., autonomous: primary motor cortex) the more we practice (40). When you consider this evidence alongside our discussion of the movement automaticity promoted by an external focus of attention, it's not surprising that theories about the intersection of focus and high-pressure performance have emerged.

Think of performance under pressure as a continuum. At one end, we have someone performing significantly better than expected (overperforming), and, at the other end, we have someone performing significantly worse than expected (underperforming). If the ends of our continuum are the extremes, then the middle represents an athlete's average, or expected, performance. Because one couldn't explain extreme over- or underperformance in terms of a miraculous change to strength, speed, or skill, any significant change in performance has to be hiding in the head. And, if this is so, it can be argued that a shift in focus is what led to the short-term optimization or disintegration of performance. This leads us back to Gray, who asked a simple question: What do baseball players focus on when they are on a streak or in a slump?

To answer this question, Gray (26) strung together three clever experiments. In experiment 1, Gray had 10 collegiate baseball players (experts) and 10 recreational baseball players (novices) practice within a virtual hitting simulator, which had been validated against live play and shown to transfer to real hitting scenarios (27). Each group performed under three different practice conditions (100 swings per condition). To assess how focus affected batting performance, Gray used what is known as a dual-task scenario. Specifically, between 300 and 800 milliseconds after the ball appeared on the virtual screen, an audible tone would sound, and the batters were required to judge whether the frequency of the tone was high or low (dual task: external environment) or whether the bat was moving up or down (dual task: external skill). Notably, when the batters had to judge tone frequency, they would've been unable to deploy significant attentional resources to skill execution, while judging the bat motion would've had the opposite effect. In line with Fitts and Posner's model, Gray found that the experts performed better when judging the sound and, thus, not focusing on the swing itself, while the novices performed better when their attention was drawn to the motion of the bat. This result is intuitive and maps onto the *constrained action hypothesis* from the standpoint that the more experience one has with a skill, the less one has to focus on the movement process underpinning it.

With evidence showing that performance is influenced by experience level and focus type, Gray wanted to see whether the natural occurrence of streaks and slumps was also associated with similar shifts in attention. To do this, Gray had the same 10 expert hitters perform another round of practice trials—500 swings in total. Enlisting the same dual tasks, the batters were randomly asked to judge either tone frequency (high or low) or swing direction (up or down) after each swing was completed. Gray was then able to go back and examine periods when the batters naturally settled into a hitting streak (a continuous streak of hits) or slipped into a slump (a continuous streak of misses). Here's the clever part: Gray was able to analyze how accurate the batters were at identifying the tone frequency and the swing direction, which provided an indication of where the batters had been focusing during the swing. The results were clear: When an expert batter is in a slump, their ability to recognize whether the bat is moving up or down improves, which is to say that they have increased their focus on the skill execution itself. To the contrary, when a batter is on a streak, they have a reduced ability to recognize the motion of the bat, which suggests that their focus is directed to an outcome feature of the skill or, at the very least, not the skill itself.

With a strong indication that underperformance could be attributed to skill-focused attention, Gray needed to add the final ingredient—pressure. So Gray recruited 12 more collegiate baseball players (experts) and had them perform 200 swings under low pressure, the same conditions as described in the previous study, and 200 swings under high pressure, with money and peer comparison used to up the stakes. The proverbial nail was now in the coffin; the results clearly showed that not only was performance negatively affected by pressure but this reduction in performance was associated with an increased ability to accurately judge whether the bat was moving up or down. Thus, Gray found a distinct relationship between skill-focused thoughts and a reduction in hitting performance in expert batters.

Pressurized Performance

Gray's observations generally fall under what is known as attentional theories of choking. As previously described, **choking** is the act of performing at a level far below one's ability due to a pressure-induced change in the way one normally controls and executes a movement (8). Simply put, when an athlete chokes under pressure, they're focusing on the wrong things at the wrong time, an attentional slipup of sorts. Despite not having absolute consensus, evidence points to *multiple routes to skill failure* that can be categorized into **dis-**

traction theories or **skill-focused theories**. Distraction theories propose that high-pressure environments degrade performance by rerouting athletes' attention to irrelevant thoughts, such as worries or consequences, or negative emotions. Skill-focused theories propose that pressure increases self-awareness and, in turn, leads athletes to focus on controlling or monitoring skill execution (18). However, as pointed out by Gray (26) and others, such as Roy Baumeister (5), Richard Masters (44), and Sian Beilock (9-11), the evidence seems to lean toward a self-focused explanation because pressure consistently triggers athletes to increase their conscious control of movement and, in doing so, literally sabotage the performance they're trying to preserve.

At this point, I wouldn't suspect that your intuition is struggling with this conclusion, considering our discussion of the constrained action hypothesis. However, there is a bit of nuance worth considering here. If you recall, Gray (26) used a relevant external focus—bat motion—and an irrelevant external focus—tone frequency. On one hand, the fact that the novices benefited from the bat focus should come as no surprise because the novices were learning to implicitly control their movement in terms of an explicit focus on the bat's interaction with the ball. On the other hand, it may have come as a surprise that the bat focus was disruptive to the expert when compared to focusing on the irrelevant sound. However, upon further inspection, this makes perfect sense. Once an expert has successfully automated their movement in terms of bat motion, the bat becomes indistinguishable from the motion itself. This allows the expert to deploy a greater proportion of their attention to relevant features of the skill not associated with skill execution itself (e.g., pitcher, ball release, launch angle, and end point). This is in no way unique to baseball, as any sport, with or without an implement, would have a similar continuum of focus points that start zoomed into skill execution and, inevitably, zoom out to goal achievement. Moreover, the evidence clearly suggests that, even if we distract an expert with a tone, the skill-focused thoughts are what ultimately oppress performance.

To showcase this last point and give a final nod to the great work of Rob Gray, we will consider the study he did with Brooke Castaneda in 2007, "Effects of Focus of Attention on Baseball Batting Performance in Players of Differing Skill Levels" (86). Similar to Gray's first experiment in 2004, the researchers recruited groups of highly skilled and less-skilled baseball players. In line with our *zoom lens* analogy, the researchers had the batters perform 40 swings under four different focus conditions, ranging from a far external to a broad internal. Using the same midswing tone as before, the batters were prompted to identify the tone as high or low (environment: irrelevant), the path of a hit ball as left or right of a target (environment: far external), the bat motion as up or down (skill: close external), or their hand motion as up or down (skill: broad internal). The results replicated and extended Gray's 2004 findings, showing that the highly skilled batters performed best when they focused on something in the environment and the less-skilled batters performed best when they focused on something to do with the skill. Specifically, the highly skilled batters' performance deteriorated the more they zoomed into their body, which means that focusing on the ball path resulted in their best performance and focusing on hand motion resulted in their worst. To the contrary, the less-skilled batters performed equally well under both skill-focused conditions, which resulted in better performances than the environment-focused conditions. While we will discuss this experience-mediated phenomenon more in the next chapter, the punch line is simple—the more automated a feature of a skill becomes, the more detrimental it is to focus on it, especially when the pressure is on.

Depressurize

Seeing as there are entire books written on this subject, I recognize that our coverage here has been brief. For those who would like to learn more, I highly recommend *Choke* by Sian Beilock, or, if you're short on time, you can watch her TED talk, "Why We Choke Under Pressure—and How to Avoid It" (90). With that said, I am hopeful that you now see the parallel between the effect an internal focus has on performance and learning and the negative effect skill-focused thoughts have on performance under pressure in highly experienced athletes. The parallel is so strong that Gabriele Wulf and Rebecca Lewthwaite (71) have referred to the performance costs associated with adopting an internal focus as *micro-choking*. I remember that it was only after reading this interpretation that I realized that choking and attentional focus weren't only related but that researchers were quite literally researching the same phenomenon from two different perspectives.

WHAT COACHES SAY

To illustrate this, let's consider three observations researchers have made. First, evidence and my own experience suggest that coaches, by chance or choice, prioritize the use of internal over external language when teaching motor skills. This has been confirmed by examining coaching behaviors in track and field (51), boxing (30), dance (29), and a diversity of collegiate sports (19). This suggests that coaches, on the whole, drift into using internal-focus cues far more than the evidence would recommend and, therefore, are encouraging athletes, at least indirectly, to focus on controlling their body actions during practice and competition.

WHAT ATHLETES THINK

Second, athletes prefer to focus on cues they're familiar with and, at least, in the short term, perform better than when they're asked to focus on cues they're unfamiliar with (45). This is not surprising because the words a coach uses to teach a skill become cloned in the thoughts of the athletes performing it. Hence, if you want to get a sense of an athlete's mental narrative, just listen to their coach. Despite this finding, there is a caveat worth considering. If individuals are provided with internal- and external-focus cues and allowed to switch between them, evidence and intuition suggest that most will inevitably choose an external focus; the key is having the option to do so (76). What's more, if we take a group of people who have identified their preferred focus and we ask them to switch their focus in the final rounds of practice, those who abandon an internal focus for an external focus will see a boost in performance, whereas those who exchange an external focus for an internal focus will see their performance degrade (66). This suggests that, even though familiarity and preference are important in the short term, there is little doubt that encouraging a shift to an external focus, in time, will lead to a higher level of performance and learning than would otherwise be possible if one depends solely on an internal focus.

Be this as it may, most athletes have a mind fully stocked with internal thoughts, ready to be deployed at any moment. The consequence of this should now be obvious. If an athlete spends the majority of their learning journey drinking the internal-cue Kool-Aid, they are inadvertently welcoming into their minds the raw material that underpins choking. While these thoughts may lie dormant once a skill has been automatized, they're still available for consideration when the heat is on. In the key moments of a competition, imagine what must be going through the head of an athlete who has been coached with internal cues their whole life—"OK, I need to make this kick; I can't let my team down. Just like coach always says, head down, stay tight, hip snap, and strike through the laces" or "This one's for the win. Elbow up, snap the wrist. Elbow up, snap the wrist." While normal circumstances might not trigger these internal thoughts, we know that pressure encourages an inward focus, leading to deautomization and performance deterioration (39). Thus, one can only assume that the more athletes have been coached to micro-manage their movement, the more likely they are to adopt an internally focused control strategy when the pressure is on.

PENICILLIN FOR PRESSURE

Finally, if my athletes' future risk of choking is tied to my present approach to coaching, then interrogating the methods used to improve their tolerance to pressure is a worthwhile exercise. Notably, just as you can't choke on a piece of food you're not chewing, you can't choke on a thought you're not thinking. Therefore, if coaches use internal language only to the degree required to *describe* a movement and prioritize external language to *cue* a movement, then they will condition their athletes to become outcome focused during skill execution, especially when combined with practice conditions that mimic the pressure of competition.

While there is no doubt that more research is needed, preliminary evidence supports this conclusion. Ong and colleagues (48), for example, showed that those who trained using an external focus of attention did not experience performance deficits when exposed to a stress-inducing posttest. Referencing the constrained action hypothesis, the researchers conclude that the automatic mode of control promoted by an external focus results in individuals who are seemingly immunized against the focus-fracturing thoughts that commonly infect the mind in stressful scenarios.

Importantly, analogies have been shown to have a similar protective effect, as novices learning a skill using an analogy (instead of a list of explicit internal and external instructions) are less susceptible to performance breakdown when exposed to a secondary task like counting backward (87, 88). While this might sound odd, asking someone to count backward while executing a movement not only introduces cognitive pressure; it also allows researchers to assess how automatic a movement has become. As such, analogies, like external cues, seem to promote movement automaticity while providing a mental focus that does well under pressure.

Thus, whether you're just starting your learning journey or you're well down the road, the right external focus (or analogy) will not only improve your ability to perform; it may just protect the performances that matter most.

SUMMARY

Just as an investment banker takes a fixed amount of money and invests it in the stock they believe will generate the greatest return, a coach takes a fixed amount of attention and invests it in the thoughts and actions they believe will generate the greatest learning. To do this effectively, however, the coach must understand the projected value of the cue they're investing their athlete's attention in. Only after this valuation has taken place can our banker and coach make an informed decision on the best investment.

The goal of this chapter was to allow you to go through this valuation process for yourself, giving you a chance to see how best to invest your athlete's attention. I argued that cues that encourage an external focus of attention will net the highest return on your athletes' attentional investment, whereas cues that encourage an internal focus will produce a much lower return and, in some cases, a loss. We discussed the historical precedence for this recommendation while considering a wide swath of evidence ranging from the lab to the field and muscles to movement. Finally, in the spirit of *National Geographic*, we examined attention in its natural habitat, showing that athletes will drift into an internal focus when under pressure and how this is directly tied to a breakdown in performance. Not to worry, however, because we also showed that the immunization for this lies partly in our ability to condition athletes to maintain an external focus in competition by first conditioning them to do so in practice.

In defining a cue as the last idea you put in your athlete's head before they move, I provided you with a one-sided suggestion, recommending that this idea always come in the form of an external cue. However, we did not dismiss internal language completely; rather, we discussed its role within our coaching loop to encourage you to use internal language, as necessary, to support your description of a movement while leveraging your infinitely larger library of external cues to coach the movement. The outcome is a coaching loop that provides you with a consistent set of linguistic placeholders to ensure you give your athlete the right information at the right time.

Be this as it may, we have not discussed the process for creating and curating the most effective external cues. The truth is, moving your athlete's focus beyond the perimeter of the body is just the start. To really understand how we build learning-rich language, we must dive into the anatomy of the cue and introduce you to the 3D cueing model.

5

CUE IT UP

Constructing Cues: A Primer

We asked a fundamental question in the last chapter: What should people focus on while they move? In answering this question, we concluded that attention is the currency of learning and that our return on investment is far higher when we focus on the outcome of a movement opposed to the process of performing it. Like coordinates on a mental map, we set a goal and allow our body to organize or reorganize, route or reroute, the optimal movement pattern required to achieve a desired outcome or arrive at a chosen destination.

On the surface, this conclusion seems like the finish line, the end of the story. As long as coaches prioritize external over internal cues, their athletes will be on the fast track to performance and learning. While this statement is almost always true, it is not the whole truth, and I would be misleading you to suggest otherwise. In actuality, the ultimate effectiveness of a cue comes down to the coach's ability to adapt their language to the athlete and create meaning that accurately represents the desired action. However, before we discuss the particulars of language, we should first establish a process for selecting and prioritizing the actions we want featured in our cues.

That's Not What I Meant!

We've all experienced the cue that backfires. With the best of intentions, we observe the way an athlete moves, target an error, deploy a cue, and watch as the error gets worse or a new set of errors emerge. While this can happen for any number of reasons, one of the most common is a blown prioritization list. You simply targeted the wrong issue and have now created a pattern that is equally, if not more, troublesome than the one that motivated the cue in the first place. Thus, to ensure that we set up our language for success, it's worth reviewing the 3P Performance Profile we discussed in chapter 1 and extending this idea to a principle of movement error prioritization.

In chapter 1, we discussed the concept of the three *P*s: *position*, *power*, and *pattern*. I argued that this was a simple heuristic, a mental model of sorts, that will help you identify whether you're dealing with a physical issue, analogous to the properties of a car, or a coordination issue, analogous to the skill of a driver. Within this comparison, I noted that *position*, our ability to dispatch the necessary mobility and stability to perform a movement, and *power*, our ability to express the associated strength and power qualities, represent two physical pillars of performance that, if limited, must be addressed as a priority or in parallel with the *pattern*, our ability to coordinate motion to achieve a goal. The interaction of the three *P*s led me to conclude that our ability to coach a *pattern* is limited by the *positions* an athlete can get into and the range of *power* available to them. In light of the book's purpose, we agreed to focus our narrative on strategies for verbally coaching the *pattern*, with a transparent understanding that coordination is affected by more than the ideas we put in our athletes' heads.

With this recap out of the way, I would like to briefly discuss our approach to unpacking patterns. As I've asserted throughout this book, a cue is only as effective as it is accurate. Meaning, you could be a cueing savant, a word-play wizard, but if your cues neglect the primary coachable movement error, then you will be left chasing shadows. Thus, we need to ensure that our language mirrors the movement goal (9) in terms of the technique required to achieve it (8). To be precise in this process, coaches must discern symptoms of a movement problem from the problem itself.

To illustrate this, imagine you are sitting lakeside on a park bench. It is a cloudless summer morning and the park is alive with runners. As each runner passes your gaze, the biomechanist in your brain can't help but blurt out an opinion. While no runner is safe from your mind's judgment, one such individual stands out for their peculiar pattern. While many of the runners have observable issues, you notice that this person has three distinct errors: (a) They are leaning so far forward, you fear for their front teeth; (b) in their attempt not to fall, the runner is reaching their leg well in front of their body; and (c) the runner's leg proceeds to fly backward in a skyward motion, giving the impression of the butt kicks one might see in a track and field warm-up. All told, the runner looks like they're trying to slow down after just being flung off a runaway skateboard, as you can see below.

Dramatics aside, this is not an unreasonable story. We've all seen this person running in our neighborhood, jogging at the park, or racing past us at the weekend 5K. Invariably, this is the same person who shows up at your facility or clinic because any combination of knee tendinopathy, iliotibial band syndrome, or plantar fasciitis is threatening their running career. The question is, from a coaching perspective, where do you start? Do you straighten them up, shorten their stride, or lift their knees? You know you will fail if you try to deploy language that addresses all three issues, so you have to place your bet and hope you identify the signal instead of the noise.

For coaches and therapists alike, this is an all-too-familiar scenario. An athlete presents with complex movement errors, and we are left to identify which error, if changed, will help the movement reorganize into a desired pattern. While we have plenty of tools to assess the physical stuff that sits beneath this pattern, we are often left with our "coach's eye" to sort out the surface-level coordination. For this reason, we need to be students of the techniques we teach and seek to understand the underpinning biomechanical, biophysiological, and biomotor attributes. In understanding a movement's blueprint, we can prioritize the physical qualities to be developed and the coordinative qualities to be coached.

Ultimately, the preconditions for effective cueing are seated within this process of error identification and prioritization. And, just as we have and will continue to discuss principles for effective cueing, it is worth discussing a principle of prioritization, a strategy for helping coaches understand whether they're targeting a movement error or its echo, which we'll call...

Positions Before Patterns

There's a saying "You can't shoot a cannon from a canoe," meaning that, if the dynamic forces produced by the cannon exceed the stabilizing forces produced by the boat, then the motion meant for the cannon ball will materialize as motion in the boat, as shown below. Similarly, during running, for example, if the dynamic forces at the hips exceed the stabilizing forces of the trunk, then any dynamic force intended for the ground will appear as unwanted motion at the back.

Coaches and therapists will commonly call these anatomical failures "energy leaks" as energy or motion emerges in joints that should otherwise be motionless for a given movement. Thus, *positions before patterns*, sometimes referred to as *proximal stability for distal mobility*, suggests that you should prioritize errors associated with motion-reducing postures before you target motion-producing patterns. Once you feel that a stable foundation for movement has been achieved, then you can chase the pattern itself by identifying the desired *range*, *rhythm*, and *rate*, that is, the desired range of motion, the rhythm or timing of that motion, and the rate or speed at which that motion should be executed.

At the risk of redundancy, let me reiterate that many energy leaks can be tied back to issues with mobility, stability, strength, and power; however, we're going to consider the implication of positions before patterns through the lens of coordination, instead of capacity. Notably, by chance or choice, athletes will adopt movement strategies that, if sustained without intervention, will become the default coordination map for the body. To change these default coordinates, we can use cues to negotiate a new movement pattern by putting an idea in our athlete's head that generates a more appealing outcome. With enough time, this appeal hardens into automaticity, and an upgraded pattern emerges.

With our prioritization principle in mind, let's see if we can apply it to our lakeside runner. As noted, you observed the following three errors. Using the right-hand column, considering our principle of positions before patterns, circle the error that should be targeted first, second, and third.

Error 1	**Excessive forward lean of the trunk**	**Priority**	1	2	3
Error 2	**Excessive forward reaching of the stride**	**Priority**	1	2	3
Error 3	**Excessive butt kicking during leg recovery**	**Priority**	1	2	3

Happy with your answers? If we start with our principle of positions before patterns, we can quickly see that the trunk (error 1), which should remain vertical and quiet to provide a stable platform from which the legs can pull-on, should be our first priority. Just as hitting a bent nail results in further bending of the nail, trying to produce force into the ground with a compromised trunk position can encourage the kind of dysfunctional leg action previously described. Cueing candidates to correct this error could include "stay tall or long," "stretch to the sky," stay zipped up," "run proud," or "lead with your belt buckle." Notably, there is one scenario in which correcting the trunk position leads to significant improvements in the other two errors; however, there is an alternative scenario in which these changes don't fully materialize, and we're still left with patterning that needs to be cleaned up. Thus, moving from position to pattern, we will now consider how to navigate errors 2 and 3.

With our last two errors, which fundamentally relate to the leg going too far forward before foot contact and too far back during leg recovery, we need to encourage our runner to deemphasize this excess forward-and-back pulling motion in favor of an up-and-down pushing action. The pushing action would bring the fringes of the technique inward, allowing our runner to hit the ground like a nail, straight on and with greater force. To do this, you can imagine a blanket lying flat on the ground. If you were to pinch the center of this blanket and lift it straight up, creating a tent-type shape, you would notice that the edges of the blanket would be brought closer together. If we map this analogy onto our runner's form, we can imagine the fringes of the blanket as the farthest point the foot reaches forward and back. To pull these fringes together, our runner needs to focus on how high and how fast they're lifting their knee, the center of our "technical blanket," if you will. In doing so, we would see a more aggressive leg-recovery strategy because our runner would need to accelerate their knee up and forward, rather than letting their leg drift farther up and behind them. Consequently, we would prioritize error 3, with the idea being that error 2 would correct itself. In this case, our cueing candidates could include "imagine you have a piece of tape on your knee, drive the tape to the sky," "drive your knees up as if to shatter a pane of glass," "cup of tea on the knee," "run away from the ground," "attack the air," or "thigh to the sky."

While our principle of positions before patterns may not fit every movement scenario, my experience, and much of the available biomechanical evidence, would suggest that you could do worse than pouring a foundation before worrying about building a house. Although more could be said here, there are volumes of books that cover technical frameworks and biomechanics. Thus, we'll pick up our story where we left off, and take a look at how we get our language to bind with our athlete's mind.

What Do You Mean?

While identifying the primary coachable error is a rate-limiting step, the real challenge lies in our ability to capture the solution in our cues. To illustrate this, let's survey your own experience. We can start with the idea that athletes need to understand the meaning of a cue for it to be effective. Think of a movement you teach all the time. Now, think of a go-to cue you use to teach or correct that movement. Flipping through your mental Rolodex, can you think of any athletes who didn't respond favorably to this prompt? Odds are you answered yes and that, upon further study, you could probably think of a number of athletes that required you to adapt your language or switch tactics to generate the change you were looking for. In these instances, we can argue that the cue's meaning accurately represents the desired action; otherwise, it wouldn't have worked for anyone. However, the unresponsive athlete is seemingly unable to drill down to this conclusion because something about the language escapes them. This happens for a variety of reasons, the simplest of which suggests that the athlete is unfamiliar with, misinterprets, or is confused by the contents of the cue or the context in which it is being applied, thus, creating a barrier to understanding.

To show you how this happens, I have listed a number of common verbs that we use as action words when coaching fast movements. Next to each verb, you will find a blank line. After you read each word, I want you to notice the image that comes to mind and write it down.

Once you're done, compare your experience to mine.

Blast _____

Snap _____

Burst _____

Whack _____

Drive _____

Punch_____

Dig _____

Pop _____

Explode _____

Shatter _____

Hammer _____

Launch _____

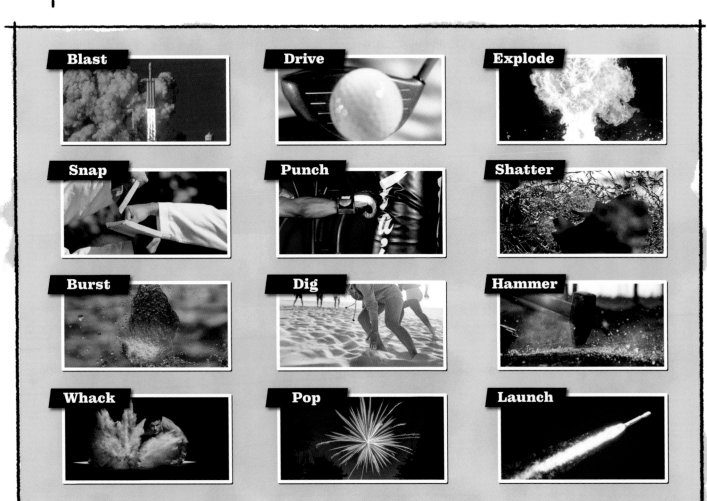

Did your interpretation of the words match mine? Odds are there were a few verbs that provoked a common visual; however, my guess is that your mind summoned pictures that were perceptually unique to you, a reflection of your past. In the same way that we had contrasting views of a common word, so too will the brushstrokes of our cues paint a different picture in our athlete's mind than it does our own. More often, however, this does not limit the athlete's ability to understand and correctly interpret what has been said. For example, imagine a coach is trying to help their athlete produce more power during a lateral bound and cues them to "explode off the ground." In this scenario, the coach selects the word *explode* because they feel the power produced during a building explosion, for example, maps onto the power they would like the athlete to generate during the bound. As long as the athlete envisions or senses the same powerful explosion, let's say an image of exploding pumpkins comes to mind because they recently watched "Exploding Pumpkins" on YouTube, then the integrity of the cue is maintained and should be effective.

Issues arise when the meaning of the cue is somehow misinterpreted by the athlete. For example, imagine our same coach is teaching an athlete how to catch the barbell during the Olympic lift, known as the snatch (see figure 5.1). To catch the bar effectively, the athlete's wrists need to go from neutral (during the pull) to slightly extended (as they catch the bar overhead). This is often referred to as the turnover, as the bar literally turns over as it goes from being pulled upward to resting atop the athlete's hands in the catch. To accentuate this action, our coach encourages the athlete to "snap the bar," as in "snap the bar into place." In the coach's mind, the word *snap* can suggest one object snapping into two (e.g., "snap a pencil") or two objects snapping into one (e.g., "snap a button"), where both scenarios are associated with a rapid, sharp sound or sensation (i.e., *pop*, *crack*, *snap*, etc.). In the context of the snatch, the second definition describes the desired action and, therefore, the desired interpretation of the cue, as the hand and forearm should *snap* together via the wrist allowing the bar to *snap* into place above one's base of support. Despite this logic, we can imagine a scenario where, at best, the athlete doesn't understand what the coach means or, at worst, misinterprets the cue all together, possibly perceiving that their coach wants them to snap the bar back instead of up (i.e., the wrist "snaps apart" instead of "snaps together"), causing excessive extension at the wrist and a compromised shoulder at the end of the movement.

FIGURE 5.1   The snatch.

SETUP   **1ST PULL**   **2ND PULL**

For every cue that hits the mark and makes a positive effect, there are many more that never even make it to the muscle. My experience suggests that coaches have a habit, often implicitly, of assuming this is a failure of the athlete. We hear comments like "slow learner," "doesn't listen," "practice player," or some other euphemism directed at the athlete's intelligence or comprehension. While communication is a two-player game, athletes have long assumed the role of scapegoat for their coaches' communication failures.

Just as John Wooden said "You haven't taught until they've learned," we can equally say that you haven't communicated until they've understood. By this logic, the coach has the responsibility to recognize when there's been a misunderstanding or misinterpretation and make the appropriate course correction. This is not difficult to do as long as coaches look for the echoes of understanding in the faces, postures, and movements their athletes adopt. Even better, when deploying a new cue, get in the habit of asking your athletes to "put the cue in your own words" or "explain what the cue means to you." This way you get premovement feedback about an athlete's grasp of the thoughts you are sending them into action with.

Once we realize that every cue is on trial and our athletes' experiences and perceptions serve as judge, jury, and executioner, we can start working toward developing cueing behaviors that will consistently result in a favorable verdict. To do this, however, we must recognize that, even if we understand the movement we are teaching and the errors we would like to correct, we still need a mechanism, a framework, with which to adapt our language to the athlete in front of us. To neglect this responsibility is to join a long list of coaches whose idea of adapting involves saying the same cue louder and more often.

Without getting ahead of ourselves, let's briefly explore how coaches can adapt their language, converting their cues to fit the needs of their athletes. To begin, remember there is no such thing as universally effective cues, as our ability to understand language and, thus, the content of cues, is directly related to *when* we've lived, *where* we've lived, and *whom* we've lived and associated ourselves with. Thus, no one will fault you for opening with your own road-tested cues; however, failure to adapt in the face of confusion borders on negligence. At the end of the day, we have to be unselfish communicators, which means we need to explore language that speaks to the experiences of our athletes.

3RD PULL/TURNOVER   **CATCH**   **RECOVERY**

If we re-join our coach teaching the catch portion of the snatch, let's see if we can't help them evolve their cue "snap the bar" and improve their athletes' comprehension. Assuming we want to maintain the cue's meaning, we can either subtract, add, or change the language within the cue.

SAY LESS

In principle, to avoid an unnecessary tax on working memory, we want to say the most with the least. This requires us to practice what we might call **lean cueing**, where we work to identify the least number of words required to impart the greatest meaning. Thus, if you've ever given a long soapbox speech, let's say before a squat, such as "OK, now remember, I want you to keep your chest up and stay long; focus on driving your hips to the low box, keeping your knees aligned; get low, and power out of the bottom," and your athletes gave you that glassy-eyed look as if to say "So what do you want me to do?," then you know the importance of lean cueing. We've all done this and, inevitably, provided a summary that is, hopefully, a one- or two-line external cue articulating the prioritized idea for the next rep.

In keeping with this idea, we will also find that an effective cue can often be consolidated into one or two action words. For example, a coach working with a sprinter may initially cue them to "push the ground back as explosively as you can," which articulates what to do—"push the ground back"—and how to do it—"as explosively as you can." As with most features of human language, a sort of slang emerges, and we can shorten the cue to "explode off the ground" without losing meaning. Inevitably, the coach may compress this cue into a single word "explode," which they may accent with a loud clap to convey the fast, violent motion the cue should promote.

The common feature in both of these examples is that we're able to lose words without losing meaning. Now, if we consider our cue in question, "snap the bar," do you think it is a candidate for word reduction? If you consider the fact that our athlete misinterpreted the intended meaning (i.e., snapping the bar back, instead of up), then we are justified in saying that the cue suffered from too little, instead of too much, information. Thus, we may find that adding language is a more desirable solution in this circumstance.

SAY MORE

Just as too much information can overpower working memory, too little information can result in underpowered insights. For example, consider our sprinter who, after some cue consolidation, was able to respond to the cue "explode" with the same fluency as "push the ground back as explosively as you can." Now, imagine that an aspiring sprinter joins our experienced sprinter's training group. We can picture a situation where the coach tells the group to "explode" before a sprint start, forgetting, for a moment, that our aspiring sprinter has no context on what or where they should be "exploding." Listening in while our newbie considers this cue, we wouldn't be surprised by any of these thoughts: "Explode up or out?" "Explosive arms, legs, or both?" "Explode toward the finish or away from the start?" Ultimately, our aspiring sprinter is left to their own devices, requiring them to make an educated guess as to what their coach means. At this point, the athlete could guess correctly, sensing that the coach wants them to "explode out"; they could guess incorrectly, focusing on an "explosive leg action" that is more quickness in the air than power on the ground; or they could abandon the entire cueing enterprise and revert to type, "just run fast."

In truth, most of this confusion and misinterpretation can be avoided if coaches take the time to provide a high-quality description and demonstration before delivering the cue; however, for a cue to stand on its own, it will require two fundamental pieces of information: a *what* and a *how*, that is, what the athlete should do to achieve a desired outcome—"push the ground back"—and how they should go about achieving it—"as explosively as you can." If a coach provides only the *what*, then the athlete is left to interpret how best to accomplish this: "powerfully," "gradually," "quickly," or "quietly." Similarly, if a coach provides only the *how*, then the athlete is left to identify the best-fitting goal: "move this, move that" or "go here, go there." Thus, quickly recognizing that our aspiring sprinter had lost the plot, our coach could have unfolded "explode" by providing a more complete version of the cue with full context: "To be clear, I want you to focus on exploding out by pushing hard off the blocks."

If we apply this logic to our cue, "snap the bar," we can see that it suffers from not having a clear goal and, thus, a clear *what*. Specifically, because the word *snap* can be interpreted as snap apart or snap together, it is easy to see how an athlete might interpret this cue to mean that the wrist and arm should snap apart, sending the bar backward and compromising the finish position. To avoid this, we need to clarify our goal, bringing our *what* into high definition by adding a *where*. For example, "snap the bar to the ceiling" provides minimal room for misinterpretation and, in this case, implicitly encourages the desired technique of snapping the bar up, instead of back. As we will discuss in chapter 6, we can elevate the visual value of this cue if we tack on an analogy at the end: "Snap the bar to the ceiling just like you were trying to snap a wet towel." By adding the analogy, we provide a comparable movement scenario that requires similar wrist mechanics. Assuming the athlete has snapped a towel before, they can map the sense of snapping a towel onto that of snapping a bar. By leveraging an existing movement memory trace, we lower the barrier to learning.

SAY IT DIFFERENTLY

If adding or subtracting language isn't working and you're targeting the right movement error with a well-worn cue, then you may want to think about refreshing your language all together. Unlike external cues, internal cues have a language cap, as the number of available phrases is the same as the number of available joints and muscles in the body. Once you've told someone to "focus on extending your hips," for example, you've fundamentally hit internal cueing bedrock. Where do you turn if this cue doesn't work? Fortunately, we can tap into our arsenal of external cues, which allow you to trigger the same movement in nearly infinite ways. The reason for this comes down to the linguistic properties of external language and, as we'll see, analogies.

To illuminate this idea, we can imagine a baseball coach who is trying to help one of his pitchers achieve greater leg drive off the mound. To do this, the coach tells the pitcher to focus "on extending hard through your hip and knee." While this cue may provide some descriptive value, it is disconnected from the entire pitching motion and could likely do with a reboot. To do this, our coach needs to identify the technical goal—extend through the hip, knee, and ankle in concert with upper-body motion—and how that goal should be achieved—maximize horizontal power by rapidly pushing toward home plate. With this information in mind, our coach can start curating external cues that will speak to the varied preferences of his pitchers. Notably, if our pitching coach questioned the utility of designing multiple cues only to choose one, we could remind them that just as they like to try on several pairs of shoes before they buy, so too would their athletes appreciate the opportunity to try out several mind-sets before they set their minds. With our pitching coach open to this viewpoint, we can now consider a sample of cues that, while different, maintain the core meaning the coach hopes to convey (see next page).

While these cues target the lower body, the language doesn't detract from the ultimate goal of throwing a fast, accurate pitch, as the energy and direction captured in each cue maps to the overall essence of the throwing motion—forward momentum. All we are doing is exploring different ways to encourage rapid extension moments at the hip, knee, and ankle, which we know will lead to improved horizontal power and, with the right amount of linking from lower to upper body, an improvement in pitch speed. By cataloguing different cues that maintain a common meaning, our coach can quickly adapt to the distinct needs of each athlete, while pulling from this cue warehouse any time a drifting mind needs an attentional boost.

As a final exercise, let's see how we might apply this approach to our snatch technique cue "snap the bar to the ceiling." Remember, we're at a point in the motion when the bar is accelerating vertically and the arms are transitioning from a flexed, high-pull position to an extended, catch position, creating a stiff, stable upper body to receive and control the bar overhead.[1]

---

[1] While the cue "snap the bar to the ceiling" suggests a constant vertical rise of the bar, the reality is that, as the load gets heavier, the vertical movement of the bar will be less. As such, there will come a point when the athlete will need to *pull* themselves under the bar if they're going to catch it. At this point, cues will typically shift from "getting the bar to the ceiling" to "getting under the bar." The mechanics are the same; however, the cue serves to change the mental strategy used to receive the bar overhead.

"TO ATTACK PITCH SPEED, WE NEED TO ATTACK THE MOUND. ON YOUR NEXT PITCH I WANT YOU TO FOCUS ON..."

"...blasting off the rubber"

"...exploding toward home"

"...driving the rubber away"

"...pushing harder to the plate"

"SNAP THE BAR TO THE CEILING"

"Whip the bar through the ceiling"

"Pull straight and snap late"

"Violently, pull yourself under the bar"

Now, it's your turn. As we did in chapter 4, I want you to identify a movement, a core technical error or outcome within that movement, and a common cue you use to teach or correct that phase of the motion. Once you've mapped this out, please use the lines to come up with three external cues that impart the same meaning; try adding, subtracting, or changing your language. For each cue you convert, circle the strategy you used.

Movement: _____

Movement error or outcome: _____

Baseline cue: _____

Converted cue 1: _____

Circle the strategy   ADD   SUBTRACT   CHANGE

Converted cue 2: _____

Circle the strategy: ADD   SUBTRACT   CHANGE

Converted cue 3: _____

Circle the strategy: ADD   SUBTRACT   CHANGE

How'd you do? Did you find this exercise easy or difficult? While some will find that they have a natural affinity for cue creation, many won't. In truth, I was one of those who felt cemented to the language I had grown comfortable coaching with. As a by-product, I found it difficult to pry myself out of my cueing comfort zone and far too easy to revert to my rigid cueing ways. However, I was not deterred, nor should you be, because cueing is a habit and habits can be transformed with the right tools.

As coaches, we are quite familiar with the evidence-based tools and systems required to drive change. Nutritionists design meal plans to target the macro- and micronutrient needs of athletes. Strength coaches design programs with exacting detail to ensure that each rep, set, and load is periodized to deliver timely results. Therapists plan out each phase of a return-to-play process by considering the time and exercises required to repair and rebuild the injured regions of the body. Thus, if we recognize the importance and necessity of the systems we use to drive *what* we do, would logic not suggest that equal importance and necessity should be awarded to a set of systems that show us just *how* to do it?

PART 1: CUEING IN 3D

If you're like me, you take great care in getting to the airport early, especially when departing a foreign city. This means you're checking flight times and grabbing directions before booking that 4:00 a.m. taxi the night before. If you think about it, so much of life is guided, quite literally, by a similar navigation algorithm.

You set an alarm clock in the morning, based on where you're going and the time you need to be there. When deciding where to go for lunch, the sandwich joint across the street or the salad shop down the road, you consider how much time you have before your next meeting. And, even in sport, take soccer and rugby, for example, players must quickly calculate if they can cover enough ground to take the shot or score the try, or if they're better off passing the ball. In all cases, we are sculpting the elements of experience—space and time.

Think about it. Whether it be a thought or an action, we are navigating a space—an environment—and doing so in a certain amount of time. While space and time are often the province of our subconscious, it doesn't make their impact on behavior any less real. From deciding how quickly to push the chair in for your grandmother at Christmas dinner to how fast you need to run to slip through a narrowing set of elevator doors, your brain is flat out calculating your goal in terms of the physical space to be explored and the time required to explore it.

Intellectuals have long considered space and time to be fundamental to human thought. From famed German philosopher Immanuel Kant, who is often quoted as saying that "space and time are the framework within which the mind is constrained to construct its experience of reality," to Albert Einstein, who echoed this view when he said that "space and time are modes in which we think," there is plenty of scholarly clout supporting this view. However, go no further than to navigate your own head*space*, and you will find infinite examples of *time*-based thinking that constructs your reality across a vast landscape of past, present, and future.

So why is this important to our story, and how does it relate to cueing? Simple, if all motion can be described in terms of space and time, which it can, and all thinking is constrained by the fabric of space and time, which it is, then we can argue that our cues should contain a similar motion-inducing DNA. And just as human DNA is composed of function-bearing genes, it shouldn't surprise you that a cue has a genetic code of its own, one that is composed of genes for distance, direction, and description (31).

Just as an actual GPS requires coordinates, a longitude and a latitude, a cue requires a *distance* and a *direction* to define the space that will become the subject of focus. Together, distance and direction describe both the physical space to be navigated, go here or there, and the mental space required to navigate it, focus on this or that. However, space is only half the story because a cue must also convey an element of time. Without this feature, an athlete would have no way of knowing how best to move through a defined space—"fast or slow, I just don't know." Fortunately, to account for this timing element, a cue must contain a *description* of the movement by way of action language—"*hammer* the ground," "*push* the bar," or "*drive* through the attacker"—or analogy—"hammer the ground like you're *hammering a nail*," "push the bar like you're *pushing someone out of the way of a car*," or "drive through the attacker like you're trying to *bury them*." Collectively, the three *D*s—distance, direction, and description—create the mental model, or the framework, that coaches can use to quickly adapt their language to fit individual needs in terms of a desired movement outcome.

Before we dive into each *D* separately, let's go through a couple of examples to make sure we can spot each *D*. Here are three cues that have each *D* labeled appropriately.

Direction

"Focus on smashing the dumbbells through the ceiling"

Description

Distance

Direction

"Focus on bursting out of the blocks"

Description

Distance

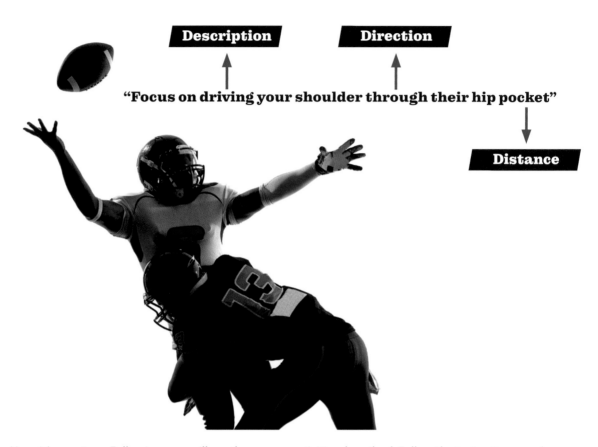

Now, it's your turn. Following, you will see three more activities described. Follow the instructions, and we will review at the end.

▶ **Example 1**

For each identified word within the example cue, label it as either the distance, direction, or description; each label should only be used once.

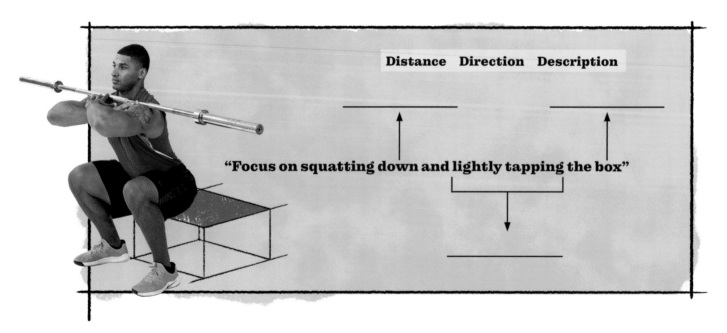

▶ **Example 2**

After reading the cue, draw a line connecting the target word(s) to the target *D*; each label should only be used once.

Distance   Direction   Description

"Focus on exploding past the farthest cone"

▶ **Example 3**

Identify a movement and a target movement error or outcome. Use the last line to create an external cue that contains all three *D*s, labeling each *D* as you did in example 2 by drawing a line connecting the target word(s) to the target *D*; each label should only be used once.

Movement name: _____

Movement error or outcome: _____

Cue: _____

Distance   Direction   Description

With an understanding of how to identify the DNA within each cue, you are in a position to discuss how to manipulate each *D* to serve the athlete you are working with and the context you are working in. Chapter 4 taught us how to categorize cues. Now, we will consider the process of creating them.

Distance

In chapter 4, we compared cueing to the zoom lens on a camera, suggesting that we have a close-internal cue (e.g., focusing on wrist motion during a pass) when we're fully zoomed in and a far-external cue (e.g., focusing on the intended receiver of the pass) when we're fully zoomed out. While the evidence clearly showed that our focus should remain beyond the perimeter of the body, we have yet to provide any evidence for the relative merit of close- versus far-external cues. Fortunately, a strong research narrative exists.

To ensure clarity, we will discuss the distance conveyed within our cues in terms of implement-based (e.g., baseball and golf) and non-implement-based movements (e.g., sprinting and jumping).

ANSWERS
Example 1: Distance = "box"; Direction = "down"; Description = "lightly tapping"
Example 2: Distance = "cone"; Direction = "past"; Description = "exploding"

IMPLEMENT-BASED MOVEMENTS

Golf and baseball have been particularly useful in studying the effects of focus distance on motor learning and performance. As you'll recall from chapter 4, Wulf and colleagues (19) found that novice golfers had better chip-shot accuracy when they focused on "the pendulum-like motion of the club," a close-external cue, opposed to focusing on "the ball's arc and . . . target," a far-external cue, which provides preliminary evidence that focus distance influences the benefits of an external focus of attention.

Naturally, if novices appear to benefit from a close external focus, researchers wondered if the same would be true for expert golfers. To answer this question, Bell and Hardy (32) recruited 33 skilled golfers with a registered handicap below 9.4. Participants were broken down into three groups. Each group practiced using either an internal focus on the "motion of the arms . . . and . . . the hinge in the wrists through impact"; a close-external focus on the "clubface through the swing, in particular, keeping the clubface square through impact"; or a far-external focus on the "flight of the ball . . . and . . . the direction in which they intended to set the ball." Similar to Wulf's work, participants tried to chip a ball as close to a 22-yard (20 m) flagstick as possible. Using their assigned focus, participants performed 10 warm-up shots followed by three blocks of 10 shots under normal conditions and two blocks of 10 shots under high-anxiety conditions. As expected, the external-focus groups, under both conditions, were significantly more accurate than the internal-focus group. However, relevant to our discussion of distance, our experts performed best using a far-external focus compared to a close-external focus.

If we consider these findings alongside the results that Rob Gray found in baseball, the intersection between attentional focus and distance is revealed. Simply put, expert performance is optimized when the external focus is an outcome (far) compared to an implement (close), while the opposite is true for novices (8, 20). For experts, a secondary benefit of a far-external focus is that it reduces any unnecessary conscious control of their movement, which we know is more detrimental to the experienced than to the inexperienced (3). This finding makes sense when considered in terms of our discussion of choking. Novices, having little experience, benefit from anchoring their movement to an implement's motion, while experts, who have long since integrated the implement into their motor memory, are better off trusting their movement and giving it a clear outcome to achieve. Practically speaking, it's not that experts don't benefit from a close-external focus, because they do (e.g., 30); it's just that, when performance is the goal, especially in the midst of a stress-laden practice or competition, coaches should consider prioritizing a far- over a close-external focus, bringing the desired outcome into high definition.

Let me be clear. I don't believe we have enough evidence, nor does my experience suggest, that experts, in all circumstances, need focus on the furthest outcome. There will be plenty of times, especially if a change to technique is desired, that experts will need to focus on the motion of the bat, club, racket, or hurley. However, as an athlete advances in skill, so too can their focus begin to advance from implement to outcome.

NON-IMPLEMENT-BASED MOVEMENTS

Imagine you are at the NFL Combine and you just stepped up to the line at the broad jump. Having just seen your number one competitor set a Combine record, your heart starts racing because you know you have consistently beaten that distance in training. With a nod to your training buddy, they casually drop a mini-band near the new record, giving you a visual mark. Taking a final deep breath, you load up and explode out.

While fictionalized, this story is anything but. Without fail, any time my athletes lined up for broad-jump work, you could count on the mini-bands coming out to mark everyone's best. Similarly, when the boys would step up to the Vertec, a vertical jump device with tabs to delineate jump height, they would inevitably ask me to swipe away the tabs just below their personal best, leaving a clear target. So why is this behavior so common during jumping tasks? What is it about a visual target that gives the athlete a sense that they can achieve a better performance than without it?

To answer this question, Jared Porter and his colleagues formulated a series of studies to see if focus distance influenced jump distance. In their first study, Porter and his team (33) showed that undergraduate students with no broad-jump experience jumped significantly farther when they focused externally on "jumping as far past the start line as possible" compared to internally on "extending your knees as rapidly as possible." With no surprises here, Porter recruited another group of undergraduate students to evaluate the effects of increasing the focus distance (22). Using the same close-external cue previously noted, Porter added a far-external focus, having participants focus on "jumping as close to the cone [set 3 yards (3 m) from the start line] as possible." Interestingly, Porter found that the far-external focus generated a significantly larger broad jump than did the close-external focus. In a final study, Porter recruited Division I athletes and compressed the cues from his first two studies into one (21). Aligned to the results noted in the implement-based section, both external-focus conditions produced significantly farther jumps than did the internal-focus condition, with the far-external focus leading to the best overall jump distance. Thus, Porter and his colleagues found that athletes and nonathletes alike benefit more from using a far- compared to a close-external focus.

"Focus on bursting toward the <u>ceiling</u>"

If we combine the findings from the implement- and non-implement-based research, the form and function of this *distance gene* are revealed. To start, let's agree that mastery, in part, is the capacity to fully attend to a movement outcome without the need to consciously consider the process. Thus, whether or not an implement is involved, we can state that the more experience an athlete has with a movement, the more likely they are to benefit from a far-external focus. In contrast, the less experienced an athlete is with a movement, the more likely they are to benefit from a close-external focus. Remember, these are considerations, not mandates, because there is plenty of scope to expand this area of research to a larger library of movements. That said, the evidence clearly shows that the *distance*[2] woven into a cue will have a material impact on performance and, as such, should be seen as one of the variables that can be manipulated if a change in pattern or performance is desired (9).

MANIPULATING DISTANCE

As you probably noticed from the examples discussed earlier, very rarely will the cue explicitly mention distance. Rather, the cue will provide a person, place, or thing, collectively known as *nouns*, at which the athlete is meant to focus their attention. For example, consider the two cues at right that are meant to encourage improved jump height during the vertical jump.

While the underpinning purpose of each cue is the same, to maximize jump height, the cues encourage this outcome, in one case, by focusing on the arrival because the ceiling is where I am going and, in the other, by focusing on the departure because the floor is where I have come from. Thus, the noun is the source of the distance and, therefore, the target word to change if you want to advance or withdraw one's focus.

In keeping with the flow of this example, consider another set of cues for hitting a tennis ball.

"Focus on bursting away from the <u>floor</u>"

[2] Note that some evidence shows that attainability influences the distance effect. For example, Cheryl Coker (9) showed that, while external compared to internal cues resulted in farther horizontal jump distance, setting a cone (i.e., external focus) at the farthest distance a participant had jumped resulted in better jump performance than setting a cone at a fixed 3-yard (3 m) distance. This suggests that attainability may play a role in the salience of the external focus. That is, one is likely to give greater effort if something is achievable opposed to not. This should be considered when setting distance parameters within cues, especially for ballistic, power-based activities.

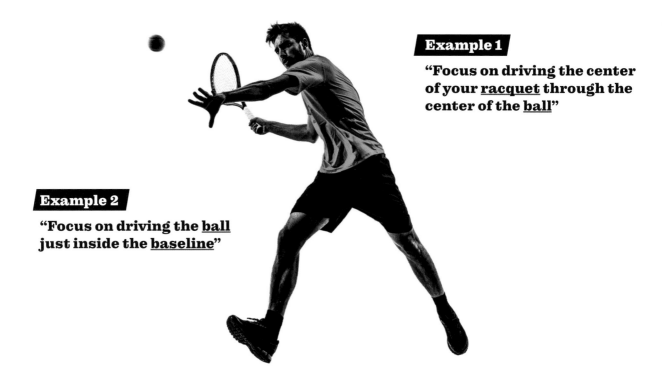

Example 1

"Focus on driving the center of your <u>racquet</u> through the center of the <u>ball</u>"

Example 2

"Focus on driving the <u>ball</u> just inside the <u>baseline</u>"

Unlike our jumping cues, which used a single noun to convey distance, it is common for cues directed at implement-based skills to leverage two nouns, connecting the action of the implement or ball to the outcome itself. As we can see in example 1, racket and ball collaborate to invite a close-external focus because racket motion is an echo of the movement pattern. In contrast, example 2 is a far-external focus because the ball and baseline align to advance focus to the outcome. As was the case with the previous set of cues, the noun holds the key for manipulating where focus is deployed and, in this way, controls the zoom lens on your cue.

Direction

To ensure our cue accurately represents the physical space we would like our athlete to navigate, we can add a direction to our distance. If distance indicates where in space we should focus attention, then the direction indicates whether we are moving to or from that point in space. To illustrate this component of the cue, consider the following example.

Example 1

"Focus on pushing the dumbbells <u>away</u> from the bench"

Example 2

"Focus on pushing the dumbbells <u>toward</u> the ceiling"

While both cues are encouraging an explosive movement, example 1 does so by telling the athletes to "push . . . away," and example 2 prompts the athletes to "push . . . toward," an obvious directional difference. It is interesting to note that the cues also shift from a close distance, dumbbell from bench, to a far distance, dumbbell to ceiling. This is not surprising as distance and direction combine to define the space the athlete is moving through. Thus, a cue that encourages an athlete to move toward something is almost always a far-external cue, while a cue that encourages an athlete to move away from something is almost always a close-external cue. This is logical because we will commonly move away from something close and toward something farther away. Here are a few more examples to help convey this point.

"Pull <u>from</u> the ground"
——— vs ———
"Pull <u>to</u> your pocket"

"Drive the ground <u>away</u>"
——— vs ———
"Drive hard <u>into</u> the space"

"Explode <u>off</u> the track"
——— vs ———
"Explode <u>through</u> the finish"

While it is clear that there is a directional component in most cues, there is virtually no research on the topic. That is, we do not know if movement is best served by focusing on moving away from the start or toward the finish. However, if we reinterpret Porter and colleagues' research as evaluating direction, instead of distance, it is possible to unveil some insights. Recall that the researchers used a close-external cue, "jump as far past the start line as possible," and a far-external cue, "jump as close to the cone as possible," during a broad jump. In the case of the close-external cue, we can see that "past the start line" is an *away* reference and "close to the cone" is a *toward* reference. By this account, we could conclude that, just as far-external cues result in better jump performance compared to close-external cues, so too do *toward*-external cues result in better jump performance compared to *away*-external cues.

While this view of Porter's work is possible, I would caution you not to overly rely on this interpretation until more research has been completed. Instead, I encourage you to consider the nature of the movement you are teaching and evaluate whether a shift in the directionality of the cue could be useful in improving the athlete's understanding and execution of the movement. For example, a throwing action is a total-body motion requiring coordinated action from the lower and upper body. In the case of pitching, for example, we could argue that a coach is justified in telling the pitcher to push *away* from the mound or *toward* home plate when cueing the lower body; however, you wouldn't tell the pitcher to throw *away* from the mound. Rather, cues directed at the upper body would focus the pitcher on the ball in terms of the plate and, thus, require a *toward* orientation. This illustrates that the skill or the portion of the skill you are targeting ultimately dictates whether the directionality of focus can be manipulated.

Let's consider two more examples to make sure this point sticks. A shoulder press, for example, is subject to a directional shift because one can focus on pushing the bar *away* from the ground or *toward* the ceiling, with both cues encouraging a vertical bar path that is guided by an external focus. While intuition would rightly suggest that starting with a *toward* cue is logical because the weight is literally moving toward the ceiling, there is no harm in shifting the focus *away* from the floor, ground, or some other object beneath the load being lifted. Note that most movements where a weight is being lifted will be subject to directionality, where you can move *away* from a surface and *toward* a ceiling or *away* from one wall and *toward* another.

This same logic holds for non-implement-based skills because one can move *away* from the ground and *toward* the sky or *away* from a start and *toward* a finish (think sprinting, jumping, and agility). Equally, even if the movement is not dynamic, as would be the case for any variety of bridging or planking, coaches can talk about stretching, or getting long, as a surrogate for referencing spine position. In these instances, it would be equally valid to say something like "from head to heel, focus on stretching *away* from the wall (behind you)" as it would be to say "from head to heel, focus on getting long *toward* the wall (in front of you)." Thus, whether the movement is static or dynamic, implement based or not, directionality, where appropriate, can be used to set a reference point from which to move. In this way, we can view the *direction gene* as the compass within the cue.

Finally, just as the noun served as the part of speech we manipulate when shifting the distance within the cue, the *preposition* is the part of speech we manipulate when changing the direction of the cue. You can reference the examples previously noted, as well as the following list of words, which includes some of the most common prepositions contained within cues.

Away	*Toward*
From	*To*
Out of	*Into*
Off of	*Through*

Using one or more of these prepositions, fill in the blanks contained within these cues to give them a direction.

"As you finish the lift, focus on getting tall_____ the ceiling"

"Focus on accelerating the ball straight _____ the wall"

Description

Continuing to draw on our DNA analogy, we can say that, in addition to defining the movement space, *distance* and *direction* give the cue sight and are responsible for the mental imagery that follows a well-formulated external cue. Without fail, telling someone to "_____ off the ground" or "_____ the barbell through the ceiling" will establish the virtual environment for a movement to be considered before permitting the body to bring it to life. However, as indicated by the blanks, the cue requires one final ingredient, a *description*.

If *distance* and *direction* give a cue the power to see, then the *description* gives a cue the power to move. That is, the action *verb*, for example, *push*, *drive*, *snap*, and *punch*, *describes* how the movement should be performed, breathing life into the cue and, in the process, defining the timing or pace of the pattern. As we've already discussed, the verb gives the cue it's energy, or vitality, and is also the part of speech that people will be most sensitive to. Recall our verb experiment from earlier. Even though we both read the same verb, our minds' sensory interpretation of those verbs differed to varying degrees. Thus, the key is to identify a verb that is interpreted as intended and conveys the movement timing you'd like to see the athlete use to navigate the movement space. Learn to do this effectively, and you'll see athletes respond to your cues with the same ease that a light responds to the flip of a switch. When done with precision, effective cueing appears to give you direct access to the motor system, as if you are speaking to the neurons themselves.

SPEAKING OF MOVEMENT

To begin, I want you to read four lists of words and simply notice what happens in your mind and body, taking a moment to reflect after each set of words.

▶ Word List 1	▶ Word List 2	▶ Word List 3	▶ Word List 4
Capture	*Wade*	*Sit*	*Grip*
Struggle	*Swim*	*Recline*	*Squeeze*
Thrash	*Glide*	*Relax*	*Fight*
Escape	*Float*	*Sleep*	*Finish*

So what did you notice? Did the words stay on the page, or did they jump into your mind? Did you have a physical response to any of the lists? Did you notice an increase in tension after reading lists 1 and 4 or possibly a reduction in tension after reading lists 2 and 3? Whatever your experience, I want you to reflect on it and commit it to memory.

Let's now consider a second set of lists. As before, read each list carefully, and simply observe how your mind and body react.

▶ Word List 1	▶ Word List 2	▶ Word List 3	▶ Word List 4
Room	*Patio*	*Bed*	*Bar*
Chair	*Ball*	*Desk*	*Bench*
Table	*Umbrella*	*Lamp*	*Rack*
Cup	*Lawn*	*Rug*	*Plate*

How was your experience this time? Similar or different? Did these lists tell a story or trigger an emotional response? While an image likely appeared in your mind, I would be confident that these words lacked the motion and emotion of our first set of lists. Would you agree? By contrasting these two sets of lists, we can start to see why verbs, action words, are so very important. They are the heartbeat of the cue and what gives language life. If not for verbs, how else would we *sit* in a chair, *lay* on a lawn, *write* at a desk, or *lift* a bar?

While this might seem trivial and obvious to most, this is where our story takes an interesting turn. If you recall, in chapter 3 we talked about Daniel Wolpert, and I mentioned his TED talk, "The Real Reason for Brains." As we discussed, Dr. Wolpert provided a very convincing narrative that the only reason we have brains is to move—end of story. Filtered by neuroscience and motor control, he argued that the brain exists as a vehicle to literally move us up Maslow's hierarchy of needs, for example, from hungry to full, outside to inside, and danger to safety. While this is a great reason for a brain, we know that a brain does more than move us; it is also quite good at moving others.

Dr. Friedemann Pulvermüller is a professor who teaches the neuroscience of language at the Free University of Berlin. In 2016, Dr. Pulvermüller recorded a video for the website Serious Science in which he asked the question "What is language good for?" to which he answered "Language is a tool for action," a tool for coordinating the movement of others (34). While this might strike you as a clever use of metaphor, Dr. Pulvermüller sees this as a statement of fact, a proclamation as literal in intention as that of Dr. Wolpert's. And, just as Dr. Wolpert believes the reason we have brains is to move ourselves, Dr. Pulvermüller believes the reason we have language is to move others, and he has the evidence to back it up.

Interested in understanding how the brain derives meaning from language, Dr. Pulvermüller and his colleagues designed a number of experiments to peer inside subjects' brains while they processed written and spoken language. In a series of studies, Pulvermüller and his team (35, 36) found that, when subjects read verbs about the lower body (e.g., *kick, run, jump*) or the upper body (e.g., *press, lift, grab*), the specific regions in the motor cortex responsible for those actions would fire. In agreement with our discussion of ideo-motor theories of motor control, the *ideas* contained within a verb triggered the brain regions in charge of transforming those ideas into *movement*.

Encouraged by this finding, Pulvermüller and his colleagues set out to see if subjects would recognize and respond to action verbs faster when brain regions associated with those actions were activated using transcranial magnetic stimulation. Sure enough, when regions of the motor cortex implicated in upper- or lower-body movement were activated, subjects could identify action verbs associated with those respective body regions much faster. This supported earlier findings and showed that the brain partly establishes a verb's meaning by activating the same brain regions responsible for carrying out those actions, a phenomenon often referred to as **embodied cognition**.

While understanding how meaning is derived from single verbs is important, we know that action words are rarely used in isolation. Thus, researchers extended these findings to action sentences, or what we might refer to as verbs in context. This is important for cueing because we often use verbs that, without context, would leave the motor system with little to go on. For example, the word *accelerate* is often associated with the lower body and *push* with the upper body; however, we have no issue with telling an athlete to "accelerate the bar" during a bench press or "push the ground away" during a sprint. Thus, verbs are conceptually diverse and often depend on the words around them to illuminate the intended meaning.

To this last point, Raposo and his colleagues (37) set out to see how the brain processed verbs in isolation (e.g., *kick*), in literal sentences (e.g., *kick* the ball), or in nonliteral figures of speech (e.g., *kick* the bucket). Similar to Pulvermüller, Raposo found that single verbs and verbs within literal sentences activated regions of the motor cortex associated with the body segments responsible for carrying out those actions, with no such motor-cortex activation occurring when subjects processed nonliteral sentences. Thus, the brain, like the body, operates from a principle of specificity, generating meaning from words and sentences by recruiting the same brain regions that are responsible for bringing those words into the physical world. This provides direct support for the importance of the 3D cueing model because each *D* supports the others in generating motor meaning.

In agreement with this finding, van Dam and colleagues (38) found that brain regions responsible for movement differentially responded to basic action verbs (e.g., *to move, to attack, to take*) versus specific action verbs (e.g., *to push, to hit, to grasp*), which suggested that, the more specific the action word, the greater the recruitment of brain regions associated with production of that coordinative signature. This is an extremely valuable finding because it supports the need for cueing specificity and a cueing model for achieving that specificity. Thus, when teaching sprinting, for example, a basic cue might be to "sprint fast." However, this cue lacks nuance and would leave the athlete to technically execute the sprint with no guidance. If cue clarity were desired, we would deploy a specific cue and ask the athlete to "explode off the track as you climb through acceleration." As we can see, the specific cue is still in service of "sprinting fast" but does so by providing the motor system with external guidance that is void of internal interference. Hence, an outcome can be technical in nature as long as it is delivered through an external filter and is aligned with the ultimate goal of the movement.

Finally, to establish the functional link between action words and motor actions, researchers set out to see if they could increase or decrease motor performance by manipulating the timing of verb presentation. In a clever set of studies, Véronique Boulenger and her colleagues (39, 40) had subjects perform a basic reaching task under two distinct conditions.

▶ **Condition 1**

Subjects started with their hand on a pad with their eyes fixed on a screen. When the subjects saw a white cross, they were instructed to reach out and grasp a cylinder positioned 16 inches (40 cm) in front of the pad. The instant their hand left the pad, a string of letters would appear on the screen. If the letters formed a word, the subjects were instructed to continue grabbing the cylinder, and, if the letters didn't form a word, the subjects were to bring their hand back to the pad.

▶ **Condition 2**

The experimental conditions were the same, with the only difference being that, instead of a white cross triggering the movement, a letter string would appear on the screen. If the letters formed a word, the subjects were to grab the cylinder, and, if they didn't, the subjects' hand was to remain on the pad.

In condition 1, processing verbs while moving resulted in reduced hand acceleration toward the cylinder compared to processing nouns. This suggests that the processing of action words while performing a motor action somehow interfered with the production of that movement. This makes sense if we go back to the brain imaging and recognize that the same motor regions are partly responsible for generating verb meaning and producing meaningful movement. Categorically, this is on par with patting your head and rubbing your tummy because both scenarios ask the motor cortex to entertain competing responsibilities simultaneously.

In condition 2, the results reversed, with verbs triggering a faster acceleration toward the cylinder compared to nouns. Moreover, the peak wrist accelerations were significantly faster in condition 2 than in condition 1. Thus, verbs served to activate or trigger the motor system when delivered right before the movement, with the opposite being true when delivered during the movement. From a coaching perspective, a very clear story emerges. Not only do we need to select contextually relevant verbs; we also need to recognize that the processing of those verbs is better served before the movement. If we take the evidence noted above and marry it with our discussion of attention, this recommendation should be intuitive. Thus, unless we are using a sound (e.g., pop, pop, pop) or a verb (e.g., push, push, push) to cue rhythm, we should be silent during the set.

LANGUAGE THAT MOVES US

In the previous section, we got a glimpse of the interaction between language and the motor system, clearly showing that action words are woven into our motor actions, forming a perfect partnership. However, this is where our story starts to get interesting, as researchers have now shown that the action in words can actually leak out into the motor system, automatically triggering the subtlest of movements. If you reflect on your lived experience, you already know this. Whether it was the lyrics in a song, the words in a speech, or the cues from a coach, all of us have had moments when language physically and emotionally *moved* us.

To establish this as a material phenomenon and not simply a turn of phrase, Victor Frak, Tatjana Nazir, and their colleagues (41, 42) formulated a series of studies. The researchers had subjects grip a force-instrumented cylinder while listening to verbs and nouns. Remarkably, the researchers observed that grip force would automatically increase when subjects heard an action verb; however, no such change was found in response to nouns. These results were extended when researchers showed that verbs embedded in affirmative sentences (e.g., Fiona *lifts* the dumbbells) triggered an increase in grip force, whereas the same verbs in negative sentences (e.g., Fiona doesn't *lift* the dumbbells) did not trigger an increase in grip force, suggesting, once again, that context matters. More recently, researchers showed that, when subjects stood on a force platform and read sentences conveying low physical effort (e.g., "The boxer is *carrying* his gym bag") and high physical effort (e.g., "The boxer is *carrying* his large punching bag"), side-to-side postural sway increased during the sentences that noted high physical effort (26).

Considering this evidence collectively, we can confidently state that verbs in context are the closest thing we have to speaking the language of the motor system. That said, I would like to draw your attention to one important fact. If you review the examples I have pulled from the papers or, better yet, reading the selection of papers yourself, you won't find any language that would be classified as internal. Thus, the evidence we have covered clearly aligns to the contents of external cues, generally, and the 3D cueing model, specifically. Moreover, this evidence lends itself to the topic of our next chapter, analogies, as many of the sentences used in the research require a motor comparison, which is to say that you are triggered to understand the motion depicted in the sentence by mapping it onto your own motor system; hence, the movement leakage noted above.

MANIPULATING DESCRIPTION

To close out our final *D*, I would like to briefly consider strategies for selecting and manipulating the action words within our cues. As previously noted, the motor system is clever and highly sensitive to the context with which a verb is delivered. Thus, the better a cue represents the biomechanical attributes of the movement we are trying to promote, the easier it will be for our brains to get the language to our limbs. While the misinformed coach may take this as an invitation to give their athletes a list of biomechanical rules, we know the limitations associated with this approach. Instead, we must hide the biomechanics in an attention-friendly cue, and we know that the best place to hide biomechanics is in the verb.

To illustrate this, let's deconstruct two plausible cues for the dumbbell bench press.

Cue 1

"Focus on **pushing** the dumbbells **toward** the ceiling"

Cue 2

"Focus on **punching** the dumbbells **through** the ceiling"

Before commenting, let's interrogate your own intuition about these cues (circle either answer).

Which cue would promote greater power production?	Cue 1	Cue 2
Which cue would promote greater dumbbell control?	Cue 1	Cue 2
Which cue triggers a stronger emotional response?	Cue 1	Cue 2

I would imagine that your intuition answered these questions quickly. And, based on everything we've discussed, this makes sense because language is embodied within the motor system responsible for giving it life. This is why language, especially action language, triggers a visceral response in us.

Now, for some deconstruction. What do you think of when you hear the word *punch*? Exactly, someone or something getting punched. And *push*? Much the same, someone or something getting pushed. Which word is faster? *Punch* suggests a fast movement with a short contact time, while *push* suggests a slower movement with a long contact time. By way of analogy, our brain maps the dominant context in which *punching* and *pushing* occur and quickly summons a motor response aligned to this interpretation of the verb. Thus, if I wanted to promote a slow, controlled movement, possibly because the athlete was a beginner or the load was very heavy, then I would select *push*. In contrast, if I wanted to advocate for a fast, violent movement, likely because I am chasing speed and power, then I would select *punch*. It's not that one verb is better than the other; rather, it is simply a case of identifying the best verb for the biomechanics you want to promote.

To ensure that we understand this concept, let's consider one more example. As you'll recall, the meaning of a verb can be modified by its neighbors within a sentence. Thus, there will be times when you need to shift *distance* or *direction* to modify the motor system's interpretation of the verb's meaning. For example, see if you can spot the technical difference in the following two sprint cues.

Cue 1

"Focus on <u>driving into</u> the ground"

Cue 2

"Focus on <u>driving off</u> the ground"

To help you, here are a few questions (circle either answer).

Which cue is better for athletes lacking force production?	Cue 1	Cue 2
Which cue promotes a shorter ground-contact time?	Cue 1	Cue 2
Which cue is better for athletes with a heavy ground contact?	Cue 1	Cue 2

As we can see, the verb is the same; however, by manipulating the preposition, the element of the cue that gives it *directionality*, we instantly shift the biomechanical feel. By "driving into" something, I am suggesting that the athlete's effort is in one direction, which likely would support greater force production *into* the ground. Conversely, by "driving off" something, I am suggesting that the athlete needs to quickly reverse direction after contact, which would likely support a shorter ground-contact time and possibly an improved expression of reactivity *off* the ground (i.e., a lighter touch).

As we can see, each *D* plays a role in crafting the biomechanics suggested within the cue. However, the *description*, the verb, gives the cue the power to turn words into actions. Thus, get the verb right, and you can manipulate *distance* and *direction* to tune the cue to the needs of the movement. So important is our ability to get these three *D*s to dance that we'll consider some final principles for consistently building the next best cue (see figure 5.2 for the 3D cueing model).

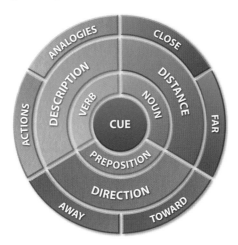

FIGURE 5.2 3D cueing model.

One, Two, or Three *D*s

Words are a vehicle used to impart meaning, a vessel for sharing ideas. Consequently, clear communication works only when coaches and athletes find common meaning in the language that fills the space between them. Ultimately, words are symbols with no inherent meaning other than what we assign them, which is why we have to be sensitive to the fact that people will understand and interpret meaning based on their own encyclopedia of experiences. Like most things, language is shaped by the environment, and, therefore, we cannot assume that the meaning intended is always the meaning received.

While no one expects the first cue to always be the right cue, we are responsible for adapting to our athletes' linguistic preferences and the context surrounding the movement we are teaching. Fortunately, the 3D cueing model was designed to support this kind of flexible coaching. However, knowing the principles behind each *D* doesn't mean your athletes will get the most out of your using this model. Thus, we will lay out principles for the effective application of the model.

PRINCIPLE 1: START WITH THREE

As we've already discussed, cues come in all shapes and sizes; some are short, some are long, some go boom, and some go bong. At the end of the day, it really isn't about the physical cue. Rather, it is about the meaning that can be extracted from the cue; meaning is what matters. Be this as it may, we have to start with the words, with the cue, and use our athlete's response as the feedback loop to sculpt our language until it fits. For this reason, when giving an athlete a cue for the first time, it is best to start with all three *D*s, reducing the likelihood of a mistranslation.

Here, you'll find two examples with explanations that we will leverage as we discuss principles for applying the 3D cueing model.

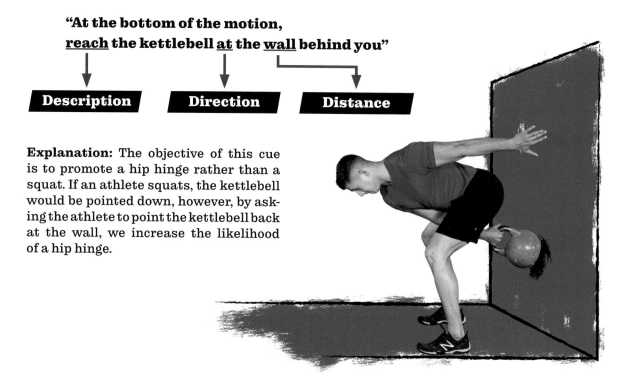

**"At the bottom of the motion,
reach the kettlebell at the wall behind you"**

Description   **Direction**   **Distance**

Explanation: The objective of this cue is to promote a hip hinge rather than a squat. If an athlete squats, the kettlebell would be pointed down, however, by asking the athlete to point the kettlebell back at the wall, we increase the likelihood of a hip hinge.

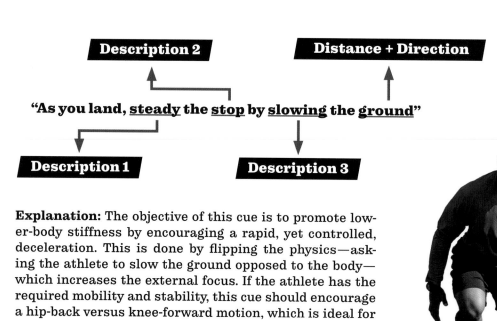

Description 2   **Distance + Direction**

"As you land, steady the stop by slowing the ground"

Description 1   **Description 3**

Explanation: The objective of this cue is to promote lower-body stiffness by encouraging a rapid, yet controlled, deceleration. This is done by flipping the physics—asking the athlete to slow the ground opposed to the body—which increases the external focus. If the athlete has the required mobility and stability, this cue should encourage a hip-back versus knee-forward motion, which is ideal for deceleration and knee health. We use three related verbs and a dash of alliteration to increase memorability and focus.

Now, it's your turn. Using the same format as earlier in the chapter, come up with two 3D cues of your own. Identify a movement and a target movement error or outcome. Use the last line to create an external cue that contains all three *D*s, labeling each *D* as I previously did by drawing a line connecting the target word(s) to the target *D*.

3D Cueing Practice 1

Movement name: _____

Movement error or outcome: _____

Cue: _____

Distance   Direction   Description

3D Cueing Practice 2

Movement name: _____

Movement error or outcome: _____

Cue: _____

Distance   Direction   Description

PRINCIPLE 2: SHIFT THE *D*'S

Once we've established what we might call the baseline cue, we can start to tune our language in the same way that you tune a guitar, one string at a time, or, in this case, one word at a time. First, though, a few points are necessary.

Point 1: Unless your cue backfires, triggering a counterproductive or harmful movement pattern, let your language marinate in your athlete's mind. While I have no rules about how to do this, I suggest you allow the athlete to try out the cue for at least two or three sets of a movement. This is your time to enhance your listening and observational skills, evaluating the marriage between the cue and the movement. Take this nonverbal evidence and any verbal feedback your athlete provides, and you should have all the information you need to know whether to invite the cue on a second date or move on.

Point 2: There are usually two circumstances where you will shift your language:

1. You have early evidence that your cue didn't hit the mark and you (a) decide to focus on the same movement error but with a new cue or (b) realize that you were cueing the wrong error and summon a new baseline cue. In the case of *b*, you go back to principle 1, and, in the case of *a*, you start shifting *D*s.

2. You have been using a cue to good effect; however, you notice that the potency is wearing off, what we might call cue fatigue. Still wanting to focus on a specific portion of the pattern, you want to come up with a fresh cue that maintains the desired focus. Again, in this circumstance, you will start shifting *D*s.

What do I mean by shifting *D*s? Simple. You will refresh your cue by introducing a new action word, changing the directionality of the cue, manipulating the focus distance, or using any combination thereof. Note that there are no rules here. You can shift one of the *D*s or make changes to all three. You may also come up with a brand-new cue; however, the principle still holds because you are still shifting the *D*s.

Here is a clever way to think about this. Imagine a combination padlock, one with three rotating number dials. Now, imagine that each one of those dials represents one of our *D*s. In the case of your baseline cue, you are making an educated guess around the right combination of *distance*, *direction*, and *description*. If you get the *D*s correct, you will see the pattern unlock and a new movement emerge; however, if the *D*s are wrong (for that athlete), the pattern won't free itself. Thus, as you would with any lock, you simply try a new combination of *D*s until the right pattern is released (see figure 5.3).

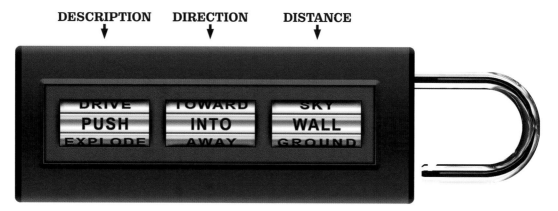

FIGURE 5.3   Padlock analogy for the application of the 3D cueing model.

Using these same cues, let's see what this looks like in practice.

Baseline Cue

"At the bottom of the motion, <u>reach</u> the kettlebell <u>at</u> the <u>wall</u> behind you"

Cue option 1

"At the bottom of the motion, <u>push</u> the kettlebell <u>into</u> the <u>wall</u> behind you"

Cue option 2

"At the end of the motion, <u>stretch</u> the bottom of the bell <u>away</u> from your shirt <u>collar</u>"

 the

Baseline Cue

"As you land, <u>steady</u> and <u>stop</u> by <u>slowing</u> the <u>ground</u>"

Cue option 1

"As you land, <u>decelerate</u> the <u>drop</u>"

Cue option 2

"As you land, <u>absorb</u> the <u>floor</u>"

It's your turn again. Taking your two baseline cues from the previous section, see if you can come up with two additional options by switching the *D*s. There's one rule, though: Only write down cues you'd actually use.

3D Cueing Practice 1

Movement 1 | Baseline cue: _____

Movement 1 | Cue option 1: _____

Movement 1 | Cue option 2: _____

3D Cueing Practice 2

Movement 2 | Baseline cue: _____

Movement 2 | Cue option 1: _____

Movement 2 | Cue option 2: _____

PRINCIPLE 3: SHORTEN AND SEE

If you've used the first two principles effectively, then we can assume you have established one or more effective cues for the pattern you are trying to promote. Another way to think of this is that you've established shared meaning with your athlete. Through words, you have implanted a movement idea in your athlete's head, and they have fully accepted it. At this point, we can start to trim the cue or consolidate it, maintaining meaning while reducing any unnecessary taxation on working memory. Notably, by shortening the cue, we can elevate the status of the verb, prioritizing the action in the athlete's mind. Moreover, we can explore various linguistic tricks, such as alliteration and rhyme, to increase mental stickiness (23). This is all in service of creating a cue that can deliver a short, punchy reminder, especially in the midst of competition.

Let's revisit our cues once more to see if we can shorten and sharpen the language. You will notice that I have pulled one cue for the kettlebell swing and one for the lateral bound.

Baseline Cue

"At the bottom of the motion, <u>push</u> the kettlebell <u>into</u> the <u>wall</u> behind you"

Shortened Cue

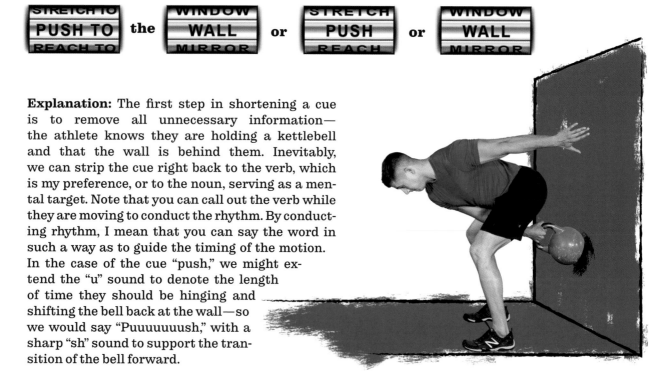

STRETCH TO / **PUSH TO** / REACH TO   **the**   WINDOW / **WALL** / MIRROR   **or**   STRETCH / **PUSH** / REACH   **or**   WINDOW / **WALL** / MIRROR

Explanation: The first step in shortening a cue is to remove all unnecessary information—the athlete knows they are holding a kettlebell and that the wall is behind them. Inevitably, we can strip the cue right back to the verb, which is my preference, or to the noun, serving as a mental target. Note that you can call out the verb while they are moving to conduct the rhythm. By conducting rhythm, I mean that you can say the word in such a way as to guide the timing of the motion. In the case of the cue "push," we might extend the "u" sound to denote the length of time they should be hinging and shifting the bell back at the wall—so we would say "Puuuuuuush," with a sharp "sh" sound to support the transition of the bell forward.

Alliteration upgrade: "<u>Push</u>, <u>Punch</u>, and <u>Pause</u>"

Explanation: This cue expands meaning without expanding word count. <u>Push</u> maps to our original cue, <u>punch</u> references the forward acceleration of the kettlebell, and <u>pause</u> is highlighting the moment at the top of the motion where the bell should appear to float. This strategy works very well for bi-phasic movements (i.e., an up and down, an eccentric and concentric, a shortening and lengthening), especially those movements that are continuous, speed dependent, and rhythmical.

Rhyme upgrade: "<u>Tap</u> and <u>snap</u>"

Explanation: Again, we are expanding the cues meaning, as <u>tap</u> is now referencing the simulated idea of <u>tapping</u> a wall, supporting the intent of our original cue, and then <u>snapping</u> references the forward projection of the bell and the sense that the upper- and lower-body snap together in a vertical position to complete the top of the swing.

Baseline Cue

"As you land, <u>steady</u> and <u>stop</u> by <u>slowing</u> the <u>ground</u>"

Shortened Cue

 the ground or

Explanation: Within our shortened cue, we can strip away "as you land," as the athlete would now be well aware that this is the portion of the movement being targeting. Similarly, we no longer need three words to describe how the athlete should land. Instead, we can select the word that best captures the interaction between the athlete and the ground or, simpler still, the interaction itself (knowing the athlete is aware the reference point is the ground.

Alliteration upgrade: "<u>Stiffen</u>, <u>Steady</u>, and <u>Stop</u>"

Explanation: We see how alliteration can be used to wrap the phases of a movement in a memorable form. In this case, <u>stiffen</u> is the feeling we want the athlete to have as they land; <u>steady</u> encourages a controlled decent, and <u>stop</u> puts the why in the what by outlining the movement goal.

Rhyme upgrade: "<u>Stop</u> the <u>drop</u>"

Explanation: Here we use rhyme to pump up memorability without losing meaning. In this case, the word <u>stop</u> suggests a fairly abrupt end to motion. The emotion and power of the cue is also subtly enhanced by using the word <u>drop</u>, which is cousins with the word <u>fall</u>, both suggesting an uncontrolled decent towards the floor. Thus, "<u>stop the drop</u>" has a strong sense of urgency, which is important if one needs to land and quickly move in another direction.

Now, your turn. Taking one of your baseline cues from the previous section, see if you can come up with two new shortened cues, taking advantage of alliteration and rhyme where it makes sense. There's still one rule: Only write down cues you'd actually use.

3D Cueing Practice 1

Movement 1 | Baseline cue: _____

Movement 1 | Cue option 1: _____

Movement 1 | Cue option 2: _____

3D Cueing Practice 2

Movement 2 | Baseline cue: _____

Movement 2 | Cue option 1: _____

Movement 2 | Cue option 2: _____

As you can see, our shortened cues would provide little value had we not started with our original 3D cue. However, once a layer of meaning has been established, coaches can shorten and sharpen language, improving transmission speed, while also reducing storage requirements. Notably, not only is this valuable for coaching individual athletes; this same principle can serve team sports when coaches are trying to identify and develop common language around plays and on-field calls—short and sharp leaves a mark.

A final point here. The ultimate sign of an effective cue is the rate at which it becomes redundant with the movement itself. Meaning, the quicker the cue infects the mind and shifts the movement to a new normal, the quicker the athlete can discard the excess verbal packaging. In a way, we can think of cues as fuel for movement, where the best cues leave limited cognitive pollution, while providing a sustainable source of informational energy to the motor system. In the end, we want our athletes to become independent movers through language that supports their learning journey, rather than being a source of dependence.

PART 2: CUE TIPS

To help frame this section, I would like to first pause and address some potential questions that might be rolling around in your head. For starters, you have probably noticed that, while I use quite a bit of analogy within the narrative of this book, I have yet to invite analogies to participate in our cueing examples. There's a simple explanation for this. We needed to first establish an understanding of the 3D cueing model and using what I call **real-world cues**, or cues that reference the physical environment around the athletes, before we can appreciate the power of **simulated cues**, or cues that leverage analogy to draw a connection between a movement and a virtual scenario that lives within the athlete's mind. As you'll notice, analogies are so fundamental to motor learning that I have dedicated the entirety of chapter 6 to them.

Second, as you started designing your own cues using some of the strategies throughout this book, my guess is that you hit a number of roadblocks with certain movements or specific errors. Meaning, you identified patterns where you felt you had no other choice but to deploy an internal cue. For example, how would you use an external cue to promote hip extension during a glute bridge or a kettlebell swing? Similarly, how would you talk about things like dorsiflexion and hip flexion in sprinting or spine position in squatting? These movements challenged me for years. The reason these movements puzzle us is because they have no obvious connection to an environmental feature, which leaves us to deploy cues like "hips to the sky" or "keep your spine long," which purists may dismiss for their internal essence. Admittedly, the vast majority of the cues I've used so far reference the whole movement and hide technical information within the formulation of the cue; however, I recognize that you're still going to want linguistic strategies for dealing with part of a motion. Don't fret because the following sections are designed to give you the detail about the detail. Thus, in the spirit of speed dating, we will go on a to-the-point tour of my favorite cue tips, which should elevate your command of even the most nuanced of movements.

Converting Cues

As we discussed in chapter 4, it's not that we have to completely dispose of all internal language. That would be ludicrous. Rather, it is a matter of knowing where and when to put it within the learning narrative. In my own work, if I use internal language, it falls within the DESCRIBE it portion of the coaching loop or, off the field, in the context of a video analysis session. Despite having a home for internal language, there are still those tricky features of a movement—often, isolated joint motion—that make it difficult for us "external cuers" to ensure that the last idea entering our athletes' heads stays beyond the perimeter of their body.

To illustrate this, try to come up with an external cue for the following movement scenarios. You can assume that the coach has explained the biomechanical error using internal language (DESCRIBE it); however, they want to identify an external cue (CUE it) that the athlete can use to guide movement execution. Again, the same rule applies: Write down only cues you'd actually use.

Scenario 1

A coach is working with an athlete on the quality of their landing mechanics during a vertical jump (landing on two legs). The coach notices that the athlete is always landing on their toes, causing them to lose balance and step forward. The coach wants to come up with an external cue, rather than simply saying "dorsiflex your ankles."

External cue: _____

Scenario 2

A coach is working with an athlete on their spinal position during the first 10 yards (9 m) of an acceleration sprint. The coach has stayed away from saying things like "chest up," "spine straight," or "back flat"; however, the coach's current external cues, "stay long" and "stay straight," aren't working because the athlete is still very flexed during the sprint. The coach wants to come up with an external cue but is struggling for ideas.

External cue: _____

If you've never attempted this before, I can empathize with any struggles you may have encountered. However, with a quick shift of perspective, we can move from feeling limited to limitless, and all it takes is some cloth and a bit of tape.

Cue Cloth

When I started out as a coach, I was obsessed with coaching ankle dorsiflexion. Because this neutral ankle position is mechanically advantageous for absorbing and producing force, you would often hear me shouting "toes up" or "ankles locked" when teaching landing mechanics during jumping or foot strike during sprinting. However, it wasn't long after I read Gabriele Wulf's 1998 paper that I started reevaluating this practice and exploring new ways to externally cue.

While whole-body external cues directed at "pushing the ground" or "exploding through the barbell" were intuitive, individual joint corrections were less so. In trying to solve this problem, I kept going back to the same question: How do you cue joint motion without mentioning the joint? Inevitably, I reflected on the cues that Wulf had used in her early balance studies, "keep your feet at the same height" versus "keep the markers at the same height," and recognized that an external cue can not only be subtle; it can also be quite close to the body.

As it turns out, my athletes had been literally wearing the solution to my cueing conundrum all along. Clothing is a perfect surrogate for referencing joint motion when you don't want to mention the joint. Shortly after this realization made its way into my cueing lineup, "toes up" was replaced by "laces up," and "ankles locked" became "laces locked to socks." As fashion continued to inform my language, I quickly found that most hip movements could be prompted by referencing a "belt buckle," a "waistband," or "pockets"; hip extension converted to "lead with your belt buckle" or "proud pockets"; and hip flexion, referencing the waistband, turned into "bow with your band" or "bow with your buckle." Similarly, when talking about a neutral spine, we can upgrade our language by saying "zip up your jacket"; "tall T-shirt"; "tension through your top"; or, simply, "stand proud"—no clothing required. By using everyday clothing items, we can simplify the movement message, stay just beyond the perimeter of the body, and articulate a clear external goal for the subtlest of movements.

"Tall T-shirt"

"Lead with your belt buckle"

While clothing is a valuable asset in all cueing toolboxes, it's not the only cue tool we can use to nudge nuance out of the motor system. To the contrary, you may find that using a few strips of sticky tape is an even better strategy for getting your athletes out of that movement slump.

Cue Tape

I first heard about using tape to cue movement after watching a video that I believe was posted by Dr. Will Wu, a professor at California State University, Long Beach, who has done extensive work on cueing and performance. In the video, Dr. Wu showed how you can use tape on the joints to help an athlete simplify a movement problem while maintaining an external focus. The second I saw this video, my mind was flooded with ideas and former athletes who I knew would've benefited from this strategy. I quickly went to work applying this new method with my athletes.

One of the most profound movement changes I've ever observed came off the back of using tape to sort out a posture issue during a sprint start. We were a few weeks out from the NFL Combine, and this athlete was still exiting his start with a flexed posture, which suffocated the force he would otherwise have access to during his first two strides. We had tried every cue I could come up with, and nothing could break this guy out of his hunchback. That's when I pulled out two strips of sticky tape.

At this point, the athlete was up for anything, so I explained that we were going to try a slightly different approach to straightening out his posture. I put a strip of tape across his upper back, from shoulder to shoulder, and a second strip of tape across his low back, just above his waistband (I used the same athletic tape one would use to wrap or strap an ankle). I then said two things to the athlete: (a) "Show me how you'd get these two pieces of tape closer together," to which he responded by extending his back and getting taller. (b) "Show me how you would get these two pieces of tape farther away from each other," to which he responded by flexing his back. Seeing as the athlete did exactly what I expected, I set up the cue for our next sprint: "OK, on our next sprint start, I want you to focus on smashing those two pieces of tape together as you explode off the line." The athlete smirked, suggesting that he knew what I was up to, and he got into his three-point stance. As I watched, I crossed my fingers, hoping this would work. Not long after he started to move, the verdict was in. Not only did he get out of his stance faster, at least, by my assessment; he did so by transitioning into the elusive neutral-spine position we'd been chasing for weeks. As he walked back, he had the kind of grin on his face that told me he had felt what I had seen—the lightbulb was on.

While I had found success using this approach long before any research emerged, I was very pleased when James Becker and Will Wu (43) published a pilot study supporting the efficacy of this strategy. Working with four elite high jumpers who had been identified as needing to improve posture during their run-up, the researchers had the athletes perform a baseline jump using their normal focus strategy and a series of intervention jumps, using a novel cueing strategy (all jumps were performed at a standard bar height that the athletes were used to using in training). Specifically, the researchers placed a piece of athletic tape on each athlete's shirt, just in front of their belly button, and cued the athletes to "lead with the tape" as they entered the curve of the run-up. After performing two practice trials with the cue, the athletes performed a third repetition, which served as a post-measurement. Using a suite of biomechanical assessments, the results showed that the cue tape promoted an upright posture, increased horizontal velocity into the penultimate step, and increased vertical velocity at the end of takeoff. All told, this evidence echoed my own experience using tape and established a solid foundation for more research to be done (e.g., see Abdollahipour et al. (1), for a study using a tape marker to improve an aerial maneuver in gymnastics, and De Giorgio et al. (12), for a novel study using colored cleats to promote improved soccer skills).

While we will reference the use of tape again in our final three chapters, I want to leave you with a very simple strategy for the effective application of cue tape. In my experience, you will never need more than one or two pieces of tape for any given cueing scenario. Typically, you will use one piece of tape when you want to align a given joint or body segment with an environmental feature and two pieces of tape when you want to encourage a specific technical orientation between two joints in the body. Thus, if I want superior hip flexion and knee drive during sprinting, I can put a piece of tape on the athletes' knees and tell them to "push the tape to the finish." Similarly, going back to our dorsiflexion example, I could easily put a piece of tape on the athletes' laces and tell them "tape to the clouds." In contrast, if I want alignment within the body, say a neutral spine during a hip-hinge motion, I could put a piece of tape on their upper and lower back and simply tell the athletes to "keep the tape aligned" or "keep the tape close" during the movement. We could continue like this, but, hopefully, these examples illuminate the concept well enough for you to apply it to your own movement scenarios.

PART 3: CLARIFYING INTERNAL CUES

Over the years, I have had the opportunity to entertain many a challenging question concerning the possible benefits of an internal focus. Coming from a field whose language is borrowed from kinesiology and anatomy, I am never surprised when people look for holes in the evidence, hoping to find that one case when the internal outperforms the external. However, to date, I have yet to find an argument or article that provides compelling evidence against the thesis of this book.

The truth is, there really is no need to engage in an internal versus external debate, as both language categories have a role in our coaching loop. As Rob Gray often says on the *Perception & Action* podcast, internal language is good for *describing* movement (the *what*), and external language is good for *coaching* it (the *how*). For this reason, I have maintained an "as-needed" policy on internal language in the DESCRIBE it portion of the coaching loop, leaving external language to fully occupy the CUE it slot. That said, if I were you, I would still want to familiarize myself with the strongest arguments in support of allowing internal cues to lead the mind through movement. Hence, the following section will outline three of the most interesting questions I have received.

Mind–Muscle Connection

Question 1

Should internal cues be used to promote muscle growth (hypertrophy) since research has shown that they increase muscle activation to a greater degree than external cues?

I love this question, as it brings me back to my coaching roots, as many of my earliest ideas around cueing came from working with bodybuilders and seeing how well they responded to what I now realize were internal cues. To answer this question, however, we need to understand that there are two primary pathways to muscle growth: a tension-mediated pathway and a metabolic-mediated pathway (28). The tension-mediated pathway benefits from the ability to generate greater tension through the muscle by way of lifting a heavy mass or accelerating that mass faster, while the metabolic-mediated pathway benefits from increased muscle activation associated with the high-volume, high-fatigue lifting protocols common to bodybuilding.

The evidence we have discussed clearly shows that an external focus leads to increased movement force (15, 18), increased movement speed (27), increased movement endurance (4, 17), and improved movement kinematics (13, 14, 25), while an internal focus has been shown to increase muscle activation (6, 7) beyond that of an external focus. This latter finding has led a number of authors to advocate for internal-focus instructions during strength training, citing the idea of a mind–muscle connection, especially if the goal is to increase lean-muscle mass (5, 24).

While there is no evidence that an internal focus supports the maximal expression of strength, power, or speed, there is one study that points to a possible benefit of an internal focus to upper-body muscle hypertrophy. Dr. Brad Schoenfeld and colleagues (44) had 30 untrained males engage in a strength-training study (three sessions a week and four sets of 8-12 repetitions per exercise) that consisted of performing a standing biceps curl and seated leg press using either an internal focus ("squeeze the muscle") or an external focus ("get the weight up"). Thus, the only difference in the two groups was the consistent use of the internal or external cue. After eight weeks, the results showed that the internal-focus group did achieve larger gains in upper-body muscle hypertrophy; however, no such differences emerged in the lower body. There were no differences in strength gains; however, the absolute scores showed that the lower-body gains were higher in the external-focus group, with the opposite being true for upper-body gains.

So how do we balance this finding with everything we've discussed so far? Simple. Let the evidence plus your movement goals guide your strategy. If your athlete is performing a single-joint exercise and you want to acutely increase local muscle activation, then you could argue that an internal focus would be acceptable, and maybe even advisable, especially for the upper body. However, the second you shift to a multijoint movement and strength, power, speed, or movement efficiency becomes your goal, the evidence clearly shows that you should trust in an external focus.

Expert Advice

Question 2

As one's experience increases, isn't it necessary to provide internal cues, especially if nuanced technical refinements are desired?

This is a tricky question; however, I believe the evidence can help us get close to an answer. First, research has consistently shown that highly experienced athletes are less sensitive to the differences between internal and external cues than those with less or no experience (i.e., novices). Practically speaking, this means that, when you have an expert perform their skill using either their normal focus, an internal focus, or an external focus, there is a growing body of evidence showing no difference between some or all of the conditions (e.g.,

11, 29). For example, my own research (45) showed that highly experienced sprinters responded similarly to no instructions ("perform to the best of your ability"), an internal focus ("focus on driving your legs back as explosively as you can"), and an external focus ("focus on driving the ground back as explosively as you can") when asked to sprint 10 m (11 yards). Wulf (29) had a similar response from a group of Cirque du Soleil acrobats performing a basic balance task while on a force platform.

So how do we explain these null findings? Is there something about being an expert that makes a person immune to the effects of internal cues? Or is it possible that experts might even benefit from focusing internally? Well, no, not exactly, as we've already covered a number of studies showing that internal cues can be just as detrimental to experts as they are to novices (e.g., 16, 30). So, what now? Well, I believe there are two ways to examine the null findings observed by Wulf and my own research team. First, any time you work with experts, especially over the brief period of one testing session, you have to recognize that there is a high likelihood of observing a **ceiling effect**, or the phenomenon where the performance of an individual is already so high that any changes prompted by the cues would be virtually undetectable within one session. Considering the small margins observed in elite sprint finals, it wouldn't be unreasonable to explain my findings through this lens.

A second explanation, which I outline in "Experience Level Influences the Effect of Attentional Focus on Sprint Performance," is this idea of abstraction, which presupposes that highly experienced athletes are better able to shed a cue's verbal carcass and extract its core meaning, regardless of whether the cue was internal or external. Thus, rather than playing servant to the exact phrase, the athlete interprets the broader meaning, converting internal or external language into the common mental currency they normally use when performing that movement and, hence, the reason the studies, including my own, examining this phenomenon have found that the control condition results in the same outcome as the cued conditions. Practically speaking, when we cued our sprinters to "drive your legs" versus "drive the ground," they could have intuited the same meaning from both cues; in essence, they got the gist (10). Now, this shouldn't be taken as an invitation to inundate expert athletes with internal cues because there is no evidence suggesting they respond better to them. Rather, the way I think about this is that expert athletes' movements are so well engrained that they are less susceptible to the performance degradation commonly associated with an internal focus. In contrast, novices depend far more on a literal reading of the cue and, therefore, are less likely to reinterpret the meaning, allowing them to reap the rewards of an external focus and, equally, the penalties of an internal focus.

If you're still wondering about those nuanced technical refinements, I would remind you that we can still outline those changes during a video analysis session or during the DESCRIBE it and DEBRIEF it sections of our coaching loop, using the clothing- and tape-based strategies that we previously noted to capture technical nuance in the CUE it section. Moreover, I believe you'll find our discussion of analogies in chapter 6 quite illuminating when it comes to the level of nuance you can pack into a customized cue.

Body Awareness

Question 3

Don't we need body awareness to develop and refine movement patterns? If so, isn't this a form of internal focus, as I'm focusing on how my body feels?

Without fail, when I give a presentation on cueing, someone will raise their hand and ask my opinion about body awareness, with an undertone that suggests they think my position on internal cueing would place me in opposition to mental states promoting self-awareness. To the contrary, I think body awareness is paramount to an athlete's overall movement health and should be included in any holistic learning environment. And I can hold this view because body awareness is not the same thing as an internal cue, despite what first impressions might suggest.

When we give an internal or external cue, we are asking the motor system to do something. In contrast, when we ask athletes to be aware, we are asking them to observe what the motor system has done. Thus, awareness requires something to have taken place, or how else would you be aware of it? Sometimes, in workshops, I will explain this as command-based cues (top down: projecting a sensory goal out into the motor system), the ones we've been discussing, versus notice-based cues, those of the awareness variety (bottom up: take an inventory of the just-experienced sensory episode). In practice, I am a huge fan of building body awareness through a process of establishing a shared vocabulary. This involves working with the athlete to generate a series of notice-based cues that describe how a movement feels in its totality. (McPherson, Collins, and Morris (46) refer to these cues as holistic or rhythm based; see also (2).) The common feature is that they are often monosyllabic words referencing the spatiotemporal signature of the whole movement. For example, following is a list of notice-based cues I use to help athletes describe how they felt during a sprint.

Light	*Heavy*
Quick	*Slow*
Relaxed	*Stiff*
Loose	*Tight*
Balanced	*Unbalanced*
Neutral	*Rotated*
Lengthened	*Compressed*
Tall or long	*Short*
Big	*Small*

When I first apply this approach, I will ask targeted questions during the DEBRIEF it portion of the coaching loop: "Did your contacts feel light or heavy?" "Did your hips feel loose or tight?" "Did your trunk feel tall or short?" and so on. I have found this approach preferable to simply asking the athletes "How did you feel?" which typically receives a barely audible "Fine." With time, the athletes will take on this vocabulary, possibly including their own descriptive language, which allows for rich discussions following each repetition.

Notably, as the experience level of an athlete improves, we can start using feeling- or emotion-based language in a similar capacity as we would the external cues we've discussed to this point. For example, I might cue an athlete to feel long, light, or loose on their next repetition. Now, this does not provide any direct information about the mechanics required to achieve such a sensory state and, thus, should not be confused with an internal focus. In contrast, this defines a sensory end point, the state or feeling you want to achieve during or at the end of the movement. Thus, just as gravity provides feedback about how effective we are on our bicycle, these feeling- or emotion-based words (including our action verbs) can provide real-time feedback on how one is organizing their movement, allowing the athlete to self-correct and explore until feeling and movement become one.

SUMMARY

Cues are the vehicle we use to navigate the terrain of the mind in hopes that we will arrive at a desired movement destination. However, before we can select the appropriate vehicle, we must first identify the movement end state we desire. To do this, we must be precise and ever evolving in our ability to prioritize the physical qualities to be trained and the movement patterns to be coached. By deploying the three Ps and leveraging our principle of positions before patterns, we increase the odds of identifying the right movement destination.

With our destination in mind, we have the information needed to select the best cue for the trip. However, like any journey, there will be unknowns along the way, and we need to be prepared to adapt. Hence, if a cue falls flat or runs out of gas, we need to have the right tools to get our cue back on track. I shared such a tool kit in the form of our 3D cueing model, where *distance*, *direction*, and *description* serve as the genetic material that turns mere words into motor actions. With the three *D*s in mind, we discussed three principles for effectively applying this model: *start with three*, *shift the D*, and *shorten and see*. These three principles operate like a user's manual, ensuring your athletes get the most out of your application of the 3D cueing model.

Finally, we tapped our inner MacGyver and discussed how we can use clothing and tape to capture the nuance and subtlety offered within the motor system. Like Bear Grylls with a Swiss Army knife, you will be able to use cloth and a few strips of sticky tape to nudge the most challenging of movements with the clearest of cues. However, to borrow the words of philosopher Alfred Korzybski, we know that "the map is not the territory" and that there are plenty of unknowns waiting to be known. Be this as it may, we can use today's knowledge to elevate the good in our coaching while eradicating the bad, moving the likelihood of our success from chance to choice.

In support of this last point, we will venture to the final stop on our journey and entertain a discussion on the use of analogies and our human capacity to understand the new in terms of the old. We will venture into the world of the imagination and explore what is possible when we use relatable experiences to trigger remarkable movements.

GOING ANALOG

6

Analogies: A Primer

The language we've considered to this point has, by all accounts, been literal in nature. By this I mean that the external cues I've shared and encouraged you to create have emphasized literal features of the athletes' environment: "move the *bar* here," "kick the *ball* there," "push toward the *ceiling*," or "drive off the *line*." And, granted, cues like "push the ground away" and "blast through the bar" require some mental abstraction (seeing as one can't literally push the ground away or actually blast through a bar), but the language itself is dressed in the literal.

However, you and I both know that literal doesn't always cut it. This is especially true when you're teaching an athlete, especially a younger athlete, a movement for the first time. Invariably, you find yourself saying things like "move *as if*," "it's *kind of like*," or "have you *ever seen*" in an attempt to help your athlete understand the present in terms of their past. This is why a coach might trade "be stiff" for "stiff as a board," "get long" for "get long like LeBron," or "pop off the ground" for "pop like a pogo stick" because each turn of phrase explains the movement feature—be stiff, get long, or pop off—in terms of someone or something the athlete already knows—a board, LeBron, a pogo stick. And, while it can feel like we're disappointing our professors by reverting to such commonplace language, we're all too familiar with the look a good analogy gets, the one that, if it could speak, would say "Oh, I get it" or "Now, I know what you mean."

So what is it about this nonliteral language that can be so helpful in unlocking the complexities of movement? How is it that athletes can improve their takeoff during acceleration by simply pretending they're a jet or, equally, clean up their hip hinge during a deadlift by imagining they're holding two heavy bags of groceries while trying to close a car door? The answer to this question is firmly grounded in the mind's innate ability to understand the new in terms of the old or the novel in terms of the known, which is to say, the mind's capacity for analogy.

Analogy and its friends, metaphor, simile, and idiom, are comparisons between two things based on some shared quality or relationship. And, while this chapter will focus on verbal analogies, you can be sure that the mind uses analogy in virtually every moment when meaning is required. How else would you know that handles are for pulling, knobs are for twisting, buttons are for pressing, stairs are for walking, and seats are for sitting? Surely, there was a moment when you first came into contact with each of these worldly items and had to make a decision about what to do. Invariably, by chance or choice, Mom or Dad, you learned how to use these everyday objects, and I would guess that you no longer pull when you see a knob or twist when you see a handle. Instead, your mind references a long history of knobs and handles and, by way of analogy, says "this is kind of like that" and proceeds to act as if "this" is in fact "that."

As you will see, an analogy is a sort of mental molecule that helps us make meaning. In the same way that mitochondria power our cells, analogies power our minds, allowing us to use association and comparison to expand and refine both our knowledge of the world and the way we move through it. However, before we dive into our discussion of how to design movement-centric analogies, it is instructive to first consider how the mind has come to depend on these quick-witted meaning makers. In doing so, you'll come to understand how words become inseparable from the thoughts, images, and emotions they incite and, similarly, how it is that a single phrase can clarify things for some and completely confuse others.

A disclaimer, however, is necessary before we continue. I have taken liberties with the depth we will travel to acquire an understanding of how our minds came to depend on analogies for making meaning. As such, those who would like to stay in the shallows and progress to the practical are encouraged to jump ahead in this chapter to Part 1: Mental Maps.

Something From Nothing

Swiss-born Jean Piaget is by all accounts the most influential developmental psychologist of his era. Author of countless books, Piaget is most well known for his theories on cognitive development, which, to this day, influence how psychologists think about our transition from wordless ground dwellers to upright storytellers. Of interest to us, is Piaget's work on the genesis of language and the process by which our potential for speech is realized.

In their book, *The Psychology of the Child*, Piaget and Inhelder insightfully note that "if the child partly explains the adult, it can also be said that each period of his development partly explains the periods that follow" (20). Thus, if we want to look under the hood of language, we must first understand the developmental tools we use to build it.

Unlike many mammals in the animal kingdom, we come into this world helpless and completely dependent on our parents. When you consider that a baby giraffe is walking within an hour of its birth, it's amazing that animals like ourselves, with no meaningful way to communicate or escape a potential predator, have done so well. However, not all is lost, as what we give up with delayed speech and movement, we gain back in the form of one of the most powerful learning tool kits on earth.

For starters, while born language-less, we are delivered with a number of helpful reflexes. Notably, these include the sucking reflex, where babies reflexively suck when the roof of their mouth is touched, and the grasping reflex, where babies reflexively grab anything that brushes the palm of their hand. These reflexes, as well as a handful of others, provide babies with a "welcome to this world" starter kit and serve as the seedlings from which complex movement and language emerge.

Working alongside these reflexes is a broad network of sensory tools: sight, smell, hearing, taste, and touch, just to name a few. These senses provide babies with a front-row seat to reality, helping them construct the world they will soon star in, one experience at a time. At this early stage of development, however, babies have limited ability to consider an experience, which is to say, think about it, unless they are in the midst of it. Even then, babies don't stay focused for long because their attention has the novelty-seeking dial turned way up. This is why telling babies to stop crying is wasted breath, while rattling a new toy in front of them is quite effective. So the interesting question is how do babies go from having nothing in their minds to something on their minds?

To answer this question, ask yourself this: How would you come to recognize and interact with a world, let alone speak and think about it, without a substantial base of experiences within it? Logic suggests you wouldn't. Hence, when babies are born, they spend their first year, and all their years thereafter, interrogating their surroundings and building sensory-motor representations based on the environment from which they're derived. To put it another way, just as vinyl records and cassette tapes are analog versions of an artist's recording, our sensory-motor system builds analog versions of our lived experience, providing babies with the mental representations, or the memories, required to support language. To brighten this idea, consider the following observations that chart a course from the first time babies see a banana to the first time they can say the word *banana*.

▶ **Observation 1**

Over a series of distinct moments, babies will come to know that bananas are yellow (sight) with a smooth skin and a textured core (touch). They have a subtly sweet aroma (smell) and flavor (taste), and, when you bite them, they make no noise (sound). These experiences amalgamate to first define *banana* in the language of babies' senses.

▶ **Observation 2**

In time, babies will come to understand a banana in terms of their sensory experience of it. Hence, babies might see a banana and start to cry for it because the sight of the fruit hits replay on the sensory recording in their heads, alerting them to their desire to relive this sensory experience.

▶ **Observation 3**

Once the concept of banana is adequately represented in babies' minds, they will be able to cry for the fruit even when one isn't present because, now, the idea of a banana lives beyond their experience of it. This is one of the reasons the transition from age two to three is called the "terrible twos"; toddlers are developing concepts of the things they want faster than they can verbalize that they want them.

▶ **Observation 4**

Inevitably, babies realize that they can communicate their desire by pointing at or bringing the banana to their parents, a far better solution for everyone involved. Fast-forward, and the pointing that grew out of crying has now matured into the spoken word *banana* or, more than likely, *ba* or *nana*, at first.

This example highlights a couple of key features about development. For one, in the early years of life, action is a surrogate for thinking, as it is strictly through our actions that we can sample the world, building the mental representations we will inevitably require to speak about and interact within it. Once these actions fill up the mind's vinyl collection with enough sensory information, we can hit playback and start mashing up our own ideas and concepts through thought. At this point, our external world has become integrated into our internal world, which produces the necessary scaffolding for language to emerge.

To summarize and fill in a few gaps, we come into this world with reflexes that incite movement. Armed with our senses, this reactive movement kick-starts our exploration of the world and the sensory information it offers. With each experience, sensory information is analogized into our nerves, creating mental representations of the world that allow us to predict future states (e.g., when you see an apple and a banana, your mind quickly computes the sensory experience tagged to eating each type of fruit, and you inevitably choose the piece of fruit you prefer). In time, we trade in our reflexive movement for voluntary actions, accelerating our ability to bottle up new sensory experiences. We inevitably learn that we can mimic others or play make-believe, test-driving what it's like to be a mommy, daddy, doctor, or dog. This child's play is anything but, as each symbolic action is an attempt to further analogize a lived experience into a considered thought. In time, our language emerges and is tagged to these stored experiences, leaving the two indistinguishable from one another. In the end, we can state that experience is analogous to our sense of it, sense is analogous to our thought of it, and thought is analogous to our language for it. The gravity of this means that it is analogy all the way down and that language is only as meaningful as the sensory experiences it represents.

The Offspring of Experience

If language is linked to and defined by the experiences it mirrors, then we would expect to see evidence for this within the brain. A reasonable hypothesis might be that, if action precedes language, which it does, and language is built from the perceptions associated with those actions, which it is, then the brain regions responsible for action and perception would overlap with those responsible for understanding language. For this hypothesis to be true, however, we would want to see evidence that, when we hear an analogy such as

"Get out of the blocks as if a venomous snake is right behind you," the visual and motor regions of your brain burst into action, as if this fiction were indeed fact.

In his witty and accessible book, *Louder Than Words*, Benjamin Bergen takes us on an epic journey through the canals of comprehension, and, in doing so, provides compelling evidence that the way our minds make meaning is by "simulating what it would be like to experience the things that language describes" (3). And, when Bergen uses the term *simulation*, or, more specifically, **embodied simulation**, he doesn't mean this in the metaphorical sense; he literally means that, when "we listen to or read sentences, we simulate seeing the scenes and performing the actions that are described . . . by using our motor and perceptual systems" (3).

This should sound somewhat familiar to you because we've already shown that action words, or verbs, are processed in the same brain centers as those responsible for enacting them. Thus, when we hear the word *punch* or we physically throw a punch, our brains rely on common motor regions to both comprehend and execute this action. The question you may be asking yourself, however, is, what does any of this have to do with analogies and helping people move better?

To answer this question, first, let me ask you to entertain a series of short thought experiments.

What does a bottle rocket have in common with a vertical jump?

_____

_____

What does a table have in common with a push-up?

_____

_____

What does a hammer have in common with a sprint?

_____

_____

Welcome back. Did you find it difficult to compare the object to the movement, or were you able to find the commonalities? Odds are, once your mind got rolling, you found it quite natural to separate the wheat from the chaff, or the similar from the different. For example, when comparing the vertical jump to the bottle rocket, did any of your observations include the fact that both concepts involve something moving upward at a fast rate? Equally, when comparing the table to the push-up, did you note that both involve a flat surface? Finally, when considering the relationship between a hammer and a sprint, did your mind transform the arms or legs of a virtual sprinter into metal-headed objects commonly used to hit things? While you likely used different words to describe these similarities, I'd be confident that our interpretations aren't miles apart.

Did I somehow read your mind? No, to the contrary. What we've just experienced is the brain's propensity to find patterns, to identify the parallels hiding beneath the surface of the seemingly distinct. And it is at this juncture that the power of analogy starts to reveal itself. Specifically, analogies feed on the mind's infinite capacity for association, propagating learning by inviting us to map features from something we're familiar with onto something we're not. For this reason, children learn one plus one, for example, not by memorizing meaningless squiggles on a page but, instead, by first learning to add 🍎+🍎 or maybe even ⛄+⛄.

In this case, two apples or two snowmen serve as an analogy for the concept of two. In time, a child learns that two and its pals not only represent the things we can see but also the things we can't, such as time, speed, space, and force. This suggests that, just as analogies help us understand the new in terms of the old, they're equally good at helping us understand the abstract in terms of the concrete.

This latter observation is supported by the fact that, when learning language, children master concrete nouns, such as *chair*, *ball*, *stairs*, and *bed*, before they master related verbs, such as *sit*, *throw*, *climb*, and *lay*, which, by comparison, are far more abstract (9). On reflection, this observation isn't surprising because you could imagine how difficult it would be to understand motion without first understanding what is moving and where it is moving to. This suggests, once again, that the concrete provides the scaffolding for the abstract.

If we closely examine language, we will see further evidence for this scaffolding everywhere we look. How else would you *run* for office, *grasp* an idea, or *nail* an interview? Equally, you wouldn't be able to *throw in the towel*, *roll with the punches*, or *get saved by the bell* if not for the mind's analogical prowess. Echoing this point in *Surfaces and Essences: Analogy as the Fuel and Fire of Thinking*, Douglas Hofstadter and Emmanuel Sander state the following.

> *If one never trusted a single analogy, how could one understand anything in this world? What, other than one's past, can one rely on in grounding decisions that one makes when facing a new situation? And of course all situations are in fact new, from the largest and most abstract ones down to the tiniest and most concrete ones. There isn't a single thought that isn't deeply and multiply anchored in the past. (12)*

It's hard to refute this view when you consider that our use of analogy (or metaphor to be exact) is so common that we utter one every 25 words (5, 11), or about six a minute (8, 15), providing further support that our minds really do run on analogy.

Playing Charades

But what about movement? While it is clear that we build many of our concepts from recycled ideas, what isn't clear yet is how the mind transforms a familiar analogy into meaningful motion. Fortunately, we've laid the foundation to understand how this conversion takes place, so now we will turn our attention back to the idea of simulation.

Did you ever play charades growing up? For those unfamiliar with this game, someone silently acts out a word or short phrase while everyone on their team frantically guesses who or what they are. When playing with my kids, for example, my daughter might gallop around the room holding an invisible set of reins, and we'll yell out "horse," or my son might start crawling around the room, stopping every so often to sniff a toy, and we quickly say "dog." Adults, in contrast, may attempt to act out phrases such as *run the show*, *climb the ladder*, or *turn it around*. In both cases, the game of charades illustrates how good we are at turning language back into the actions or objects it represents.

As noted earlier, we do this by rapidly running language through a simulator, activating the portions of the brain required to bring those actions forward. This neural overlap allows for a seamless transition between thinking and doing, as our brains extract meaning by converting language back into the sensory-motor signals from which it originally emerged. Once language has been converted back into its raw form, the brain is free to draw associations that enhance our understanding and integration of that information. This is why, after showing my daughter a basketball for the first time, she was able to instinctively respond by saying "Oh, kind of like a soccer ball." Equally, this is why my son, three at the time, could understand the difference between holding his tennis racket like it was "standing up" versus "lying down," quickly realizing that the latter position improved his chance of hitting the ball over the net. In my daughter's case, her mind identified the raw features of a soccer ball, round, rubbery, bounceable, and light, and mapped them onto the thing I was calling a basketball. In my son's case, he was able to use a set of positions he was familiar with, standing up versus lying down, to understand how to hold his tennis racket. In both cases, my children used analogical reasoning to make the foreign familiar.

These examples fully reveal why analogies are so effective for teaching movement. Like a computer, our brains can unzip an analogical file, extracting and simulating the raw features, leaving these remnants to be repurposed by the motor system during the ensuing movement. Said differently, the mind can translate an analogy into the common positions and patterns the motor system is in charge of producing. Thus, our spine can become a "chain being pulled in either direction," our hips a "bucket of water that shouldn't be spilled," and our legs a set of "pistons firing on all cylinders."

MOTION

If our brains automatically distill action from language by activating the brain regions in charge of perceiving and producing it, then we might expect to see this cognitive priming influencing actual movement. A phenomenon known as the *action–sentence compatibility effect* confirms this expectation. Specifically, after reading a sentence about forward motion (e.g., "close the drawer" or "you handed Jerry the ball"), you are faster to indicate that the phrase made sense when you have to move your hand forward to press a button, while the reverse is true for sentences involving backward motion (e.g., "open the drawer" or "Jerry handed you the ball") (10).

This effect provides strong support that our minds extract the motion- or pattern-based features of language, and, in the moments following the processing of that language, leave the mind briefly primed to deploy a comparable physical action (4). Importantly, this evidence suggests that language can literally put motion on the mind, providing support that analogies may help an athlete understand an unfamiliar pattern by learning it in terms of a familiar one.

PICTURE

While the pattern-based qualities of a cue, regardless of whether they are in the form of an analogy, are important, we also want our language to convey information about specific body positions. Thus, when saying things like "stand straight as a pencil," "stretch like a band being pulled at both ends," or "strike the ground as you would a match," it's valuable to know if the mind can simulate the orientation and shape of these objects, allowing their essence to carry through to our coordination.

To test this, researchers had subjects read sentences that clearly suggested a vertical orientation (e.g., "Dennis hammered the nail into the floor") or a horizontal orientation (e.g., "Dennis hammered the nail into the wall") (18). Shortly after confirming they understood the sentence, an object was projected on a screen, and subjects responded by pressing a button to indicate whether the object had been mentioned in the preceding sentence. The results showed that the subjects recognized objects faster when the objects were in the same orientation as the objects described in the sentence. Hence, reading the sentence "John put the pencil in the cup," primed subjects to identify a pencil in a vertical position, with the opposite being true for the sentence "John put the pencil in the drawer."

This evidence suggests that the mind simulates the implied orientation of an object and, thus, primes itself to be able to perceive that orientation. Notably, this same research group extended this finding to shape, showing that reading about an object's shape primes the mind to perceive it (19). In practical terms, this means that an athlete struggling to adopt a given body position, for example, a flat back during a tackle, may benefit from an analogy that draws their attention to a familiar object with a similar shape and orientation, say a tabletop. Because the mind perceives shape and orientation in their raw form, the motor system can quickly map "stay flat like a table" or "don't tip the table" right onto the body during tackling.

TROJAN HORSE

Although this chapter's focus is on analogies, the evidence and insights we've considered to this point apply equally well to literal language processing. It's not as if analogies are simulated and literal language is not.

To the contrary, all language is run through a perception–action simulator, which, in turn, provides the basis for the sense we get when we understand something. So what, specifically, is it about analogies that makes them so helpful when it comes to learning movement?

Unlike a literal cue, which explicitly highlights one major movement feature, a well-designed analogy can implicitly alert the athletes to a number of movement characteristics without a large increase in word count. For example, consider the vertical jump analogy "load and explode like a spring." Within this cue hides a multitude of movement factors that would otherwise need to be addressed, one discrete cue at a time. First, as anyone who's used a spring can attest, the more force you put into those metal coils, the more energy you get back. This echoes the expression of force we would like the athletes to mirror as they load and explode off the ground. Second, when loaded vertically, springs will project vertically, which maps to the direction of the jump. Moreover, it's easy for the mind to extend this analogy to the spring of a pogo stick, visualizing extreme pogoers flying skyward as they clear a barrier. Third, springs are very good at absorbing energy, which plays into the control we'd like to see during landing. Thus, even though the base analogy targets the takeoff, spin-offs such as "absorb the landing like the suspension of a car" or "lighten the landing like the shocks on a mountain bike" spring to mind and can be used to build a richer visual picture. All in all, this analogy is a triple threat, a trojan horse, if you will, sneaking in three cues for the price of one.

As we've just seen, analogies work by presenting the mind with a scenario or image that can be compared to an upcoming movement. The mind is then able to simulate the actions (do this) and perceptions (sense that) triggered by the prompt, allowing the athlete to test-drive the contents of the cue. Because an object's motion and structure are implied within the analogy, the athlete is able to extract more relevant information about the movement than is typically available in a literal cue. Thus, in the same way that we like to say "a picture is worth a thousand words," we might say that analogies are too.

The art in all of this is finding the "right" analogy, the one that prompts an "aha," instead of a "huh?" Using yourself as a test case, consider the analogies presented in this book. Is it fair to say that some of the analogies have spoken to you and others have not? Without question, you said yes, and that's OK because the experiences I pull from, the simulations I run, are different from yours. It's not a matter of good or bad, right or wrong; to the contrary, it's about identifying the best analogy for the movement and the athlete performing it. This is why individualization is so important, as each athlete's personal language locker stores a unique set of experiences from which to simulate a cue's meaning. Thus, one athlete's "push like a piston" is another athlete's "blast like a bullet." And it is for this reason that we will return to the shallows and test-drive a model coaches can use to ensure their analogies and athletes go hand in glove.

PART 1: MENTAL MAPS

As we've now seen, the mind runs on analogy. From my daughter's comparing a soccer ball to a basketball to my comparing a vertical jump to a spring, we can see that our ability to analogize is vast, spanning obvious comparisons, such as objects' roundness, to less obvious comparisons, such as objects' ability to store and release energy. And, though it is easy to spot a clever analogy—"as you land the jump, grab for your pistols like you're in an old Western movie"—it's far more difficult to come up with one—"sidestep the defender like _____." However, it need not be this way. To the contrary, once armed with an analogy's anatomy, you can quickly come up with any number of familiar comparisons that will assist your athlete in trading in their current movement pattern for a newer model.

To ease our way into understanding the inner workings of analogy, let's start with a series of activities that will wake up your analogical engine and reveal three different types of analogies available to you as a coach. For each activity, see if you can spot the source of the comparison between the analogy, what we will call the **base**, and the movement, what we will call the **target**. There are no rules here, so jot down any and all relevant comparisons that jump to mind. To help you get started, I have included an example at the beginning of each activity.

Activity 1: Trading Places   *Example*

Analogy: "Pull up as you would if you were hanging off the face of a cliff."

Base: Pulling up the face of a cliff

Target: Wide-grip pull-up

Source of Comparison:

This analogy provides two primary comparisons: One is emotive and will influence effort, and the other is kinematic and will influence technique. The source of emotion comes from the fear associated with "hanging on for dear life," which should trigger an increase in grip and effort. The source of the technique comes from the fact that you would hold onto a cliff in a manner similar to the hold in a wide-grip pull-up and, because the body cannot swing forward, it must be pulled straight up, which reduces any attempt to use forward leg motion to create momentum during the pull.

Your Turn

Analogy: "Push the bar like you are pushing heavy building debris off of you."

Base: Pushing heavy building debris off of you

Target: Barbell bench press

Source of Comparison:

_____

_____

_____

_____

Analogy: "Blast off the start line like you're being chased up a hill."

Base: Being chased up a hill

Target: Acceleration or sprint

Source of Comparison:

_____

_____

_____

_____

How'd it go? Were you able to find one or more relevant sources of comparison for the two analogies you tackled? Did you notice, as suggested by the activity title, that each analogy mapped the target movement onto a scenario that required the same motion? If you didn't, go back and take a look; you'll realize that scaling a cliff, pushing heavy debris, and escaping a pursuer maps nicely onto the pull-up, bench press, and sprint. In each of these examples, which we will call **scenario-based analogies**, I asked you to consider an analogous scenario that highlighted features that I wanted you to map onto the movement. In the pull-up, these features included the force-inducing adrenaline that accompanies a cliff-hanger and the technical constraints that are standard to climbing a vertical face. Similarly, the analogies used for the bench press and the sprint were equally provocative, inciting visuals that would encourage heightened force production. What's more, to effectively push heavy debris off you, you must generate a large, concentrated force in the vertical direction; while sprinting up a hill, especially if being chased, requires you to lift your knees and gradually rise or risk a collision between your face and the dirt. The cool thing is that, if you're an athlete, these implicit features are automatically downloaded in the form of "I can imagine what that feels like." However, if you're the coach, you need to explicitly create the analogy that will map onto the target-movement feature—some assembly required.

Now that we've looked under the hood of scenario-based analogies, consider a movement you commonly teach, and see if you can create your own analogy using this strategy, identifying the sources of comparison that would trigger a desired movement response.

Scenario-Based Analogy: "_____

_____"

Base: _____

Target: _____

Source of Comparison:

_____

_____

_____

_____

_____

Activity 2: Virtually Real — *Example*

Analogy: "Sprint as if to balance a cup of tea on your knee at the end of each stride."

Base: A cup of tea on your knee

Target: Sprinting at maximal velocity

Source of Comparison:

Don't be dismayed by my use of knee, as I am well aware that I referenced a body part in this analogy. The body part mentioned is stripped of any meaningful reference to body motion, leaving it drained of the movement constraints common to its internal cueing cousin. In fact, the use of knee in this analogy is akin to the use of cup of tea because both words reference objects in space. Thus, this cue triggers a simulation of what we would need to do to achieve the goal of balancing a cup of tea on our knee, a goal that obviously requires our upper thigh to be parallel to the sky, which is a desirable position for anyone trying to sprint as fast as they can.

Your Turn

Analogy: "Front squat as if there are vertical pillars just in front of each weight plate."

Base: Vertical pillars just in front of each weight plate

Target: Front squat

Source of Comparison:

_____

_____

_____

_____

Analogy: "Backpedal as if there is a hot bowl of soup on your head and you don't want to spill it."

Base: Soup on your head

Target: Backpedal

Source of Comparison:

_____

_____

_____

_____

I like to call these "as if" analogies because you are asking the athlete to "move as if" an object or physical constraint were present. This alerts a comparison between one's actual movement scenario and the same scenario with a virtual constraint. Thus, we can refer to these analogies as **constraint-based analogies**, a play on the well-known constraint-based approach to motor-skill learning. These analogies work by establishing a mental rule that serves to guide how the movement should be performed. While these analogies lack the emotive power of those considered in activity 1, they're well positioned to influence the way movement patterns are organized. In the sprint example, the "cup of tea on the knee," provides salient insights on the height of the lead thigh as an athlete finishes their stride. Notably, if the lead leg is insufficiently recovered, the thigh will have an excessive downward slope, resulting in Grandma's fine china sliding off the table and crashing to the floor. With the front squat, the "vertical pillars" immediately alert the athlete to a movement barrier. In this case, the barrier requires a precise focus on a vertical bar path, limiting how far forward the bar and, thus, the body can drift. Finally, the backpedal trades in a cup for a bowl but uses a similar analogical logic to that of the sprint. That is, to balance a bowl of soup on one's head requires the head to stay level and still, a capacity valued in those with effective backpedal technique. Mind you, if cups of tea and bowls of soup aren't your thing, don't despair because one could just as easily balance cups of coffee, bowls of cereal, or books for that matter, as long as the analogy gets the right idea in the athlete's mind.

Now that we've peeked behind the curtain of constraint-based analogies, consider another movement you commonly teach and see if you can create your own analogy using this strategy, identifying the sources of comparison that would trigger a desired movement response.

Constraint-Based Analogy: " _____
"
_____

Base: _____

Target: _____

Source of Comparison:

_____

_____

_____

_____

_____

Activity 3: Shape-Shifter   *Example*

Analogy: "Sidestep like a rubber ball bouncing off a wall."

Base: Rubber ball bouncing off a wall

Target: Side step or change of direction

Source of Comparison:

Here, we invite a comparison between the kinetics of a rubber ball bouncing and that of an athlete changing direction. Notably, a rubber ball, also known to some as a super ball, is made of dense rubber and is able to store and release immense energy, giving kids hours of fun seeing how high they can make this small sphere bounce. This feature of a rubber ball maps nicely onto the rate of recoil we would like to see when an athlete strikes the ground with the intention of sidestepping an opponent.

Your Turn

Analogy: "Stay long and hinge as a teeter-totter (seesaw) hinges on a fixed point."

Base: Teeter-totter hinges on a fixed point

Target: Romanian deadlift

Source of Comparison:

_____

_____

_____

_____

Analogy: "Rise through the sprint like a jet taking off."

Base: Jet taking off

Target: Sprint or acceleration

Source of Comparison:

_____

_____

_____

_____

Here, we explored what we'll call **object-based analogies**. This type of analogy is by far the most abstract because it requires an athlete to map a feature of an inanimate object onto an animate body. However, this flavor of analogy also provides tremendous scope for purposeful creativity, as coaches can consider how the shape, material, or behavior of a given object might illuminate a subtle feature of a movement skill that is otherwise outside the reach of human-centric language. This is why a comparison between the action of a rubber ball and a sidestepping athlete may paint a far richer picture than an action verb in isolation. Similarly, triggering the thought of a teeter-totter brings about images of a straight board hinging about a fixed axis, analogous to a straight body hinging about a fixed hip. What's more, if you were on *Jeopardy* and, after selecting "fast things for $200," Alex Trebek were to read "rapidly accelerating, its strong frame gradually rises over a fixed distance," no one would blame you if "Who is Usain Bolt?" popped into your mind just as easily as "What is a jet?" The point is that, when we reference a thing, our mind can quickly access all the qualities of that thing. Once that thing is in our mind, we can marry it to the movement it is meant to influence and, voilà, our mind gives birth to a hybrid creation straight out of an episode of *Rick and Morty*: Rubber Ball Boy, Mr. Woodman Teeter-Totter, and the Human Jet. Joking aside, as we've seen with simulation, our mind can test-drive the contents of a cue on its way to making meaning, leaving the motor system to interpret rubbery-ness, teeter-totter-ness, and jet-ness. The outcome is a brain that has synthesized the relevant kinetic and kinematic qualities that should be woven into the next rep. As an aside, we may also find ourselves drawing comparisons between human motion and the motion of other animals (e.g., "hop like a bunny," "crawl like a bear," or "land softly like a cat"), especially if we work with kids. As such, we can invite the mind to mesh a movement with these animalistic alternatives by creating **animal-based analogies.**

Now that we've seen what object-based analogies (and animal-based analogies) can offer, consider a final movement you commonly teach, and see if you can create your own analogy using this strategy, identifying the sources of comparison that would trigger a desired movement response.

Object-Based (or Animal-Based) Analogy: "_____"

Base: _____

Target: _____

Source of Comparison:

Structure-Mapping

At the beginning of this section, I said that we are far better at spotting analogies than we are at creating them. However true this statement may have been a few pages ago, the activities you just completed should've given you a nice boost of analogical assurance. For this reason, we can now fully consider the cellular makeup of an analogy and the factors that differentiate the analogies that work from those that don't.

Dr. Dedre Gentner is a professor of psychology and education at Northwestern University, in Evanston, Illinois. Of her many achievements, Gentner is best known for her seminal work on analogy, which she clearly lays out in her 1983 paper, "Structure-Mapping: A Theoretical Framework for Analogy" (21). As the title suggests, Gentner has proposed **structure-mapping** to explain how the mind uses analogy to drive learning by taking features of something we're familiar with and mapping them onto something we're not. Notably, this is how children build up category membership, as displayed in "this is my bucket of *balls*" or "this drawer is for my *dolls*, and this one is for my *blocks*." The same can be said for concept membership because individuals can apply an understanding of *roundness* to a ball just as easily as they can an orange or the sun. By equal measure, individuals can come to recognize the concept of *explosiveness* within an actual explosion just as easily as they can an argument between strangers or a defensive lineman's effort after the snap. Thus, our analogical operating system allows us to literally map our ever-changing external world onto our ever-growing internal world.

But what is actually being mapped when we use analogies? Gentner argues that, any time we make one of these comparisons, we are mapping **object-attributes** and **object-actions** such that the former represents features of a thing (e.g., tall, short, arm, leg, strong, weak, etc.) and the latter represents the inter*actions* between things (e.g., push, strike, dance, bounce; at least one thing interacts with another). Practically speaking, an object-attribute, for the most part, is immutable, or static; it is what it is. In contrast, object-actions suggest motion and the possibility of emergence (sparks can emerge when metal strikes a rock just as running can emerge when a leg strikes the ground). If you go back to our examples, you will see that the meaning we mapped from the base analogy onto the target movement came in the form of attributes and actions. Take the jet analogy, for example. The jet's *attributes* we wanted mapped onto the sprint included a long and strong frame, while the jet's *actions* we wanted mapped onto the sprint included rapid acceleration and a gradual rise.

Gentner goes on to discuss how object-attributes and object-actions work together to determine the overall effect and stickiness of an analogy. To illustrate this, I want you to imagine a computer program that is designed to rate your analogy; we'll call it Analogous. Analogous is a simple software program that requires you to input your base analogy and target movement. With this information, Analogous compares the base to the target and rates how well one maps onto the other. This rating is based on the number of common attributes and the number of common actions, each of which is visualized on a sliding scale, where the left-most position represents no overlap and the right-most position represents complete overlap. To illustrate the analogical sweet spot, let's consider some examples using our fictional software.

► Complete Overlap

As we can see, no new information can be accessed when the base analogy is the same as the target movement. This reinforces that the contrast between the analogy and the movement is needed to reveal the relevant similarities. For example, if we use a constraint-based analogy, while there is a direct movement-to-movement comparison, the analogy, say "a cup of tea on the knee," contains strategic differences that implicitly alert the athlete to the importance, in this case, of knee lift.

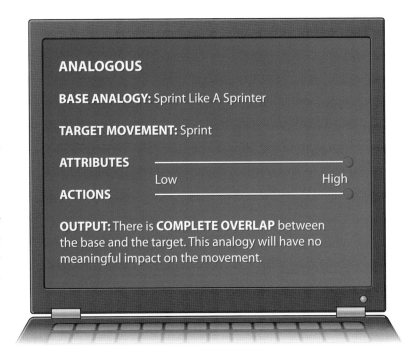

► No Overlap

If there are no salient attributes or actions connecting the analogy to the movement, then there will be no useful information that can be extracted from the comparison. Sometimes, there is overlap, but the overlap is apparent only to the coach because they're familiar with the comparison, while the athlete is not. Thus, athletes will be able to map features only from analogies that contain content they're familiar with.

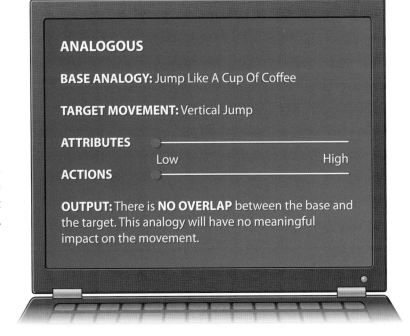

► ## Action Overlap

If actions overlap, then the analogy may serve to reinforce the direction (e.g., move here or there) or speed (e.g., move quickly or slowly) of the motion; however, these analogies may be less effective at directly shifting a specific body shape or state. Once again, we can use scenario-based analogies that involve comparable motion as exemplars of action overlap. Notably, these analogies can directly influence the movement pattern by suggesting how it should be performed (e.g., quickly, slowly, deliberately, chaotically, gradually, or rapidly).

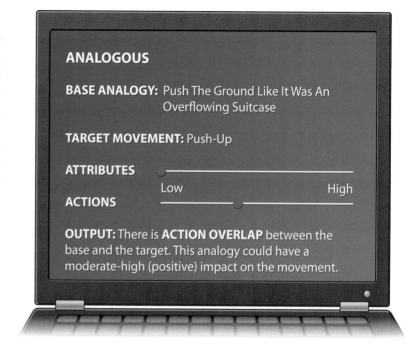

ANALOGOUS

BASE ANALOGY: Push The Ground Like It Was An Overflowing Suitcase

TARGET MOVEMENT: Push-Up

ATTRIBUTES

Low   High

ACTIONS

OUTPUT: There is **ACTION OVERLAP** between the base and the target. This analogy could have a moderate-high (positive) impact on the movement.

► ## Attribute Overlap

If attributes overlap, then the analogy may serve to reinforce a specific body shape (e.g., long or short) or state (e.g., stiff or relaxed); however, the analogy will have limited effect on the actual movement pattern unless the analogy alerts the athlete to relevant actions. Mapping attributes is particularly important for the postural components of movement. For example, object-based analogies, with their comparisons of material (e.g., stiff as steel) or shape (e.g., straight as a pencil), are very effective at encouraging a shift in body position and, therefore, exploiting attribute overlap.

ANALOGOUS

BASE ANALOGY: Stiff As A Board During The Push-Up

TARGET MOVEMENT: Push-Up

ATTRIBUTES

Low   High

ACTIONS

OUTPUT: There is **ATTRIBUTE OVERLAP** between the base and the target. This analogy could have a moderate (positive) impact on the movement.

▶ **Action/Attribute Overlap**

If actions and attributes overlap, then the base analogy will likely have a positive influence on the positions and patterns of the target movement. A risk to be aware of, however, is that analogies with too much overlap can become overly general and, thus, lack the contrast needed to alert the athlete to a specific feature of the movement you'd like them to target. That said, the scenario- and constraint-based analogies we previously discussed should provide a nice balance of overlap and contrast to ensure that the right messages are relayed to the athlete.

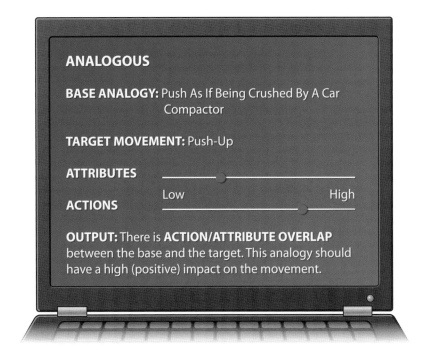

ANALOGOUS

BASE ANALOGY: Push As If Being Crushed By A Car Compactor

TARGET MOVEMENT: Push-Up

ATTRIBUTES ———————————○—————————————

Low   High

ACTIONS ——————————————————○————

OUTPUT: There is **ACTION/ATTRIBUTE OVERLAP** between the base and the target. This analogy should have a high (positive) impact on the movement.

In principle, there is no perfect analogy, just the perfect analogy for you. That's why my "cup of tea" might be your "cup of coffee," but, in the end, if we're asked to "balance *it* on our knee at the end of each stride," we can comply just the same, bringing our thigh to the sky as we run on by. This highlights the value of Gentner's structure-mapping theory. Once you understand the movement feature you want to nudge, you can choose from a seemingly infinite catalog of comparisons. The key is to make sure that the attributes or actions the analogy highlights are in fact the attributes or actions you want the athlete to focus on during the movement. Considering the importance of this, the next section will guide you through the exact movement-centric qualities you'll want to hide inside the casing of your analogies.

PART 2: SIMILARITY

Hannah Arendt, famed philosopher and celebrated storyteller, once said that "storytelling reveals meaning without committing the error of defining it" (1). Equally, we could say that analogies reveal complexity without committing the error of explaining it. This perspective helps polish the fact that analogies, like external cues, are able to encourage complex movement without the aid of complex knowledge. Thus, just as we can drive a car with no insight into its mechanics, we can also move a body with no awareness of its anatomy.

Be this as it may, a coach on the other side of an analogy will not be granted the same blissful ignorance. Unlike athletes, coaches benefit from having a comprehensive understanding of the movement features they seek to influence. This knowledge aids the coach in mining for analogical gems that make those qualities shine. Before a coach can start digging around their mind's quarry, however, they must first know the actions or attributes they're digging for. For this, we will enlist the help of our 3P Performance Profile one final time.

As you'll recall, all analogies map actions or attributes from a familiar analogical base onto an unfamiliar or less-familiar movement target. We noted that attributes tend to be static in nature, exemplified by their ability to illuminate a body shape, as in "stretch your rotator cuff by turning your upper body into the shape of a *W*," or body state, as in "get stiff as if you were about to take a punch from Mike Tyson." Reflecting back to our 3P Performance Profile, which *P* captures both shape and state? You got it—*position*. Remember that position represents the specific body positions or postures an athlete must attain to execute a given movement pattern. For example, a coach would expect to see a *straight* spine during a sprint, while they would expect to see a *curved* spine during a front flip. In principle, if there are body positions that should be held constant during a movement, such as a neutral spine while squatting, or achieved at a specific time point, say the figure-four position that accompanies ground contact in sprinting, then a useful analogy might be one that captures those positions.

In contrast to attributes, actions reference dynamic relationships within the body (e.g., how a set of joints interact to create motion) and between the body and the environment (e.g., the magnitude and direction of force into the ground). Again, upon reflection, we can easily see how *power* and *pattern* represent the actions a coach might look to intensify within an analogy. Recall that power references the requisite strength and power qualities (kinetics) anchored to a given movement. Thus, an analogy can help an athlete to express these qualities through the imagery it triggers (e.g., fly off the line like "a rocket off a ramp" or "a daredevil being shot from a cannon"). Practically speaking, analogies that give power a platform will inform the pace of a movement in the same way that different action verbs do.

Pattern, on the other hand, references the coordinative qualities (kinematics) aligned to a given movement. Hence, analogies can be used to illustrate a pattern of motion using a relatable example. Thus, you may ask an athlete performing an Olympic lift to imagine there is a wall in front of them, providing a constraint-based analogy that will directly influence bar motion. Similarly, a pitcher who drifts off their line may benefit from imagining they are pitching down a narrow hallway, which leverages a scenario-based analogy that may straighten their throw. In both examples, the analogy unveils a visual that will most certainly influence the organization of the pattern if attended to with the same intensity as if it were real.

At work here is what we can call the **principle of similarity**, which states that an analogy will affect a movement to the degree it represents a relevant feature of that movement. As previously noted, these features include attributes (position) and actions (power and pattern). Thus, when designing analogies, coaches can use the 3P Performance Profile as a checklist of sorts, verifying that, on its way to influencing a movement, the selected analogy is capturing one or more of these performance qualities. By applying the principle of similarity, coaches are encouraged to be critical consumers of the biomechanics they observe and the analogies they use to influence it.

To help illustrate and support your application of the principle, I have created two examples for you to consider, the first of which is completed for you as a reference. In each example, there is a picture of a movement and four possible analogies. Your job is to select the analogy that you feel best suits the movement (note that more than one analogy may apply). Once you've made your selection, use the 3P Performance Profile checklist to mark the features being mapped onto the movement.

► **Example 1: Jump**

As we can see in the first example, some of the analogies seem to fit, while others definitely do not. Notably, while an "uppercut" may align to the motion of the upper body during a jump, it fails to make sense when directed at the lower-body motion needed to "explode off the ground." Similarly, exploding "off the ground like an arrow from a bow" would fail to hit the target with most athletes because arrows tend to fly horizontally, while a vertical jump is, well, vertical. Our last two analogies, both of which are scenario based, make sense, as they map a relatable sport movement onto the movement skill being taught. As such, "jump as if to rebound a basketball" or "jump as if to catch a fly ball" would serve to support maximal vertical projection. In both cases, the analogy reflects the desired position because a jump is a jump; the desired power because both scenarios encourage maximal vertical displacement; and the desired pattern because, once again, a jump is a jump. Both analogies accentuate the performance outcome by encouraging the mind to run a simulation of a movement that, if executed as intended, would maximize jump height. Had the coach wanted to work on the landing or a nuanced technical feature of the jump itself, then a different set of analogies would have needed to be considered. Again, the key is to ensure that the analogy hides the key technical feature(s) you're looking to target within a relatable visual prompt.

OK, it's your turn. Considering the movement, pick the analogy that would best support its execution, and identify which features of the movement—position, power, or pattern—the analogy is nudging.

▶ **Example 2: Sprint**

For the second example, you probably noticed that two of the analogies mapped onto the sprint, and two were slightly off. Notably, one uses a sledgehammer to strike concrete using a vertical motion, while an axe is used to strike a tree using a horizontal motion. Granted, both analogies impart the power we want to see during sprinting; the difference in motion characteristics would suggest that the axe would provide a more relatable comparison. Similarly, sprinting upstairs, which requires a delicate balance of horizontal and vertical focus, overlaps with sprinting to a far greater degree than sprinting up a ladder, which is a vertically biased motion. As such, if you agreed that the axe and stairs would provide better companionship for our sprint than the other options, then you also likely noticed that, in addition to mapping features of the pattern, both analogies encourage the power one expects to see in a well-executed sprint.

With the principle of similarity in hand, you are well on your way to designing representative analogies. Just as we use the 3P Performance Profile to profile and prioritize athletic qualities, we can use the same three factors to reverse engineer biomechanically sound comparisons. However, to ensure your analogy is welcome in your athlete's mind, we need to consider one final ingredient.

PART 3: FAMILIARITY

Let's play a matching game. Here, you'll find six pictures with two possible choices, an A and a B option. After reviewing each picture, check the box next to the label that you'd use to describe the image.

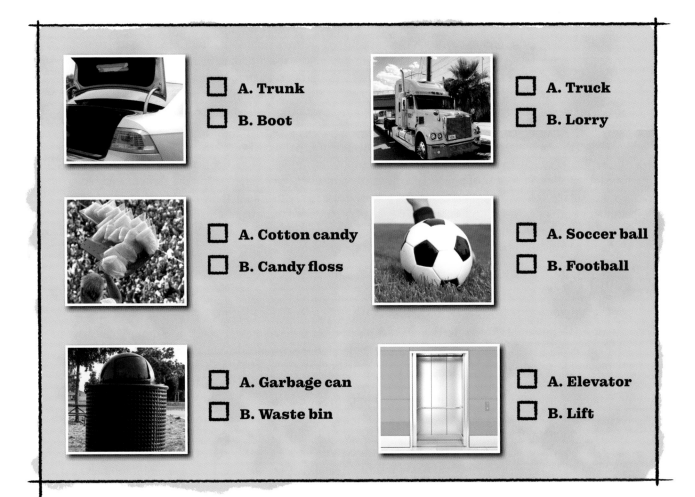

☐ A. Trunk	☐ A. Truck
☐ B. Boot	☐ B. Lorry
☐ A. Cotton candy	☐ A. Soccer ball
☐ B. Candy floss	☐ B. Football
☐ A. Garbage can	☐ A. Elevator
☐ B. Waste bin	☐ B. Lift

Invariably, you found yourself drawn to either all the A or all the B options. For my friends west of the Atlantic, you most certainly gravitated toward A options, while my friends on the other side of the pond proudly claimed the B options. As an American, I am partial to putting my *groceries in the trunk*, rather than my *shop in the boot*, and my *garbage in a can*, rather than my *waste in a bin*. However, after moving to Ireland in 2016 to join Irish Rugby, those preferences quickly changed, as did my perception of the universality of the English tongue. For my fellow Americans, if you've never been to Ireland or Great Britain, you might not know what I mean, so let me explain.

East of the Atlantic, you don't go on vacation; you go on holiday. At the airport, you stand in a queue, instead of a line. At your hotel, you'll take the lift to the first floor, which you'll find puzzling, until the receptionist, seeing your confusion, says "We call the second floor the first floor, which makes this the ground floor." At dinner, you'll ask where the bathroom is only to be told that "the toilet is down the hall and to the left." Finally, when trying to find that perfect companion to your sandwich, you'll quickly learn that fries are chips, chips are crisps, and the funny thing on the menu called goujons is code for chicken strips.

While this variance in vernacular can appear harmless, if not humorous, my perspective shifted once I went from touring Ireland to coaching there. See, even though I had already started writing this book and, therefore, was well aware of the importance of language specificity, I was still surprised when my analogies flopped. Surprise, however, soon gave way to solutions as my *analogizer* kicked into high gear, creating regionally relevant phrases that might just do the trick. This meant *field* was out and *pitch* was in; players no longer *cut* but, rather, *sidestepped*; and when we ran, we stopped lifting *cleats to clouds* and started lifting *boots to belts*.

In time, I converted my foreign phrases into local lingo by getting to know the people who were now my players and converting American football slang into rugby-relevant jargon.

While coaching in a foreign country is the ultimate test of one's linguistic latitude, every coach, to some degree, faces a similar challenge. It doesn't take long to realize that nodding heads or a bit of chatter are preferred responses to a cue than a sea of straight faces staring back in somber silence. As such, coaches, at least the effective ones, inevitably come to realize that athletes, at a minimum, must be familiar with the language they're hearing and, ideally, be able to connect with those words at some deeper level, what we can call the **principle of familiarity**.

While the take-home here is obvious—know your athletes—what's less obvious is knowing how to do this efficiently and effectively. For instance, coach–athlete interactions are often confined to practice, which limits time for substantive conversations. What's more, conversations will often focus on the contents of training and not on the contents of athletes' lives. This leaves coaches with little in the way of meaningful insights about their athletes. Thus, coaches need to be acutely aware of the type of information they should be listening for during conversations and on the training floor. With the right information in hand, coaches can lower the barrier to learning by translating their athletes' mental narratives into the ones they use to coach them.

Culture

In the words an athlete speaks and the behaviors they assume hides the culture that formed them.

Here, I use the word *culture* in the broadest sense, to reflect the environments and social groups that shape people's values, beliefs, behaviors, and language. Notably, it was my incomplete understanding of the Irish culture and the colloquial speech that accompanies it that initially limited the clarity of my communication. However, the same thing could happen to a coach from Seattle working with an athlete from New Orleans or a therapist from Chicago working with a patient from San Diego, as each city possesses its own unique features, which are passed down to those who call it home. Add in the subculture of one's family and their local community, and you have yourself a bona fide individual that should be treated as such.

While you shouldn't need more than intuition to convince yourself that culture shapes our understanding of analogies, an interesting set of studies highlight this in a clever way. Using the table tennis forehand as the target movement, a research group from the University of Hong Kong asked native English speakers to participate in an analogy-learning study. The participants assigned to the analogy group were told to "pretend to draw a right-angled triangle with the bat [paddle] and . . . strike the ball while bringing the bat up the hypotenuse of the triangle." After 300 practice trials, this group demonstrated a strong learning effect that was maintained even when the participants had to simultaneously count backward (14).

Here's where it gets interesting. In a related study, the researchers translated the right-angle analogy into Cantonese and asked a group of Chinese participants to apply it to the same forehand shot (17). This time, however, the researchers did not see a performance benefit. In fact, postexperimental interviews revealed that most of the participants found the analogy confusing. Intrigued by this finding, the researchers set out to see if they could identify a culturally appropriate analogy that would replicate the findings from their original study. Assisted by native Cantonese speakers, the research group swapped the right triangle for a mountain, asking a new group of Chinese participants to "move the bat as though it is traveling up the side of a mountain." Sure enough, this new analogy did the trick, and the researchers were able to replicate their original findings (16).

This thin slice of evidence taps our intuition and reminds us that only through listening to our athletes can we get to know the beings behind the biomechanics. Remember, it's our athletes' use and understanding of language, not our own, that determine their ability to understand cues and analogies. This is why listening is so critical to analogy formation, as hiding within our athletes' language is the raw material needed to create analogies that appeal to the individual. A simple way to unlock this raw material is to ask your athletes to come up with their own analogies, ask them to explain what your analogies mean to them, or give them a few analogies to choose from. In all cases, you'll get a sense of your athletes' language preferences and ensure you are using analogies that are calibrated to them.

Generation

If an individual's culture is a reflection of where they grew up, then their generation is a reflection of when they grew up. And, just as culture embeds itself in language, so too does an individual's generation color the way they think and speak. For example, when I was growing up in the 1990s, if we liked something, we said it was "cool," and, when we were relaxing, we said we were "chillin.'" However, not long after the turn of the century, I started hearing my athletes say "coolin'" in response to the standard pretraining "What's up, man?" Ultimately, those born into a given generation are bound to the pop culture, technology, events, and slang of the time, grounding their perception of the present, to some degree, in the past. How else do we get phrases like "back in my day" or "kids these days"? We all know that the time period we grew up in stays with us, allowing us to enjoy those nostalgic moments that bring us back to "a simpler time."

I first became sensitive to the interaction between individuals' generations and language when I worked as a personal trainer in college. During those years, I realized that, while my degree was teaching me how to program for a diversity of goals, it wasn't teaching me how to communicate with a diversity of people; those lessons took place on the training floor. Over the course of a day, for example, I could have a 55-year-old professor preparing for a triathlon, a 25-year-old engineering student wanting to put on lean mass, a 70-year-old retiree trying to maintain function, and a 16-year-old high school student training to make their varsity squad. In each case, I had to learn how to sync my language to theirs, translating reps and sets into cues that connect.

As I transitioned into strength and conditioning, my sensitivity to generational differences faded, as I worked with a fairly homogeneous group of athletes who were within a 10-year age bracket. Because those early years had me in the same age bracket as my athletes', it wasn't difficult to connect on a generational level. As time passed, however, I kept getting older, while my athletes stayed the same age. Inevitably, this age gap widened, and I started noticing that my movie quotes weren't getting the same laughs and I no longer recognized the music being played in my weight room. Someone even had to explain to me that flossing was now a dance, as well as a part of good dental hygiene.

There were times, in fact, when this generation gap seemed to widen right before my eyes. One such moment occurred after a training session toward the end of an NFL Combine prep period. I had brought the boys up to debrief the session and set the tone for the next day. I remember telling the athletes that "we had a good session; however, *the hay isn't quite in the barn*." To my surprise and everyone else's amusement, one of the athletes blurted out "What the hell does that mean?" After the hecklers had settled down and my own laughter subsided, I responded by refurbishing the metaphor and telling the athlete that "the app on your phone isn't done downloading," which was met with approving nods and a final bit of laughter.

These moments always remind me that being a good coach is about more than textbook knowledge. We also need street smarts, which means that we need to be up on the trends, the things *kids these days* are into. And, with the pace at which innovation is accelerating, it is a case of adapt or die. Take music, for example. Over the course of 50 years, we went from vinyl records to eight-tracks and tapes to CDs, and, now, we're in the age of digital music and streaming services. Over a similar period, we went from only having phones in our homes to only having phones in our pockets, and, now, we're in an era when our smart devices do everything short of cooking us breakfast. In the past 25 years alone, we've seen the rise of the Internet, the professionalization of gamers, and the first taste of driverless cars. We now tweet and like more than we meet and talk; we get our information from Google, our rides from Uber, and our stuff from Amazon; and it won't be long before Netflix is hitting up the Buggles to produce a new single, "On Demand Killed the Television Star."

These changes are neither good nor bad; they just are. However, just as you'll get left behind professionally if you don't stay up to speed with research and technology, you'll get left behind personally if you don't adapt your language to your athletes'. This doesn't mean you have to scrap your favorite music and start playing *Call of Duty*; however, it does mean that you need familiarize yourself with your athletes' generation and seek to understand their lived experiences. In doing so, you'll collect more of the raw material needed to create the analogies that will be the tick to your athletes' talk.

Experience

While culture and generation are important, they're not the whole story, as people are far more than the circumstances into which they're born. We enter this world as individuals, each containing a unique set of predispositions that play out in the way we think, the way we behave, and, ultimately, the decisions we make. With each decision, no matter the importance, we gain new experiences, all of which add to the perceptions and actions on which language is based.

While any experience can serve as the reference on which an analogy is created, evidence suggests that understanding our athletes' physical experiences might reap the most relevant rewards. Intuitively, this makes sense because an analogy between familiar and unfamiliar movements would have greater structural overlap than an analogy involving an abstract comparison, with the likes of a rubber ball, let's say. This isn't suggesting that object-based analogies aren't valuable; they are, especially when trying to convey nuance. However, it may simply be the case that scenario- and constraint-based analogies map more movement features within a relatable context. If this is true, it stands to reason that one would process language about familiar movements differently than unfamiliar movements.

As it turns out, Sian Beilock, whom we met back in chapter 4, also has an interest in how we derive meaning from language and has done some of her own work on embodied simulation. Specifically, Beilock and her team were interested to know how individuals' experiences with movement impacted the way they processed language depicting those movements. In their first study, Beilock and her team invited expert hockey players and novices with no hockey experience to complete the sentence–image matching task (18, 19), which was previously described in this chapter. Remember, this involves reading a sentence, seeing an image, and then pressing a *yes* or *no* key to indicate whether the image had been mentioned in the sentence. In this case, the researchers used a blend of hockey and nonhockey actions to test whether the expert hockey players processed hockey-centric language differently than the novices. The results showed that, while the experts and novices were similar in speed and accuracy when matching nonhockey images, the experts were indeed faster in matching hockey images (13). From an embodied simulation perspective, this result makes sense because the expert hockey players already have motor representations of the actions being described, which allows them to simulate and identify those actions faster than the novices can. For this explanation to stand, however, we'd expect to see processing differences when we peer inside those experts' brains.

To test this, Beilock and her colleagues invited another group of expert hockey players and novices into the lab. This time, the researchers had the groups listen to sentences depicting hockey actions and everyday actions (e.g., "The hockey player finished the shot" vs. "The individual pushed the cart") while lying in an fMRI scanner. The results showed that, while the brains of both groups responded similarly to everyday action sentences, the expert hockey players consistently activated their premotor cortex to a greater degree than did the novices when listening to hockey-action sentences (2). When we consider the role of the premotor cortex in action planning and intentional movement, it makes sense that the expert hockey players' brains would activate the same brain centers responsible for performing the actions depicted in the sentences. The novices, on the other hand, wouldn't have this experience-dependent motor memory. This would require them to use general sensory-motor centers, such as the primary motor cortex, to comprehend these actions. And, as it turns out, this is exactly what the researchers found.

When you consider that the same neural specificity is observed when expert dancers watch videos of their dancing discipline (6, 7), we can start to appreciate how connected the brain truly is, as one's physical experiences directly influence how their brains process visual and auditory information, even when they're not moving. As coaches, this suggests that we can use an athlete's movement history to formulate analogies that, in addition to overlapping conceptually, might also overlap neurologically, potentially lowering the threshold to comprehension and learning. Thus, when a strength coach working in rugby compares the body position during a scrum to the body position during a squat, the athlete can easily map the sensations of one onto the other. Equally, if an athlete is able to execute sprint drills to good effect but struggles to perform the real thing, then the coach can draw an analogy back to those drills. This allows the athlete to, once again, map the sensations of a past experience onto a present one. In understanding your athlete's lived experiences, notably, those of a physical nature, you'll have the final piece of raw material needed to create analogies that stick.

SUMMARY

Analogies are as fundamental to thinking and learning as oxygen is to breathing and living. From the hidden analogies of everyday speech to those obviously designed to persuade—"not buying this stock would be like refusing free money"—analogies form the building blocks of communication. Despite their ubiquity, analogies are often left to collect dust in many a coach's toolbox, commonly used by chance instead of choice. My hope is that, if you're reading these words, you now see analogies for what they are, a catalyst for learning and an indispensable coaching tool.

As our journey revealed, our earliest actions and perceptions form the sensory foundations on which language is built. Consequently, we learned that we extract meaning from language partly through a process of embodied simulation. Hence, the mental machinery we use to kick a ball is the same mental machinery we use to comprehend the phrase "kick a ball." In essence, our brains have been optimized for efficiency, leveraging common sensory-motor brain centers to act, speak, and think. The net result is a mind that operates similar to a mail room, taking all new, incoming sensory information and sorting it in terms of existing mental categories.

Knowing this, I argued that coaches can leverage this existing knowledge to help athletes learn new movement concepts. Highlighting the work of Dedre Gentner, we discussed how minds use structural-mapping, taking the features of a base analogy and mapping them onto the same features of a target movement. Thus, joints can move like *well-oiled hinges*, muscles can stretch like *rubber bands*, and speed can be deployed like you're *dodging a car*. In each case, our brains synthesize the raw sensory-motor material embedded in the analogy and reapply it to the subsequent movement.

To do this effectively, however, coaches must leverage the principles of similarity and familiarity (see figure 6.1). The former states that the analogy and movement must have something in common. Notably, the analogy must convey a shift in movement position, power, or pattern. The latter, on the other hand, requires the athletes to be familiar with the content of the prescribed analogy. Across dimensions of culture, generation, and experience, we find the raw material needed to create these individualized analogies. To access this raw material, coaches need only provide their athletes with an opportunity to speak and listen intently when they do.

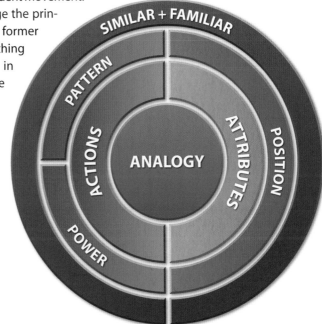

FIGURE 6.1   Model for creating effective analogies.

PART III
CUE

Over a decade has passed since my first NFL Combine. In that time, I've had the unique opportunity to support hundreds of NFL prospects transition to NFL pros. Each one of those athletes stands out in my mind, clear as the day I met them. I'll never forget their stories, their struggle, their triumph, and, at times, their failure. The reason for this is straightforward: I lived those stories, shared those struggles, took part in that triumph, and, yes, faced those failures. And, therein, lies an important truth about coaching: It is impossible to divorce our athletes' journey from our own. While we create cues, design drills, and formulate feedback, they're the ones responsible for the focus, execution, and reflection necessary to make those coaching efforts worthwhile. For this reason, it is the responsibility of coaches, trainers, therapists, and teachers to be at their best so they can help their athletes, clients, patients, and students be at theirs.

The gravity of this responsibility never leaves my side. It's the stomachache I get when I start worrying more about the program in my mind than the person on the pitch. It's that little voice that reminds me to scan eye contact, body language, and movement for the echo of my effectiveness. It's the knowledge that athletes don't need a boss, they need a business partner, one that can play their role without always trying to play others'. Ultimately, great coaches know how to build great relationships, which, if they could talk, would say something like this:

> *"I am the space between you and your athlete. I'm wide enough for a two-way road but often used as a one-way street. I'm strengthened when two seek to understand one another and weakened when they do not. Respect me and a bridge is formed, turning words into meaning and back again. Disrespect me and that bridge is never built, leaving each to stand on opposite sides of a river of confusion. In the end, one needs to only show up, look up, listen up, and speak up to reap the full rewards of what I can offer."*

This relationship, the space between you and your athletes, is sacred. And, although we've talked about filling this space with movement-based language, our impact will go well beyond the patterns we teach. See, an athlete isn't aware of all that goes into a cue, nor should they be. All they're aware of is whether the cue made sense and had an effect on the way they moved. Thus, first, by using language that is customized to your athletes, you send the signal that you understand them and, consequently, listen to and care about them. Second, if those cues consistently result in positive performance shifts, then the athletes will associate their relationship with you to the learning and motivation that follow. Ultimately, you're just teaching movement, but, to do so effectively, you must use the communication strategies on which every great relationship is built.

Today, I think of cueing as being synonymous with connecting. It is central to building an effective coach—athlete relationship and as important to the training process as is the program itself. However, the challenge with language is that the evidence for its effectiveness is far clearer to its recipient than to its creator. Thus, we depend on our athlete as a source of feedback to calibrate, update, and refresh language in line with their learning needs. The models you've learned about are designed to help do just that, putting you in a position to adapt to the ever-changing needs of your athlete.

That said, putting you in a position to master the art of adaptive coaching is different than having mastered it. Therefore, this final section will, first, provide you with a road map intended to help you develop a habit around the cueing skills we've discussed. From there, we will venture through 25+ movement sequences, outlining examples that will apply the strategies we've covered in this book. Collectively, the road map and examples contained in part III, supported by the models outlined in part II and the science explored in part I, will put you in a position to chart a (habit-forming) course to upgrade your coaching language, leaving your athletes to reap the rewards each step of the way.

THE ROAD MAP

7

Habits: A Primer

As each coach found their spot on the gym floor, I found mine at the front of the room. Seeing as the group had just finished the final activity of the course, the room was still buzzing with energy as everyone discussed the cues and analogies they'd come up with for their chosen movement.

The course, by all accounts, had been successful. Engagement was high, presentations were clear, and the activities were filled with rich discussions on the nuances of coaching language. I had done what I had come to do: I taught, and they learned, at least that's what I thought.

As the group finally settled down, a sea of faces looked at me, waiting for my closing remarks. After reminding them that they now had the tools to critically evaluate and upgrade their coaching language, I asked if there were any questions.

After wading through the momentary silence, a young man finally spoke up, announcing to the group "Yeah, I have a question." He continued by saying "I took your course two years ago and, like today, I found the information very useful. However, my question concerns what I should do next to make sure these ideas stick when I'm actually coaching?"

Without thinking, I started to give my canned response on how "this is just the starting line" and how he'll need to "go out and practice," but then I hesitated. I realized that I'd neglected a pretty important detail: He'd already taken this course. And, if my "go into this world and make it a better place" speech didn't work then, why would it suddenly work now?

I quickly redirected from comment to question and asked the coach to explain what he'd done after completing the course the first time. Giving the question some thought, the coach shared "When I got done with the course two years ago, I was eager to start using external cues and analogies within my coaching. I worked hard at it for the first few weeks; however, I noticed that, when I couldn't come up with a good cue, I'd go back to using the cues I was comfortable with, many of which were internal. After about a month, I had reverted back to my old cueing ways."

As I reflected on the coach's answer, I was struck by its familiarity. From diet to exercise, saving money to quitting smoking, how often do people start something with the knowledge of what to do and the apparent motivation to do it only to break under the gravity of their old habits? Why would changing how you coach be any different? In principle, our coaching habits sit alongside our sleeping habits, our eating habits, our driving habits, and a thousand other habits that make up the behaviors that define who we are. The sobering truth was that, up until that moment, I had been convinced that my words were enough to change those used by coaches.

Not wanting to dismiss this coach's vulnerability with a "well, it takes time" or "patience and practice is the key," I took a slightly different approach. I remembered that there had been another coach in the course whose analogies seemed to captivate her group throughout the day. Interested to see what we might gain from her coaching journey, I asked her to tell us how she'd become so obviously good at creating analogies. With everyone in the room echoing their interest, the coach said, "Well, I also took your course two years ago and found the information very helpful. I had always enjoyed using analogies and found that clients responded well to them. This course backed my intuitions and gave me the tools to create analogies as opposed to waiting for them to pop into my mind." Sensing the room wanted more, I asked the coach to walk us through her process for developing this skill. The coach continued, "At first, the change felt effortful and, at times, uncomfortable, as I was trying to come up with new cues on the spot; however, I stuck with it, knowing the benefit outweighed the cost, and, after several months, my language had shifted to the point where I didn't need to think about it anymore."

Here, we have two coaches with a similar set of experiences. They work at the same gym, went through the same course, and bought into the same messages. Why is it, then, that one of the coaches emerged victorious, behavior changed, while the other one had admitted defeat, reverting back to his old cueing ways? While there could be many reasons for this outcome, we can be certain of one thing: A large portion of the answer lives within the science of behavior change.

THE HABIT INSTINCT

How many times have you read a book, attended a course, or gone to a conference and said "Love it; I'm going to start applying these ideas immediately," only to find yourself right back where you started, uncertain as to where it all fell apart? Equally, how many times have you seen an athlete fail to adjust their eating, recovery, or sleeping habits, despite being armed with education, a plan, and a mechanism for accountability? The simple truth is, behavior change is hard for everyone. And, even though we, the coaches, spend most of our days trying to help others shift their habits, it doesn't necessarily mean we're any better at upgrading our own.

Therefore, to get the words off these pages and into your athletes' heads, we need to discuss how you, to the degree that is required, will go about upgrading your coaching language. To do this, we'll get out the pen and paper and start to chart a course for change, helping you to create a road map that will guide your journey from "I will" to "I am."

A Habit Is Born

In the highly pragmatic book *Atomic Habits* (1), James Clear compares habits to atoms, illustrating how the habit is the smallest and most directly controllable unit of behavior change. To see this, picture what you consider to be (un)healthy people. To understand their behavior, we would need to drill down to the singular habits on which their behavior is based. To do this, we would, first, break down their behavior into the categories that influence health, such as diet, exercise, sleep, stress management, and work–life balance. We would then break down each category into its relevant habits, which, in the case of diet, might include their breakfast, lunch, dinner, and snacking habits. Once we're at the level of the habit, choices and actions become observable and, thus, subject to analysis and the possibility of change.

In his critically acclaimed book *The Power of Habit* (2), Charles Duhigg defines a **habit** as a choice that was once deliberate and conscious that has now turned into something we do automatically without even thinking. As such, habits represent the reflexive decisions we make when navigating life's most common circumstances. From what we do when we first get up in the morning (e.g., check phone, go for a run, or meditate) to what we do right before we go to bed (e.g., watch TV, take a warm shower, or read a book), habits represent our default settings. As Duhigg points out, however, at first, habit formation is anything but reflexive. Whether we're learning how to ride a bike or trying to improve our coaching language, when faced with a new situation that requires us to make a decision (move here or there; say this or that), we must deploy a significant amount of effort and concentration. It's only after the repetitions of that choice have accumulated and the novelty has dissipated that we're able to perform these acts with mindless ease.

This should sound familiar because it is fundamentally the same process that we've been discussing in regard to motor learning. In fact, habit formation is considered to be a type of implicit learning, which, as you'll recall, is a form of learning that doesn't require our explicit knowledge or permission. This is why, if not kept in check, habits can emerge that serve our immediate desires—"one more _____ won't hurt"—rather than our best interest. Now, there is nothing malicious at work here. There is no devil on one shoulder and angel on the other. Rather, the brain does what it's designed to do. It suggests solutions that tend to be safe, easy, and immediately gratifying: *why cook when we can order a pizza*; *that email can wait, let's see how many likes our selfie has*; *we can start going to the gym tomorrow, let's get a little more sleep*. If we obey this inner voice often enough, a memory of this decision is constructed, automated, and moved into our unconscious for safekeeping—a habit is born.

Once a habit has fully matured and is no longer under the scrutiny of the conscious mind, it will stay buried, operating in blissful ignorance until the day we decide to dig it up, crack it open, and tinker. However, as coaches, we're uniquely qualified to comment on just how hard this tinkering can be. Whether a movement or a habit, it makes no difference; once something has become entrenched in the mind, it is remarkably difficult to change. In fact, many would argue that we cannot change what has been ingrained; instead, we are simply trying to convince the brain to give some preferred habit a promotion: *packing a healthy lunch*, *organizing my daily schedule*, *meditating before bed*. As challenging as it might be to introduce new habits and paint over old ones, it's not impossible. All we need to get started is an understanding of what makes these automated decisions tick.

The Habit Loop

A habit, at its core, is a decision. It's a decision to do one thing, go for a run, instead of another, turn on the TV. Inevitably, if you consistently make the same decision to go for a run when you get home from work, then we can say you've developed a habit, in this case, of going for a run when you get home from work. The question is why? Why do some people continue to choose their sneakers while others choose their remotes?

To answer this question, we'll refer back to the works of James Clear (1) and Charles Duhigg (2). Both authors talk about four fundamental phases of habit formation. The first phase is the **cue**. Yes, that's right. Before a decision can be made, something needs to be either in our mind or in the physical environment, cueing us to act. For our runner, the cue might be their running shoes inside the door when they get home, while our TV enthusiast might live in a flat, so the TV is the first thing they see upon entering their apartment.

In principle, the job of the cue is to trigger the second phase, the **craving**, which, to borrow a line from James Clear, "is the motivational force behind every habit." If Simon Sinek were to describe a craving, he would say that it is the habit's *why*, its purpose, its reason for existing. The craving is what drives us to take the actions necessary to satisfy it. As such, our runner could run to satisfy any number of cravings. Maybe they enjoy the euphoria of the runner's high, the total-body equivalent to the tingle one gets after brushing their teeth, or maybe they love ice cream, justifying their nightly scoop of mint chocolate chip with a run around the block. Equally, our TV watcher may crave a reprieve from the mental weight of work just as easily as they crave the enjoyment that comes from binge watching the newest Netflix series. Ultimately, the craving doesn't matter as long as it provides a strong enough motivational stimulus for our third phase, the **response**, which is simply the process of acting out the habit.

Once the response has been actioned, our final phase is triggered, the **reward**. Practically speaking, the reward is what satisfies the craving; it is the achievement of the goal, the prize at the bottom of the cereal box. Thus, our runner craving the runner's high is rewarded by the endorphin spike they get after their run, while our TV watcher craving the mental reprieve is rewarded every time they're lost in the fiction of their favorite show. In both cases, if the reward is strong enough, the craving is recharged, ready to be cued the next time our runner and watcher get home from work.

Like a table missing a leg, if a habit is missing even one of these phases, it cannot be sustained. Echoing this point, James Clear (1) notes the following.

> If a behavior is insufficient in any of the four stages, it will not become a habit. Eliminate the cue and your habit will never start. Reduce the craving and you won't experience enough motivation to act. Make the behavior difficult and you won't be able to do it. And if the reward fails to satisfy your desire, then you'll have no reason to do it again in the future. Without the first three steps, a behavior will not occur. Without all four, a behavior will not be repeated. (p. 129)

Collectively, these four phases participate in what Charles Duhigg (2) calls a habit loop: a loop that is initiated when a craving is cued and completed when a response is rewarded. And, like any feedback loop, the more often the cue predictably results in the desired reward, the stronger the habit becomes. Now, if the habit is a positive one, say packing a salad for lunch, it's unlikely that you'll be too concerned about the cue, craving, and reward powering it. However, if a change in job means that you start trading in your leafy greens for the company buffet, then you might suddenly find yourself interested in the particulars of the habit loop, especially if it starts rewarding your waistline as often as it does your taste buds. Dramatics aside, if we recognize that one of our habits is in need of an adjustment, then the first thing we must do is identify the cue and the reward enabling it. Only then can we begin the process of tinkering with each phase until a new habit is formed.

THE HABIT OF CUEING

Now that we understand how habits are formed, we can start designing the road map we'll use to upgrade our own. To do this, we must first decide which habit we want to nudge, which, in our case, is going to be the *habit of cueing*. Because this is an existing habit for coaches, we don't need to try to create a new behavior; instead, we're simply going to explore the cue, craving, and reward steering our current approach to *cueing* movement.

What Cues You to *Cue*?

I think it is fair to say that you won't find this first question difficult to answer. In principle, our job is to help our athletes move better. Therefore, our cue to *cue* is the physical presence of our athletes and their expectation that we'll provide them with information that will help them execute a given movement with greater precision and performance.

Can you think of any other triggers that cue you to *cue*?

_____

_____

_____

What Craving Is Your *Cue* Trying to Satisfy?

While the answer to this question might seem obvious, there are a few possibilities here. The first possible craving is the desire to have your *cue* positively affect the movement itself. In this case, if a coach's *cue* results in a positive shift in coordination or performance, then the craving would be rewarded and reinforced. The second possible craving is the desire to feel like you're connecting with your athlete and being understood. Here, a coach is looking for feedback that suggests that the athlete understands the *cue* and values the coach's contribution. While you might come up with other cravings, these are the most likely candidates because one craving focuses on winning over the movement, while the other craving focuses on winning over the mind.

Can you think of any other cravings your cue is trying to satisfy?

_____

_____

_____

What Type of *Cues* (Responses) Do You Use?

Over the previous six chapters, I've built the case that movements work best when preceded by an external cue or analogy. However, as you now know, many of us, by chance or choice, have ended up promoting internal cues to a far greater degree than evidence (and my personal experience) would suggest. Thus, it is important to take an honest look at your current approach to *cueing* and recognize where it falls within the continuum of cues (chapter 4: internal ↔ external ↔ analogy). By doing this, we'll be able to screen our current cueing habits and, in the process, identify which features need to be maintained, updated, or discarded altogether.

Using the following pie chart, draw in the slices and associated percentages that you feel represent your current approach to cueing. I have included my own pie chart as an example.

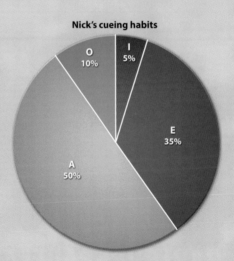

Nick's cueing habits

O = OTHER: Statements not explicitly directed at the movement. For example, general encouragement ("Let's go!"), focus statements ("It's time to concentrate"), and motivational prompts ("You've worked hard for this").

I = INTERNAL CUES: Cues that prompt a focus on limb motion, joint motion, or muscle activation.

E = EXTERNAL CUES: Cues that prompt a focus on an outcome or an interaction with the environment to achieve an outcome.

A = ANALOGY: Cues that prompt a mental image comparing the movement to a familiar scenario, constraint, or object.

Your cueing habits

What Reward Is Your *Cue* Trying to Achieve?

Once you've outlined your craving, in principle, you've outlined the reward you desire. As such, assuming your craving aligns with those mentioned previously, the reward you're chasing includes a positive shift in coordination, connection, or both. Remember that, if we clearly understand the reward we're craving, we'll update our response, our *cue*, to achieve it. However, if the only reward we crave, let's say, is the personal satisfaction that the *cue* makes sense to us (the coach) and we neglect to pay attention to the influence the message has on the athlete, then we won't absorb the information required to know if an adjustment to our language is even needed. We discussed this very point in chapter 1, stressing the importance of looking for the echo of our impact on the way our athlete moves, leveraging *silent sets* to check for learning.

How does the presence or absence of a reward acutely influence your approach to *cueing*, if at all?

_____

_____

_____

If it hasn't already dawned on you, I'd like to call your attention to something. Specifically, in the context of this book and our discussion of coaching language, if you think about it, our cueing habit loop actually lives within our coaching communication loop (see chapter 4). That is, the athletes' physical execution of the movement, DO it, cues us to come up with a *cue* for their next rep, CUE it, whose content is a reflection of the change we crave to see in the athlete, which is then rewarded (or not) during the next rep, DO it, and subsequent discussion, DEBRIEF it. Simply put, our short loop, CUE it, DO it, and DEBRIEF it, is our habit loop. And, if we're going to change or upgrade this habit, we're going to need to put an action plan in place.

HABIT UPGRADE: A THREE-STEP PROCESS

Having outlined the anatomy of our cueing habit loop, we can now consider a three-step process that you can use to kickstart the change that'll inevitably become your new normal. Each step has been given a recommended rollout window, with step 1, *observe*, spanning one week; step 2, *act*, spanning four weeks; and step 3, *become*, representing all time thereafter. My hope is that this plan provides you with the strategies and guidance I wish I had when initially learning how to reboot my own cueing habits.

STEP 1 | WEEK 1 | OBSERVE

While I asked you to reflect on your current use of cues, which you represented as percentages of a pie, the truth is, you can't truly understand your cueing habits until you observe them in action. To do this, you can adopt one (or more) of the following strategies, which range from low to high effort, where an increase in effort is associated with an increase in the accuracy of the observation. Once you've identified the best strategy or strategies for you, use week 1 to observe your cueing habits and establish a baseline.

▶ Strategy 1: Think About It

Here, all you need to do is mentally observe yourself in action. Focusing on the CUE it component of your coaching loop, you'll take time to notice how the quantity and quality of your language impacts the way your athletes move. To guide this reflective practice, answer the following questions at the end of each training session or, at the very least, the end of each training day.

- *Quantity:* How many cues, on average, did I use when coaching my athlete(s) to move?
- *Quality:* What type of cues did I use when coaching my athlete(s) to move?
- *Impact:* How efficient and effective were my cues at changing the way my athlete(s) moved?

As you start to reflect on and answer these questions, notice the way context influences how you communicate. Do you say more or less, emphasizing internal or external cues based on whether you're in the gym versus on the field; working with novices versus experts; or coaching an athlete returning from injury versus one preparing for a competition? Ultimately, we're trying to identify the circumstances that trigger you to over-cue or misplace internal language within the CUE it, as opposed to the preceding DESCRIBE it portion of our coaching loop.

▶ Strategy 2: Write It Down

While everyone should be able to roll out strategy 1, some of you will wish to take a more rigorous and, possibly, more accurate approach. In this case, you'll still extract the quantity, quality, and impact of your cueing; however, this time, you'll carry a notebook with you and answer the following questions, ideally, at the end of each training session or, at the very least, each training day. Remember, these questions are specifically targeted at the CUE it component of your coaching loop.

Session Cueing Reflection

Total #/50 _____

I primarily used external language and analogies when cueing.

1   2   3   4   5   6   7   8   9   10

My external cues had a positive impact on movement performance.

1   2   3   4   5   6   7   8   9   10

My analogies had a positive impact on movement performance.

1   2   3   4   5   6   7   8   9   10

I provided one cue at a time, minimizing information overload.

1   2   3   4   5   6   7   8   9   10

My athlete(s) understood and connected with my cues.

1   2   3   4   5   6   7   8   9   10

Give yourself a score between 1 and 10 for each question and tally up the total out of 50. The higher your score, the more your current behaviors align with the recommendations discussed in this book. It is worth noting that it will take you a few sessions until your score stabilizes. Once you've identified this stable score, say it is 35, then you have what we referred to earlier as your baseline (double your score to see it as a percentage out of 100: e.g., $35 \times 2 = 70$ percent). With your baseline score in hand, you can strategically use this reflective practice activity to track progress over time.

▶ Strategy 3: Record It

As impactful as strategy 2 can be, it is still subject to errors of memory. As such, to up the rigor of your self-reflection, you also have the option of recording one or more of your training sessions during week 1. To do this, you can use either video and audio, which is equipment intensive and usually requires a third person to video the session, or record yourself using a voice recording app on your phone and a wired mic that goes into your headphone jack.[1] Companies like Instamic have created an affordable, wireless mic that is controlled by your phone and downloads straight to your computer via USB. Whichever method you choose, you'll have a recording of the session, which you can then analyze using the five questions outlined in strategy 2. Alternatively, for those who have the time and interest, you can literally count the number of internal cues, external cues, and analogies you used during the session, providing you with an accurate breakdown of your cueing habits for that session.

WEEK 1 SUMMARY

The goal of week 1 is to simply get a handle on how you currently cue by taking an inventory of the impact each prompt has on the way your athletes move. Note the following:

- Which cues get the laughs and the nods
- Which cues shift coordination the quickest
- Which cues get repeated back to you or among the group
- Which cues, when given the option, do your athletes come up with on their own

If we know where to look, the science on which this book is based will appear before your very eyes. Collectively, this should help to make the invisible visible, providing you with a clear understanding of your cueing habits and, in turn, any changes you'd like to make.

WEEK 1 REFLECTION

With week 1 in the books, I want you to recognize that you've taken the first and most difficult step in upgrading the way you coach movement. It doesn't matter whether you uncovered a number of coaching blind spots or you found out that you were pretty good at this cueing stuff; you now have a foundation from which to grow. However, this opportunity will soon fade if you don't take action. Thus, to help you capitalize on your week 1 effort, I've crafted a number of strategies that will help you progressively upgrade your cueing habits.

STEP 2 | WEEKS 2-5 | ACT

While some of you will choose to go at this "cold turkey," changing your cueing habits through brute force, most of you will benefit from taking a more progressive approach. Regardless of the path you choose, I have designed two compounding strategies to help you along the way. The first strategy, *swap*, is meant to help you (re)organize your existing language locker, while the second strategy, *prep*, is about helping you upgrade the future language you put in it.

---

[1] Make sure you get consent from your clients, students, athletes, or patients before recording one of your coaching sessions. This is important, especially if you are working with minors.

▶ Strategy 1: Swap

For the first strategy, I don't want you to focus on coming up with new cues. Instead, you're going to work on (re)organizing your existing coaching language. To do this, I want you to think back to the coaching loop from chapter 4. As you'll recall, we noted that internal and external language can be used when describing a movement, while external language and analogies should be prioritized when cueing it. This ensures that the athlete understands *what* to do (DESCRIBE it) and *how* to do it (CUE it). Problems can arise, however, when you allow too much internal language to leak into your cues, leaving athletes with more knowledge than know-how.

To overcome this common problem, I want you to perform a sleight of hand on your cueing habit. Over the next two weeks, during the CUE it component of your coaching loop, notice when you use internal language as opposed to external language. If you find yourself giving an athlete an internal cue, don't worry about it, and don't correct it; just let the cue ride and see how the athlete responds (the questions from step 1 will support your reflection here). Now, for the sleight of hand. With a clear picture of how your athlete responded to the internal cue, I want you to swap it for a comparable external cue (or analogy) before their next set. To illustrate how you might do this, consider the following example, which outlines a cue swap for the wide-grip pull-up.

This swap serves two purposes. First, it will provide you with a natural opportunity to compare internal and external cues, and, second, the mere presence of an internal cue will start to trigger you to swap it out for an equivalent external cue on subsequent sets. Ultimately, your goal is to progressively move your internal language into the DESCRIBE it component of your coaching loop, allowing your external language and analogies to be the sole tenants of the CUE it component.

Set 1 | Internal Cue

"At the top of the pull, squeeze your shoulder blades down and back"

The Swap

Set 2 | Analogy

"At the top of the pull, bend the bar like an old-school strongman"

Here are some practical tips to remember:

- This works best if you're disciplined in providing only one cue at a time.
- You can continue to use internal language as long as it is followed by an external cue or analogy (e.g., "To jump higher, you'll need to *extend your legs* much faster. To do this, I want you to focus on *exploding off the ground*, like you're trying to touch the ceiling").
- The benefits of an external over an internal cue will be more acutely visible in novices than in experts. This is partly due to the fact that experts are closer to their performance ceiling, and, thus, acute changes are harder to see.
- It's not that internal language can't promote improved movement performance; it can, just not to the same degree or consistency as external language. This is why it is so easy to become dependent on internal cues, as they lull you into a false sense of security.

By the end of two weeks, if you're consistent, you'll have successfully organized your language locker, with internal and external language sitting on the DESCRIBE it shelf and external language and analogies sitting on the CUE it shelf. With spring cleaning out of the way, we can now shift our attention to the strategies that'll help you upgrade and automate your growing inventory of external cues and analogies.

▶ Strategy 2: Prep

By assessing and adapting your current approach to cueing, you've established the mental hooks on which to hang the models for building external cues (chapter 5) and analogies (chapter 6). As such, we're almost ready to apply these strategies in live situations; however, before we run, we must walk, and, in our case, this means crafting our cues in preparation for a session before we attempt to compose them during one.

This is as simple as it sounds. Over these final two weeks, I want you to make two small adjustments to the way you approach presession planning. The first thing I'd like you to do is add a *cueing column*[2] to the existing exercise, set, rep, and load columns that currently make up your programming template (see table 7.1). This should be easy for those of you who use a tabular system (e.g., Excel) to program; however, if you're using a program design software, then this capability might not be available to you. If this is true for your situation, then I suggest you write down your cues in the same notebook you used for your reflective practice. Alternatively, you can create a cueing grid similar to the one depicted in table 7.2.

Once you've found a home for your newly created cues, the next thing I'd like you to do is identify when and where you'll create them. To do this, I'd like you to identify a *trigger* (what will cue you to plan your cues), a *time* (when you will plan your cues), and a *place* (where you will plan your cues). Here's an example:

> **Trigger:** Weekly phone alert—Program design
>
> **Time:** Wednesdays from 2:00–4:00 p.m.
>
> **Place:** Table at favorite coffee shop

Now, it's your turn. Take a moment to identify your trigger, time, and place for planning your cues.

> **Trigger:** _____
>
> **Time:** _____
>
> **Place:** _____

---

[2] It is important that the cues that go in the cue column are in fact cues and *not* descriptive language. See chapter 4 and The Cueing Grid section later in this chapter for clarity on the difference between cues and descriptions.

Once you've created space in your schedule for planning your prompts, you're ready to start using our models to design a new generation of cues to accompany your veteran vocab. Note, however, that, if you haven't read chapters 5 and 6, I'd encourage you to go back and familiarize yourself with our cue creation models (see figure 5.2 on page 131 and figure 6.1 on page 173).

TABLE 7.1 Example of a Program With an Integrated Cueing Column

Movement name	Sets	Reps	Load	Cues or analogies	
A Front squat	1	6	150 lb (68 kg)	1	4
	2	6	160 lb (73 kg)	2	5
	3	6	170 lb (77 kg)	3	6
A Wide-grip pull-up	1	6	+15 lb (7 kg)	1	4
	2	6	+20 lb (9 kg)	2	5
	3	6	+25 lb (11 kg)	3	6
B One-arm one-leg dumbbell Romanian deadlift	1	8	50 lb (23 kg)	1	4
	2	8	55 lb (25 kg)	2	5
	3	8	60 lb (27 kg)	3	6
B One-arm dumbbell bench press	1	10	35 lb (16 kg)	1	4
	2	10	40 lb (18 kg)	2	5
	3	10	45 lb (20 kg)	3	6

TABLE 7.2 Example of a Template for Outlining and Anchoring Cues to a Specific Movement and the Associated Movement Errors or Phases

Movement name		
Movement phase or error	**External cues**	**Analogies**
1	1	1
	2	2
	3	3
2	1	1
	2	2
	3	3
3	1	1
	2	2
	3	3

Here are some practical tips to remember:

- It is helpful to write down your existing external cues and analogies before you focus too heavily on trying to come up with new cues for new cues' sake.
- When using the models to come up with new cues, it is helpful to have a common movement error or phase in mind or a specific athlete for whom the cue is designed.
- This strategy should be used well beyond two weeks. By documenting your cues, you build up a literal language locker and continuously improve your capacity for cue creation.

SUMMARY OF WEEKS 2-5

A positive consequence of using models to plan your cues is that, well, you'll get very good at using them. In a way, this is akin to your mind downloading a new piece of software much like Neo downloaded kung fu in his first days out of the Matrix. And, just as Neo had to learn to harness this new skill by fighting Morpheus in his mind, you'll have to engage in your own mental battle as you learn how to create cues from scratch. However, once this software is fully downloaded, you'll find that you'll stop using the model and, instead, the model will start using you. Instantly, you'll know if a cue's *distance* is close or far, *direction* is toward or away, and *description* is action or analogy. Without thinking, you'll be able to manipulate a cue until it serves the athlete and the movement they're learning.

REFLECTION ON WEEKS 2-5

I'd like to tell you that this change will happen in exactly 14 days, 6 hours, and 54 minutes; however, learning doesn't work like that. What I can tell you is that, the more work you put into our preceding strategies, the better and, likely, faster you'll find yourself controlling language, as Neo did the Matrix. Ultimately, if you want to learn how to bend language to your will, you must accept the challenge, put in the time, and embrace the discomfort that accompanies change.

STEP 3 | WEEKS 6+ | BECOME

To explain the final step, I'd like to revisit James Clear's *Atomic Habits* once more. Of all the valuable insights Clear shares, I found his discussion of the *habit x identity* interaction to be one of the most transformative. In discussing habit change, Clear outlines three levels, which he analogizes to "layers of an onion" (1).

The outer layer represents **outcome**, which are the goals one hopes to achieve by changing a habit. In our case, outcomes would include improved coordination, connection, and performance. The middle layer represents **process**, which are the strategies, the responses, that define the habit. In our case, process is defined by focusing on the promotion of external language and analogies while cueing. The inner layer represents **identity**, which reflects the beliefs and values that give the habit meaning. In our case, the identity associated with the outcomes and processes previously noted is one that values truth, growth, and the pursuit of coaching excellence.

In summarizing these layers, Clear (1) states that "outcomes are about what you get; processes are about what you do; [and] identity is about what you believe" (p. 108). Clear goes on to argue that many attempts at behavior change fail due to an over-focus on changing outcomes and processes and an under-focus on changing identity. In essence, we act out our identity, what we value, with every decision we make. Hence, if we want to change a habit, we must change the identity inspiring it.

Therefore, if you want your cueing habit to fully surrender itself to this new path, you must adopt an authentic belief in the ideas outlined in this book. You must recognize that it's not about a one-off coaching strategy; it's about becoming a better coach. And, in principle, this is exactly what steps 1 and 2 were designed to help you do. Once you believe and trust in these cueing concepts, you're ready to deploy them live within your training sessions. You're ready to freestyle, adapt on the fly, and use our cueing models in the seconds you have between an athlete finishing a rep and expecting you to share an insight that will make the next one better. Having committed to using our models in preparing a session, you're now ready to start using them during one.

Over the coming weeks, if you haven't already, I'd like you to start using our principles for cue creation and adaptation in the midst of your training sessions. This means shifting the distance, direction, or description of your cues as needed, creating analogies in real time and modifying those analogies to fit the needs of the individual. By taking this final step, you're introducing a central ingredient to making your new cueing habit stick—vulnerability. You are, behaviorally, stating that you value upgrading your coaching language more than you fear the discomfort that comes from change.

Be assured that you will make mistakes; you will feel uncomfortable; and you will, at times, sound silly. This is normal. For each time you embrace a mistake, you embrace vulnerability; and only through vulnerability do you alert your cueing habit that you are committed to change, no matter what. I promise you that, if you stay the course, your language will adapt and your athletes will be better for it.

FISHING FOR CUES

We've all heard the saying "Give a man a fish and you feed him for a day; teach a man to fish and you feed him for a lifetime." As an educator, I do my best to live by these words. However, that's not always easy to do, as many prefer the quick fix: "tell me what to do," "give me the tool," "show me the exercise." And, in truth, the quick fix makes a lot of sense when you consider the magnitude of information we have to process relative to our capacity to process it.

Thus, I recognize the extraordinary effort that is required to read a book and attempt to change an entrenched behavior that, for many, has operated untouched or unnoticed for years. However, if you're reading these words, you've gone against the grain, committed to the hard path, and shed your natural affinity for the quick fix. That said, there is plenty of road left to travel. And, while I am confident that you now have the road map and the skills to navigate what lies ahead, there is no doubt that you'll need help along the way.

In many ways, we're like the aspiring fisherman. While learning to fish is our goal, our goal becomes irrelevant if we starve to death on our way to achieving it. For this reason, I felt it critical to provide you with the cueing equivalent to a fridge full of fish. Over the next three chapters, I'd like to invite you to step into my coaching mind and explore my personal language locker, taking whatever you need to evolve your own.

Broken up by strength (chapter 8), power (chapter 9), and speed (chapter 10), these chapters give you a chance to explore cueing grids for 27 movements. Using the structure of our coaching communication loop (chapter 4) as a guide, each cueing grid reflects the principles and models we've been discussing throughout this book. To ensure you get the most out of the next three chapters, I will talk you through the logic of the cueing grids and walk you through some examples.

The Cueing Grid

Each cueing grid is broken down into two sections and laid out across three pages. Section 1, page 1, maps to the DESCRIBE it + DEMONSTRATE it components of our coaching loop and provides suggested language for describing a movement. Section 1 is further broken down into Setup Language, which provides the phrases a coach can use to ensure that the athlete is in the correct position before they move, and Execution Language, which provides the phrases a coach can use to describe how the movement should be performed.[3]

---

[3] Throughout the Setup Language and the Execution Language subsections, you'll see a mix of internal and external language. This mix of language aligns with our discussion of the type of language that occupies the DESCRIBE it component of our coaching loop. However, I want you to notice that there is still a heavy emphasis on external language and analogy. As such, do not feel like you have to use excessive internal language if there is a simpler or more interesting way to phrase it.

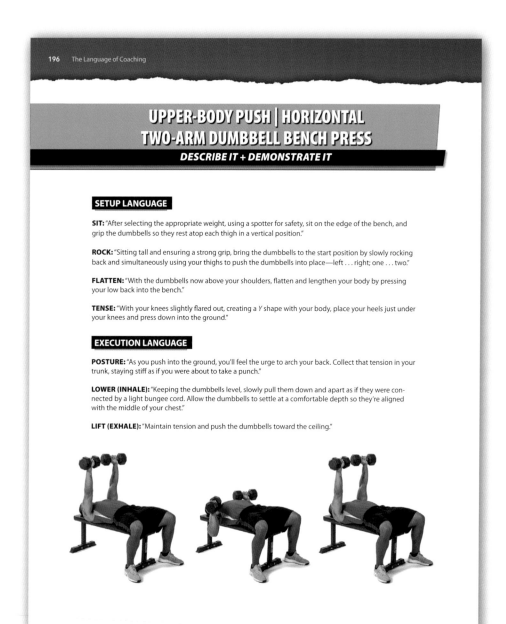

UPPER-BODY PUSH | HORIZONTAL
TWO-ARM DUMBBELL BENCH PRESS
DESCRIBE IT + DEMONSTRATE IT

SETUP LANGUAGE

SIT: "After selecting the appropriate weight, using a spotter for safety, sit on the edge of the bench, and grip the dumbbells so they rest atop each thigh in a vertical position."

ROCK: "Sitting tall and ensuring a strong grip, bring the dumbbells to the start position by slowly rocking back and simultaneously using your thighs to push the dumbbells into place—left . . . right; one . . . two."

FLATTEN: "With the dumbbells now above your shoulders, flatten and lengthen your body by pressing your low back into the bench."

TENSE: "With your knees slightly flared out, creating a *Y* shape with your body, place your heels just under your knees and press down into the ground."

EXECUTION LANGUAGE

POSTURE: "As you push into the ground, you'll feel the urge to arch your back. Collect that tension in your trunk, staying stiff as if you were about to take a punch."

LOWER (INHALE): "Keeping the dumbbells level, slowly pull them down and apart as if they were connected by a light bungee cord. Allow the dumbbells to settle at a comfortable depth so they're aligned with the middle of your chest."

LIFT (EXHALE): "Maintain tension and push the dumbbells toward the ceiling."

While Setup Language will vary based on movement type (e.g., a bench press requires more setup than a vertical jump), Execution Language follows a formula. Specifically, under execution, you'll always see a description for posture, as every movement, to some degree, is limited by postural control (see *positions before patterns* in chapter 5). From posture, you'll see descriptions for each phase of movement, where *phase* is defined as a continuous motion path. For example, the bench press has two phases: a lowering phase, when the weight is lowered from a starting position, and a lifting phase, when the weight is then lifted back up. In contrast, a vertical jump has three phases: a load phase, when the athlete rapidly loads down; an explode phase, when the athlete rapidly explodes up; and a land phase, when the athlete lands the jump.[4] Section 1 concludes with the movement sequence on which the descriptive language is based, providing a visual example of how one might demonstrate the movement.

---

[4] You'll notice that the terms used to describe the phases will change across chapters 8-10. This is a function of selecting terms that best describe the speed of the phase. As such, *lift* is used for slower strength-based movements, while *explode* is used to describe faster power-based movements. Additionally, I had considered organizing the movement cues by common movement error; however, organizing the cues by phase is a more generalizable approach, and, by targeting the phase, you'll also target the movement errors common to that phase.

Section 2, page 2, maps to the CUE it + DO it components of our coaching loop and provides two types of external cues. The first type of external cue, the classic cue, provides four cues for posture and each phase of movement. Each cue is designed based on our 3D cueing model (chapter 5). Hence, distance, direction, and description are varied across the cues.

The second type of cue, which applies our cue-tape strategy from chapter 5, showcases how coaches can guide the most nuanced of movement patterns by applying (cue) tape[5] to the body. Each set of cues is preceded by a description of where the tape should be placed. The cues then describe where the tape should be cued to move, which, in turn, guides the motion of the body, no internal language necessary.

CUE IT + DO IT

POSTURE
- "Stay long and get strong."
- "Flatten into the bench."
- "Stay glued to the bench."
- "Stretch from wall to wall."

LOWERING PHASE
- "Pull the dumbbells apart."
- "Pull the dumbbells to the ground."
- "Resist the dumbbells as you lower."
- "Push through the floor."

LIFTING PHASE
- "Drive the dumbbells toward the ceiling."
- "Punch the dumbbells toward the sky."
- "Push the dumbbells away from the bench."
- "Squeeze the dumbbells together at the top."

POSTURE
Setup: Place a piece of white tape on the outside of each shoulder, a piece of white tape on the outside of each knee, and a piece of yellow tape on the outside of each hip.
Cue 1: "Stretch the white pieces of tape away from each other."
Cue 2: "Keep the pieces of the tape in a straight line."

LOWERING PHASE
Setup: Place a piece of yellow tape on each wrist and a piece of white tape on each elbow.
Cue 1: "Keep the yellow and white tape stacked through the motion."
Cue 2: "Drive the white (elbow) tape down toward the ground."
Cue 3: "Drive the white (elbow) tape away from each other (and toward the walls)."

LIFTING PHASE
Setup: Place a piece of yellow tape on each wrist and a piece of white tape on each elbow.
Cue 1: "Keep the yellow and white tape stacked through the motion."
Cue 2: "Drive the yellow (wrist) tape up toward the ceiling."
Cue 3: "Drive the white (elbow) tape toward each other."

[5] As you'll recall from chapter 5, you can use athletic-type tape. Note that you should use only one tape orientation per rep or set. This means you will target one movement phase at a time, which should be standard practice anyway. Notably, when it makes sense, you can reference clothing as a surrogate for the direct application of a piece of tape (e.g., referencing the shoe instead of placing a piece of tape on the shoe).

Section 2 continues on page 3 and outlines an analogy for posture and each phase of movement. Each analogy is based on our analogy model (chapter 6). Thus, the analogies are either scenario, constraint, or object based, with each analogy referencing either a movement action, attribute, or both.

POSTURE
"Stay stiff like someone is going to punch you in the stomach."

LOWERING
"Drive your elbows out and down as if to compress a spring, using the energy on the way up."

LIFTING
"Drive upward as if to shatter a pane of thick glass."

Just as section 1 concludes with a movement sequence, each set of cues and analogies is anchored to a set of visuals. The classic cues overlay a biomechanical line to help transform a flat image into a dynamic movement. The cue tape places actual markers on the body, enhancing your understanding of where the tape goes and how it should move. Finally, the analogies are brought to life using rich visuals designed to mirror the type of image that might actually jump to mind.

You may be wondering where the DEBRIEF it component of our coaching loop has gone. Don't worry; it wasn't kicked off the team since chapter 4. The reality is, as you know, that the debrief is a fluid process that provides the coach and the athlete with an opportunity to discuss the preceding movement. This discussion could result in a cue being maintained, updated, or changed altogether. As such, further discussion of a movement may leverage the language outlined in section 1, while the cues that emerge from the debrief will pull from the language described in section 2. Thus, there was no explicit need to have a third section titled DEBRIEF it.

SUMMARY

To wrap up, let's revisit the two coaches we met at the beginning of the chapter. The first coach, as you'll recall, was unable to fully realize the habit change he'd hoped to make, while the second coach did. In light of everything we've now learned about habit (re)formation, how might we explain these findings, and what recommendations could we give to the first coach?

For starters, before either coach had ever taken my course, the second coach had already developed a habit of using analogies. She'd already developed a craving for the improved coordination, the reward, that often followed an analogy, the response. In principle, she'd walked into the course with step 1 of our road map complete, aware of the relationship between language and learning. She'd also engaged in a version of step 2, as she was already integrating effective cueing behaviors into her coaching. Thus, her cueing habit was built on a strong foundation, and, therefore, all she needed were the strategies to shift this behavior from chance to choice.

The first coach, on the other hand, hadn't engaged in the same level of coaching introspection and, consequently, was learning about much of this information for the first time. He was pursuing a destination without a road map. As such, he would've gained insights from taking a week to reflect on his current approach to cueing (step 1); benefited from (re)organizing his language locker based on our DESCRIBE it and CUE it coaching loop components (step 2: swap); and profited from learning how to build up his inventory of cues using our cue creation models (step 2: prep). Collectively, these steps would've developed his belief in the outlined cueing principles and slowly introduced him to the change that would have become his new normal. In time, he would have become confident in bringing these principles into live coaching scenarios, trying out cues that, in the past, he would've never thought of or, potentially, been comfortable using (step 3).

While I failed to give our *coaches* these insights on the day, I am forever indebted to them, as their experiences ensured that I wouldn't fail you. You now have everything I have to give. And, while there is, undoubtedly, more to say on the topic, I've said all I can. Thus, it is time for me to stop talking, so you can start.

STRONG CUEING

8

The following pages contain nine movements commonly used to develop strength. Movements are organized by region (upper or lower body), type (push or pull), direction (vertical or horizontal) for upper body, and position (one leg, two legs, or split) for lower body. While specific exercises have been selected to illustrate each movement, it is important to recognize that any number of exercises could've been used.

As discussed in chapter 7, the movements are organized into cueing grids, which are broken down into two sections that collectively map to our *coaching communication loop* (chapter 4). Section 1 provides the language and imagery that support our DESCRIBE it and DEMONSTRATE it phases, and section 2 provides the language and imagery that support our CUE it and DO it phases. While the cueing grids are self-explanatory, a detailed description of how to interpret them is provided in chapter 7 in the section titled The Cueing Grid (page 189).

Some Things to Remember

1. The movement descriptions (i.e., DESCRIBE it) serve two purposes: (1) They provide example coaching phrases that you can use to describe the movement or a portion of it, and (2) they provide you, the coach, with an indication of the biomechanics involved. These are NOT scripts and rarely, if ever, would you need to say everything I have shared, especially if you provide a high-quality demonstration. As such, take what you need, no more, no less, and shed the description once your athlete understands the movement by name. This way you can focus on creating short cues (i.e., CUE it) that will effectively guide focus from one repetition to the next.

2. Even though I have provided multiple external cues (and analogies) for each phase of movement, we should only give our athletes one cue per rep. As you'll recall, this is due to the limitations of both attention and working memory. Therefore, we build learning one movement, one repetition, and one focus at a time.

3. The cues and analogies provided do not represent an exhaustive list. For this reason, I encourage you to come up with your own cues and analogies in addition to using the ones provided. You can use the 3D Cueing Model (chapter 5) and the Analogy Model (chapter 6) to help you during the cue creation process.

UPPER-BODY PUSH | HORIZONTAL
TWO-ARM DUMBBELL BENCH PRESS
DESCRIBE IT + DEMONSTRATE IT

SETUP LANGUAGE

SIT: "After selecting the appropriate weight, using a spotter for safety, sit on the edge of the bench, and grip the dumbbells so they rest atop each thigh in a vertical position."

ROCK: "Sitting tall and ensuring a strong grip, bring the dumbbells to the start position by slowly rocking back and simultaneously using your thighs to push the dumbbells into place—left . . . right; one . . . two."

FLATTEN: "With the dumbbells now above your shoulders, flatten and lengthen your body by pressing your low back into the bench."

TENSE: "With your knees slightly flared out, creating a Y shape with your body, place your heels just under your knees and press down into the ground."

EXECUTION LANGUAGE

POSTURE: "As you push into the ground, you'll feel the urge to arch your back. Collect that tension in your trunk, staying stiff as if you were about to take a punch."

LOWER (INHALE): "Keeping the dumbbells level, slowly pull them down and apart as if they were connected by a light bungee cord. Allow the dumbbells to settle at a comfortable depth so they're aligned with the middle of your chest."

LIFT (EXHALE): "Maintain tension and push the dumbbells toward the ceiling."

CUE IT + DO IT

POSTURE

- ▸ "Stay long and get strong."
- ▸ "Flatten into the bench."
- ▸ "Stay glued to the bench."
- ▸ "Stretch from wall to wall."

LOWERING PHASE

- ▸ "Pull the dumbbells apart."
- ▸ "Pull the dumbbells to the ground."
- ▸ "Resist the dumbbells as you lower."
- ▸ "Push through the floor."

LIFTING PHASE

- ▸ "Drive the dumbbells toward the ceiling."
- ▸ "Punch the dumbbells toward the sky."
- ▸ "Push the dumbbells away from the bench."
- ▸ "Squeeze the dumbbells together at the top."

POSTURE

Setup: Place a piece of white tape on the outside of each shoulder, a piece of white tape on the outside of each knee, and a piece of yellow tape on the outside of each hip.

Cue 1: "Stretch the white pieces of tape away from each other."

Cue 2: "Keep the pieces of the tape in a straight line."

LOWERING PHASE

Setup: Place a piece of yellow tape on each wrist and a piece of white tape on each elbow.

Cue 1: "Keep the yellow and white tape stacked through the motion."

Cue 2: "Drive the white (elbow) tape down toward the ground."

Cue 3: "Drive the white (elbow) tape away from each other (and toward the walls)."

LIFTING PHASE

Setup: Place a piece of yellow tape on each wrist and a piece of white tape on each elbow.

Cue 1: "Keep the yellow and white tape stacked through the motion."

Cue 2: "Drive the yellow (wrist) tape up toward the ceiling."

Cue 3: "Drive the white (elbow) tape toward each other."

POSTURE

"Stay stiff like someone is going to punch you in the stomach."

LOWERING

"Drive your elbows out and down as if to compress a spring, using the energy on the way up."

LIFTING

"Drive upward as if to shatter a pane of thick glass."

UPPER-BODY PUSH | VERTICAL
TWO-ARM DUMBBELL SHOULDER PRESS
DESCRIBE IT + DEMONSTRATE IT

SETUP LANGUAGE

STAND: "After selecting the appropriate weight, using a spotter if needed, bring the dumbbells up so they hover just above your shoulders."

ALIGN: "Ensure that your elbows sit under the dumbbells and just in front of your shoulders as if you were holding two waiter's trays."

GET TALL: "Before pressing, get tall like a tree, reaching the top of your head to the ceiling like branches while driving down through the ground like roots, allowing the tension to develop throughout your trunk."

EXECUTION LANGUAGE

POSTURE: "As you drive down through the ground and begin to press, you'll feel the urge to arch your back. Store that tension in your trunk by staying stiff as if someone were about to swing a bat at your stomach."

LIFT (EXHALE): "Press the dumbbells straight up toward the ceiling until the middle of the dumbbells are vertically aligned with the middle of your shoulders."

LOWER (INHALE): "Slowly lower the dumbbells back into place just above your shoulders, resisting the urge to drop the dumbbells (like the elevator in the Tower of Terror)."

CUE IT + DO IT

POSTURE

▸ "Stand proud."
▸ "Get tall through the press."
▸ "Stay long through the press."
▸ "Don't let the weight shrink you."

LIFTING PHASE

▸ "Punch straight to the sky."
▸ "Press away from the floor."
▸ "Push up through the ceiling."
▸ "Push down into the ground."

LOWERING PHASE

▸ "Resist the DBs as you lower."
▸ "Control the DBs as you lower."
▸ "Keep the DBs flat as you lower."
▸ "Lower the DBs at the same speed."

POSTURE

Setup: Place a piece of yellow tape on the upper chest and a piece of white tape above the waistband.

Cue 1: "Keep the pieces of tape stacked."

Cue 2: "Don't let the tape move as you press; maintain spacing."

LIFTING PHASE

Setup: Place a piece of yellow tape on each wrist and a piece of white tape on each elbow.

Cue 1: "Keep the yellow and white tape stacked through the motion."

Cue 2: "Drive the yellow (wrist) tape up toward the ceiling."

Cue 3: "Drive the white (elbow) tape toward each other."

LOWERING PHASE

Setup: Place a piece of yellow tape on each wrist and a piece of white tape on each elbow.

Cue 1: "Keep the yellow and white tape stacked through the motion."

Cue 2: "Drive the white (elbow) tape down toward the ground."

Cue 3: "Drive the white (elbow) tape away from each other (and toward the walls)."

POSTURE

"Get tall like a tree."

LIFTING

"Press up as you would if you were opening a heavy roll-up garage door."

LOWERING

"Lower the dumbbells as you would a heavy box from a high shelf."

UPPER-BODY PULL | HORIZONTAL
ONE-ARM ONE-LEG DUMBBELL ROW
DESCRIBE IT + DEMONSTRATE IT

SETUP LANGUAGE

HINGE: "After selecting the appropriate weight, approach the bench (or box) so that you're a foot (30 cm) or so away. With the dumbbell in the same hand as the leg that is down, hinge forward, allowing the opposite leg to rise while the free hand rests lightly on the bench for balance."

LENGTHEN: "Hinging forward so your trunk is almost parallel to the ground, focus on lengthening, from head to heel, by reaching the bottom of your shoe toward the wall behind you."

SOFTEN: "With the body in a long, stable position, allow yourself to soften (or bend) your bottom knee, and bring your whole body closer to the ground like an elevator going down a floor."

EXECUTION LANGUAGE

POSTURE: "Stay long, from head to heel, reaching the top of your head to one wall and the bottom of your shoe to the other."

LIFT (EXHALE): "With your arm straight and the dumbbell just in front of your knee, pull the weight up toward your pocket, ending the motion once it is at or just below your hip."

LOWER (INHALE): "Maintaining a long, flat (tabletop) body position, resist the pull of the weight as you slowly lower the dumbbell back to its starting point."

CUE IT + DO IT

POSTURE

▶ "Stretch from wall to wall."
▶ "Lengthen and reach back."
▶ "Stay flat through the pull."
▶ "Stay long through the pull."

LIFTING PHASE

▶ "Pull to your pocket."
▶ "Pull away from the floor."
▶ "Pull toward the ceiling."
▶ "Pull along a vertical line."

LOWERING PHASE

▶ "Resist the weight."
▶ "Slow down the weight."
▶ "Control to the bottom."
▶ "Fight the pull of gravity."

POSTURE

Setup: Place a piece of white tape on the outside of each shoulder, a piece of white tape on each shoe, and a piece of yellow tape on the outside of each hip.

Cue 1: "Stretch the white pieces of tape away from each other."

Cue 2: "Keep the pieces of tape in a straight line."

LIFTING PHASE

Setup: Place a piece of white tape on each elbow.

Cue 1: "Drive the tape to the sky."

Cue 2: "Drive the tape away from the ground."

Cue 3: "Pull the dumbbell through the tape."

LOWERING PHASE

Setup: Place a piece of white tape on each elbow.

Cue 1: "Slow the descent of the tape."

Cue 2: "Lower the tape at a constant speed."

Cue 3: "Keep the dumbbell under the tape as you lower."

POSTURE

"Get long and strong like a chain being pulled in both directions."

LIFTING

"To keep the dumbbell moving straight, imagine you're dragging it up a concrete wall."

LOWERING

"Resist the weight like someone is trying to pull it out of your hands."

UPPER-BODY PULL | VERTICAL | PULL-UP
DESCRIBE IT + DEMONSTRATE IT

SETUP LANGUAGE

GRIP: "Get a strong grip on the bar, with your hands positioned slightly wider than shoulder-width apart."

HANG ON: "Before you start to pull, allow yourself to hang on for a moment, ensuring you are in a long, stable body position and your body is no longer swaying."

EXECUTION LANGUAGE

POSTURE: "Stay long, from head to heel, reaching the top of your head to the ceiling and the bottom of your shoes to the floor."

LIFT (EXHALE): "With your arms straight and grip strong, begin to pull yourself straight up until your chin just clears the bar. You have the option of keeping your legs straight or pulling your knees up into a sitting position as you rise."

LOWER (INHALE): "After pausing and squeezing the bar for just a moment at the top, allow yourself to slowly return to your starting position, unfolding your body back to straight if you had brought your legs up."

CUE IT + DO IT

POSTURE

▶ "Get long."
▶ "Get tight."
▶ "Stay parallel to the wall."
▶ "Stay connected through the pull."

LIFTING PHASE

▶ "Pull up through the ceiling."
▶ "Pull the bar down to the floor."
▶ "Squeeze the bar as you pull."
▶ "Bend the bar as you pull."

LOWERING PHASE

▶ "Resist the weight."
▶ "Slow down the descent."
▶ "Control to the bottom."
▶ "Fight the pull of gravity."

POSTURE

Setup: Place a piece of yellow tape on the upper back (or chest) and a piece of white tape on the lower back (or above the waistband).

Cue 1: "Keep the tape stacked."

Cue 2: "Don't let the pieces of tape get closer as you pull."

LIFTING PHASE

Setup: Place a piece of white tape on each elbow and a piece of yellow tape in the center of the back.

Cue 1: "Drive the white (elbow) tape to the floor."

Cue 2: "Pull the yellow (back) tape to the bar."

Cue 3: "Bring the white (elbow) tape toward each other."

LOWERING PHASE

Setup: Place a piece of white tape on each elbow and a piece of yellow tape in the center of the back.

Cue 1: "Slowly allow the white (elbow) tape to arc out and up."

Cue 2: "Slowly lower the yellow (back) tape to the ground."

Cue 3: "Allow the white (elbow) tape to arc away from each other."

LOWER-BODY PUSH | TWO-LEG FRONT SQUAT
DESCRIBE IT + DEMONSTRATE IT

SETUP LANGUAGE

GRIP: "After selecting the appropriate weight, using a spotter if needed, step up and center yourself directly under the bar so it rests in the space between your shoulders and neck. Once the bar is secure, select your preferred grip (overhand is pictured)."

STEP BACK: "With your elbows forward and arms flat like a table, lift the bar up and off the hooks in the rack, stepping back, one . . . two, to a shoulder-width or slightly wider position. Exact foot position and outward flare should be based on the individual."

EXECUTION LANGUAGE

POSTURE: "Stay long and strong, from head to hip, and keep your elbows pointing forward as if to shoot lasers through the wall."

LOWER (INHALE): "Maintaining a proud, upright trunk, lower toward the ground by allowing your hips to slide back and your knees to slide forward as if you were sitting down onto a low box."

LIFT (EXHALE): "Once you have reached a comfortable depth, focus on standing straight up by pushing the floor away."

CUE IT + DO IT

POSTURE

- ▶ "Keep the bar level."
- ▶ "Get tall as you squat down."
- ▶ "Get long as you squat down."
- ▶ "Stay proud through the squat."

LOWERING PHASE

- ▶ "Squat down."
- ▶ "Pull the floor into you."
- ▶ "Squat down and back."
- ▶ "Sit down behind the bar."

LIFTING PHASE

- ▶ "Push off the floor."
- ▶ "Drive to the ceiling."
- ▶ "Blast from the bottom."
- ▶ "Explode through the roof."

POSTURE

Setup: Place a piece of yellow tape on the upper chest and a piece of white tape above the waistband.

Cue: "Don't let the pieces of tape get closer as you squat."

LOWERING PHASE

Setup: Place a piece of white tape on each hip and a piece of yellow tape on each knee.

Cue 1: "Push the white (hip) tape down and back at the wall."

Cue 2: "Push the white (hip) tape behind the yellow (knee) tape."

Cue 3: "Keep the yellow (knee) tape aligned with your shoes."

LIFTING PHASE

Setup: Place a piece of white tape on each hip and a piece of yellow tape on each knee.

Cue 1: "Drive the white (hip) tape up toward the ceiling."

Cue 2: "The white (hip) tape should move before the yellow (knee) tape."

Cue 3: "Keep the yellow (knee) tape aligned with your shoes."

POSTURE

"Spine of steel."

LOWERING

Squat down as if to gently tap a box full of explosives." (Using a real box will help with this analogy.)

LIFTING

"Stand straight up as if you were sandwiched between two walls." (A pole can be held in front of the athlete to give the illusion of a wall.)

LOWER-BODY PUSH | ONE-LEG SQUAT TO BENCH
DESCRIBE IT + DEMONSTRATE IT

SETUP LANGUAGE

STANCE: "Using a box or a bench, set up so you're standing a foot (30 cm) or so in front of it. Once set, lift your nonsquatting leg so it hovers just above the ground."

REACH: "You can then reach out your arms like you're handing someone a medicine ball, which will help you balance. Alternatively, you may choose to hold a weight, which will typically require you to keep your hands close to your chest."

EXECUTION LANGUAGE

POSTURE: "Stay long and strong, from head to hip, and keep your arms outstretched."

LOWER (INHALE): "Maintaining a proud chest, lower toward the bench by allowing your hips to slide back and your knees to slide forward until you feel a light tap on the bench."

LIFT (EXHALE): "Once you have tapped the bench, focus on standing straight up by driving toward the ceiling."

CUE IT + DO IT

POSTURE

- ▶ "Stay proud as you sit."
- ▶ "Get tall as you tap."
- ▶ "Get long as you squat."
- ▶ "Lengthen as you squat."

LOWERING PHASE

- ▶ "Tap the bench."
- ▶ "Sit down and back."
- ▶ "Squat, tap, and stand."
- ▶ "Reach back for the bench."

LIFTING PHASE

- ▶ "Push off the ground."
- ▶ "Drive through the roof."
- ▶ "Burst from the bottom."
- ▶ "Explode off the floor."

POSTURE

Setup: Place a piece of yellow tape on the upper chest and a piece of white tape above the waistband.

Cue: "Don't let the pieces of tape get closer as you squat."

LOWERING PHASE

Setup: Place a piece of white tape on each hip and a piece of yellow tape on each knee.

Cue 1: "Drive the white (hip) tape down and back at the bench."

Cue 2: "Push the white (hip) tape behind the yellow (knee) tape."

Cue 3: "Keep the yellow (knee) tape pointed at the wall."

LIFTING PHASE

Setup: Place a piece of white tape on each hip and a piece of yellow tape on each knee.

Cue 1: "Drive the white (hip) tape up toward the ceiling."

Cue 2: "The white (hip) tape should move before the yellow (knee) tape."

Cue 3: "Keep the yellow (knee) tape pointed at the wall."

POSTURE

"Squat as if you were holding a heavy medicine ball." (To amplify this analogy, have the athlete alternate between reps with and without a real medicine ball.)

LOWERING

"Imagine you have lasers coming out of your knees; point the lasers at the wall."

LIFTING

"Stand straight up as if you were standing on the edge of a cliff." (You can have the athlete stand on a strip of tape to enhance the illusion of a cliff's edge.)

LOWER-BODY PUSH | REAR FOOT ELEVATED SPLIT SQUAT
DESCRIBE IT + DEMONSTRATE IT

SETUP LANGUAGE

STANCE: "After selecting the appropriate weight, stand flush to the bench so your calves almost touch the edge. With your back foot on the ground, step forward as you would to set up for a split squat. Shift most of your weight onto your front leg, and slowly bring your back foot up (you may need to adjust your distance from the bench), resting the top of your shoe on the edge of the bench." (Based on the weight lifted, some athletes may prefer to set the weight on the floor, get into the split position, and then squat down to pick up the dumbbells.)

EXECUTION LANGUAGE

POSTURE: "Stay long and strong, from head to knee, and keep most of your weight balanced through the front foot, using the back foot for stability."

LOWER (INHALE): "Maintaining a proud chest, lower toward the ground by allowing your back knee to glide back and down toward the bench while your front knee gently slides forward. You will feel your weight shift back as you descend into the squat."

LIFT (EXHALE): "Once you've reached a comfortable depth, drive up and forward at the same angle you followed as you lowered into the squat position. You should finish standing tall, with your weight, once again, centered over your front foot."

CUE IT + DO IT

POSTURE

- ▶ "Stay proud as you squat."
- ▶ "Lengthen as you lower."
- ▶ "Get taller as you descend."
- ▶ "Lift (your chest) as you lower."

LOWERING PHASE

- ▶ "Drive down and back."
- ▶ "Glide back at an angle."
- ▶ "Pull yourself back into the floor."
- ▶ "Slide back toward the bench."

LIFTING PHASE

- ▶ "Drive the ground away."
- ▶ "Push the floor down and back."
- ▶ "Drive up through the ceiling."
- ▶ "Push up and away from the bench."

POSTURE

Setup: Place a piece of white tape on each shoulder, a piece of yellow tape on each hip, and a piece of white tape on each knee.

Cue 1: "Keep the pieces of tape aligned through the movement."

Cue 2: "Keep the yellow (hip) tape between the two pieces of white tape."

LOWERING PHASE

Setup: Place a piece of white tape on the inside of each knee and a piece of yellow tape on the outside of each knee.

Cue 1: "Drive the rear white (knee) tape down and back below the bench."

Cue 2: "Push the rear white (knee) tape behind the front yellow (knee) tape."

LIFTING PHASE

Setup: Place a piece of white tape on each hip and a piece of yellow tape on each knee.

Cue 1: "Drive the white (hip) tape up toward the ceiling."

Cue 2: "Drive the white (hip) tape above the yellow (knee) tape."

POSTURE

"Squat as if you are balancing a book on the top of your head."

LOWERING

"Imagine that your back knee is the head of a hammer and the nails you're trying to hit are just under the bench." (Short: "Hammer the nail.")

LIFTING

"Imagine your hip is a fist; punch up through the top of your head."

LOWER-BODY PULL | TWO-LEG ROMANIAN DEADLIFT
DESCRIBE IT + DEMONSTRATE IT

SETUP LANGUAGE

GRIP: "After selecting the appropriate weight, address the bar, and grasp it such that your hands are placed slightly wider than shoulder-width apart."

STEP BACK: "With a firm grip on the bar (prone grip is pictured) and a strong neutral trunk position, use your legs to slowly rise to a standing position, stepping back from the rack hooks, one . . . two."

EXECUTION LANGUAGE

POSTURE: "Stay long and strong, from head to hip, and keep your arms straight, elbows out, and grip firm."

LOWER (INHALE): "Maintaining a proud, upright trunk, hinge toward the ground by allowing your hips to flex and slide back as if you were bumping your car door shut. Your knees should be slightly bent; however, they should not move during the descent."

LIFT (EXHALE): "Once you've reached a comfortable depth, maintain your trunk position and hinge back up, pushing the floor away as you drive your hips up and forward."

CUE IT + DO IT

POSTURE

- "Bow over the bar."
- "Lengthen as you lower."
- "Finish parallel to the floor."
- "Stay proud through the hinge."

LOWERING PHASE

- "Hide your front pockets."
- "Push (your hips) back at the wall."
- "Back (your hips) away from the bar."
- "Show the ceiling your back pockets."

LIFTING PHASE

- "Stand tall (or get vertical)."
- "Snap up to the ceiling."
- "Take (or steal) the bar away from the floor."
- "Accelerate the bar away from the floor."

POSTURE

Setup: Place a piece of yellow tape on the upper chest and a piece of white tape above the waistband.

Cue 1: "Don't let the pieces of tape get closer as you hinge."

Cue 2: "Drive the yellow (chest) tape away from the white (waist) tape as you hinge."

LOWERING PHASE

Setup: Place a piece of yellow tape on the outside of each shoulder and a piece of white tape on the outside of each hip.

Cue 1: "Drive the white (hip) tape up and back at the wall (or away from the bar)."

Cue 2: "Push the white (hip) tape back and away from the yellow (shoulder) tape."

Cue 3: "Keep the yellow (shoulder) and white (hip) tape aligned through the hinge."

LIFTING PHASE

Setup: Place a piece of yellow tape on the outside of each shoulder and a piece of white tape on the outside of each hip.

Cue 1: "Accelerate the yellow (shoulder) tape above the white (hip) tape (or to the ceiling)."

Cue 2: "Drive the white (hip) tape up and through the yellow (shoulder) tape."

Cue 3: "Trace a quarter circle with the yellow (shoulder) tape."

LOWER-BODY PULL | ONE-LEG ROMANIAN DEADLIFT
DESCRIBE IT + DEMONSTRATE IT

SETUP LANGUAGE

STANCE: "After selecting the appropriate weight, shift all your weight to one leg, allowing a slight bend, or softening, of the loaded knee. With your weight now shifted, maintain a straight line, from head to heel, and allow a slight hinge at your hips so that your free leg drifts back and just off the ground."

EXECUTION LANGUAGE

POSTURE: "Stay long and strong, from head to heel, and keep your arms straight, elbows back, and grip firm."

LOWER (INHALE): "Maintaining a proud, upright trunk, hinge toward the ground by allowing your free heel to rise up and back at the same speed as your upper body descends. The knee of your loaded side should remain slightly bent throughout the motion."

LIFT (EXHALE): "Once you've reached a comfortable depth, maintain your neutral position, from head to heel, and hinge back up, pushing the floor away as you drive your hips up and forward."

CUE IT + DO IT

POSTURE

▸ "Lengthen as you lower."
▸ "Stretch from wall to wall."
▸ "Get proud as you hinge."
▸ "Be unbendable as you bow."

LOWERING PHASE

▸ "Hide your front pockets."
▸ "Move your heel before your head."
▸ "Put your footprint on the back wall."
▸ "Push your heel back and up the wall."

LIFTING PHASE

▸ "Stand tall (or get vertical)."
▸ "Snap up to the ceiling."
▸ "Take (or steal) the dumbbells from the floor."
▸ "Accelerate the dumbbells from the floor."

POSTURE

Setup: Place a piece of yellow tape on the outside of each shoulder and a piece of white tape on the outside of each shoe.

Cue 1: "Don't let the pieces of tape get closer as you hinge."

Cue 2: "Drive the yellow (shoulder) tape away from the white (shoe) tape as you hinge."

LOWERING PHASE

Setup: Place a piece of yellow tape on the outside of each shoulder and a piece of white tape on the outside of each shoe.

Cue 1: "Drive the white (shoe) tape up and back at the wall (or away from the dumbbells)."

Cue 2: "Push the white (shoe) tape back and away from the yellow (shoulder)."

Cue 3: "Keep the yellow (shoulder) and white (shoe) tape aligned through the hinge."

LIFTING PHASE

Setup: Place a piece of yellow tape on the outside of each shoulder and a piece of white tape on the outside of each shoe.

Cue 1: "Accelerate the yellow (shoulder) tape above the white (shoe) tape (or to the ceiling)."

Cue 2: "Drive the white (shoe) tape under the yellow (shoulder) tape as you rise."

Cue 3: "Trace a quarter circle with the yellow (shoulder) tape."

POSTURE

"From head to heel, imagine you're a bungee being pulled at both ends."

LOWERING

"Imagine you have chalk on your heel and there is a brick wall behind you; use your heel to draw a straight line."

LIFTING

"Imagine your chest is chained to the ground and you must break the chain as you drive up."

POWERFUL CUEING

The following pages contain eight plyometric movements commonly used to develop power. Movements are organized by type (jump, bound, hop, throw, toss, or pass), direction (vertical, horizontal, or rotational), and initiation (countermovement or noncounter-movement).

   As discussed in chapter 7, the movements are organized into cueing grids, which are broken down into two sections that collectively map to our *coaching communication loop* (chapter 4). Section 1 provides the language and imagery that support our DESCRIBE it and DEMONSTRATE it phases, and section 2 provides the language and imagery that support our CUE it and DO it phases. While the cueing grids are self-explanatory, a detailed description of how to interpret them is provided in chapter 7 in the section titled The Cueing Grid (page 189).

Some Things to Remember

1. The movement descriptions (i.e., DESCRIBE it) serve two purposes: (1) They provide example coaching phrases that you can use to describe the movement or a portion of it, and (2) they provide you, the coach, with an indication of the biomechanics involved. These are NOT scripts and rarely, if ever, would you need to say everything I have shared, especially if you provide a high-quality demonstration. As such, take what you need, no more, no less, and shed the description once your athlete understands the movement by name. This way you can focus on creating short cues (i.e., CUE it) that will effectively guide focus from one repetition to the next.

2. Even though I have provided multiple external cues (and analogies) for each phase of movement, we should only give our athletes one cue per rep. As you'll recall, this is due to the limitations of both attention and working memory. Therefore, we build learning one movement, one repetition, and one focus at a time.

3. The cues and analogies provided do not represent an exhaustive list. For this reason, I encourage you to come up with your own cues and analogies in addition to using the ones provided. You can use the 3D Cueing Model (chapter 5) and the Analogy Model (chapter 6) to help you during the cue creation process.

COUNTERMOVEMENT | VERTICAL JUMP
DESCRIBE IT + DEMONSTRATE IT

SETUP LANGUAGE

STANCE: "Set your feet so they're slightly wider than shoulder-width apart. Standing tall, bring your arms up, and hold them in a position similar to that of a throw-in in soccer (football) or a line-out in rugby."

EXECUTION LANGUAGE

POSTURE: "Stay long and strong, from head to hip—body silent; legs and arms violent."

LOAD (INHALE): "Maintaining a proud chest, accelerate toward the ground by driving your hips down and back as if evenly loading two vertical springs (your legs). At the same time, focus on throwing your arms down and back, helping load your hips (or springs) with downward force."

EXPLODE (EXHALE): "Once you've reached a comfortable depth (where you've maximized your sense of spring, or elastic tension), focus on exploding skyward, accelerating your arms as if to catch a ball at its highest point."

LAND: "After maximizing hang time, you'll begin to fall back toward earth. Right before impact, reaccelerate your arms down and back, as this will help your hips slide back into position as you absorb the ground."

CUE IT + DO IT

POSTURE

- ▸ "Stay long as you load."
- ▸ "Be proud as you drop."
- ▸ "Stretch the front of your shirt as you dip."
- ▸ "Get tall through the air."

LOADING PHASE

- ▸ "Load and explode."
- ▸ "Pull yourself into the ground."
- ▸ "Sit back between your heels."
- ▸ "Lower along a straight line."

EXPLODING PHASE

- ▸ "Push the floor away."
- ▸ "Explode off the ground."
- ▸ "Accelerate toward the sky."
- ▸ "Drive up and through the ceiling."

LANDING PHASE

- ▸ "Absorb the floor."
- ▸ "Pull the ground into you."
- ▸ "Gradually stop the drop."
- ▸ "Throw your hands back as you brake."

POSTURE

Setup: Place a piece of yellow tape on the upper chest and a piece of white tape above the waistband.

Cue 1: "Don't let the pieces of tape get closer together as you load."

Cue 2: "Drive the yellow (chest) tape up and away from the white (waist) tape as you load."

LOADING PHASE

Setup: Place a piece of white tape on the outside of each hip and a piece of yellow tape on the outside of each knee.

Cue 1: "Drive the white (hip) tape down and back."

Cue 2: "Push the white (hip) tape behind the yellow (knee) tape."

Cue 3: "Keep the yellow (knee) tape pointing straight ahead."

EXPLODING PHASE

Setup: Place a piece of yellow tape on the upper chest and a piece of white tape above the waistband.

Cue 1: "Drive the yellow (chest) tape to the sky."

Cue 2: "Smash the white (waist) tape through the yellow (chest) tape."

Cue 3: "Stack the pieces of tape at the peak of the jump."

LANDING PHASE

Setup: Place a piece of white tape on the outside of each hip and a piece of yellow tape on the outside of each knee.

Cue 1: "Drive the white (hip) tape down and back."

Cue 2: "Push the white (hip) tape behind the yellow (knee) tape."

Cue 3: "Keep the yellow (knee) tape pointing straight ahead."

POSTURE

"Keep your posture zipped up."
(Short: "Zip up.")

LOADING

"Accelerate down as if
to compress a spring,
using the energy on the
way up." (Short: "Coil" or
"Load the spring.")

EXPLODING

"Explode up as if to
catch a football at its
highest point." (Short:
"Get up" or "Catch it.")

LANDING

"Imagine your knees are headlights; as you land, keep
the headlights pointed forward." (Short: "Headlights.")

COUNTERMOVEMENT | HORIZONTAL JUMP
DESCRIBE IT + DEMONSTRATE IT

SETUP LANGUAGE

STANCE: "Step to the line, and set your feet so they're slightly wider than shoulder-width apart. Standing tall, bring your arms up, and hold them in a position similar to that of a throw-in in soccer (football) or a line-out in rugby."

EXECUTION LANGUAGE

POSTURE: "Stay long and strong, from head to hip—body silent; legs and arms violent."

LOAD (INHALE): "Maintaining a proud chest, accelerate toward the ground by driving your hips down and back as if to evenly load two vertical springs (your legs). At the same time, focus on throwing your arms down and back, helping load your hips (or springs) with downward force."

EXPLODE (EXHALE): "Once you've reached a comfortable depth (where you've maximized your sense of spring, or elastic tension), focus on exploding out and up, accelerating your arms out toward your intended landing spot."

LAND: "After maximizing hang time, you'll begin to fall back toward earth, like the flight of a thrown ball. In preparation for landing, start to bring your legs up and forward as if to fold yourself in half. Right before impact, reaccelerate your arms down and back, as this will help your hips slide back into position as you absorb the ground."

CUE IT + DO IT

Note: The colored outlines signify the different phases of the movement.

POSTURE

- ▸ "Lengthen as you load."
- ▸ "Stay proud as you dip."
- ▸ "Keep tension in your T-shirt as you sit."
- ▸ "Get long as you launch off the line."

LOADING PHASE

- ▸ "Dip and rip."
- ▸ "Fall (or tip) forward as you load."
- ▸ "Load along a straight line."
- ▸ "Slice the air (with your hands) as you lower."

EXPLODING PHASE

- ▸ "Push the line away."
- ▸ "Drive away from the ground."
- ▸ "Explode toward the cone."
- ▸ "Blast out beyond the cone."

LANDING PHASE

- ▸ "Soak up the ground."
- ▸ "Pull the pitch into you."
- ▸ "Slow down the dip (or drop)."
- ▸ "Slice the air (with your hands) as you land."

POSTURE

Setup: Place a piece of yellow tape on the upper chest and a piece of white tape above the waistband.

Cue 1: "Don't let the pieces of tape get closer together as you load."

Cue 2: "Drive the yellow (chest) tape up and away from the white (waist) tape as you load."

LOADING PHASE

Setup: Place a piece of white tape on the outside of each hip and a piece of yellow tape on the outside of each knee.

Cue 1: "Drive the white (hip) tape down and back."

Cue 2: "Push the white (hip) tape behind the yellow (knee) tape."

Cue 3: "Keep the yellow (knee) tape pointing straight ahead."

EXPLODING PHASE

Setup: Place a piece of yellow tape on the upper chest and a piece of white tape above the waistband (or on the outside of each hip).

Cue 1: "Drive the yellow (chest) tape to the cone."

Cue 2: "Smash the white (waist) tape through the yellow (chest) tape."

Cue 3: "Align the pieces of tape as you drive off the line."

LANDING PHASE

Setup: Place a piece of white tape on the outside of each hip and a piece of yellow tape on the outside of each knee.

Cue 1: "Drive the white (hip) tape down and back."

Cue 2: "Push the white (hip) tape behind the yellow (knee) tape."

Cue 3: "Keep the yellow (knee) tape pointing straight ahead."

POSTURE

"Imagine a band is pulling you into the ground; focus on getting long as you burst through the band." (Short: "Break the band.")

LOADING

"Load down and forward as you would right before hitting a ski jump (or ramp)."

EXPLODING

"Explode out as if to jump across a fast-flowing river." (Constraint: Use a cone, line, or piece of tape on the ground to reference the shoreline.)

LANDING

"Imagine you are landing in a puddle and trying not to splash." (Short: "Make it ripple.")

COUNTERMOVEMENT | VERTICAL HOP

DESCRIBE IT + DEMONSTRATE IT

SETUP LANGUAGE

STANCE: "With your feet close together, shift all your weight to one leg, and lift your other foot up so it hovers just above the ground. Standing tall, bring your arms up, and hold them in a position similar to that of a throw-in in soccer (football) or a line-out in rugby."

EXECUTION LANGUAGE

POSTURE: "Stay long and strong, from head to hip—body silent; legs and arms violent."

LOAD (INHALE): "Maintaining a proud chest, accelerate toward the ground by driving your hips down and back as if to load a spring (your leg). At the same time, focus on throwing your arms down and back, helping load your hips (or springs) with downward force."

EXPLODE (EXHALE): "Once you've reached a comfortable depth (where you've maximized your sense of spring, or elastic tension), focus on exploding skyward, accelerating your arms as if to catch a ball at its highest point."

LAND: "After maximizing hang time, you'll begin to fall back toward earth. Right before impact, reaccelerate your arms down and back, as this will help your hips slide back into position as you absorb the ground."

CUE IT + DO IT

POSTURE

- ▶ "Lengthen as you lower."
- ▶ "Sight straight as you sit."
- ▶ "Show the wall your shirt as you drop to the dirt."
- ▶ "Stretch up toward the sky."

LOADING PHASE

- ▶ "Drop and pop."
- ▶ "Accelerate into the ground."
- ▶ "Lower in line with your laces."
- ▶ "Cut through the air (with your hands) as you load."

EXPLODING PHASE

- ▶ "Push the ground away."
- ▶ "Get away from the grass."
- ▶ "Drive up toward the ceiling."
- ▶ "Accelerate through the air."

LANDING PHASE

- ▶ "Be silent as you sit."
- ▶ "Pull the floor into you."
- ▶ "Decelerate through the drop."
- ▶ "Cut the air (with your hands) as you drop."

POSTURE

Setup: Place a piece of yellow tape on the upper chest and a piece of white tape above the waistband.

Cue 1: "Don't let the pieces of tape get closer together as you load."

Cue 2: "Drive the yellow (chest) tape up and away from the white (waist) tape as you load."

LOADING PHASE

Setup: Place a piece of white tape on the outside of each hip and a piece of yellow tape on the outside of each knee.

Cue 1: "Drive the white (hip) tape down and back."

Cue 2: "Push the white (hip) tape behind the yellow (knee) tape."

Cue 3: "Keep the yellow (knee) tape pointing straight ahead."

EXPLODING PHASE

Setup: Place a piece of yellow tape on the upper chest and a piece of white tape above the waistband.

Cue 1: "Drive the yellow (chest) tape to the sky."

Cue 2: "Smash the white (waist) tape through the yellow (chest) tape."

Cue 3: "Stack the pieces of tape at the peak of the hop."

LANDING PHASE

Setup: Place a piece of white tape on the outside of each hip and a piece of yellow tape on the outside of each knee.

Cue 1: "Drive the white (hip) tape down and back."

Cue 2: "Push the white (hip) tape behind the yellow (knee) tape."

Cue 3: "Keep the yellow (knee) tape pointing straight ahead."

POSTURE

"Imagine you have a big number 54 on the front of your shirt. Make sure we can always see that number. (Short: "Show your number.")

LOADING

"Load straight down as if you were in a very narrow alley (or hallway)."

EXPLODING

"Explode up as if you were trying to touch the bottom of a basketball net." (Short: "Get the net.")

LANDING

"Land as if you were in a room where a baby had just fallen asleep." (Short: "Don't wake the baby.")

Shhhh

COUNTERMOVEMENT | LATERAL BOUND
DESCRIBE IT + DEMONSTRATE IT

SETUP LANGUAGE

STANCE: "With your feet close together, shift all your weight to the leg opposite the direction you'll bound, lifting your other foot up so it hovers just above the ground. Standing tall, bring your arms up, and hold them in a position similar to that of a throw-in in soccer (football) or a line-out in rugby."

EXECUTION LANGUAGE

POSTURE: "Stay long and strong, from head to hip—body silent; legs and arms violent."

LOAD (INHALE): "Maintaining a proud chest, accelerate toward the ground by driving your hips down and back, as if to load a spring (your leg). At the same time, focus on throwing your arms down and back, helping load your hips (or springs) with downward force."

EXPLODE (EXHALE): "Once you've reached a comfortable depth (where you've maximized your sense of spring, or elastic tension), focus on exploding up and away (laterally) from where you started, accelerating your arms as if to catch a ball at its highest point."

LAND: "After maximizing hang time, you'll begin to fall back toward earth. Right before impact, reaccelerate your arms down and back, as this will help your hips slide back into position as you absorb the ground."

CUE IT + DO IT

POSTURE

- "Stay long as you lower."
- "Look up as you load."
- "Keep the number on your T-shirt visible to everyone."
- "Stay vertical in flight."

LOADING PHASE

- "Bend and blast."
- "Coil into the ground."
- "Fall in (or laterally) as you load."
- "Hammer (your hands) back as you bend."

EXPLODING PHASE

- "Push away from the pitch."
- "Snap off the ground."
- "Fly over (or across) the arch (or rainbow)."
- "Drive out and up (to the cone or line)."

LANDING PHASE

- "Gently accept the ground."
- "Pull the pitch into you."
- "Squeeze the brakes at the bottom."
- "Hammer (your hands) back as you brake."

POSTURE

Setup: Place a piece of yellow tape on the upper chest and a piece of white tape above the waistband.

Cue 1: "Don't let the pieces of tape get closer together as you load."

Cue 2: "Drive the yellow (chest) tape up and away from the white (waist) tape as you load."

LOADING PHASE

Setup: Place a piece of white tape on the outside of each hip and a piece of yellow tape on the outside of each knee.

Cue 1: "Drive the white (hip) tape down and back."

Cue 2: "Push the white (hip) tape behind the yellow (knee) tape."

Cue 3: "Keep the yellow (knee) tape pointing straight ahead."

EXPLODING PHASE

Setup: Place a piece of yellow tape on the upper chest and a piece of white tape above the waistband.

Cue 1: "Drive the yellow (chest) tape up and out."

Cue 2: "Keep the pieces of tape stacked throughout the arc of the bound."

LANDING PHASE

Setup: Place a piece of white tape on the outside of each hip and a piece of yellow tape on the outside of each knee.

Cue 1: "Drive the white (hip) tape down and back."

Cue 2: "Push the white (hip) tape behind the yellow (knee) tape."

Cue 3: "Keep the yellow (knee) tape pointing straight ahead."

POSTURE

"Imagine there is a chain pulling your shoulder to your opposite foot; break the chain as you bound." (Short: "Break the chain.")

LOADING

"Load as you would if you were about to make a front-on tackle." (Short: "Load for impact.")

EXPLODING

"Explode up and out as if you were bounding over an open flame." (Short: "Get over the fire.")

LANDING

"Land as you would on a thin sheet of ice." (Short: "Don't break the ice.")

NONCOUNTERMOVEMENT | SQUAT TO THROW
DESCRIBE IT + DEMONSTRATE IT

SETUP LANGUAGE

STANCE: "Set your feet so they're slightly wider than shoulder-width apart. Holding the medicine ball at your chest, elbows pointing down, lower into a quarter- to half-squat position."

EXECUTION LANGUAGE

POSTURE: "Stay long and strong, from head to hip; coil like a spring ready to release."

EXPLODE (EXHALE): "Once you've reached a comfortable depth (where you've maximized your sense of spring, or elastic tension), focus on exploding skyward, accelerating the ball in an effort to project it as high as you can."

LAND: "Maintain sight on the ball as you land naturally (tall, with a slight bend in your hips and knees). The ball should come straight back down, which may require you to step out of the way (do *not* attempt to catch the ball)."

CUE IT + DO IT

POSTURE

- "Stay long."
- "Be proud."
- "Support under the ball."
- "Keep the ball at your collar."

EXPLODING PHASE

- "Explode off the ground."
- "Drive the ground away."
- "Accelerate the ball to the sky."
- "Project the ball as high as you can."

POSTURE

Setup: Place a piece of yellow tape on the upper chest and a piece of white tape above the waistband.

Cue 1: "Don't let the pieces of tape get closer together as you explode."

Cue 2: "The yellow (chest) tape leads the white (waist) tape as you explode."

EXPLODING PHASE

Setup: Place a piece of yellow tape on the upper chest and a piece of white tape above the waistband.

Cue 1: "Drive the yellow (chest) tape to the sky (or up through the ball)."

Cue 2: "Smash the white (waist) tape through the yellow (chest) tape."

Cue 3: "Stack the pieces of tape at the peak of the throw."

POSTURE

"Create tension as if the ball were chained to the ground."
(Short: "Tension and blast.")

EXPLODING

"Imagine you are fully submerged and must explode up and out of the water."
(Short: "Get out of the water.")

NONCOUNTERMOVEMENT | VERTICAL TOSS
DESCRIBE IT + DEMONSTRATE IT

SETUP LANGUAGE

STANCE: "Set your feet so they're slightly wider than shoulder-width apart. Keeping your arms straight (and elbow-less), hinge at the hip (just like a Romanian deadlift) until the ball hovers just off the ground and between your shoes."

EXECUTION LANGUAGE

POSTURE: "Stay long and strong, from head to hip; body should be dinner table flat."

EXPLODE (EXHALE): "Once you've reached a comfortable depth (where you've maximized your sense of spring, or elastic tension in the hamstrings), focus on exploding (hinging) skyward, accelerating the ball in an effort to project it (vertically) as high as you can."

LAND: "Maintain sight on the ball as you land naturally (tall, with a slight bend in your hips and knees). The ball should come straight back down, which may require you to step out of the way (do *not* attempt to catch the ball)."

CUE IT + DO IT

POSTURE

- ▶ "Stay flat."
- ▶ "Be proud."
- ▶ "Bow over the ball."
- ▶ "Stay parallel to the ground."

EXPLODING PHASE

- ▶ "Accelerate the ball away from the ground."
- ▶ "Drive the ball vertically."
- ▶ "Whip the ball to the sky."
- ▶ "Release the ball high into the sky."

POSTURE

Setup: Place a piece of white tape on the outside of each hip and a piece of yellow tape on the outside of each knee.

Cue 1: "Don't let the white (hip) tape drop as you hinge down."

Cue 2: "Keep the white (hip) tape above the yellow (knee) tape."

EXPLODING PHASE

Setup: Place a piece of yellow tape on the upper chest or outside of each shoulder and a piece of white tape on the outside of each hip.

Cue 1: "Drive the yellow (chest) tape up through the ball (or to the sky)."

Cue 2: "Smash the white (waist) tape through the yellow (chest) tape."

Cue 3: "Stack the pieces of tape at the peak of the throw."

POSTURE

"Hinge as though there were a high box just below your hips, preventing you from squatting down." (Short: "Don't bump the box.")

EXPLODING

"Release the ball vertically as if there were a wall behind you." (Short: "Get the ball up the wall.")

NONCOUNTERMOVEMENT | CHEST PASS
DESCRIBE IT + DEMONSTRATE IT

SETUP LANGUAGE

DISTANCE: "Before squatting, stand up and reach toward the wall. There should be 1-2 feet (30-61 cm) between the ball and the wall. When first learning this movement, start close to the wall, especially if the medicine ball doesn't have much bounce. Later on (or if using a bouncy medicine ball), you can move back, allowing for an increased focus on power."

STANCE: "Standing parallel to the wall, set your feet so they're slightly wider than shoulder-width apart. Holding the medicine ball at your chest, elbows pointing down, lower into a quarter- to half-squat position."

EXECUTION LANGUAGE

POSTURE: "Stay long and strong, from head to hip; body should be 'zipped up.'"

EXPLODE (EXHALE): "Once you've reached a comfortable depth, place an imaginary target on the wall where you'd like the ball to hit (target should be parallel with the ball). Focusing on the target, accelerate the ball at the wall, minimizing movement in the trunk and lower body."

CATCH: "If the medicine ball is *not* bouncy (i.e., a dead ball), then you will catch it with your arms still outstretched. If the medicine ball is bouncy (i.e., a reactive ball), then you will need to absorb the ball by softening (bending) your elbows as the ball rebounds off the wall."

CUE IT + DO IT

POSTURE

- ▸ "Collar up, ball up."
- ▸ "Stay square to the wall."
- ▸ "Keep the ball at chest height."
- ▸ "Focus on where you want the ball to hit the wall."

EXPLODING PHASE

- ▸ "Get the ball away from you."
- ▸ "Drive the ball along a straight line."
- ▸ "Accelerate the ball into the wall."
- ▸ "Project the ball through the wall."

POSTURE

Setup: Place a piece of yellow tape on the outside of each shoulder and a piece of white tape on the outside of each shoe.

Cue 1: "Keep the yellow (shoulder) and white (shoe) tape stacked."

Cue 2: "Keep the yellow (shoulder) tape aligned over the middle of each shoe."

EXPLODING PHASE

Setup: Place a piece of yellow tape on the outside of each shoulder and a piece of white tape on the outside of each hand.

Cue 1: "Drive the white (hand) tape at the wall."

Cue 2: "Finish with the white (hand) tape in front of the yellow (shoulder) tape."

Cue 3: "Drive the ball away from the yellow (shoulder) tape."

POSTURE

"Set up like you were about to pass a basketball to a teammate."

EXPLODING

"Imagine someone has wrapped your upper body in duct tape, pinning your arms to your sides. Drive the ball at the wall as if to break the tape." (Short: "Break the tape.")

NONCOUNTERMOVEMENT | ROTATIONAL THROW
DESCRIBE IT + DEMONSTRATE IT

SETUP LANGUAGE

DISTANCE: "Before squatting, stand up and reach your inside arm toward the wall. There should be less than a foot (30 cm) between your hand and the wall. When first learning this movement, start close to the wall, especially if the medicine ball doesn't have much bounce. Later on (or if using a bouncy medicine ball), you can move back, allowing for an increased focus on power."

STANCE: "Standing perpendicular to the wall, set your feet so they're slightly wider than shoulder-width apart. Cradling the medicine ball just outside of your pocket, lower into a quarter- to half-squat position. Allow yourself to rotate slightly toward the ball, creating tension through your trunk and hips."

EXECUTION LANGUAGE

POSTURE: "Stay long and strong, from head to hip; body should be 'zipped up.'"

EXPLODE (EXHALE): "Once you've reached a comfortable depth, place an imaginary target on the wall where you'd like the ball to hit (target should be parallel with the ball). Focusing on the target, accelerate the ball at the wall, allowing your hips and trunk to rotate as they would if you were hitting a tennis ball."

CATCH: "If the medicine ball is *not* bouncy (i.e., a dead ball), then you will catch it with your arms still outstretched. If the medicine ball is bouncy (i.e., a reactive ball), then you will need to absorb the ball by softening (bending) your elbows as the ball rebounds off the wall."

CUE IT + DO IT

POSTURE

- ▸ "Collar up, ball down."
- ▸ "Hide the ball from the wall."
- ▸ "Keep the ball next to your pocket."
- ▸ "See the spot on the wall you want the ball to strike."

EXPLODING PHASE

- ▸ "Belt buckle and ball should face the wall."
- ▸ "Guide the ball along a straight line."
- ▸ "Whip the ball into the wall."
- ▸ "Smash the ball through the wall."

POSTURE

Setup: Place a piece of white tape on the front of each hip.

Cue 1: "As you load, rotate so that the outside (hip) tape is behind the inside (hip) tape."

Cue 2: "Rotate until the ball and the outside (hip) tape are behind the inside (hip) tape."

EXPLODING PHASE

Setup: Place a piece of white tape on the front of each hip.

Cue 1: "Drive the outside (hip) tape at the wall with the ball."

Cue 2: "Accelerate the ball on a straight line from the outside (hip) tape to the wall."

Cue 3: "Throw the ball so that you finish with both pieces of (hip) tape facing the wall."

POSTURE

"Load as you would if you were just about to swing a softball bat." (Other analogies can be created by referencing tennis, golf, and hockey, just to name a few.)

EXPLODING

"Whack the wall and burst the ball." (Accentuate this analogy by verbalizing the *whack* and adding a clap when the ball hits the wall.)

WHACK!

FAST CUEING

10

The following pages contain 10 movement skills commonly associated with the expression of speed, especially in the context of field and court sports. Movements are organized by direction (linear and multidirectional) and type (e.g., acceleration, crossover, and backpedal).

As discussed in chapter 7, the movements are organized into cueing grids, which are broken down into two sections that collectively map to our *coaching communication loop* (chapter 4). Section 1 provides the language and imagery that support our DESCRIBE it and DEMONSTRATE it phases, and section 2 provides the language and imagery that support our CUE it and DO it phases. While the cueing grids are self-explanatory, a detailed description of how to interpret them is provided in chapter 7 in the section titled The Cueing Grid (page 189).

Some Things to Remember

1. The movement descriptions (i.e., DESCRIBE it) serve two purposes: (1) They provide example coaching phrases that you can use to describe the movement or a portion of it, and (2) they provide you, the coach, with an indication of the biomechanics involved. These are NOT scripts and rarely, if ever, would you need to say everything I have shared, especially if you provide a high-quality demonstration. As such, take what you need, no more, no less, and shed the description once your athlete understands the movement by name. This way you can focus on creating short cues (i.e., CUE it) that will effectively guide focus from one repetition to the next.

2. Even though I have provided multiple external cues (and analogies) for each phase of movement, we should only give our athletes one cue per rep. As you'll recall, this is due to the limitations of both attention and working memory. Therefore, we build learning one movement, one repetition, and one focus at a time.

3. The cues and analogies provided do not represent an exhaustive list. For this reason, I encourage you to come up with your own cues and analogies in addition to using the ones provided. You can use the 3D Cueing Model (chapter 5) and the Analogy Model (chapter 6) to help you during the cue creation process.

LINEAR SPEED | THREE-POINT START
DESCRIBE IT + DEMONSTRATE IT

SETUP LANGUAGE

STEP: "With both feet on the start line, hip-width apart, step back, one . . . two, so that both feet are now between 1 to 1.5 foot lengths away from the line."

DRAG AND DROP: "Drag your dominant kicking leg straight back so that, when you drop your knee to the ground, it is parallel with (or slightly behind) the toe of your opposite shoe (still hip-width apart). You are now kneeling, with toes tucked in a vertical posture, looking down the track or field."

FALL: "With your hands positioned as if you were holding two glasses of water, fall forward, placing your fingers on the edge of the start line. Your thumbs and pointer fingers should form right triangles with the ground, with your thumbs aligned with the middle of your shoulders."

LIFT AND LOAD: "Slowly bring your hips up and forward as if a wall were behind you. Then, bring the hand on the side of the forward leg back so that it aligns with your hip pocket. At this point, you should be in the position pictured in the first image below."

EXECUTION LANGUAGE

POSTURE: "From head to hip, stay long and strong—'tension through length.'"

LEG ACTION (The PUSH): "Both legs PUSH out and up at the same angle as the front shin; the trunk parallels the front shin during the PUSH; and the PUSH ends once a straight line is achieved from head to heel."

LEG ACTION (The PUNCH): "After the initial PUSH, the back leg glides over the ground as the knee punches forward, until the thigh and body create a 90-degree angle.

"PUSH and PUNCH finish at the same moment; the action is then reversed to initiate the next stride."

ARM ACTION: "The front arm is straight while the hand pushes the start line forward. With the arm acting like a wall, the legs, especially the front leg, push back, creating tension in the body. To initiate the start, the up arm is violently thrown forward as the down arm is thrown back. This movement serves to break the inertia and kick-start forward momentum."

CUE IT + DO IT

POSTURE

- ▶ "Lengthen through the push."
- ▶ "Lengthen through the lift."
- ▶ "Get long off the line."
- ▶ "Stay long and low."

LEG ACTION (PUSH Emphasis)

- ▶ "Explode off the start line."
- ▶ "Push away from the start line."
- ▶ "Blast out of the blocks."
- ▶ "Drive the ground back."

LEG ACTION (PUNCH Emphasis)

- ▶ "Explode up and out."
- ▶ "Punch out of your stance."
- ▶ "Blast toward the finish."
- ▶ "Drive as you rise."

ARM ACTION

- ▶ "Throw (your forearm) at the finish."
- ▶ "Throw (your hand) at the wall."
- ▶ "Hammer (your hand) back."
- ▶ "Fire (your forearm) forward."

POSTURE

Setup: Place a piece of yellow tape on the upper back and a piece of white tape on the lower back.

Cue 1: "Smash the pieces of tape together as you drive off the line."

Cue 2: "Align the pieces of tape as you finish driving off of the line."

LEG ACTION

Setup: Place a piece of white tape on the outside of the ankle of the front leg and a piece of yellow tape on the outside of the knee of the back leg.

Cue 1: "Drive the white (ankle) tape back into the ground" (PUSH emphasis).

Cue 2: "Drive the yellow (knee) tape toward the finish" (PUNCH emphasis).

Cue 3: "Rip the pieces of tape (ankle and knee) apart as you blast off the line."

ARM ACTION

Setup: Place a piece of white tape on the down hand and a piece of yellow tape on the up hand.

Cue 1: "Throw the white tape back."

Cue 2: "Throw the yellow tape forward."

Cue 3: "Rip the pieces of tape apart as you explode toward the finish."

POSTURE

"From head to heel, imagine that your body is a chain. As you drive out, snap the chain." (Short: "Snap the chain.")

LEG ACTION (PUSH)

"Explode off the line like a cheetah is two steps behind you." (Short: "Beat the cheetah.")

LINEAR SPEED | ACCELERATION
DESCRIBE IT + DEMONSTRATE IT

EXECUTION LANGUAGE

OVERVIEW: While acceleration can be broken down into many phases for analytical purposes, when it comes to coaching, we must recognize that the athlete executes acceleration as a singular motion with a cyclical, or alternating, pattern. As such, we will treat acceleration as a single-phase movement whereby one leg PUSHes back (sometimes called backside mechanics) while the opposite leg PUNCHes forward (sometimes called frontside mechanics). Similar to the language used to cue the three-point start, we will consider separate cues for each type of leg action.

POSTURE: "From head to hip, stay long and strong—'tension through length.'"

LEG ACTION (PUSH): "The PUSH starts once the thigh and hip finish flexing, continues as the foot on the same side strikes the ground, and ends once the foot has finished PUSHing off the ground. During the PUSH, the leg should drive back at the same angle as the trunk (shin should be parallel to the trunk). If successful, the foot will strike under (or slightly in front of) the center of mass, creating enough vertical force to lift the athlete off the track and enough horizontal force to propel them down it."

LEG ACTION (PUNCH): "The PUNCH starts once the foot has finished pushing off the ground, continues as the leg on the same side travels forward, and ends once the thigh and hip have finished flexing. During the PUNCH, the thigh should immediately start to move forward, until it has created an 80- to 90-degree angle with the body. Any delay in this forward motion (characterized by the heel going to the butt, instead of the thigh moving forward) will compromise the harmony of the overall technique.

"When the PUSH and PUNCH are coordinated effectively, the athlete will appear to gradually rise like a jet taking off as they transition from acceleration to absolute speed."

ARM ACTION: "The arms, like the legs, alternate between a forward and backward motion whereby the forward motion requires the arm to flex (just as the opposite leg flexes) and the backward motion requires the arm to extend (just as the opposite leg extends)."

CUE IT + DO IT

POSTURE

- ▶ "Stay long as you push."
- ▶ "Get long as you drive."
- ▶ "Lengthen as you lift."
- ▶ "Rise through the drive."

LEG ACTION (PUSH)

- ▶ "Drive the track back."
- ▶ "Explode off the ground."
- ▶ "Push the ground away."
- ▶ "Project through the push."

LEG ACTION (PUNCH)

- ▶ "Punch through the air."
- ▶ "Drive toward the finish."
- ▶ "Punch through the finish."
- ▶ "Get away from the ground."

ARM ACTION

- ▶ "Cut the air."
- ▶ "Slice the air."
- ▶ "Throw (your arms) back."
- ▶ "Hammer (your arms) back."

POSTURE

Setup: Place a piece of yellow tape on the upper back and a piece of white tape on the lower back.

Cue 1: "Keep the tape in a straight line through the sprint."

Cue 2: "Don't let the tape get farther apart during the sprint."

Cue 3: "Drive the tape together as you drive off the ground."

LEG ACTION

Setup: Place a piece of white tape on the outside or front of each ankle and a piece of yellow tape on the outside or top of each knee.

Cue 1: "Drive the white (ankle) tape back into the ground" (PUSH emphasis).

Cue 2: "Drive the yellow (knee) tape toward the finish" (PUNCH emphasis).

Cue 3: "Rip the (opposite) pieces of tape apart as you drive off the ground."

ARM ACTION

Setup: Place one piece of yellow tape on the top of each wrist.

Cue 1: "Throw the tape back."

Cue 2: "Hammer the tape back."

Cue 3: "Drive the tape past your pockets."

POSTURE

"As you accelerate, gradually rise like a jet taking off from an aircraft carrier." (Short: "Be the jet" or "Get the jet.")

LEG ACTION (PUSH)

"Strike back and rip up the track." (Short: "Rip the track.")

LEG ACTION (PUNCH)

"Drive your knees forward as if to shatter a pane of glass." (Short: "Shatter the glass.")

ARM ACTION

"Arms are like hammers; legs are like nails. Hammer the nail." (Short: "Hammer" or "Hammer the nail.")

LINEAR SPEED | ABSOLUTE SPEED
DESCRIBE IT + DEMONSTRATE IT

EXECUTION LANGUAGE

OVERVIEW: While absolute speed can be broken down into many phases for analytical purposes, when it comes to coaching, we must recognize that the athlete executes absolute speed as a singular motion with a cyclical, or alternating, pattern. As such, we will treat absolute speed as a single-phase movement whereby one leg PUSHes down and back (sometimes called backside mechanics) while the opposite leg PUNCHes up and forward (sometimes called frontside mechanics). Note that the coaching language considered here can generally be applied to endurance running as well as it can sprinting, as both techniques overlap in the physics imposed on them.

POSTURE: "From head to hip, stay tall. Lead through the belt buckle or waistband."

LEG ACTION (PUSH): "The PUSH starts once the thigh and hip finish flexing, continues as the foot on the same side strikes the ground, and ends once the foot has finished PUSHing off the ground. During the PUSH, the leg should strike just in front of the center of mass, creating enough vertical force to lift you off the track. Where you are in relation to your maximal velocity will determine whether the additional force directed horizontally equates to an increase, maintenance, or decrease in speed."

LEG ACTION (PUNCH): "The PUNCH starts once the foot has finished pushing off the ground, continues as the leg on the same side travels up and forward, and ends once the thigh and hip have finished flexing. During the PUNCH, the thigh should immediately start to move up and forward until it has created an 80- to 90-degree angle with the body. Any delay in this upward motion (characterized by the heel going to the butt, instead of the thigh moving up) will compromise the harmony of the overall technique.

"When the PUSH and PUNCH are coordinated effectively, the front thigh (leg) will move down and back at the same instant the back thigh (leg) moves up and forward."

ARM ACTION: "The arms, like the legs, alternate between a forward and backward motion whereby the forward motion requires the arm to flex (just as the opposite leg flexes) and the backward motion requires the arm to extend (just as the opposite leg extends)."

CUE IT + DO IT

Note: The colored outlines signify the different phases of the movement.

POSTURE

- ▸ "Get tall."
- ▸ "Stretch to the sky."
- ▸ "Lengthen as you lift."
- ▸ "Lead with your belt buckle (or waistband)."

LEG ACTION (PUSH)

- ▸ "Attack the track."
- ▸ "Drive down and back."
- ▸ "Explode off the track."
- ▸ "Aggressive through the push."

LEG ACTION (PUNCH)

- ▸ "Attack the sky."
- ▸ "Punch through the sky."
- ▸ "(Drive your) thigh to the sky."
- ▸ "Aggressive through the punch."

ARM ACTION

- ▸ "Cut the air."
- ▸ "Slice the air."
- ▸ "Throw (your arms) back."
- ▸ "Hammer (your arms) back."

POSTURE

Setup: Place a piece of yellow tape on the upper back and a piece of white tape on the lower back.

Cue 1: "Keep the tape stacked through the sprint."

Cue 2: "Keep the tape aligned during the sprint."

Cue 3: "Stretch the yellow (upper) tape up and away from the white (lower) tape."

LEG ACTION

Setup: Place a piece of white tape on the outside or front of each ankle and a piece of yellow tape on the outside or top of each knee.

Cue 1: "Drive the white (ankle) tape down into the ground" (PUSH emphasis).

Cue 2: "Drive the yellow (knee) tape up toward the sky" (PUNCH emphasis).

Cue 3: "Rip the (opposite) pieces of tape apart as you drive off the ground."

ARM ACTION

Setup: Place a piece of yellow tape on the top of each wrist.

Cue 1: "Throw the tape back."

Cue 2: "Hammer the tape back."

Cue 3: "Drive the tape past your pockets."

POSTURE

"Stay long and (slightly) lean like you're in a windstorm (or wind tunnel)." (Short: "Let the wind hold you" or "Lean into the wind" or "Don't get blown back.")

LEG ACTION (PUSH)

"Drive down through the track as you would if you were sprinting up a steep set of stairs." (Short: "Get up the stairs" or "Strike the stairs.")

LEG ACTION (PUNCH)

"Drive your knee (thigh) forward as if to strike up through a sparring mitt." (Short: "Hit the mitt.")

ARM ACTION

"The elbow is like a door hinge, opening as the arm moves back and closing as the arm moves forward." (Short: "Open the door.")

MULTIDIRECTIONAL SPEED | 45-DEGREE CUT
DESCRIBE IT + DEMONSTRATE IT

EXECUTION LANGUAGE

OVERVIEW: Change of direction, for which cutting is a type, refers to any movement in which an athlete stops motion in one direction (i.e., deceleration) so they can generate motion in a new direction (i.e., acceleration). In the context of the 45-degree cut, imagine an athlete is looking for a way to get past an approaching defender. With space to the defender's left or right, the athlete decides to take a 45-degree cut to attack the available space. While we will specifically look at cueing for the *cut* itself, it is important to recognize that the totality of this movement requires the *approach*, the *cut*, and the *transition*, which, in this case, is a linear acceleration (a movement we discussed earlier in the chapter).

POSTURE: "Stay square to the defender so you don't tip them off to where you're going. Your posture should remain square (i.e., 'square up') to the defender and neutral (i.e., 'proud posture' or 'be proud'). Once you start to PUSH, your posture should remain 'proud' and move in the direction of the cut (*not* bending or leaning toward the PUSH leg)."

LEG ACTION (PUSH): "As you approach the defender, start to lower your body (suddenly or gradually, based on the scenario). Once you're low enough (quarter- to half-squat depth, based on the scenario), plant the cleats of your *outside* foot firmly into the field, and PUSH yourself into the available space (45 degrees to your left or right). You can think of this as an angled acceleration step."

LEG ACTION (PUNCH): "Just as the PUSH and PUNCH work together during acceleration, they also work together during cutting. As your PUSH leg drives you in the desired direction, your (inside) PUNCH leg should lift and point in the new direction. Think of your knee like a headlight on a car; you want that headlight pointing in the direction you're headed.

"When done correctly, the PUSH and PUNCH legs work together to allow the next step out of the cut to look just like the first step in linear acceleration."

ARM ACTION: "Your arms play an important role in breaking momentum in one direction so you can redirect it in another. Just like acceleration, your opposite arm and leg work together. Your outside arm drives across your body in the same direction as your PUNCH leg while your inside arm drives back toward your PUSH leg."

CUE IT + DO IT

POSTURE

- ▸ "Square up (the defender)."
- ▸ "Stay strong as you strike."
- ▸ "Stay proud as you push."
- ▸ "Be unbreakable as you cut."

LEG ACTION (PUSH)

- ▸ "Drive the ground away."
- ▸ "Snap off the ground."
- ▸ "Push the ground away."
- ▸ "Stay low (or flat) as you push."

LEG ACTION (PUNCH)

- ▸ "Drive hard into the space."
- ▸ "Get to the outside (of the defender)."
- ▸ "Punch out of the cut (or into the space)."
- ▸ "Stay low (or flat) as you punch (out of the cut)."

ARM ACTION

- ▸ "Punch (your arm) across."
- ▸ "Throw (your arm) across."
- ▸ "Create torque as you turn."
- ▸ "Rotate (or reach) into the run."

POSTURE

Setup: Place a piece of yellow tape on the upper chest and a piece of white tape above the waistband.

Cue 1: "Keep the tape connected through the cut."

Cue 2: "Keep the yellow (chest) tape inside of your (outside) pocket."

Cue 3: "Lead with the yellow (chest) tape as you exit the cut."

LEG ACTION

Setup: Place a piece of white tape on the outside or front of each ankle and a piece of yellow tape on the outside or top of each knee.

Cue 1: "Drive the white (ankle) tape into the ground" (PUSH emphasis).

Cue 2: "Drive the yellow (knee) tape into the space" (PUNCH emphasis).

Cue 3: "Get the (opposite) pieces of tape away from each other as you drive off the ground."

ARM ACTION

Setup: Place a piece of yellow tape on top of each wrist.

Cue 1: "Punch the (outside) yellow tape toward the space."

Cue 2: "Throw the (outside) yellow tape into the space."

Cue 3: "Drive the (outside) yellow tape across your midline."

POSTURE

"Get low and lean like you're busting down a door with the side of your shoulder." (Short: "Bust down the door.")

LEG ACTION (PUSH)

"Get out of the cut like a rattlesnake is about to strike the side of your ankle." (Short: "Don't get bit.")

LEG ACTION (PUNCH)

"Imagine your knees are headlights. Point them in the direction you want to go." (Short: "Light the path.")

ARM ACTION

"Imagine your trunk is a spinning top. Throw your arms across your body to spin the top in the direction you want to go." (Short: "Spin the top.")

MULTIDIRECTIONAL SPEED | SIDE-STEP CUT
DESCRIBE IT + DEMONSTRATE IT

EXECUTION LANGUAGE

OVERVIEW: Change of direction, for which the side-step cut is a type, refers to any movement in which an athlete stops motion in one direction (i.e., deceleration) so they can generate motion in a new direction (i.e., acceleration). In the context of the side-step cut, imagine an athlete is looking for a way to get past an approaching defender. With space to the defender's left or right, the athlete decides to sidestep the defender and attack the available space. While we will specifically look at cueing for the *cut* itself, it is important to recognize that the totality of this movement requires the *approach*, the *cut*, and the *transition*, which, in this case, is a linear acceleration (a movement we discussed earlier in the chapter).

POSTURE: "Stay square to the defender so you don't tip them off to where you're going. Your posture should remain square (i.e., 'square up') to the defender and neutral (i.e., 'proud posture' or 'be proud'). Once you start to PUSH, your posture should remain "proud" and move in the direction of the cut (*not* bending or leaning toward the PUSH leg)."

LEG ACTION (PUSH): "As you approach the defender, start to lower your body (suddenly or gradually, based on the scenario). Once you're low enough (quarter- to half-squat depth, based on the scenario), plant the cleats of your *outside* foot firmly into the field and PUSH yourself laterally (90 degrees to your left or right) while staying square to the direction you're running."

LEG ACTION (PUNCH): "Just as the PUSH and PUNCH work together during acceleration, they also work together during the side step. As your PUSH leg drives you laterally, your (inside) PUNCH leg should lift and laterally drift, still pointing straight ahead.

"When done correctly, the PUSH and PUNCH legs work together to allow the next step out of the side step to look just like the first step in linear acceleration."

ARM ACTION: "Your arms should mirror the opposite leg through the side step and rapidly switch as you exit the side step into acceleration. Note that your arms are critical for shifting lateral momentum into linear acceleration, hence the need to be aggressive as you exit the side step."

CUE IT + DO IT

POSTURE

- ▸ "Square up (the defender)."
- ▸ "Stay strong as you step."
- ▸ "Stay proud as you push."
- ▸ "Be unbendable as you step."

LEG ACTION (PUSH)

- ▸ "Explode off the ground."
- ▸ "Step out of the way."
- ▸ "Drive as you (laterally) drift."
- ▸ "Stay low (or flat) as you step."

LEG ACTION (PUNCH)

- ▸ "Explode into the space."
- ▸ "Step into the space."
- ▸ "Shift to the outside (of the defender)."
- ▸ "Stay low (or flat) as you punch (out of the step)."

ARM ACTION

- ▸ "(Arms) loose as you move laterally."
- ▸ "(Arms) silent (during step) and then violent (during sprint)."
- ▸ "Throw (your arms) back (during sprint)."
- ▸ "Hammer (your arms) back (during sprint)."

POSTURE

Setup: Place a piece of yellow tape on the upper chest and a piece of white tape above the waistband.

Cue 1: "Keep the tape connected through the step."

Cue 2: "Keep the yellow (chest) tape inside of your (outside) pocket."

Cue 3: "Lead with the yellow (chest) tape as you finish the step."

LEG ACTION

Setup: Place a piece of white tape on the outside or front of each ankle and a piece of yellow tape on the outside or top of each knee.

Cue 1: "Drive the white (ankle) tape laterally into the ground" (PUSH emphasis).

Cue 2: "Drive the yellow (knee) tape up and out into the space" (PUNCH emphasis).

Cue 3: "Get the (opposite) pieces of tape away from each other as you drive off the ground."

ARM ACTION

Setup: Place a yellow piece of tape on top of each wrist.

Cue 1: "Throw the yellow tape back as you exit the step."

Cue 2: "Hammer the yellow tape back as you exit the step."

Cue 3: "Drive the tape past your pockets as you exit the step."

POSTURE

"As you step, imagine that there is a brick wall in front of you and you must step into a doorway to get out." (Short: "Get out the door.")

LEG ACTION (PUSH)

"Step as you would if you were barefoot and trying to get off a pile of hot coals." (Short: "Get off the coals.")

LEG ACTION (PUNCH)

"Once you've sidestepped the defender (or into the space), go straight (or north) as if sprinting down a narrow hallway." (Short: "Go north.")

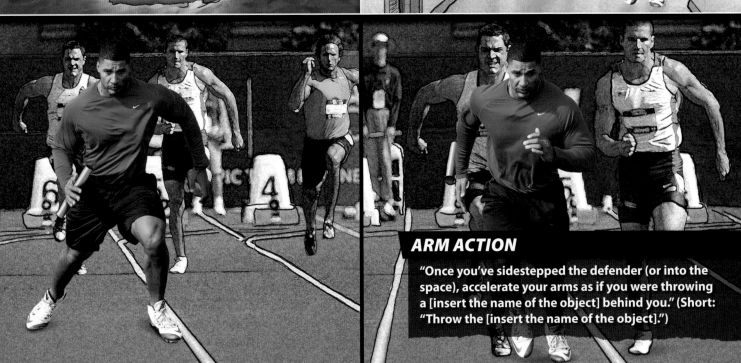

ARM ACTION

"Once you've sidestepped the defender (or into the space), accelerate your arms as if you were throwing a [insert the name of the object] behind you." (Short: "Throw the [insert the name of the object].")

MULTIDIRECTIONAL SPEED | 180-DEGREE CUT
DESCRIBE IT + DEMONSTRATE IT

EXECUTION LANGUAGE

OVERVIEW: Change of direction, for which the 180-degree cut is a type, refers to any movement in which an athlete stops motion in one direction (i.e., deceleration) so they can generate motion in a new direction (i.e., acceleration). While sport, at times, requires athletes to make such severe maneuvers, the following version depicted is associated with the Pro-Agility Drill, a test popularized by its inclusion in the NFL Combine. As a nod to my own Combine coaching roots, I felt compelled to include it here because I have used many a cue to help athletes master this deceptively difficult drill. Because we've already considered detailed (and transferable) cues for the 45-degree cut and the side-step cut, we will broaden our focus to include the *approach*, the *cut*, and the *transition*, which, in this case, is a crossover to acceleration (a movement we'll cover later in this chapter).

APPROACH: "For simplicity, we will define the *approach* as the three steps into the cut. We can refer to step 1 as the SIT step, step 2 as the PIVOT step, and step 3 as the CUT step. The key is to drop your center of mass on the SIT step (quarter to half squat); pivot, lean, and lower on the PIVOT step (quarter to half turn); and punch the (cut) line while loading the (inside) pivot leg during the CUT step. The transition from PIVOT step to CUT step should be a fast, one . . . two, tempo."

CUT: "When the *approach* is done correctly, the (outside) *cut* leg will be on or just beyond the (cut) line, with the majority of your weight shifted onto the (inside) pivot leg. Having accepted your body weight during the PIVOT step, the CUT step can be used to rapidly PUSH you off the line."

TRANSITION: "With the (inside) PIVOT leg already loaded like the front leg in a three-point start, the CUT step simply gives you the boost needed to overcome inertia. Just like the three-point start, you'll PUSH with both legs at first. Once you've created enough force, you'll drive your cut leg (tightly) across your body (what is known as a crossover). With the help of your arms, this crossover will project you into a powerful acceleration position."

CUE IT + DO IT

Note: The colored outlines signify the different phases of the movement.

APPROACH

Cut Step   Pivot Step   Sit Step

CUT

TRANSITION

APPROACH

- ▸ "Sit down" (SIT step).
- ▸ "Lower and lean" (PIVOT step).
- ▸ "Punch the line" (CUT step).
- ▸ "Get low as you get into the line."

CUT

- ▸ "Punch the line away."
- ▸ "Bounce off the line."
- ▸ "Get away from the line."
- ▸ "Be light off the line."

TRANSITION

- ▸ "Explode toward the finish."
- ▸ "Drive hard off your inside (leg)."
- ▸ "Fire (your outside knee) at the finish."
- ▸ "Punch (your outside knee) past your pocket."

APPROACH

Setup: Place a piece of yellow tape just above the waistband.

Cue 1: "Turn the tape toward [pick a target they'll be facing during the cut] as you lower."

Cue 2: "Lower the tape as you load into the line."

CUT

Setup: Place a piece of yellow tape just above the waistband.

Cue 1: "Keep the yellow (waist) tape inside of the cut step."

Cue 2: "Drive the yellow (waist) tape away from the cut step."

TRANSITION

Setup: Place a piece of yellow tape on the outside or top of each knee.

Cue 1: "Drive the yellow (knee) tape at the finish."

Cue 2: "Punch the yellow (knee) tape past your (inside) pocket."

APPROACH

"Imagine there is a triangular roof over the drill. As you approach the line, get under the roof." (Short: "Get under the roof.")

CUT

"Imagine that there is a hundred dollar bill on the line. Get the cash before your competitor does." (Short: "Get the cash.")

TRANSITION

"Keep your crossover tight as if there were a ledge right in front of you." (Short: "Stay tight to the ledge.")

MULTIDIRECTIONAL SPEED | CROSSOVER TO SPRINT
DESCRIBE IT + DEMONSTRATE IT

EXECUTION LANGUAGE

OVERVIEW: Transition movements, for which the crossover is a type, refers to any movement that is used to transition an athlete from facing one direction to another by rotating, without reducing speed. In the context of the crossover to sprint, we can imagine an athlete on defense, after getting beat to their inside or outside, must quickly cross over and sprint to try to catch the runaway attacker (offensive player). While we will specifically look at cueing for the crossover to sprint itself, it is important to recognize that the totality of this movement requires the *approach* (typically, a shuffle), the *cut*, and the *transition* (i.e., crossover to sprint).

POSTURE: "Once you realize the attacker has evaded you, you want to keep your eyes on them, maintaining a neutral ('proud') posture that, if it could speak, would say 'no way I'm getting beat.'"

LEG ACTION (PUSH): "As soon as you realize the attacker is moving outside of you, you want to rapidly lower your center of mass ('get low' or 'get down') and shift in their direction. With your weight shifted in the direction you want to move, drive off your (inside) PUSH leg, projecting yourself in the direction of the fleeing attacker."

LEG ACTION (PUNCH): "Just as the PUSH and PUNCH work together during acceleration, they also work together during the crossover. As your PUSH leg drives you in the desired direction, your (outside) PUNCH leg should lift and point in that new direction, driving tightly across your body (think of your knee like a headlight on a car; you want that headlight pointing in the direction you're headed)."

"When done correctly, the PUSH and PUNCH legs work together to allow the next step out of the crossover to look just like the first step in linear acceleration."

ARM ACTION: "Your arms play an important role in breaking momentum in one direction so you can redirect it in another. Just like acceleration, your opposite arm and leg work together. Your inside arm drives across your body and forward in the same direction as your PUNCH leg while your outside arm drives back toward your PUSH leg."

CUE IT + DO IT

POSTURE
- ▶ "Track the attacker."
- ▶ "Shadow the attacker."
- ▶ "Get long as you load."
- ▶ "Stay proud as you push."

LEG ACTION (PUSH)
- ▶ "Drive hard off the ground."
- ▶ "Push the ground away."
- ▶ "Stay low (or flat) as you launch."
- ▶ "Stay level (or flat) as you push."

LEG ACTION (PUNCH)
- ▶ "Drive hard at the attacker."
- ▶ "Chase the attacker."
- ▶ "Punch out of the crossover (or into the space)."
- ▶ "Stay level (or flat) as you punch (out of the crossover)."

ARM ACTION
- ▶ "Punch (your forearm) across."
- ▶ "Throw (your forearm) across."
- ▶ "Create torque as you turn."
- ▶ "Reach into the run."

POSTURE

Setup: Place a piece of yellow tape on the upper chest and a piece of white tape above the waistband.

Cue 1: "Keep the tape aligned during the crossover."

Cue 2: "Drive the yellow (chest) tape past your (inside) pocket."

Cue 3: "Lead with the yellow (chest) tape as you cross over."

LEG ACTION

Setup: Place a piece of white tape on the outside or front of each ankle and a piece of yellow tape on the outside or top of each knee.

Cue 1: "Drive the white (ankle) tape into the ground" (PUSH emphasis).

Cue 2: "Drive the yellow (knee) tape into the space" (PUNCH emphasis).

Cue 3: "Get the (opposite) pieces of tape away from each other as you drive off the ground."

ARM ACTION

Setup: Place a piece of yellow tape on top of each wrist.

Cue 1: "Punch the (inside) yellow tape toward the space."

Cue 2: "Throw the (inside) yellow tape into the space."

Cue 3: "Drive the (inside) yellow tape across your midline."

POSTURE

"Launch into the crossover like a missile taking off." (Short: "Launch.")

LEG ACTION (PUSH)

"Imagine that you're racing a track athlete coming out of the blocks. Drive through your crossover so you don't get beat off the line." (Have athletes face each other and race over a given distance.)

LEG ACTION (PUNCH)

"Punch your knee across as if to hit (or drive) a baseball off a low tee." (Short: "Hit the ball.")

ARM ACTION

"Imagine that your inside arm is being pulled back by a band. Snap the band as you drive out of the crossover." (Short: "Snap the band.")

MULTIDIRECTIONAL SPEED | CROSSOVER RUN
DESCRIBE IT + DEMONSTRATE IT

EXECUTION LANGUAGE

OVERVIEW: Tracking movements, for which the crossover run is a type, refers to any movement that is used to track an opponent, most commonly, during a defensive scenario. In the context of the crossover run, imagine an athlete is on defense and requires the capacity to track a forward moving attacker (offensive player) to maintain position or make a stop. In American football, this pattern allows a defensive back to maintain position on a wide receiver. Equally, in rugby, this movement allows a defender to force their opponent into touch (out of bounds) or back inside, where they're likely to get tackled by the defender or their teammate. Ultimately, the crossover run is the most effective way to move backward (at varied angles) to track a fast-moving opponent.

POSTURE: "Keep your eyes focused on the opponent (or target) at all times and maintain a neutral ('proud') posture as you track back."

LEG ACTION (PUSH): "As soon as you realize the attacker is moving, you want to rapidly lower your center of mass ('get low' or 'get down') and shift in their direction. With your weight shifted in the direction you want to move, you'll alternate between driving off your inside (PUSH) leg and your outside (PUSH) leg, projecting yourself in the direction of the evading attacker."

LEG ACTION (PUNCH): "Just as the PUSH and PUNCH work together during acceleration, they also work together during the crossover run. As your PUSH leg drives you in the desired direction, your PUNCH leg should lift and point in the same direction, driving tightly across your body (think of your knee like a flashlight; you want that flashlight pointing in the direction you're headed).

"When done correctly, the PUSH and PUNCH alternate, allowing you to accelerate, backward, at the desired angle."

ARM ACTION: "Just like acceleration, your opposite arm and leg work together. The arm opposite the PUNCH leg drives forward while the arm opposite the PUSH leg drives back."

CUE IT + DO IT

POSTURE

▸ "Track the attacker."
▸ "Shadow the attacker."
▸ "Stay square as you track."
▸ "Get long through the push."

LEG ACTION (PUSH)

▸ "Drive hard down the line."
▸ "Attack back—push, push, push."
▸ "Rapidly drive the ground away."
▸ "Stay level (or flat) as you push."

LEG ACTION (PUNCH)

▸ "Close the space."
▸ "Chase the space."
▸ "Punch down the line."
▸ "Get away from the grass."

ARM ACTION

▸ "Cut the air."
▸ "Slice the air."
▸ "Throw (your arms) back."
▸ "Hammer (your arms) back."

POSTURE

Setup: Place a piece of yellow tape on the upper chest and a piece of white tape above the waistband.

Cue 1: "Keep the tape aligned during the run."

Cue 2: "Keep the yellow (chest) tape facing the attacker as you run."

Cue 3: "Lead with the yellow (chest) tape as you run."

LEG ACTION

Setup: Place a piece of white tape on the outside or front of each ankle and a piece of yellow tape on the outside or top of each knee.

Cue 1: "Drive the white (ankle) tape into the ground" (PUSH emphasis).

Cue 2: "Drive the yellow (knee) tape into the space" (PUNCH emphasis).

Cue 3: "Get the (opposite) pieces of tape away from each other as you drive off the ground."

ARM ACTION

Setup: Place a piece of yellow tape on the top of each wrist.

Cue 1: "Throw the yellow tape back."

Cue 2: "Hammer the yellow tape back."

Cue 3: "Drive the tape past your pockets."

POSTURE

"Imagine you have laser vision like Superman. Keep those lasers pointed at your opponent's hips." (Short: "Lock in the laser.")

LEG ACTION (PUSH)

"Imagine the ground is a drum and each step is a beat. Create a loud, fast drumbeat—boom, boom, boom." (Short: "Bring the boom" or "Bring the beat.")

LEG ACTION (PUNCH)

"Once you pick your line, run like it's a cliff's edge." (Short: "Stay on the edge.")

ARM ACTION

"Imagine your forearms are metal blades like the T-1000 in *Terminator 2*, and cut through the air." (Short: "Cut (or slice) the air.")

MULTIDIRECTIONAL SPEED | DROP STEP TO SPRINT
DESCRIBE IT + DEMONSTRATE IT

EXECUTION LANGUAGE

OVERVIEW: Transition movements, for which the drop step is a type, refers to any movement that is used to transition an athlete from facing one direction to another by rotating, without reducing speed. In the context of the drop step to sprint, imagine an athlete backpedaling to maintain defensive position and, after getting beat to their inside or outside, quickly drop stepping and sprinting to try to catch the runaway attacker (offensive player). While we will specifically look at cueing for the drop step itself, it is important to recognize that the totality of this movement requires the *approach* (commonly the backpedal), the *cut*, and the *transition* (i.e., drop step to sprint). Note that, while the crossover is typically used to make transitions between 90 and 135 degrees of rotation, the drop step is typically used to make transitions between 90 and 180 degrees of rotation. The decision to use one over the other depends on the athlete's physical quali-ties, movement preferences, and the situation.

POSTURE: "Once you realize the attacker has evaded you, you want to keep your eyes on them and main-tain a neutral ('proud') posture that mirrors (or shadows) your opponent."

LEG ACTION (PUSH): "As soon as you realize the attacker is moving outside of you, you want to rapidly lower your center of mass ('get low' or 'get down') and start to pivot (off your outside leg) in their direction of motion. Tracking the attacker will allow you to transition from pivot to PUSH, driving off your (outside) PUSH leg and projecting yourself in the direction of the escaping attacker."

LEG ACTION (PUNCH): "Just as the PUSH and PUNCH work together during acceleration, they also work together during the drop step. As your PUSH leg drives you in the desired direction, your (inside) PUNCH leg should lift, swing (open), and point in the new direction.

"When done correctly, the PUSH and PUNCH legs work together to allow the next step out of the drop step to look just like the first step in linear acceleration."

ARM ACTION: "Your arms play an important role in transferring momentum from one direction so you can redirect it in another. Just like acceleration, your opposite arm and leg work together. Your outside arm drives across your body and forward in the same direction as your PUNCH leg while your inside arm drives back toward your PUSH leg."

CUE IT + DO IT

POSTURE

- "Track the attacker."
- "Mirror their motion."
- "Stay square as you push."
- "Stay proud as you push."

LEG ACTION (PUSH)

- "Explode backward."
- "Push the ground away."
- "Push through the pivot."
- "Stay level (or flat) as you push."

LEG ACTION (PUNCH)

- "Explode into the space behind you."
- "Open into the space behind you."
- "Punch through the pivot."
- "Swing or sweep (your leg) open."

ARM ACTION

- "Hammer (your inside elbow) back."
- "Throw (your inside elbow) back."
- "Create torque as you turn."
- "Elbow the air as you turn."

POSTURE

Setup: Place a piece of yellow tape on the upper chest and a piece of white tape above the waistband.

Cue 1: "Keep the tape connected during the drop step."

Cue 2: "Drive the tape back as you push into the drop step."

Cue 3: "The yellow (chest) tape should track the attacker as you pivot into the drop step."

LEG ACTION

Setup: Place a piece of white tape on the outside or front of each ankle and a piece of yellow tape on the outside or top of each knee.

Cue 1: "Drive the white (ankle) tape back into the ground" (PUSH emphasis).

Cue 2: "Swing the yellow (knee) tape into the space" (PUNCH emphasis).

Cue 3: "Get the (opposite) pieces of tape away from each other as you drive off the ground."

ARM ACTION

Setup: Place a piece of yellow tape on the back or outside of each elbow.

Cue 1: "Drive the (inside) yellow tape back."

Cue 2: "Throw the (inside) yellow tape back."

Cue 3: "Hammer the (inside) yellow tape back."

Imagine you have a spotlight coming out of your chest like Iron Man. Keep the spotlight pointed at the offensive player at all times." (Short: "Keep the light on 'em.")

LEG ACTION (PUSH)

"Explode back and away as if someone were about to tackle you."

LEG ACTION (PUNCH)

"Imagine your body is a door. Throw the door open as you drive back." (Short: "Open the door.")

ARM ACTION

"Drive your inside elbow back and around as if to whack a tackle dummy." (Short: "Whack the dummy.")

MULTIDIRECTIONAL SPEED | BACKPEDAL
DESCRIBE IT + DEMONSTRATE IT

EXECUTION LANGUAGE

OVERVIEW: Tracking movements, for which the backpedal is a type, refers to any movement that is used to track an opponent, most commonly, during a defensive scenario. In the context of the backpedal, imagine an athlete is on defense and requires the capacity to track a forward-moving attacker (offensive player) to maintain position or make a stop. In American football, this pattern allows a defensive back to maintain position on a wide receiver running downfield. Equally, in rugby, this movement allows a defender to get back into a defensive line. Ultimately, the backpedal is the most effective way to move straight back over short distances, with the crossover run available to the defender if an increase in speed (or moving at an angle) is required.

POSTURE: "Keep your eyes focused on the opponent (or target) at all times, stay square, and maintain a neutral ('proud') posture as you backpedal."

LEG ACTION (PUSH): "As soon as you realize the attacker is moving, you want to rapidly lower your center of mass ('get low' or 'get down'), dropping into a quarter-squat position. With your weight lowered and forward, you'll move backward by quickly PUSHing the ground away in an alternating pattern—'pop, pop, pop.'"

LEG ACTION (LIFT): "While one leg is PUSHing, the opposite leg will be LIFTing. This subtle pattern requires you to flex your knee so that you can, once again, rapidly extend and PUSH the ground away on the next stride.

"The head, trunk (posture), and thigh (upper leg) should remain stable (or silent), with all visible movement coming from your knees extending and flexing and your arms alternating with this action."

ARM ACTION: "Your arms will make much smaller movements than they do when you are sprinting; however, they will still alternate, moving forward as the opposite leg is PUSHing and backward as the opposite leg is LIFTing."

CUE IT + DO IT

POSTURE
- ▸ "Parallel the attacker."
- ▸ "Stay in front of the attacker."
- ▸ "Stay square as you push."
- ▸ "Stay proud as you push."

LEG ACTION (PUSH)
- ▸ "Rapidly drive backward."
- ▸ "Quickly push the ground away."
- ▸ "Flick the ground away."
- ▸ "Stay low (or level) as you push."

LEG ACTION (LIFT)
- ▸ "Flick your heel (to your back pocket)."
- ▸ "Lift your heel (just off the ground)."
- ▸ "Hide your heel (behind your hamstring)."
- ▸ "Get off the ground as quickly as you can."

ARM ACTION
- ▸ "Rapid (arm) swing."
- ▸ "Quick (arm) swing."
- ▸ "Slice the air."
- ▸ "Cut the air."

POSTURE
Setup: Place a piece of yellow tape on the upper chest and a piece of white tape above the waistband.

Cue 1: "Don't let the tape get closer as you backpedal."

Cue 2: "Keep the yellow (chest) tape in front of the white (waist) tape."

Cue 3: "Make sure the attacker can see the yellow (chest) tape."

LEG ACTION
Setup: Place a piece of white tape on the outside or front of each ankle and a piece of yellow tape on the outside or top of each knee.

Cue 1: "Drive the white (ankle) tape into the ground" (PUSH emphasis).

Cue 2: "Flick the white (ankle) tape in front of the yellow (knee) tape" (PUSH emphasis).

Cue 3: "Lift the white (ankle) tape behind the yellow (knee) tape" (LIFT emphasis).

ARM ACTION
Setup: Place a piece of yellow tape on the back or outside of each wrist.

Cue 1: "Drive the yellow tape back."

Cue 2: "Swing the yellow tape back."

Cue 3: "Swing the yellow tape past your pockets."

POSTURE

"Imagine you have a book (or another object) resting on top of your head. Don't let the book fall off." (Short: "Balance the book.")

LEG ACTION (PUSH)

"Imagine you have rubber bands sewn into your shorts and shoes. As you backpedal, quickly stretch those bands." (Short: "Stretch the bands.")

LEG ACTION (LIFT)

"Imagine you're barefoot and standing on scorching hot asphalt. Get off the ground as quickly as you can." (Short: "Get off the ground.")

ARM ACTION

"Imagine your arms are the clapper inside the Liberty Bell. Ring that bell as quickly as you can." (Short: "Ring the bell.")

REFERENCES

Chapter 1

1. Bjork, EL, and Bjork, RA. Making things hard on yourself, but in a good way: Creating desirable difficulties to enhance learning. In *Psychology and the Real World: Essays Illustrating Fundamental Contributions to Society*. Gernbacher, MA, Pew, RW, Hough, LM, and Pomerantz, JR, eds. New York: Worth, 56-64, 2011.

2. Brady, F. The contextual interference effect and sport skills. *Perceptual and Motor Skills* 106:461-472, 2008.

3. Cahill, L, McGaugh, JL, and Weinberger, NM. The neurobiology of learning and memory: Some reminders to remember. *Trends in Neuroscience* 24:578-581, 2001.

4. Farrow, D, and Buszard, T. Exploring the applicability of the contextual interference effect in sports practice. *Progress in Brain Research* 234:69-83, 2017.

5. Guadagnoli, MA, and Lee, TD. Challenge point: A framework for conceptualizing the effects of various practice conditions in motor learning. *Journal of Motor Behavior* 36:212-224, 2004.

6. Johnson, L, Burridge, JH, and Demain, SH. Internal and external focus of attention during gait re-education: An observational study of physical therapist practice in stroke rehabilitation. *Physical Therapy* 93:957-966, 2013.

7. Kantak, SS, and Winstein, CJ. Learning—performance distinction and memory processes for motor skills: A focused review and perspective. *Behavioural Brain Research* 228:219-231, 2012.

8. Morin, J-B, Slawinski, J, Dorel, S, Couturier, A, Samozino, P, Brughelli, M, and Rabita, G. Acceleration capability in elite sprinters and ground impulse: Push more, brake less? *Journal of Biomechanics* 48:3149-3154, 2015.

9. Porter, JM, and Beckerman, T. Practicing with gradual increases in contextual interference enhances visuomotor learning. *Kinesiology: International Journal of Fundamental and Applied Kinesiology* 48:244-250, 2016.

10. Porter, JM, and Magill, RA. Systematically increasing contextual interference is beneficial for learning sport skills. *Journal of Sports Sciences* 28:1277-1285, 2010.

11. Porter, JM, and Saemi, E. Moderately skilled learners benefit by practicing with systematic increases in contextual interference. *International Journal of Coaching Science* 4:61-71, 2010.

12. Porter, JM, Wu, W, and Partridge, J. Focus of attention and verbal instructions: Strategies of elite track and field coaches and athletes. *Sport Science Review* XIX:199-211, 2010.

13. Schmidt, RA, and Bjork, RA. New conceptualizations of practice: Common principles in three paradigms suggest new concepts for training. *Psychological Science* 3:207-218, 1992.

14. Shea, JB, and Morgan, RL. Contextual interference effects on the acquisition, retention, and transfer of a motor skill. *Journal of Experimental Psychology: Human Learning and Memory* 5:179, 1979.

15. Soderstrom, NC, and Bjork, RA. Learning versus performance: An integrative review. *Perspectives on Psychological Science* 10:176-199, 2015.

16. Weyand, PG, Sternlight, DB, Bellizzi, MJ, and Wright, S. Faster top running speeds are achieved with greater ground forces not more rapid leg movements. *Journal of Applied Physiology* 89:1991-1999, 2000.

17. Wulf, G. *Attention and Motor Skill Learning*. Champaign, IL: Human Kinetics, 2007.

18. Wulf, G. Attentional focus and motor learning: A review of 15 years. *International Review of Sport and Exercise Psychology* 6:77-104, 2013.

19. Wulf, G, McConnel, N, Gartner, M, and Schwarz, A. Enhancing the learning of sport skills through external-focus feedback. *Journal of Motor Behavior* 34:171-182, 2002.

20. Young, W, McLean, B, and Ardagna, J. Relationship between strength qualities and sprinting performance. *Journal of Sports Medicine and Physical Fitness* 35:13-19, 1995.

21. PGA Tour. Funny golf tip from J.C. Anderson. December 2010. www.youtube.com/watch?v=qQVFhqAKcMg.

Chapter 2

1. Anderson, BA. A value-driven mechanism of attentional selection. *Journal of Vision* 13:7, 2013.

2. Anderson, BA. The attention habit: How reward learning shapes attentional selection. *Annals of the New York Academy of Sciences* 1369:24-39, 2016.

3. Baird, B, Smallwood, J, Mrazek, MD, Kam, JW, Franklin, MS, and Schooler, JW. Inspired by distraction: Mind wandering facilitates creative incubation. *Psychological Science* 23:1117-1122, 2012.

4. Baker, J, Côte, J, and Abernethy, B. Sport-specific practice and the development of expert decision-making in team ball sports. *Journal of Applied Sport Psychology* 15:12-25, 2003.

5. Baker, J, Côté, J, and Abernethy, B. Learning from the experts: Practice activities of expert decision makers in sport. *Research Quarterly for Exercise and Sport* 74:342-347, 2003.

6. Bjork, EL, and Bjork, RA. Making things hard on yourself, but in a good way: Creating desirable difficulties to enhance learning. In *Psychology and the Real World: Essays Illustrating Fundamental Contributions to Society.* Gernbacher, MA, Pew, RW, Hough, LM, and Pomerantz, JR, eds. New York: Worth, 56-64, 2011.

7. Brault, S, Bideau, B, Kulpa, R, and Craig, C. Detecting deceptive movement in 1 vs. 1 based on global body displacement of a rugby player. *International Journal of Virtual Reality* 8, 2009.

8. Connor, JD, Crowther, RG, and Sinclair, WH. Effect of different evasion maneuvers on anticipation and visual behavior in elite Rugby League players. *Motor Control* 22:18-27, 2018.

9. Conway, AR, Cowan, N, and Bunting, MF. The cocktail party phenomenon revisited: The importance of working memory capacity. *Psychonomic Bulletin & Review* 8:331-335, 2001.

10. Coyle, D. *The Little Book of Talent: 52 Tips for Improving Your Skills.* New York: Bantam, 2012.

11. Craig, A. Interoception: The sense of the physiological condition of the body. *Current Opinion in Neurobiology* 13:500-505, 2003.

12. Csikentmihalyi, M. *Flow: The Psychology of Optimal Experience.* New York: HarperCollins, 1990.

13. Downar, J, Crawley, AP, Mikulis, DJ, and Davis, KD. A cortical network sensitive to stimulus salience in a neutral behavioral context across multiple sensory modalities. *Journal of Neurophysiology* 87:615-620, 2002.

14. Ericsson, A, and Pool, R. *Peak: Secrets From the New Science of Expertise.* Boston: Houghton Mifflin Harcourt, 2016.

15. Ericsson, KA. Deliberate practice and acquisition of expert performance: A general overview. *Academic Emergency Medicine* 15:988-994, 2008.

16. Ericsson, KA, Krampe, RT, and Tesch-Römer, C. The role of deliberate practice in the acquisition of expert performance. *Psychological Review* 100:363, 1993.

17. Fan, J, McCandliss, BD, Fossella, J, Flombaum, JI, and Posner, MI. The activation of attentional networks. *Neuroimage* 26:471-479, 2005.

18. Fecteau, JH, and Munoz, DP. Salience, relevance, and firing: A priority map for target selection. *Trends in Cognitive Sciences* 10:382-390, 2006.

19. Fitts, PM. Categories of human learning. In *Perceptual–Motor Skills Learning.* Melton, AW, ed. New York: Academic Press, 1964.

20. Fitts, PM, and Posner, MI. *Human Performance.* Belmont, CA: Brooks/Cole, 1967.

21. Gallagher, W. *New: Understanding Our Need for Novelty and Change.* New York: Penguin, 2011.

22. Gegenfurtner, A, Lehtinen, E, and Säljö, R. Expertise differences in the comprehension of visualizations: A meta-analysis of eye-tracking research in professional domains. *Educational Psychology Review* 23:523-552, 2011.

23. Guadagnoli, MA, and Lee, TD. Challenge point: A framework for conceptualizing the effects of various practice conditions in motor learning. *Journal of Motor Behavior* 36:212-224, 2004.

24. Güllich, A. Many roads lead to Rome: Developmental paths to Olympic gold in men's field hockey. *European Journal of Sport Science* 14:763-771, 2014.

25. Hambrick, DZ, Oswald, FL, Altmann, EM, Meinz, EJ, Gobet, F, and Campitelli, G. Deliberate practice: Is that all it takes to become an expert? *Intelligence* 45:34-45, 2014.

26. Kahneman, D. *Thinking, Fast and Slow.* New York: Macmillan, 2011.

27. Killingsworth, MA, and Gilbert, DT. A wandering mind is an unhappy mind. *Science* 330:932-932, 2010.

28. Levitin, DJ. *The Organized Mind: Thinking Straight in the Age of Information Overload.* New York: Penguin, 2014.

29. Locke, EA, and Latham, GP. *A Theory of Goal Setting & Task Performance.* Englewood Cliffs, NJ: Prentice Hall, 1990.

30. Locke, EA, and Latham, GP. Building a practically useful theory of goal setting and task motivation: A 35-year odyssey. *American Psychologist* 57:705, 2002.

31. Macnamara, BN, Moreau, D, and Hambrick, DZ. The relationship between deliberate practice and performance in sports: A meta-analysis. *Perspectives on Psychological Science* 11:333-350, 2016.

32. Magill, R, and Anderson, D. Augmented feedback. In *Motor Learning and Control: Concepts and Applications.* 11th ed. New York: McGraw-Hill Education, 2017.

33. McVay, JC, and Kane, MJ. Why does working memory capacity predict variation in reading comprehension? On the influence of mind wandering and executive attention. *Journal of Experimental Psychology: General* 141:302, 2012.

34. Menon, V, and Uddin, LQ. Saliency, switching, attention and control: A network model of insula function. *Brain Structure and Function* 214:655-667, 2010.

35. Mooneyham, BW, and Schooler, JW. The costs and benefits of mind-wandering: A review. *Canadian Journal of Experimental Psychology/Revue canadienne de psychologie expérimentale* 67:11, 2013.

36. Paus, T. Primate anterior cingulate cortex: Where motor control, drive and cognition interface. *Nature Reviews Neuroscience* 2:417, 2001.

37. Petersen, SE, and Posner, MI. The attention system of the human brain: 20 years after. *Annual Review of Neuroscience* 35:73-89, 2012.

38. Posner, MI. *Attention in a Social World.* United Kingdom: Oxford University Press, 2011.

39. Posner, MI, and Fan, J. Attention as an organ system. *Topics in Integrative Neuroscience* 31-61, 2008.

40. Posner, MI, and Rothbart, MK. Research on attention networks as a model for the integration of psychological science. *Annual Review of Psychology* 58:1-23, 2007.

41. Ptak, R. The frontoparietal attention network of the human brain: Action, saliency, and a priority map of the environment. *The Neuroscientist* 18:502-515, 2012.

42. Raichle, ME. The brain's default mode network. *Annual Review of Neuroscience* 38:433-447, 2015.

43. Raichle, ME, MacLeod, AM, Snyder, AZ, Powers, WJ, Gusnard, DA, and Shulman, GL. A default mode of brain function. *Proceedings of the National Academy of Sciences* 98:676-682, 2001.

44. Raichle, ME, and Mintun, MA. Brain work and brain imaging. *Annual Review of Neuroscience* 29:449-476, 2006.

45. Randall, JG, Oswald, FL, and Beier, ME. Mind-wandering, cognition, and performance: A theory-driven meta-analysis of attention regulation. *Psychological Bulletin* 140:1411, 2014.

46. Smallwood, J, and Schooler, JW. The restless mind. *Psychological Bulletin* 132:946, 2006.

47. Sridharan, D, Levitin, DJ, and Menon, V. A critical role for the right fronto-insular cortex in switching between central-executive and default-mode networks. *Proceedings of the National Academy of Sciences* 105:12569-12574, 2008.

48. Tucker, R, and Collins, M. What makes champions? A review of the relative contribution of genes and training to sporting success. *British Journal of Sports Medicine* 46:555-561, 2012.

49. Uddin, LQ. Salience processing and insular cortical function and dysfunction. *Nature Reviews Neuroscience* 16:55, 2015.

50. Unsworth, N, and McMillan, BD. Mind wandering and reading comprehension: Examining the roles of working memory capacity, interest, motivation, and topic experience. *Journal of Experimental Psychology: Learning, Memory, and Cognition* 39:832, 2013.

51. Ward, P, Hodges, NJ, Starkes, JL, and Williams, MA. The road to excellence: Deliberate practice and the development of expertise. *High Ability Studies* 18:119-153, 2007.

52. James, W. *The Principles of Psychology*. New York: Dover Publications, 1890.

53. Gladwell, M. *Outliers: The Story of Success*. United Kingdom: Hachette, 2008.

54. Damasio, A. *Descartes' Error: Emotion, Reason, and the Human Brain*. New York: Putnam, 1994.

Chapter 3

1. Adolphs, R, Cahill, L, Schul, R, and Babinsky, R. Impaired declarative memory for emotional material following bilateral amygdala damage in humans. *Learning & Memory* 4:291-300, 1997.

2. Akkal, D, Dum, RP, and Strick, PL. Supplementary motor area and presupplementary motor area: Targets of basal ganglia and cerebellar output. *Journal of Neuroscience* 27:10659-10673, 2007.

3. Atkinson, RC, and Shiffrin, RM. Human memory: A proposed system and its control processes. In *Psychology of Learning and Motivation*. Elsevier, 89-195, 1968.

4. Baddeley, A. The episodic buffer: A new component of working memory? *Trends in Cognitive Sciences* 4:417-423, 2000.

5. Baddeley, A. Working memory: Looking back and looking forward. *Nature Reviews Neuroscience* 4:829, 2003.

6. Baddeley, A. Working memory: Theories, models, and controversies. *Annual Review of Psychology* 63:1-29, 2012.

7. Baddeley, AD, and Hitch, G. Working memory. In *Psychology of Learning and Motivation*. Elsevier, 47-89, 1974.

8. Ballanger, B, Thobois, S, Baraduc, P, Turner, RS, Broussolle, E, and Desmurget, M. "Paradoxical kinesis" is not a hallmark of Parkinson's disease but a general property of the motor system. *Movement Disorders* 21:1490-1495, 2006.

9. Barclay, JR, Bransford, JD, Franks, JJ, McCarrell, NS, and Nitsch, K. Comprehension and semantic flexibility. *Journal of Verbal Learning and Verbal Behavior* 13:471-481, 1974.

10. Bergson, H. *Matter and Memory*. New York: Macmillan, 1911.

11. Biran, Md. *The Influence of Habit on the Faculty of Thinking*. Baltimore: Williams & Wilkins, 1929.

12. Bower, GH. Mood and memory. *American Psychologist* 36:129, 1981.

13. Boyd, LA, and Winstein, CJ. Cerebellar stroke impairs temporal but not spatial accuracy during implicit motor learning. *Neurorehabilitation and Neural Repair* 18:134-143, 2004.

14. Broadbent, DE. *Perception and Communication*. New York: Pergamon Press, 1958.

15. Buszard, T, Farrow, D, Verswijveren, S, Reid, M, Williams, J, Polman, R, Ling, FCM, and Masters, RSW. Working memory capacity limits motor learning when implementing multiple instructions. *Front Psychol* 8:1350, 2017.

16. Cahill, L, Haier, RJ, Fallon, J, Alkire, MT, Tang, C, Keator, D, Wu, J, and Mcgaugh, JL. Amygdala activity at encoding correlated with long-term, free recall of emotional information. *Proceedings of the National Academy of Sciences* 93:8016-8021, 1996.

17. Cahill, L, Prins, B, Weber, M, and McGaugh, JL. \gb\-adrenergic activation and memory for emotional events. *Nature* 371:702, 1994.

18. Casasanto, D, and Dijkstra, K. Motor action and emotional memory. *Cognition* 115:179-185, 2010.

19. Cowan, N. Evolving conceptions of memory storage, selective attention, and their mutual constraints within the human information-processing system. *Psychological Bulletin* 104:163, 1988.

20. Cowan, N. The magical number 4 in short-term memory: A reconsideration of mental storage capacity. *The Behavioral and Brain Sciences* 24:87-185, 2001.

21. Cowan, N. The magical mystery four: How is working memory capacity limited, and why? *Current Directions in Psychological Science* 19:51-57, 2010.

22. Craik, FI, and Lockhart, RS. Levels of processing: A framework for memory research. *Journal of Verbal Learning and Verbal Behavior* 11:671-684, 1972.

23. Craik, FI, and Tulving, E. Depth of processing and the retention of words in episodic memory. *Journal of Experimental Psychology: General* 104:268, 1975.

24. Cushion, CJ, and Jones, R. A systematic observation of professional top-level youth soccer coaches. *Journal of Sport Behavior* 24:354, 2001.

25. DeLong, MR, and Wichmann, T. Circuits and circuit disorders of the basal ganglia. *Archives of Neurology* 64:20-24, 2007.

26. Dijkstra, K, Kaschak, MP, and Zwaan, RA. Body posture facilitates retrieval of autobiographical memories. *Cognition* 102:139-149, 2007.

27. Doyon, J, Bellec, P, Amsel, R, Penhune, V, Monchi, O, Carrier, J, Lehéricy, S, and Benali, H. Contributions of the basal ganglia and functionally related brain structures to motor learning. *Behavioural Brain Research* 199:61-75, 2009.

28. Eichenbaum, H. *The Cognitive Neuroscience of Memory: An Introduction.* New York: Oxford University Press, 2011.

29. Eichenbaum, H. Two distinct stages of memory consolidation. In *The Cognitive Neuroscience of Memory: An Introduction.* New York: Oxford University Press, 317-350, 2011.

30. Elbert, T, Pantev, C, Wienbruch, C, Rockstroh, B, and Taub, E. Increased cortical representation of the fingers of the left hand in string players. *Science* 270:305-307, 1995.

31. Ford, PR, Yates, I, and Williams, AM. An analysis of practice activities and instructional behaviours used by youth soccer coaches during practice: Exploring the link between science and application. *Journal of Sports Sciences* 28:483-495, 2010.

32. Fried, I, Haggard, P, He, BJ, and Schurger, A. Volition and action in the human brain: processes, pathologies, and reasons. *Journal of Neuroscience* 37:10842-10847, 2017.

33. Fried, I, Katz, A, McCarthy, G, Sass, KJ, Williamson, P, Spencer, SS, and Spencer, DD. Functional organization of human supplementary motor cortex studied by electrical stimulation. *Journal of Neuroscience* 11:3656-3666, 1991.

34. Gaser, C, and Schlaug, G. Brain structures differ between musicians and non-musicians. *Journal of Neuroscience* 23:9240-9245, 2003.

35. Glickstein, M, and Stein, J. Paradoxical movement in Parkinson's disease. *Trends in Neurosciences* 14:480-482, 1991.

36. Haslinger, B, Erhard, P, Altenmüller, E, Hennenlotter, A, Schwaiger, M, Gräfin von Einsiedel, H, Rummeny, E, Conrad, B, and Ceballos Baumann, AO. Reduced recruitment of motor association areas during bimanual coordination in concert pianists. *Human Brain Mapping* 22:206-215, 2004.

37. Herculano-Houzel, S. The human brain in numbers: A linearly scaled-up primate brain. *Frontiers in Human Neuroscience* 3:31, 2009.

38. Isen, AM, Shalker, TE, Clark, M, and Karp, L. Affect, accessibility of material in memory, and behavior: A cognitive loop? *Journal of Personality and Social Psychology* 36:1, 1978.

39. Jahanshahi, M, Jenkins, IH, Brown, RG, Marsden, CD, Passingham, RE, and Brooks, DJ. Self-initiated versus externally triggered movements: I. An investigation using measurement of regional cerebral blood flow with PET and movement-related potentials in normal and Parkinson's disease subjects. *Brain* 118:913-933, 1995.

40. James, W. *The Principles of Psychology*. New York: Dover Publications, 1890.

41. Jenkins, IH, Jahanshahi, M, Jueptner, M, Passingham, RE, and Brooks, DJ. Self-initiated versus externally triggered movements: II. The effect of movement predictability on regional cerebral blood flow. *Brain* 123:1216-1228, 2000.

42. Kane, MJ, and Engle, RW. The role of prefrontal cortex in working-memory capacity, executive attention, and general fluid intelligence: An individual-differences perspective. *Psychonomic Bulletin & Review* 9:637-671, 2002.

43. LePort, AK, Mattfeld, AT, Dickinson-Anson, H, Fallon, JH, Stark, CE, Kruggel, F, Cahill, L, and McGaugh, JL. Behavioral and neuroanatomical investigation of highly superior autobiographical memory (HSAM). *Neurobiology of Learning and Memory* 98:78-92, 2012.

44. Lim, I, van Wegen, E, de Goede, C, Deutekom, M, Nieuwboer, A, Willems, A, Jones, D, Rochester, L, and Kwakkel, G. Effects of external rhythmical cueing on gait in patients with Parkinson's disease: A systematic review. *Clinical Rehabilitation* 19:695-713, 2005.

45. Lisberger, SG, and Thach, WT. The cerebellum. In *Principles of Neural Science*. 5th ed. Kandel, ER, Schwartz, JH, Jessell, TM, Siegelbaum, SA, Hudspeth, AJ, eds. New York: McGraw-Hill, 2013.

46. Loukas, C, and Brown, P. Online prediction of self-paced hand-movements from subthalamic activity using neural networks in Parkinson's disease. *Journal of Neuroscience Methods* 137:193-205, 2004.

47. Magill, RA, and Anderson, DI. Memory components, forgetting, and strategies. In *Motor Learning and Control: Concepts and Applications*. 11th ed. New York: McGraw-Hill Education, 2017.

48. Maguire, EA, Gadian, DG, Johnsrude, IS, Good, CD, Ashburner, J, Frackowiak, RS, and Frith, CD. Navigation-related structural change in the hippocampi of taxi drivers. *Proceedings of the National Academy of Sciences* 97:4398-4403, 2000.

49. Maguire, EA, Valentine, ER, Wilding, JM, and Kapur, N. Routes to remembering: The brains behind superior memory. *Nature Neuroscience* 6:90, 2003.

50. Manto, M, Bower, JM, Conforto, AB, Delgado-García, JM, da Guarda, SNF, Gerwig, M, Habas, C, Hagura, N, Ivry, RB, Mariën, P, Molinari, M, Naito, E, Nowak, DA, Ben Taib, NO, Pelisson, D, Tesche, CD, Tilikete, C, and Timmann, D. Consensus paper: Roles of the cerebellum in motor control—The diversity of ideas on cerebellar involvement in movement. *Cerebellum (London, England)* 11:457-487, 2012.

51. McGaugh, JL. Memory: A century of consolidation. *Science* 287:248-251, 2000.

52. McRobbie, LR. Total recall: The people who never forget. *The Guardian*. February 2017. www.theguardian.com/science/2017/feb/08/total-recall-the-people-who-never-forget.

53. Miller, EK, and Cohen, JD. An integrative theory of prefrontal cortex function. *Annual Review of Neuroscience* 24:167-202, 2001.

54. Milner, B, Corkin, S, and Teuber, H-L. Further analysis of the hippocampal amnesic syndrome: 14-year follow-up study of HM. *Neuropsychologia* 6:215-234, 1968.

55. Nachev, P, Wydell, H, O'Neill, K, Husain, M, and Kennard, C. The role of the pre-supplementary motor area in the control of action. *Neuroimage* 36:T155-T163, 2007.

56. Pessiglione, M, Seymour, B, Flandin, G, Dolan, RJ, and Frith, CD. Dopamine-dependent prediction errors underpin reward-seeking behaviour in humans. *Nature* 442:1042, 2006.

57. Potrac, P, Jones, R, and Cushion, C. Understanding power and the coach's role in professional English soccer: A preliminary investigation of coach behaviour. *Soccer & Society* 8:33-49, 2007.

58. Pulvermüller, F, Hauk, O, Nikulin, VV, and Ilmoniemi, RJ. Functional links between motor and language systems. *European Journal of Neuroscience* 21:793-797, 2005.

59. Rizzolatti, G, and Kalaska, JF. Voluntary movement: The parietal and premotor cortex. In *Principles of Neural Science*. 5th ed. Kandel, ER, Schwartz, JH, Jessell, TM, Siegelbaum, SA, Hudspeth, AJ, eds. New York: McGraw-Hill, 2013.

60. Rizzolatti, G, and Kalaska, JF. Voluntary movement: The primary motor cortex. In *Principles of Neural Science*. 5th ed. Kandel, ER, Schwartz, JH, Jessell, TM, Siegelbaum, SA, Hudspeth, AJ, eds. New York: McGraw-Hill, 2013.

61. Schacter, DL. Implicit memory: History and current status. *Journal of Experimental Psychology: Learning, Memory, and Cognition* 13:501, 1987.

62. Schacter, DL. The seven sins of memory: Insights from psychology and cognitive neuroscience. *American Psychologist* 54:182, 1999.

63. Schacter, DL, and Wagner, AW. Learning and memory. In *Principles of Neural Science*. 5th ed. Kandel, ER, Schwartz, JH, Jessell, TM, Siegelbaum, SA, Hudspeth, AJ, eds. New York: McGraw-Hill, 2013.

64. Schneider, D, Mertes, C, and Wascher, E. The time course of visuo-spatial working memory updating revealed by a retro-cuing paradigm. *Scientific Reports* 6:21442, 2016.

65. Scoville, WB, and Milner, B. Loss of recent memory after bilateral hippocampal lesions. *Journal of Neurology, Neurosurgery, and Psychiatry* 20:11, 1957.

66. Seidler, RD, Bo, J, and Anguera, JA. Neurocognitive contributions to motor skill learning: The role of working memory. *Journal of Motor Behavior* 44:445-453, 2012.

67. Squire, LR. The legacy of patient HM for neuroscience. *Neuron* 61:6-9, 2009.

68. Tulving, E. Episodic and semantic memory. In *Organisation of Memory*. Tulving, E, Donaldson, W, eds. New York: Academic Press, 1972.

69. Tulving, E. How many memory systems are there? *American Psychologist* 40:385, 1985.

70. Tulving, E, and Thomson, DM. Encoding specificity and retrieval processes in episodic memory. *Psychological Review* 80:352, 1973.

71. Vaidya, CJ, Zhao, M, Desmond, JE, and Gabrieli, JD. Evidence for cortical encoding specificity in episodic memory: Memory-induced re-activation of picture processing areas. *Neuropsychologia* 40:2136-2143, 2002.

72. Wichmann, T, and DeLong, MR. The basal ganglia. In *Principles of Neural Science*. 5th ed. Kandel, ER, Schwartz, JH, Jessell, TM, Siegelbaum, SA, Hudspeth, AJ, eds. New York: McGraw-Hill, 2013.

73. Wolpert, DM, and Flanagan, JR. Motor prediction. *Current Biology* 11:R729-R732, 2001.

74. Wu, T, Kansaku, K, and Hallett, M. How self-initiated memorized movements become automatic: A functional MRI study. *Journal of Neurophysiology* 91:1690-1698, 2004.

75. Hebb, DO. *The Organization of Behavior: A Neuropsychological Theory*. Mahwah, NJ: Lawrence Erlbaum Associates, 2009.

76. Schacter, DL. The seven sins of memory: Insights from psychology and cognitive neuroscience. *American Psychologist* 54:182, 1999.

77. Miller, GA. The magical number seven, plus or minus two: Some limits on our capacity for processing information. *Psychological Review* 63:81, 1956.

78. Foer ,J. *Moonwalking With Einstein: The Art and Science of Remembering Everything*. New York: Penguin, 2012.

79. Claparède, E. Recognition and "me-ness." In *Organization and Pathology of Thought*. Rapaport, D, ed. New York: Columbia University Press, 58-75, 1951.

80. Graf, P, and Schacter, DL. Implicit and explicit memory for new associations in normal and amnesic subjects. *Journal of Experimental Psychology: Learning, Memory, and Cognition* 11:501, 1985.

81. Schacter, DL. Implicit memory: History and current status. *Journal of Experimental Psychology: Learning, Memory, and Cognition* 13:501, 1987.

82. Eichenbaum, H. To cortex: Thanks for the memories. *Neuron* 19:481-484, 1997.

83. Soderstrom, NC, and Bjork, RA. Learning versus performance: An integrative review. *Perspectives on Psychological Science* 10:176-199, 2015.

84. Foer, J. Feats of memory anyone can do. February 2012. www.ted.com/talks/joshua_foer_feats_of_memory_anyone_can_do#t-88395.

85. Michael J Fox Parkinson's disease. April 2009. www.youtube.com/watch?v=ECkPVTZlfP8.

86. Wolpert, D. The real reason for brains. July 2011. www.ted.com/talks/daniel_wolpert_the_real_reason_for_brains.

Chapter 4

1. Al-Abood, SA, Bennett, SJ, Hernandez, FM, Ashford, D, and Davids, K. Effect of verbal instructions and image size on visual search strategies in basketball free throw shooting. *Journal of Sports Sciences* 20:271-278, 2002.

2. An, J, Wulf, G, and Kim, S. Increased carry distance and X-factor stretch in golf through an external focus of attention. *Journal of Motor Learning and Development* 1:2-11, 2013.

3. Andrieux, M, and Proteau, L. Observation learning of a motor task: Who and when? *Experimental Brain Research* 229:125-137, 2013.

4. Andrieux, M, and Proteau, L. Mixed observation favors motor learning through better estimation of the model's performance. *Experimental Brain Research* 232:3121-3132, 2014.

5. Baumeister, RF. Choking under pressure: Self-consciousness and paradoxical effects of incentives on skillful performance. *Journal of Personality and Social Psychology* 46:610, 1984.

6. Beck, EN, Intzandt, BN, and Almeida, QJ. Can dual task walking improve in Parkinson's disease after external focus of attention exercise? A single blind randomized controlled trial. *Neurorehabilitation and Neural Repair* 32:18-33, 2018.

7. Becker, KA, and Smith, PJ. Attentional focus effects in standing long jump performance: Influence of a broad and narrow internal focus. *Journal of Strength & Conditioning Research* 29:1780-1783, 2015.

8. Beilock, S. *Choke: What the Secrets of the Brain Reveal About Getting It Right When You Have To.* New York: Simon and Schuster, 2010.

9. Beilock, SL, and Carr, TH. On the fragility of skilled performance: What governs choking under pressure? *Journal of Experimental Psychology: General* 130:701-725, 2001.

10. Beilock, SL, Carr, TH, MacMahon, C, and Starkes, JL. When paying attention becomes counterproductive: Impact of divided versus skill-focused attention on novice and experienced performance of sensorimotor skills. *Journal of Experimental Psychology: Applied* 8:6-16, 2002.

11. Beilock, SL, and Gray, R. From attentional control to attentional spillover: A skill-level investigation of attention, movement, and performance outcomes. *Human Movement Science* 31:1473-1499, 2012.

12. Benjaminse, A, Otten, B, Gokeler, A, Diercks, RL, and Lemmink, KA. Motor learning strategies in basketball players and its implications for ACL injury prevention: A randomized controlled trial. *Knee Surgery, Sports Traumatology, Arthroscopy* 1-12, 2015.

13. Benjaminse, A, Welling, W, Otten, B, and Gokeler, A. Transfer of improved movement technique after receiving verbal external focus and video instruction. *Knee Surgery, Sports Traumatology, Arthroscopy* 26:955-962, 2018.

14. Bernstein, NA. *The Coordination and Regulation of Movements.* New York: Pergamon Press, 1967.

15. Castaneda, B, and Gray, R. Effects of focus of attention on baseball batting performance in players of differing skill levels. *Journal of Sport and Exercise Psychology* 29:60-77, 2007.

16. Christina, R, and Alpenfels, E. Influence of attentional focus on learning a swing path change. *International Journal of Golf Science* 3:35-49, 2014.

17. Coker, C. Combining attentional focus strategies: Effects and adherence. *Physical Educator* 76:98-109, 2019.

18. DeCaro, MS, Thomas, RD, Albert, NB, and Beilock, SL. Choking under pressure: Multiple routes to skill failure. *Journal of Experimental Psychology: General* 140:390-406, 2011.

19. Diekfuss, JA, and Raisbeck, LD. Focus of attention and instructional feedback from NCAA division 1 collegiate coaches. *Journal of Motor Learning and Development* 4:262-273, 2016.

20. Fietzer, AL, Winstein, CJ, and Kulig, K. Changing one's focus of attention alters the structure of movement variability. *Human Movement Science* 62:14-24, 2018.

21. Fitts, PM, and Posner, MI. *Human Performance.* Belmont, CA: Brooks/Cole, 1967.

22. Ford, P, Hodges, NJ, and Mark Williams, A. An evaluation of end-point trajectory planning during skilled kicking. *Motor Control* 13:1-24, 2009.

23. Freudenheim, AM, Wulf, G, Madureira, F, Pasetto, SC, and Corrêa, UC. An external focus of attention results in greater swimming speed. *International Journal of Sports Science and Coaching* 5:533-542, 2010.

24. Gokeler, A, Benjaminse, A, Welling, W, Alferink, M, Eppinga, P, and Otten, B. The effects of attentional focus on jump performance and knee joint kinematics in patients after ACL reconstruction. *Physical Therapy in Sport* 16:114-120, 2015.

25. Gokeler, A, Neuhaus, D, Benjaminse, A, Grooms, DR, and Baumeister, J. Principles of motor learning to support neuroplasticity after ACL injury: Implications for optimizing performance and reducing risk of second ACL injury. *Sports Medicine* 49:853-865, 2019.

26. Gray, R. Attending to the execution of a complex sensorimotor skill: Expertise differences, choking, and slumps. *Journal of Experimental Psychology: Applied* 10:42-54, 2004.

27. Gray, R. Transfer of training from virtual to real baseball batting. *Frontiers in Psychology* 8:2183, 2017.

28. Gray, R. Comparing cueing and constraints interventions for increasing launch angle in baseball batting. *Sport, Exercise, and Performance Psychology* 7:318, 2018.

29. Guss-West, C, and Wulf, G. Attentional focus in classical ballet: A survey of professional dancers. *Journal of Dance Medicine & Science* 20:23-29, 2016.

30. Halperin, I, Chapman, DW, Martin, DT, Abbiss, C, and Wulf, G. Coaching cues in amateur boxing: An analysis of ringside feedback provided between rounds of competition. *Psychology of Sport and Exercise* 25:44-50, 2016.

31. Hitchcock, DR, and Sherwood, DE. Effects of changing the focus of attention on accuracy, acceleration, and electromyography in dart throwing. *International Journal of Exercise Science* 11:1120-1135, 2018.

32. Hodges, N, and Williams, AM. *Skill Acquisition in Sport: Research, Theory and Practice.* New York: Routledge, 2012.

33. Hommel, B, Müsseler, J, Aschersleben, G, and Prinz, W. The theory of event coding (TEC): A framework for perception and action planning. *Behavioral and Brain Sciences* 24:849-878, 2001.

34. Ille, A, Selin, I, Do, MC, and Thon, B. Attentional focus effects on sprint start performance as a function of skill level. *Journal of Sports Sciences* 31:1705-1712, 2013.

35. Jeannerod, M. The representing brain: Neural correlates of motor intention and imagery. *Behavioral and Brain Sciences* 17:187-202, 1994.

36. Kim, T, Diaz, JJ, and Chen, J. The effect of attentional focus in balancing tasks: A systematic review with meta-analysis. *Journal of Human Sport and Exercise* 12:463-479, 2017.

37. Komar, J, Chow, J-Y, Chollet, D, and Seifert, L. Effect of analogy instructions with an internal focus on learning a complex motor skill. *Journal of Applied Sport Psychology* 26:17-32, 2014.

38. Lee, DN, Lishman, JR, and Thomson, JA. Regulation of gait in long jumping. *Journal of Experimental Psychology: Human Perception and Performance* 8:448, 1982.

39. Liao, CM, and Masters, RSW. Self-focused attention and performance failure under psychological stress. *Journal of Sport & Exercise Psychology* 24:289-305, 2002.

40. Lohse, K, Wadden, K, Boyd, L, and Hodges, N. Motor skill acquisition across short and long time scales: A meta-analysis of neuroimaging data. *Neuropsychologia* 59:130-141, 2014.

41. Lohse, KR, Jones, M, Healy, AF, and Sherwood, DE. The role of attention in motor control. *Journal of Experimental Psychology: General* 143:930-948, 2014.

42. Lohse, KR, Sherwood, DE, and Healy, AF. How changing the focus of attention affects performance, kinematics, and electromyography in dart throwing. *Human Movement Science* 29:542-555, 2010.

43. Marchant, DC, Greig, M, and Scott, C. Attentional focusing instructions influence force production and muscular activity during isokinetic elbow flexions. *Journal of Strength & Conditioning Research* 23:2358-2366, 2009.

44. Masters, RS. Knowledge, knerves and know how: The role of explicit versus implicit knowledge in the breakdown of a complex motor skill under pressure. *British Journal of Psychology* 83:343-358, 1992.

45. Maurer, H, and Munzert, J. Influence of attentional focus on skilled motor performance: Performance decrement under unfamiliar focus conditions. *Human Movement Science* 32:730-740, 2013.

46. Miles, GF. Thinking outside the block: External focus of attention shortens reaction times in collegiate track sprinters. In *College of Science and Health Human Performance*. La Crosse: University of Wisconsin, 2018.

47. Muller, H, and Loosch, E. Functional variability and an equifinal path of movement during targeted throwing. *Journal of Human Movement Studies* 36:103-126, 1999.

48. Ong, NT, Bowcock, A, and Hodges, NJ. Manipulations to the timing and type of instructions to examine motor skill performance under pressure. *Frontiers in Psychology* 1:1-13, 2010.

49. Park, SH, Yi, CW, Shin, JY, and Ryu, YU. Effects of external focus of attention on balance: A short review. *Journal of Physical Therapy Science* 27:3929-3931, 2015.

50. Parr, R, and Button, C. End-point focus of attention: Learning the "catch" in rowing. *International Journal of Sport Psychology* 40:616-635, 2009.

51. Porter, JM, Wu, W, and Partridge, J. Focus of attention and verbal instructions: Strategies of elite track and field coaches and athletes. *Sport Science Review* XIX:199-211, 2010.

52. Prinz, W. Perception and action planning. *European Journal of Cognitive Psychology* 9:129-154, 1997.

53. Raisbeck, LD, Suss, J, Diekfuss, JA, Petushek, E, and Ward, P. Skill-based changes in motor performance from attentional focus manipulations: A kinematic analysis. *Ergonomics* 59:941-949, 2016.

54. Redgrave, P, Rodriguez, M, Smith, Y, Rodriguez-Oroz, MC, Lehericy, S, Bergman, H, Agid, Y, DeLong, MR, and Obeso, JA. Goal-directed and habitual control in the basal ganglia: Implications for Parkinson's disease. *Nature Reviews: Neuroscience* 11:760-772, 2010.

55. Rocha, PA, Porfirio, GM, Ferraz, HB, and Trevisani, VF. Effects of external cues on gait parameters of Parkinson's disease patients: A systematic review. *Clinical Neurology and Neurosurgery* 124:127-134, 2014.

56. Rohbanfard, H, and Proteau, L. Learning through observation: A combination of expert and novice models favors learning. *Experimental Brain Research* 215:183-197, 2011.

57. Schorer, J, Baker, J, Fath, F, and Jaitner, T. Identification of interindividual and intraindividual movement patterns in handball players of varying expertise levels. *Journal of Motor Behavior* 39:409-421, 2007.

58. Schutts, KS, Wu, WFW, Vidal, AD, Hiegel, J, and Becker, J. Does focus of attention improve snatch lift kinematics? *Journal of Strength & Conditioning Research* 31:2758-2764, 2017.

59. Scott, MA, Li, F-X, and Davids, K. Expertise and the regulation of gait in the approach phase of the long jump. *Journal of Sports Sciences* 15:597-605, 1997.

60. Shea, CH, and Wulf, G. Enhancing motor learning through external-focus instructions and feed-back. *Human Movement Science* 18:553-571, 1999.

61. Spaulding, SJ, Barber, B, Colby, M, Cormack, B, Mick, T, and Jenkins, ME. Cueing and gait improve-ment among people with Parkinson's disease: A meta-analysis. *Archives of Physical Medicine and Rehabilitation* 94:562-570, 2013.

62. Stoate, I, and Wulf, G. Does the attentional focus adopted by swimmers affect their performance? *International Journal of Sports Science and Coaching* 6:99-108, 2011.

63. Vance, J, Wulf, G, Tollner, T, McNevin, N, and Mercer, J. EMG activity as a function of the performer's focus of attention. *Journal of Motor Behavior* 36:450-459, 2004.

64. Vereijken, B, Emmerik, REv, Whiting, H, and Newell, KM. Free(z)ing degrees of freedom in skill acquisition. *Journal of Motor Behavior* 24:133-142, 1992.

65. Vidal, A, Wu, W, Nakajima, M, and Becker, J. Investigating the constrained action hypothesis: A movement coordination and coordination variability approach. *Journal of Motor Behavior* 1-10, 2017.

66. Weiss, SM, Reber, AS, and Owen, DR. The locus of focus: The effect of switching from a preferred to a non-preferred focus of attention. *Journal of Sports Sciences* 26:1049-1057, 2008.

67. Wolpert, DM, Ghahramani, Z, and Jordan, MI. An internal model for sensorimotor integration. *Science* 269:1880-1882, 1995.

68. Wulf, G, and Dufek, JS. Increased jump height with an external focus due to enhanced lower extremity joint kinetics. *Journal of Motor Behavior* 41:401-409, 2009.

69. Wulf, G, Dufek, JS, Lozano, L, and Pettigrew, C. Increased jump height and reduced EMG activity with an external focus. *Human Movement Science* 29:440-448, 2010.

70. Wulf, G, Lauterbach, B, and Toole, T. The learning advantages of an external focus of attention in golf. *Research Quarterly for Exercise and Sport* 70:120-126, 1999.

71. Wulf, G, and Lewthwaite, R. Effortless motor learning? An external focus of attention enhances movement effectiveness and efficiency. In *Effortless Attention: A New Perspective in Attention and Action*. Bruya, B, ed. Cambridge, MA: MIT Press, 75-101, 2010.

72. Wulf, G, and Lewthwaite, R. Optimizing performance through intrinsic motivation and attention for learning: The OPTIMAL theory of motor learning. *Psychonomic Bulletin & Review* 23:1382-1414, 2016.

73. Wulf, G, McConnel, N, Gartner, M, and Schwarz, A. Enhancing the learning of sport skills through external-focus feedback. *Journal of Motor Behavior* 34:171-182, 2002.

74. Wulf, G, McNevin, N, and Shea, CH. The automaticity of complex motor skill learning as a func-tion of attentional focus. *The Quarterly Journal of Experimental Psychology* 54:1143-1154, 2001.

75. Wulf, G, McNevin, NH, Fuchs, T, Ritter, F, and Toole, T. Attentional focus in complex skill learning. *Research Quarterly for Exercise and Sport* 71:229-239, 2000.

76. Wulf, G, Shea, C, and Park, JH. Attention and motor performance: Preferences for and advantages of an external focus. *Research Quarterly for Exercise and Sport* 72:335-344, 2001.

77. Zachry, T, Wulf, G, Mercer, J, and Bezodis, N. Increased movement accuracy and reduced EMG activity as the result of adopting an external focus of attention. *Brain Research Bulletin* 67:304-309, 2005.

78. Gallwey, TW. *The Inner Game of Tennis: The Classic Guide to the Mental Side of Peak Performance*. New York: Random House, 2010.

79. Chater, N. *The Mind Is Flat: The Remarkable Shallowness of the Improvising Brain*. New Haven, CT: Yale University Press, 2018.

80. Wulf, G. *Attention and Motor Skill Learning*. Champaign, IL: Human Kinetics, 2007.

81. Bijl, P. 10 step plan to the perfect power gybe. January 2016. http://pieterbijlwindsurfing.com/tutorialpowergybe.

82. Wulf, G, Hoss, M, and Prinz, W. Instructions for motor learning: Differential effects of internal versus external focus of attention. *Journal of Motor Behavior* 30:169-179, 1998.

83. James, W. *The Principles of Psychology*, Vol. 2. New York: Henry Holt and Company, 1890.

84. Stock, A, and Stock, C. A short history of ideo-motor action. *Psychological Research* 68:176-188, 2004.

85. Wulf, G, McNevin, N, and Shea, CH. The automaticity of complex motor skill learning as a function of attentional focus. *The Quarterly Journal of Experimental Psychology* 54:1143-1154, 2001.

86. Castaneda, B, and Gray, R. Effects of focus of attention on baseball batting performance in players of differing skill levels. *Journal of Sport and Exercise Psychology* 29:60-77, 2007.

87. Liao, C-M, and Masters, RS. Analogy learning: A means to implicit motor learning. *Journal of Sports Sciences* 19(5):307-319, 2001.

88. Lam, WK., Maxwell, JP., and Masters, RSW. Analogy versus explicit learning of a modified basketball shooting task: Performance and kinematic outcomes. *Journal of Sports Sciences* 27(2):179-191, 2009.

89. Choosing music over meds, one man's quest to retrain his brain to overcome dystonia. *Globe and Mail*. https://youtu.be/IpcXkV_ex8Y.

90. Beilock, SL. Why we choke under pressure—and how to avoid it. November 2017. www.ted.com/talks/sian_leah_beilock_why_we_choke_under_pressure_and_how_to_avoid_it?language=en.

91. Wulf, G. Attentional focus and motor learning: A review of 15 years. *International Review of Sport and Exercise Psychology* 6(1):77-104, 2013.

92. McNevin, NH, Shea, CH, and Wulf, G. Increasing the distance of an external focus of attention enhances learning. *Psychological Research* 67:22-29, 2003.

93. Bernstein, NA. *The Coordination and Regulation of Movements*. New York: Pergamon Press, 1967.

Chapter 5

1. Abdollahipour, R, Wulf, G, Psotta, R, and Palomo Nieto, M. Performance of gymnastics skill benefits from an external focus of attention. *Journal of Sports Sciences* 1-7, 2015.

2. Becker, KA, Georges, AF, and Aiken, CA. Considering a holistic focus of attention as an alternative to an external focus. *Journal of Motor Learning and Development* 1-10, 2018.

3. Beilock, SL, Carr, TH, MacMahon, C, and Starkes, JL. When paying attention becomes counterproductive: Impact of divided versus skill-focused attention on novice and experienced performance of sensorimotor skills. *Journal of Experimental Psychology: Applied* 8:6-16, 2002.

4. Bredin, SS, Dickson, DB, and Warburton, DE. Effects of varying attentional focus on health-related physical fitness performance. *Applied Physiology, Nutrition, and Metabolism* 38:161-168, 2013.

5. Calatayud, J, Vinstrup, J, Jakobsen, MD, Sundstrup, E, Brandt, M, Jay, K, Colado, JC, and Andersen, LL. Importance of mind-muscle connection during progressive resistance training. *European Journal of Applied Physiology* 116:527-533, 2016.

6. Calatayud, J, Vinstrup, J, Jakobsen, MD, Sundstrup, E, Colado, JC, and Andersen, LL. Mind-muscle connection training principle: Influence of muscle strength and training experience during a pushing movement. *European Journal of Applied Physiology* 117:1445-1452, 2017.

7. Calatayud, J, Vinstrup, J, Jakobsen, MD, Sundstrup, E, Colado, JC, and Andersen, LL. Influence of different attentional focus on EMG amplitude and contraction duration during the bench press at different speeds. *Journal of Sports Science* 36:1162-1166, 2018.

8. Castaneda, B, and Gray, R. Effects of focus of attention on baseball batting performance in players of differing skill levels. *Journal of Sport and Exercise Psychology* 29:60-77, 2007.

9. Coker, C. Optimizing external focus of attention Instructions: The role of attainability. *Journal of Motor Learning and Development* 4:116-125, 2016.

10. Corbin, JC, Reyna, VF, Weldon, RB, and Brainerd, CJ. How reasoning, judgment, and decision making are colored by gist-based intuition: A fuzzy-trace theory approach. *Journal of Applied Research in Memory and Cognition* 4:344-355, 2015.

11. Couvillion, KF, and Fairbrother, JT. Expert and novice performers respond differently to attentional focus cues for speed jump roping. *Frontiers in Psychology* 9:2370, 2018.

12. De Giorgio, A, Sellami, M, Kuvacic, G, Lawrence, G, Padulo, J, Mingardi, M, and Mainolfi, L. Enhancing motor learning of young soccer players through preventing an internal focus of attention: The effect of shoes colour. *PloS One* 13:e0200689, 2018.

13. Ducharme, SW, Wu, WF, Lim, K, Porter, JM, and Geraldo, F. Standing long jump performance with an external focus of attention is improved as a result of a more effective projection angle. *Journal of Strength & Conditioning Research* 30:276-281, 2016.

14. Gokeler, A, Benjaminse, A, Welling, W, Alferink, M, Eppinga, P, and Otten, B. The effects of attentional focus on jump performance and knee joint kinematics in patients after ACL reconstruction. *Physical Therapy in Sport* 16:114-120, 2015.

15. Halperin, I, Williams, KJ, Martin, DT, and Chapman, DW. The effects of attentional focusing instructions on force production during the isometric mid-thigh pull. *Journal of Strength & Conditioning Research* 30:919-923, 2016.

16. Ille, A, Selin, I, Do, MC, and Thon, B. Attentional focus effects on sprint start performance as a function of skill level. *Journal of Sports Sciences* 31:1705-1712, 2013.

17. Marchant, DC, Greig, M, Bullough, J, and Hitchen, D. Instructions to adopt an external focus enhance muscular endurance. *Research Quarterly for Exercise and Sport* 82:466-473, 2011.

18. Marchant, DC, Greig, M, and Scott, C. Attentional focusing instructions influence force production and muscular activity during isokinetic elbow flexions. *Journal of Strength & Conditioning Research* 23:2358-2366, 2009.

19. McNevin, NH, Shea, CH, and Wulf, G. Increasing the distance of an external focus of attention enhances learning. *Psychological Research* 67:22-29, 2003.

20. Perkins-Ceccato, N, Passmore, SR, and Lee, TD. Effects of focus of attention depend on golfers' skill. *Journal of Sports Sciences* 21:593-600, 2003.

21. Porter, JM, Anton, PM, Wikoff, NM, and Ostrowski, JB. Instructing skilled athletes to focus their attention externally at greater distances enhances jumping performance. *Journal of Strength & Conditioning Research* 27:2073-2078, 2013.

22. Porter, JM, Anton, PM, and Wu, WF. Increasing the distance of an external focus of attention enhances standing long jump performance. *Journal of Strength & Conditioning Research* 26:2389-2393, 2012.

23. Read, K, Macauley, M, and Furay, E. The Seuss boost: Rhyme helps children retain words from shared storybook reading. *First Language* 34:354-371, 2014.

24. Schoenfeld, BJ, and Contreras, B. Attentional focus for maximizing muscle development: The mind-muscle connection. *Strength & Conditioning Journal*, 2016.

25. Schutts, KS, Wu, WFW, Vidal, AD, Hiegel, J, and Becker, J. Does focus of attention improve snatch lift kinematics? *Journal of Strength & Conditioning Research* 31:2758-2764, 2017.

26. Stins, JF, Marmolejo-Ramos, F, Hulzinga, F, Wenker, E, and Canal-Bruland, R. Words that move us: The effects of sentences on body sway. *Advances in Cognitive Psychology* 13:156-165, 2017.

27. Vance, J, Wulf, G, Tollner, T, McNevin, N, and Mercer, J. EMG activity as a function of the performer's focus of attention. *Journal of Motor Behavior* 36:450-459, 2004.

28. Winkelman, N. Theoretical and practical applications for functional hypertrophy: Development of an off-season strategy for the intermediate to advanced athlete. *Professional Strength & Conditioning* 16, 2009.

29. Wulf, G. Attentional focus effects in balance acrobats. *Research Quarterly for Exercise and Sport* 79:319-325, 2008.

30. Wulf, G, and Su, J. An external focus of attention enhances golf shot accuracy in beginners and experts. *Research Quarterly for Exercise and Sport* 78:384-389, 2007.

31. Winkelman, NC. Attentional focus and cueing for speed development. *Strength & Conditioning Journal* 40:13-25, 2018.

32. Bell, JJ, and Hardy, J. Effects of attentional focus on skilled performance in golf. *Journal of Applied Sport Psychology* 21:163-177, 2009.

33. Porter, JM, Ostrowski, EJ, Nolan, RP, and Wu, WF. Standing long-jump performance is enhanced when using an external focus of attention. *Journal of Strength & Conditioning Research* 24:1746-1750, 2010.

34. Pulvermüller video, August 2016. http://serious-science.org/neuropragmatics-and-language-5989

35. Pulvermüller, F, Härle, M, and Hummel, F. Walking or talking? Behavioral and neurophysiological correlates of action verb processing. *Brain and Language* 78:143-168, 2001.

36. Pulvermüller, F, Härle, M, and Hummel, F. Walking or talking? Behavioral and neurophysiological correlates of action verb processing. *Brain and Language* 78:143-168, 2001.

37. Raposo, A, Moss, HE, Stamatakis, EA, and Tyler, LK. Modulation of motor and premotor cortices by actions, action words and action sentences. *Neuropsychologia* 47:388-396, 2009.

38. van Dam, WO, Rueschemeyer, SA, and Bekkering, H. How specifically are action verbs represented in the neural motor system: An fMRI study. *Neuroimage* 53:1318-1325, 2010.

39. Boulenger, V, Roy, AC, Paulignan, Y, Deprez, V, Jeannerod, M, and Nazir, TA. Cross-talk between language processes and overt motor behavior in the first 200 msec of processing. *Journal of Cognitive Neuroscience* 18:1607-1615, 2006.

40. Boulenger, V, Silber, BY, Roy, AC, Paulignan, Y, Jeannerod, M, and Nazir, TA. Subliminal display of action words interferes with motor planning: A combined EEG and kinematic study. *Journal of Physiology—Paris* 102:130-136, 2008.

41. Frak, V, Nazir, T, Goyette, M, Cohen, H, and Jeannerod, M. Grip force is part of the semantic representation of manual action verbs. *PLoS One* 5:e9728, 2010.

42. Aravena, P, Delevoye-Turrell, Y, Deprez, V, Cheylus, A, Paulignan, Y, Frak, V, and Nazir, T. Grip force reveals the context sensitivity of language-induced motor activity during "action words" processing: Evidence from sentential negation. *PLoS One* 7:e50287, 2012.

43. Becker, J, and Wu, WF. Integrating biomechanical and motor control principles in elite high jumpers: A transdisciplinary approach to enhancing sport performance. *Journal of Sport and Health Science* 4:341-346, 2015.

44. Schoenfeld, BJ, Vigotsky, A, Contreras, B, Golden, S, Alto, A, Larson, R, Winkelman, N, and Paoli, A. Differential effects of attentional focus strategies during long-term resistance training. *European Journal of Sport Science* 18:705-712, 2018.

45. Winkelman, NC, Clark, KP, and Ryan, LJ. Experience level influences the effect of attentional focus on sprint performance. *Human Movement Science* 52:84-95, 2017.

46. MacPherson, A, Collins, D, and Morriss, C. Is what you think what you get? Optimizing mental focus for technical performance. *The Sport Psychologist* 22:288-303, 2008.

Chapter 6

1. Arendt, H. *Men in Dark Times*. San Diego, Houghton Mifflin Harcourt, 1968.

2. Beilock, SL, Lyons, IM, Mattarella-Micke, A, Nusbaum, HC, and Small, SL. Sports experience changes the neural processing of action language. *Proceedings of the National Academy of Sciences* 105:13269-13273, 2008.

3. Bergen, BK. *Louder Than Words: The New Science of How the Mind Makes Meaning*. New York: Basic Books, 2012.

4. Borreggine, KL, and Kaschak, MP. The action–sentence compatibility effect: It's all in the timing. *Cognitive Science* 30:1097-1112, 2006.

5. Bowdle, BF, and Gentner, D. The career of metaphor. *Psychological Review* 112:193, 2005.

6. Calvo-Merino, B, Glaser, DE, Grèzes, J, Passingham, RE, and Haggard, P. Action observation and acquired motor skills: An FMRI study with expert dancers. *Cerebral Cortex* 15:1243-1249, 2005.

7. Calvo-Merino, B, Grèzes, J, Glaser, DE, Passingham, RE, and Haggard, P. Seeing or doing? Influence of visual and motor familiarity in action observation. *Current Biology* 16:1905-1910, 2006.

8. Geary, J. *I Is an Other: The Secret Life of Metaphor and How It Shapes the Way We See the World*. New York: HarperCollins, 2011.

9. Gentner, D. Why nouns are learned before verbs: Linguistic relativity versus natural partitioning. *Center for the Study of Reading Technical Report* 257, 1982.

10. Glenberg, AM, and Kaschak, MP. Grounding language in action. *Psychonomic Bulletin & Review* 9:558-565, 2002.

11. Graesser, A, Mio, J, and Millis, K. Metaphors in persuasive communication. In *Comprehension and Literary Discourse: Results and Problems of Interdisciplinary Approaches* Meutsch, D, Viehoff, R, eds. Berlin: De Gruyter, 131-154, 1989.

12. Hofstadter, D, and Sander, E. *Surfaces and essences: Analogy as the fuel and fire of thinking*. Basic Books, 2013.

13. Holt, LE, and Beilock, SL. Expertise and its embodiment: Examining the impact of sensorimotor skill expertise on the representation of action-related text. *Psychonomic Bulletin & Review* 13:694-701, 2006.

14. Liao, C-M, and Masters, RS. Analogy learning: A means to implicit motor learning. *Journal of Sports Sciences* 19:307-319, 2001.

15. Pollio, HR, Barlow, JM, Fine, HJ, and Pollio, MR. *Psychology and the Poetics of Growth: Figurative Language in Psychology, Psychotherapy, and Education*. Hillsdale, NJ: Erlbaum, 1977.

16. Poolton, JM, Masters, RS, and Maxwell, JP. The development of a culturally appropriate analogy for implicit motor learning in a Chinese population. *Sport Psychologist* 21:375-382, 2007.

17. Poolton, JM, Masters, RSW, and Maxwell, JP. Analogy learning as a chunking mechanism. In *Hong Kong Student Conference in Sport Medicine, Rehabilitation, & Exercise Science*. Hong Kong, 2003.

18. Stanfield, RA, and Zwaan, RA. The effect of implied orientation derived from verbal context on picture recognition. *Psychological Science* 12:153-156, 2001.

19. Zwaan, RA, Stanfield, RA, and Yaxley, RH. Language comprehenders mentally represent the shapes of objects. *Psychological Science* 13:168-171, 2002.

20. Piaget, J, and Inhelder, B. *The Psychology of the Child*. New York: Basic Books, 2000.

21. Gentner, D. Structure-mapping: A theoretical framework for analogy. *Cognitive Science* 7:155-170, 1983.

Chapter 7

1. Clear, J. *Atomic Habits: An Easy & Proven Way to Build Good Habits & Break Bad Ones*. New York: Penguin Random House, 2018.

2. Duhigg, C. *The Power of Habit: Why We Do What We Do in Life and Business*. New York: Random House, 2014.

INDEX

ABOUT THE AUTHOR

© Brittany Winkelman

Nick Winkelman, PhD, is the head of athletic performance and science for the Irish Rugby Football Union. His primary role is to oversee the delivery and development of strength and conditioning and sports science across all national and provincial teams. Prior to working for Irish Rugby, Winkelman was the director of education and training systems for EXOS (formerly Athletes' Performance), where he directed the development and execution of all educational initiatives. As a performance coach, he oversaw the speed and assessment component of the EXOS NFL Combine Development Program, and he supported many athletes across the NFL, MLB, NBA, national sport organizations, and military.

Winkelman completed his doctorate through Rocky Mountain University of Health Professions with a dissertation focus on motor skill learning and sprinting. He is a recognized speaker and consultant on human performance and coaching science and has publications through the UK Strength and Conditioning Association (UKSCA), National Strength and Conditioning Association (NSCA), IDEA Health & Fitness Association, Human Movement Science, and Routledge.

You read the book—now complete the companion CE exam to earn continuing education credit!

Find and purchase the companion CE exam here:
US.HumanKinetics.com/collections/CE-Exam
Canada.HumanKinetics.com/collections/CE-Exam

50% off the companion CE exam with this code

LOC2021

HUMAN KINETICS